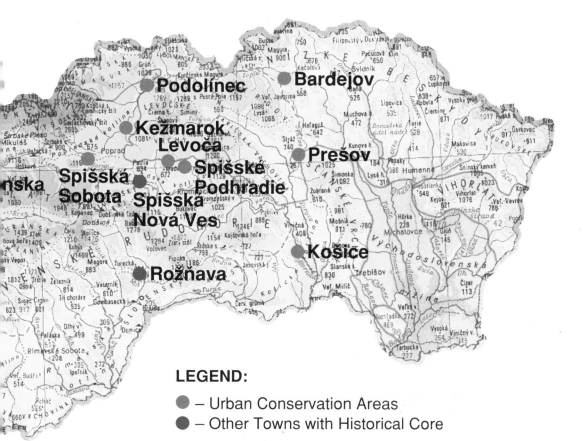

Podolinec

Bardejov

Kežmarok

Levoča

Prešov

Spišská

Podhradie

Spišská

Sobota

Spišská

Nová Ves

Košice

Rožňava

LEGEND:

● – Urban Conservation Areas
● – Other Towns with Historical Core

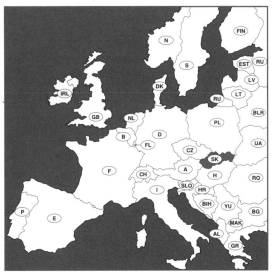

PRÍRODA

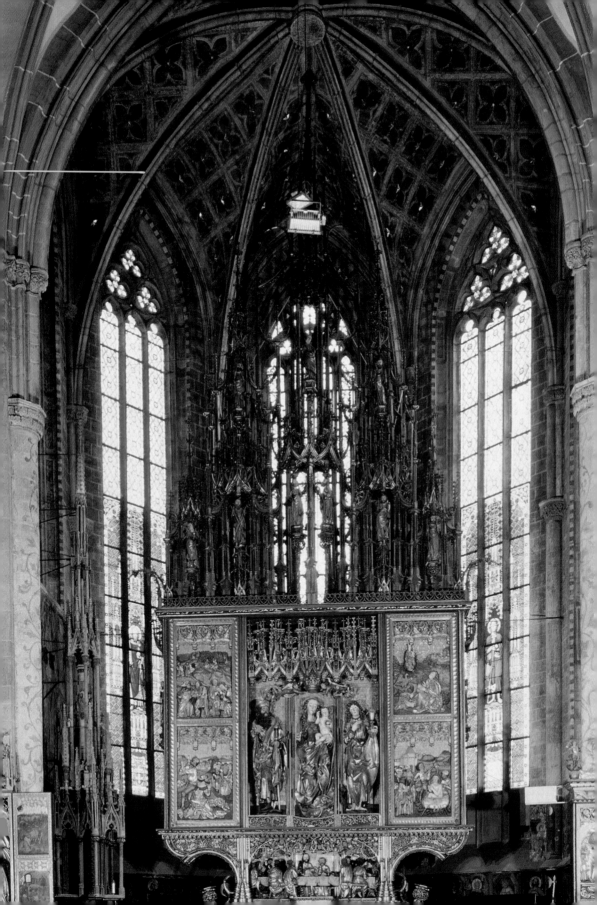

Slovakia

WALKING THROUGH CENTURIES OF CITIES AND TOWNS

Western Slovakia
11

Authors of texts:
Ľudmila Husovská, CSc., *Guilding Author*
Viera Dvořáková
Viera Floreková
Júlia Takátsová
Štefánia Tóthová
Igor Skoček

Municipal Arms:
Texts: Jozef Novák
Drawings: Ladislav Čisárik Jn.

Photos:
Jan Sláma,
Head Photographer: Ján Kováčik, Štefan Péchy,
    Jozef Sedlák, Milan Tesák, Gabriel Tököly, Tibor Takáts

Town Plans:
Dušan Šoltés

Lecturers:
Eva Križanová
Gabriela Škvarčeková

The publication was translated under the supervision of
    Ms. Elizabeth Yenchko by: Pavel Fabian, Ľubomír
    Kmeco, Silvia Nagyová and Karol Herian

Design, Cover Design, Cloth:
František Jablonovský

Revision of Text Svatava Šimková
Technical Editor Božena Braklová
Made and Printed Východoslovenské tlačiarne, a. s.,
    Košice
Issue No. 7959

64-017-00

ISBN 80-07-01134-X

Central Slovakia

Eastern Slovakia

INTRODUCTION

Slovakia, a small country in the very heart of Europe, is protected by the Carpathian Mountains on three sides and by the Danube River on the fourth. Nature has endowed her with highly varying landscape. Hills and massive mountain ranges, tranquil rivers in the downs on the northern fringe of the vast Danubian Plain, the rugged peaks and deep rocky cloughs of the High Tatras, all have effected the process of forming the characteristic features of human settlements in Slovakia over thousands of years. Not only nature but also the changing populations with their foreign cultures had strong impact on the general apearance of the country as well.

Throughout her history, Slovakia has developed multifarious methods of settlement. They were determined by frequent intercourse with various cultures, which got involved in creating material, spiritual and cultural substance of the national heritage. Abundant and fascinating historical evidences confirm inhabitation of the territory deep in remote past. The uninterrupted development of human society here is testified by a wide variety of produces of creative work. When we consider the basic factors which had contributed to this heritage, among them are the lines of communication – the long-distance trade routes – and the general structure of settlements. They both enable to re-create the atmosphere of individual phases of the country's past because they always resist the working of the time. The changes went over centuries and each age and each admixture of foreign incomers to the settlements left its traces on the country. They etched the spirit and image, to be again absorbed and further developed by the new, succeeding population. The wide variety of ways of life, speech, customs, the landscape of the country, its spirit, are unique and inimitable, and thus they create the image of the society. They are also the links with the country's past because they have resulted from transformations of local economic and cultural life, which were often caused by new incomers. Here the different experience of individual societies, states, and even continents is deeply rooted. Even today it permeates and shapes their existence.

The highly varying landscape of Slovakia determined the routes facilitating communication between neighbouring settlements, regions and countries. In the primeval times, merchants already used the mountain passes on long-distance trade routes. They supplied the local inhabitants with both utilitarian and luxury goods. But along these routes also invaders penetrated to harass the country. So the indigenious people had to protect themselves against such raids. Consequently, first fortified farmstead and settlements, forts and later castles with towers – the look-out posts – were built at strategically advantageous and important places, they guaranteed protection to the people who had settled within their walls or in the settlements attached to the base of rocky hills on which the castles usually stood. From the C12 onwards, another aspect of their development was significant: many of them were transformed into cores of market villages; subsequently, many of them evolved into bustling and rich towns in the Middle Ages, became the centres of crafts and business. Later on, favourable circumstances fostered transformation of many medieval into important economic, administrative and cultural centres, often of more than only local significance. Due to the building of railway lines in the C19, the process of changes was accelerated and many very ancient towns became principal centres of intensively developing industry.

Their rich historical associations are manifested in their outer appearance, in the abundance of architectural forms of great beauty, often multiplied by sculpture and painting. Their uniqueness is derived from the specific combination of urban structure and its skyline, which are often in unrepeatable symbiosis with their natural environment. They demonstrate their power as the machinery of progress in material and spiritual life of the society. They are chroniclers of falls and rises; they express best the need for works of art. Therefore, historic towns represent one of the most important constituents of Slovak cultural heritage.

On the pages of this book the reader will be guided through the most interesting cities and towns in Slovakia and will be told about the most attractive stages of their history. Among them are seventeen Urban Conservation Areas declared by the Slovak Government; this collection has been added descriptions of further eight towns which also represent unique historic urban structures.

Owing to the varieties of urban structures in the single regions, the text of this book is arranged into three parts. The first part is devoted to western Slovakia, the second one to central Slovakia, and the third – the last one – to eastern Slovakia. A general introduction to each of these parts brings descriptions of places of historical interest and places of nature beauties. By studying the characteristics of individual towns and cities, the reader will get acquainted with the events which shaped their urban and art-historical development and had the strongest impact on their appearance. The most valuable cultural monuments are supplied with a selection of basic data.

A city's coat of arms are an integral part of its identity, and are presented in this book as important historical documents and artistic mementoes linked to the ancient laws and bygone importance of these cities. For this reason, some of the coats of arms portrayed in this book differ from those currently in use.

Authors

Slov

ABBREVIATIONS

ATC	–	car-camping site
CHO	–	chales and cottages
RC	–	rental cottages
GH	–	guests houses
HH	–	hiking hostels
M	–	motels
av	–	average
C	–	century
CC	–	centuries
mid-C...	–	in the middle of the... th century
L	–	Latin
G	–	German
H	–	Hungarian
S	–	Slovak

General information about Slovakia is available abroad and in individual cities at these travel agencies:
SATUR a.s.; Tatratour; Slovakotour; Neckermann; Reise Kaiser; Ruefa Reisen; Fischer; and the Association of Information Centers in Liptovský Mikuláš:

Tel/fax: ++(421)(0)849-5523721; e-mail: aices@trynet.sk, web: www.ifo.sk/aices

The authors wish to thank officials of the cities of Kežmarok, Nitra, Pezinok, Podolínec, Prešov, Trenčín, and Žilina for their invaluable contributions which have been added to the text.

Western Slovakia

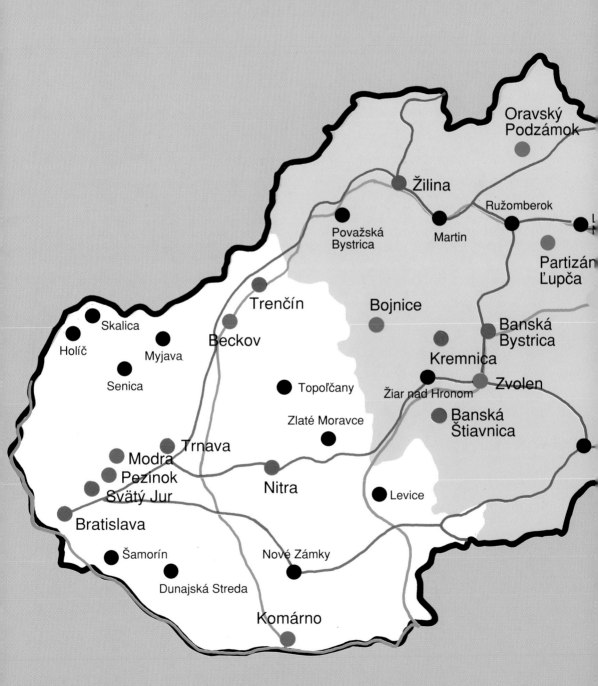

The western part of Slovakia with an area of 15,000 square kilometers spreads at approximately 16° 48' to 19° 05' Eastern latitude and from 47° 42' to 49° 05' Northern longitude. The region is a comparatively vast flat plain interrupted only rarely by undulations of the Danube and Záhorie lowlands where the richest and most fertile agricultural land is to be found. They are also the warmest regions of Slovakia. On the west and the northeast boundary, delightful ranges of mountains – the Little and White Carpathian Mountains, the Považský Inovec Hills, the Strážovské vrchy (Strážov Hills) and the Krupinská planina (Krupina Tableland) seem to stand guard of the entire lowlands. The country is full of picturesque contrasts: compact forests alternate with fertile plains; beautiful deep valleys with swampy forests; little mountain brooks feed the slow-flowing big rivers.

This region is rich in thermal springs where popular and much-visited spas, health resorts and recreational centres cater for numerous visitors. The Danube, one of the longest European major rivers, deserves special attention. Its length of 172 km on the Slovak territory offers excellent fishing; labyrinths of forests in swamps and a dense net of its branches with wide sand beaches on their banks; many nature reserves established here to preserve wildlife alternate with abundant hunting-grounds for deer, little game, and water birds. At present the project of the hydroelectric power-plant on the Danube has reached its final stage.

Most of the territory enjoys a warm, mildly dry lowland climate. The climate of the promontories of the mountain chains varies from a mildly warm to mildly cool and humid mountain climate. The southwest part of western Slovakia is known for a relatively great number of tropical days a year. Winters are milder than in any other region of Slovakia.

Extremely favourable natural conditions, very well preserved ancient trade routes, and numerous mountain passes have attracted the people to make this territory a place of habitation since the ancient times.

The oldest traces of settlement in the western Slovakia reach back to Quaternary Period, or the Pleistocene, characterized by substantial changes in geological structure which shaped the morphology of the country.

The presence of hunters on the territory of western Slovakia in the Lower Paleolithic, especially Great Inter-Glacial, is evidenced by discoveries in the lower river-basin of the River Hron, in the northern part of the Danube lowlands as well as the foot of Tríbeč, the Považský Inovec Mountains and the White Carpathian Mountains. The artifacts distributed here belonged to the Clactonian flint industry.

The existence of Mousterian flint industry constituted in the Middle Paleolithic is evidenced by finds over the southern fringes of the Myjava downs. The discovery of the skeletal remains of a woman at Šaľa upon Váh is datable to this period as well as a little sculpture of a woman called Venus of Moravany.

Remarkably numerous camp sites of the advanced Upper Paleolithic hunters confirm to the growing population of Primeval People. Numerous excavations of the Szeletien and Gravettien camp sites were unearthed between Piešťany and Trenčianska Teplá, especially near the thermal springs; the more ancient sites reached the Ilavská kotlina (Ilava valley); the later ones were excavated near Žilina.

The Middle Stone-Age, or Mesolithic, industries (from 8200 to 5000 BC) are also represented here. Scanty camping sites of the Sereď group were discovered in the loess country along the River Váh from the point marked by Sereď and spreading as far as the Little Danube.

In the New Stone-Age, or Neolithic (from 5000 to 3000 BC), a culture using pottery appeared on the territory of western Slovakia. The southwest lowlands were settled by people of the Danubian culture with stroke-ornamented pottery. They built large timber loghouses and practiced the burying of dead. The crouched burials were lying in graves. Gradually, this culture spread up along rivers more nothwards. In the Late Neolithic the Želiezovce group settled here. Archaeological finds prove the existence of bartertrade with southwest Europe.

Near the end of the New Stone Age, or Eneolithic (from 3800 to 1900 BC), also less fertile higlands were settled. The movement there occurred under the Lengyel and Baden cultures, when domesticated animals became common. The people lived in enclosed settlements. Some of them indicate an advanced, socially differentiated society.

The first produces of copper metallurgy which already appeared in the Late Eneolithic, were of foreign origin, e.g. from Transylvania. The development of copper metallurgy based on rich local sources in the Bronze-Age (from 900 to 700 BC) was very rapid.

Western Slovakia was settled by sub-groups spreading the Chłopice-Veselé and Nitra cultures, created by producers of copper objects. They occupied the northern and central part of the Danube lowlands, in the vicinity of Piešťany and Trnava, the valleys of the Nitra and Žitava rivers, and the central part of the lower Váh. After the Unětice culture distributed from Moravia and the settlements extended eastwards along the Váh and Nitra rivers, the most important domestic culture developed here. It influenced other cultures of the Bronze Age and had commercial links with remote areas.

The people of the Maďarovce culture of Slovakia (the name is derived from the village of Maďarovce where it was excavated, today's Santovka) spread along the main water flows and penetrated deep into the Považie region, into the Trenčín and Ilava hollows. Their hillforts possessing more functions are the most characteristic feature. The influences of the Mediterranean civilization of Mycenae are confirmed by many archaeological discoveries.

The Velatice culture was of greater significance for western Slovakia in the Late Bronze Age. The people of this culture used to build forts such as, for example, at Ducové. Round or elongated barrows were built over richly furnished burials of their chieftains. Očkov may be regarded as a typical example.

In the Late Iron Age, or Hallstatt period (from 700 to 400 BC), the territory of Slovakia became a part of a great cultural group which extended eastwards of the Alps. Trade contacts were maintained with the highly advanced civilization and culture in the south of Europe, for instance with Etruscan cities, whose influence penetrated here through the Alpine passes. The Kalenderberg culture spred widely over southwest Slovakia, northwards of the Danube, including the region of Piešťany and the Little Carpathian Mountains. The enormous influence of this culture is manifested in considerable differentiation of the inhabitants of open settlements and forts (Molpír near Smolenice). The evidence is also confirmed by a large number of princely burials. Amphorae sumptuously embellished with paintings and sculptural decoration are clay imitations of the original north-Italian metal models.

The invasion of the Thracians from their seats into this territory caused gradual decline of the Kalenderberg aristocrats' power and the culture of the late Hallstatt period. The short-term established Thracian culture in southwest Slovakia dwindled away after the arrival of the Celts from the south; the La Tène culture in Slovakia was formed under the Celtic influence from 400 B.C. up to the Early Christian period. The gradual occupation of the southwest Slovakia by the Celts was manifested by the maximum concentration of their settlements towards the end of the middle La Tène period. In the final stage it also influenced the culture of the more northward situated parts of western Slovakia which are in the Moravian-Slovak borderland. On the site of today's Bratislava there was a Celtic oppidum – a centre of their economic and political power over a vast area. The Celto – Dacian settlements from the end of the La Tène period were revealed in the south-western part of western Slovakia. The extension of the Dacians to this territory was closely connected with their conquest over the tribes settled along the central Danube, and with the short-term establishment of their rule here. These events also caused the movement of the Celts more to the north. They mixed with the folk settled there; thus, the new Púchov culture emerged.

After the arrival of the Celts into central Europe, the differences between the developed South and barbarian peoples of Europe started dwindling away, as the latter became more interested in the Mediterranean civilizations – Greek and Roman. More about this process may be assumed from the writings of Classical authors. To the territory of Slovakia, the Celts introduced various new civilizational ideas and technical improvements such as, for example, the mass production of pottery on a potter's wheel; they also diffused knowledge of producing various artifacts of iron, including articultural tools, and also the art of coin-stamping and money-trade. Shortly before the turn of the millennia, the Roman empire pushed its borders nothwards to the Danube after a new province, Pannonia, had been established there. Simultaneously Germanic tribes of the Quadi swept into the Danube lowlands, where they gradually replaced the Celts and Dacians. This Germanic population stayed in the fertile lowlands and valleys of southwest Slovakia during the Roman period, i.e. from C1 to C4 and diffused the so-called Romano-Barbarian culture. Under the direct influence of the Roman civilization represented by the provincial culture of Pannonia appeared only a very limited area on the left bank of the Danube. It had links with the natural frontier zone strenghtened by a system of fortifications "limes romanus". Remnants of Roman military and civilian constructions may be found in Iža – Leányvár nearby Komárno, Milanovce, Pác, Bratislava-Dúbravka, Devín and Stupava. Unique among the Roman monuments in Slovakia is Gerulata, the military station (nowadays in Bratislava-Rusovce) with a surrounding civilian settlement, which grew up outside the station. It was still lying on the territory of the Roman Empire – the Roman province of Pannonia. At the end of C2, further changes occurred as a result of Marcomannic wars. New Germanic tribes arrived in the Danube lowlands and the Roman legions invaded the barbarian territory in the valleys along the Hron, Nitra and Váh. The inscription on the rock below Trenčín Castle records the victory of the Second Roman Auxiliary Legion over the barbarian tribes at Laugaricio in 179 A.D.

At the end of C4, Rome lost its positions along the central Danube, and new ethnic groups settled temporarily in the Danubian Plain. In the period of the Great Migration (from C5 to C6) the first wave of the Slavonic tribes appeared in what is today Slovakia. The settlement of the territory by the Slavs was decisive for the course of the next centuries.

In the Early-Slavonic period (from C5 to C7), Slavs gradually spread over western Slovakia and found their new homeland on territories which had already been intensively inhabited by Germanic tribes. First, they settled along the Váh and its tributaries; later they reached the lowlands of southwest Slovakia. An independent alliance of these Slavonic tribes existed under Samo's chieftainship in 623 – 658. At the end of C7, the Avars wedged deep into the Danube lowlands, and having moved the borders of their empire westwards, they occupied vast territories here. Both populations mingled and lived together on the occupied territory in the pre-Great-Moravian period in C8. In the other areas of western Slovakia these changes were not so rapid and the continuity of Slavonic settlement is documented by the building of first fortified settlements connected with the tribal organization of the Slavs.

After the Avarian Khanate had ceased to exist at the end of C8, southwest Slovakia was again inhabited by Slavonic population. Further development influenced by first contacts with the Early-Carolingian culture and Christianity tended to the establishment of physical unity of tribes closely connected with their centres in fortified towns. Among them, Prince Pribina's Nitra and Prince Mojmír's Morava had distinguished themselves at the first third of C9 and through their unification of Nitra and Morava, the early-feudal state – Great Moravia – came into existence approximately in 833. In Slovakia the administrative organization of Great Moravia was based on a system of hillforts, for instance at Devín, Bratislava, Svätý Jur, and Nitra, which, apart from being military, productive and commercial centres, became religious centres as well. The archaeological discoveries of stone works of architecture show influences both from the West and the South-East. After the arrival of the Byzantine mission of two brothers Cyril and Methodius, who created the first Slavonic alphabet, the basis for diffusing knowledge in vernacular was founded. The legacy of the Byzantine sages did not disappear simultaneously with the disintegration of Great Moravia caused by internal frictions, rivalry and military defeat by the Old Magyars/Hungarians at the beginning of C10. Nevertheless, it diminished slowly.

In the post-Great-Moravian period, Slovakia entered the final phase of the Early Middle Ages. After the centralizing power of the administrative centre in Nitra had petered, the territorial organization collapsed entirely. Yet, in some minor centres situated to the north of the territory won by the Old Magyars/ Hungarians above the borderline marked by Trnava – Nitra – Levice, Slavonic magnates and their military retainers secured their hold on the band as demonstrated by the seat of a magnate at Ducové. These possessions began to be occupied by the Hungarians only towards the end of C 10, probably during C 11, following the unification processes in the Hungarian state. In the general organization of the state no major changes occurred as the Hungarians overtook the principles of the administrative organization of Great Moravia, including the centres in Nitra, Bratislava, Trenčín, Šintava, Sereď etc. The structure and economy of the rural settlements did not completely collapse, either; it became gradually incorporated into the Hungarian economy. The continuity of the Great-Moravian hillforts and fortified settlements is also confirmed by archaeological discoveries of intact settlement sites and dwellings from throughout CC10 – 13 which were permeated by Slavonic culture and traditions.

The king became the owner of this new state. From C11 onwards, he ruled over his estates through the administrative units – the counties. A count was the chief administrator; an important place in the hierarchy of power was secured by church and later, by aristocracy. Such a division of society gave rise to towns. Due to their wealth and loyalty to the state they received various privileges from the king which enabled them to increase their economic growth, self-defence and self-government.

The foundations of a new, urban culture in Slovakia were laid in throughout CC12 – 13. Originally, towns sprang up from market villages situated on the longdistance trade routes which run through attractive and favourable settlement sites in Slovakia. Some of them transformed economically into towns in C12. Crafts-men and merchants pursued trades there, founded workshops, shops, stocked goods, and built public and administrative buildings. The growing prosperity of towns in C13 was also legally codified; they were chartered with various rights and liberties by the king, which allowed them to control economic life,

decide on their own internal affairs, punish crime, and defend themselves against enemies.

In the course of three centuries, a dense network of towns covered Slovakia. Nowadays, they serve good examples of compact seats with definitely formed architectural appearance and patterns of social life. They were often founded near well-fortified strategic points or just outside a fortified castle, or were erected on sites of earlier fortified Slavonic forts and fortified villages. Though castles were not administered or owned by municipalities, they often became a part of the urban structure and dominated their skyline. In the Middle Ages the development, internal structure, and appearance of the towns were also influenced by foreigners, especially Italian and German colonists – specialists, who were invited by King Béla IV to revitalize the land and modernize mining technologies after the Tartars had plundered the country in 1241 – 1242.

Western Slovakia was gradually divided into several counties: Bratislava, Komárno, Nitra, and Trenčín Counties; also, a part of Esztergom County reached into this territory.

In the course of C13, nearly fifty settlements in Slovakia were granted the municipal charters. In western Slovakia, Bratislava, Nitra, Trnava, Trenčín, Komárno, and Nové Mesto nad Váhom were of greatest importance. These towns possessed large amount of economic, administrative and cultural functions. Owing to the necessity to enhance the defensive power of the country, a dense network of castles was being built simultaneously with the towns. The castles had already become a property of aristocrats – feudal lords. The process of feudalizing the society was deepened.

Another important factor stabilizing the state was the church which not only determined the religious and cultural life but was also part of the state administration; the *"loci credibili"* where authenticity of charters, agreements, administrative warrants was established or verified came into existence. In our, modern sense they had the right to notarize documents. In western Slovakia they were represented by Bratislava, Nitra, Zobor and Šahy.

The C14 was the period of economic growth of privileged towns; their significance was reflected in construction of fortifications, imposing municipal public buildings and residential houses. As strong towns emerged, so did the schools because educated people were needed to run these towns. Towns situated on the trade routes were involved in commerce and supported cultural advancement, it is evidenced by the preserved historical architecture concentrated especially in these towns presently protected as Urban Conservation Areas.

In the course of CC14 – 15, the relations in the Hungarian kingdom were steady. The economic, social and cultural development was accompanied by the granting of new charters re-establishment and confirmation of earlier ones, which concerned several towns of western Slovakia: Beckov, Hlohovec, Bánovce nad Bebravou, Modra, Pukanec, Senica, Skalica, and Topoľčany. In this period, towns and some other settlements developed their basic townplan and typical expression of architectural structure.

The C15 was marked by sharpened social conflicts. The territory of today's Slovakia became the headquarters of the resistance against military attacks of the Czech Hussites, who fought battles in western Slovakia, especially in Trnava, Skalica, and Topoľčianky. Hungarian dignitarie, both ecclesiastical and secular, supported by some patricians of the towns became the leading force among supporters of King Sigismund of Luxemburg in the struggle against them. Because of the support which they had shown the King they were rewarded by new privileges and liberties.

What concerns the structure of settlement sites in Slovakia, they differentiated further in close dependence on their main economic pursuit. Craft production and commercial activities resulting in formation of guilds constituted the basis of town's economic life. The peasants in forming villages continued to perform work on the land in accordance with their main economic background, but they turned partially to crafts as well.

The social stratification of population was also reflected in urban structure and appearance of the towns. The houses of rich burghers and patricians developed around a square or a market place. At first, the houses were erected as tower and blocklike huge constructions in the centre of the building plots. Their ground-plans were gradually expanded, and houses with a passageway or houses of a hall-type covering much of the plot arose; a continuous street flanked with rows of inter-connected houses was gradually being formed from C15 onwards. The façades of the houses were treated with quadratura, complementing the decorative stone jambs of windows and portals; the interiors boasted wall-paintings, richly wood-carved ceilings and ribbed vaults.

Stately edifices as churches, town-halls and schools, were situated in the very town centre - in the square. Craftsmen built their houses in concentric side streets, and poor quarters spread near the town walls. The defences with huge curtain walls with bastions and towers above the gates, and a moat, the town proper from the suburbs and the surrounding uninhabited country. From C13 monastic quarters were placed next to the walls; they carried out charitable and pastoral activities catering mainly to the poor and ill. Almhouses, spittals and hospitals were often located nearby the town walls.

The most impressive buildings were the town-halls; originally the home of the magistrate, after C15 the town-halls stood as solitary administrative buildings containing marketing facilities and assembly rooms, as well as representative council-halls. The parish church of monumental dimensions and rhythmically vaulted interior spaces pretentious interior furnishings were "showpieces" of economic prosperity of the town. The altars decorated with sculptures of patron saints and paintings were made in the workshops of distinguished European and domestic artists. The churches also contained tomb-stones and valuable epitaphs reminding of the merits of the deceased patricians.

The second half of C15 was a starting point for the advance of humanistic tendencies and new approach to education. In 1467 King Matthias Corvinus established the first university in Bratislava – Academia Istropolitana.

Though the discovery of the New World in 1492 terminated the Middle Ages the following development was still carrying traces of the feudal principles for a long time.

The new historical development on the territory of Slovakia and all of Europe was dictated by revolutionary events rapid changes in the society.

In C16 the process of decay of the Hungarian society culminated. The lack of a strong central authority and subsequent feudal anarchy, peasants' revolts and threat of Turkish invasion created conditions in which the country could not resist effectively attacks of enemies. The peasants' revolt in 1514 was cruelly suppressed, but the defeat of the Hungarian army by the Turks at the battle of Mohacz of 1526 was disastrous. The western part of Slovakia became an immediate neighbour of the Osman Empire. The Turks advanced rapidly northward. The Hungarian aristocrats wanted to save their lives, and sought for refuge on the territory of today's Slovakia. The Archibishop of Esztergom and the administrators of the Hungarian kingdom moved to Bratislava. In 1530 the Turks plundered the River Váh Valley region as far as Trnava and Piešťany, the Nitra Valley up to Bojnice, and along the River Hron they penetrated as far as Hronský Beňadik. About three thousand unfree settlements and villages were burnt down in southwest Slovakia, in Bratislava and Nitra Counties. After the victory of Emperor Ferdinand I in 1540 over the Turks, the Hungarian kingdom was incorporated into the Habsburg monarchy. Slovakia became its principal part, because the Transdanubian district with centres in Buda and Esztergom was seized by the Turks. Bratislava became the capital and coronation town of Hungary in 1531. In 1554 the boundary between the free country and the territory occupied by Turks was established near Nové Zámky. As the Turks approached the frontiers, the works to enhance the defensive power of towns, castles and residences of gentry, manors and villages went feverishly on.

At the same time the ideas of Reformation reached Slovakia and the new, reformed churches were established. The Habans – the anabaptists – arrived in Slovakia to escape religious persecution; they lived within a closed community of their own concentrated around farmsteads; they were unsurpassed potters, producers of majolica, well-known up to now as Haban majolica. They also made knives and were excellent blacksmiths. The Haban homestead at Veľké Leváre has been preserved as a type site.

The C17 was the period of anti-Habsburg uprisings of the Hungarian Estates, led by Bocskay, Bethlen, J. Rákoczi, Thököly and later, in C18, also by F. Rákoczi. These revolts and the Turkish occupation were the main causes of the decline of towns and villages. The Habsburg armies alternated with the insurgent armies and in the south the Turks took their place. The Osman Empire reached its climax at that period.

The establishment of the University of Trnava can be interpreted as a manifesto of the Counter-Reformation. This university was founded in 1635 and became a centre diffusing new educational trends.

The Renaissance architecture created in Slovakia under the Italian influence and by Italian architects responded to new technological as well as functional needs. It was a reaction to the verticalism of Gothic and its light supportive systems. For political reasons, emphasis was put on the construction of fortifications. The town walls were being rebuilt because of the development of new military technology – firearms, mainly guns. Therefore, modern mound fortifications of the bastion type were erected. The climax of the art of modern fortification-system construction executed by Italian engineers on the new Italian model were the towns situated in western Slovakia and conceived as citadels. The citadel of Nové Zámky (1573 – 1581) became a pattern of fortification engineering and after it had been seized by Turks, the Leopoldov fortress (1665 – 1669) substituted it.

The Renaissance style of architectural composition and performance of single architectural elements were also manifested in the rebuilding of patrician and bourgeoisie houses. The horizontal sgrafittoed façades with an attic storey above the parapet changed the character of squares; so did the houses with vaulted entrance – hallways, arcaded courtyards and oriels on the façades. Many of them are to be seen especially in Bratislava, Trnava, and Trenčín. Special arrangements of the west Slovakia architectural style were created by the wine-growing towns as Modra, Pezinok, and Svätý Jur; the ground-plans of the houses here were developed highly rationally according to clearly defined functions of individual spaces.

The new stylistic expression was also manifested in the sacral art which, owing to rigorous demands and pretensions of Protestantism, withdrew from the medieval decorativeness; in C17 a new type of a ministerial church with a tribune, or loft, appeared with simplified interior wooden furnishings. A fine example of such a magnificent church is the Jesuitical church in Bratislava, originally an Evangelical one.

In 1683, the Turkish armies were defeated near Vienna and the 150-year occupation by the Osman Empire ended.

The C18 represents a period of the gradual rebuilding and settlement of destroyed and depopulated territories of the monarchy. The town fortifications lost their significance; the towns began to grow out of their medieval plans and expanded the urban structures towards the surrounding free space outside the walls. The first census of people because of taxation was carried out in 1715 and 1720. For the whole Austro-Hungarian Empire, including the territory of Slovakia, the period of the rule of Maria Theresa was a period of gradual reconstruction and revitalization of economic, social and cultural relations. Though her reforms resulted in the monarchial absolutism, they also resulted in the development of crafts, manufactures, commercial

activities and education. Bratislava secured its position as the capital of the Hungarian Empire but the University of Trnava was moved to Buda in 1777. Simultaneously with the advancement of industry, the cultural and educational standard of towns and villages, whose number reached 3,592 at that time, rose. The activities of scholars felt stronger in the multinational monarchy. In 1787 Anton Bernolák codified the first standardized form of the Slovak literary language. Craft production and the growth of manufactures formed the basis of economic and building development. The second half of C18 was again a period of great revolutionary changes in the political and economic life of the country as well as in the social sphere and technological development. The Great French Revolution and Napoleonic wars were accompanied by the Enlightenment and the change of the social system.

New ideas were expressed in fine arts and architecture where the classical elements rooted in the antique traditions began to be used again: symmetry, straight lines, closed forms, architrave systems and more simply designed façades. The building of residential quarters continued through the expansion of the townplan. At the beginning, the Baroque monasteries, built according to the model of the Jesuitical monastery the Gesù in Rome, wedged into the urban structures.

These were four-wing complexes with a central courtyard and a sumptuously equipped church overdecorated with variety of colours and materials applied on altars, liturgical ornaments, sculptures and paintings, decorative plaster, and wonderful wrought-iron lattices. The Counter-Reformation period impacted the plan of the towns with minute sacral buildings such as chapels, votive columns, Calvaries, statues of saints, standing on pedestals usually placed on bridges in front of entrance gateways protecting the settlement, etc.

The Baroque art employed all means of fine arts in its works to increase splendour and pomp of theirs. The reconstruction of the royal castle in Bratislava into a dignified residence of the Habsburgs has all the signs of exquisite architecture: a cour d'honneur, formal garden, riding academy, orangery and aviaries. The interior boasted a monumental stairway, stately reception rooms, and it included a chapel. This magnificent castle inspired the mass building of aristocratic palaces not only in Bratislava but also in the surrounding towns. They were built according to desings of significant European, especially Austrian, architectures. Another functional element appeared in the urban structure – a county house, a construction of palatial character with a wide, horizontally developed façade. The Baroque art essentially altered the skyline of the town by soft forms of onion domes and gambrel roofs employed in dominating, monumental building as well as in details of façades, such as oriels. A special position in the development of Baroque art in Slovakia is taken by Trnava, a religious metropolis and university town, whose wonderful works of architecture and arts served as models which influenced artistic production both in its surroundings and more remote towns and districts in throughout CC17 – 18.

Towards the end of C18 and in the middle of C19, the towns saw further changes including the building of railway, a new means of transportation. In the towns new types of buildings began to appear: theatres, county-houses, and railway stations, usually situated beyond the original historical centre. A new type of residential housing (rental apartment houses) arose both in the new and old portions of towns.

The new approach of the inhabitants of towns to the surrounding nature is typical of the Romanticism of C19. In many towns, public parks and gardens copying the style of aristocratic residences, were developed on their outskirts. They were attractive for taking a rest and various holiday activities. New restaurants built there were often a destination of a family trip. The romantic veneration of Nature discovered beauties of waterways and water in general. Walks in the open air manifested the essentially changed values of the new life style programme; it also impacted the town planning. Bratislava may serve a typical example. Instead of the former town walls and the moat on the site of the present-day Hviezdoslav Square, a park-like promenade with palaces, theatres and restaurants arose. At the edges of quarters remote of the city, recreational areas were developed, such as, for example, Železná studienka or Petržalka Park. Neither Trnava nor Trenčín, having a forest below the ruins of the medieval castle, lacked behind this trend.

In the revolution 1848 – 1849, the effort to constitute the Slovak nation culminated. The demands for independent cultural, educational, and political development were pronounced with great insistance. The Bratislava Lycée bore these ideas; Ľ. Štúr became the representative of the Slovak National Revival.

The end of C19 and the beginning of C20 was a period of industrial growth related especially to technological progress. The upsurge of industry and railway transport provided an incentive for new building activity in both urban and rural districts. The towns were more densely populated and therefore expanded the built-up areas. New residential quarters were closely connected with the new traffic routes. The industrial and social development was interrupted by World War I, which caused the end of the multinational Austro-Hungarian empire and the rise of new states. On 28th October 1918, the Czechoslovak Republic was declared and Slovakia joined in the common state with Bohemia and Moravia through Martin Declaration of 30th October 1918. In the following twenty interwar years, new conditions for development of the urbanization of Slovakia, which began to be planned, were created. Extensive building activities concentrated especially on urban housing tracts, situated in the suburbs of the towns. Relatively steady conditions and continuous development of economic, social and cultural life were interrupted by World War II, when many towns and villages were destroyed. In western Slovakia due to heavy air-raids, a part of Bratislava, the entire historical part of the original anti-Turkish fortress of Nové Zámky, and

houses in Nitra, were left desolate wasteland. After 1945, industrial, social and cultural life revived. The programme of large-scale industrialization of Slovakia was launched, accompanied by enormous concentration of population in towns. The need for their rapid reconstruction of old towns and construction of new housing estates became very urgent. Some of the towns such as, for example, Senica, Topoľčany, Galanta, Levice, etc. essentially altered their appearance. Many of them, however, have saved their beautiful original structure. The towns of western Slovakia which are presented in this book belong to the best preserved and the most valuable ones from the historical point of view.

Western Slovakia with the capital city of Bratislava is interesting not only for historical and natural beauties but also for towns, villages, typical of their settlement pattern, as well as recreational centres. Besides the towns documented in greater detail on the following pages, it is necessary to mention in particular the cities of Dunajská Streda, Galanta, Komárno, Levice, Nové Zámky, Senica and Topoľčany, which are administrative, industrial, social and cultural centres.

In Komárno it is possible to see a castle and an anti-Turkish fortress and town fortifications built from C17 up to C18; they are a National Cultural Monument. Levice is known for well-preserved ruins of the original castle. Of the other thirty-six histori-cally significant towns of western Slovakia, Myjava, Skalica, and Uhrovec deserve special attention. Skalica, nearby the Moravian-Slovak border, is well-known in conjunction with the history of Great Moravia; a witness to medieval history is the Saint George's Rotunda, a National Cultural Monument. Skalica is a fine starting point to the White Carpathian Mountains; Zlatnícka dolina (valley) is a recreational area in a close neighbourhood to the town. The significance of Myjava is firmly connected with the Slovak national revival movement, with the revolution of 1848 – 1849 when the first Slovak parliament – the Slovak National Council – held its sessions here. Another National Cultural Monument – the Memorial House of the Slovak National Council, including a museum – is a reminder of those events. Uhrovec is the native town of one of the most famous personalities in Slovak history – Ľ. Štúr. His native house was converted into a museum where the visitors may learn about him and his adherents who played an eminent role in the Slovak national renaissance. The picturesqueness of the countryside is enhanced by silhouettes of castle ruins or preserved castles situated at the foothills of the Little Carpathian Mountains; Červený Kameň Castle (a National Cultural Monument) is transformed into a museum; Smolenice Castle; then ruins of Biely Kameň, Čachtice, Dobrá Voda, Korlátko, Pajštún, and Plavecký Castle are other well-known monuments. Of special interest is the in outlines reconstructed princely seat datable from throughout CC9 – 10 and located at Ducovo at the foothill of the Považský Inovec Hills nearby Piešťany. Other chains of mountains of western Slovakia are topped with ruins of Branč, Gýmeš-Jelenec, Hrušov,

Tematín, Oponice, Topoľčany, Uhrovec Castles.

Spires and onion-domes of churches and monasteries signal the presence of sacral constructions in this region; the most significant of them is the minute early medieval Saint George's Church, a National Cultural Monument, located at Kostoľany at the foot of Tríbeč Hill. Other sacral monuments are worth attention: the churches at Hamuliakovo, Kaplná, Kalinčiakovo, Klížske Hradište, Diakovce, Šamorín, Veľký Kĺíž, and the Premonstratensian monastic church in Šahy, etc.

The mansions and parks surrounding them create impressive elements in the structure of settlements in the region; they are to be found in almost every town or village. The most valuable among them are National Cultural Monuments such as, for example, the original Theresian summer residence at Holíč; the mansions in Topoľčianky, Bernolákovo, Brodzany, Moravany, Stupava, Malinovo, Malacky, Veľký Biel and Veľké Leváre provide further fine examples of country seats. Mansions in Moravany and Topoľčianky are used as recreational facilities. The A. Pushkin Museum is housed in Brodzany Mansion.

The Western Slovakia abounds in traditional handicraft folk and variety of types of folk architecture preserved ancient customs and usages. Production of pottery, especially jugs, the wearing of folk costumes and traditional cooking add to the attractiveness of this part of Slovakia. At Veľké Leváre, Plavecký Peter, and Brhlovce folk-style houses protected as Folk Architecture Conservancies have been preserved. At Brhlovce a special type of dwellings cut into rocks is to be found. Veľké Leváre are closely connected with Habans – producers of traditional majolica jugs. A preserved Haban house, formerly occupied by them, is well-known for the traditional pottery-making. Besides Modra's typical pottery performed mainly in white-and-blue but also varied in colour, another type of majolica in brown-white-and-green has been preserved and still produced at Pukanec.

A beautiful jug has always been connected with one of the most ancient drinks – wine. Wine-drinking and wine-growing may have been introduced to Slovakia by the Romans. Western Slovakia and especially the Little Carpathians belong to the most important and historically best-known wine districts.

Other manifestation of folk art are the painted ornaments on the walls of houses typical of Vajnory. Delicately embroidered folk costumes come from Chvojnica, Myjava, Láb, Stupava, Viničné, and also from Trnava, Trenčín or Piešťany, and from the region of Tekov. Slovenský Grob is well-known, besides its folk costume, for a meal typical western Slovakia - a roast of goose served with thin potato pancakes and red cabbage. Skalica, Soľčany, and Topoľčany are renown for cakes baked in a traditional oven usually used for baking bread. They are a ceremonial meal

eaten on the occasions of various festivals and celebrations. During folk art festivals held in the summer season in Myjava and in Želiezovce, folk customs, songs, and dances are performed.

The most often-visited localities of the western part of this region are those connected with the traditions of the Marian cult and pilgrimages to Šaštín and Marianka.

The spas of western Slovakia are also well-known all over the world. Piešťany is world-renown for treatment of rheumatic diseases, and Trenčianske Teplice is visited by patients who suffer from diseases of locomotion and nervous systems. Dermic diseases are treated in Smrdáky Spa.

Western Slovakia with all the recreational centres is a perfect country for spending pleasant holidays here both in the winter and summer seasons. During the summer season, very popular outdoor thermal swimming pools, or natural pools besides the rivers, and many various water reservoirs attract lovers of water sports. The greatest number of thermal swimming pools may be found in southwest Slovakia in the Danube lowlands. The finest swimming pools are in Nové Zámky, Podhájska, and Štúrovo. The swimming pools in Veľký Meder, Dunajská Streda, and Levice are well-known and much visited, as well as the swimming pools in Santovka and Vincov Les at Diakovce. Well-known bottled mineral waters come from the west-Slovakia springs at Santovka and Slatina. The Slnečné jazerá (Sunny Lakes) near Senec, Sĺňava near Piešťany, Duchonka at Topoľčany, Zelená voda at Nové Mesto nad Váhom, and Bátovce or Šutrovňa at Malé Leváre are natural pools, lakes and water reservoirs which are ideal for water sportsfans.

The centres of winter sports are situated in the mountainous part of western Slovakia. Harmónia and Zoch's Cottage near Modra, Baba near Pezinok, and Jozefské Valley near Svätý Jur are in the Little Carpathian Mountains; Bezovec near Stará Lehota is in the Považský Inovec Hills and Holuby's Cottage at Lubina.

Western Slovakia offers good fishing, hunting, and picking of forest fruits and mushrooms. There are hunting-grounds for small game in the forests of the Little and White Carpathian Mountains, the Považský Inovec Hills, and the Tríbeč Hills; the swampy forests are famous for wild boar. The Danube lowlands are known for their hunting-grounds for small game.The rivers, dams and lakes are a fisherman's paradise. The Záhorie region with pine forests and the west-Slovakia mountain ranges provide advantages of pleasant walks amidst a nice scenery combined with the picking mushrooms, raspberries, and blackberries. The beauties of the underground world can be explored in Driny Cave which is easy reach of Smolenice.

Bratislava

the Capital of Slovakia

Names: L – Posonium, Istropolis, **G** – Pressburg, **H** – Pozsony
Latitude: 48° 10' N, **Longitude:** 17° 05' E
Elevation: average 164 m, **range:** 130 – 514 m
Population: 455 000
Suburbs: Čunovo, Devín, Devínska Nová Ves, Dúbravka, Jarovce, Karlova Ves,
   Lamač, Nové Mesto, Petržalka, Podunajské Biskupice, Rača, Ružinov, Staré
   Mesto, Vajnory, Vrakuňa, Záhorská Bystrica
Means of Access: By rail: routes No. 301 and 310, 110, 120, 130, 131, 132; By road:
   E 65 = 75 = D2 = 2 from Hungary and the Czech Republic; E 58 from Austria;
   E 61 = D 61 to Trnava and east; other route Nos. 2, 63, 502
Accommodations: Hotels: Bratislava, Danube, Devín, Dukla, Echo, Fórum, Kyjev,
   Nivy, Perugia, Sorea, Turist, Penzión No. 16, Clubhotel Slovan, PLUS Penzión,
   Penzión Gremium, Chez David, Eva, Marco, Slov-air, ATC Zlaté Piesky; Botels
   Fairway and Gracia; bed-and-breakfast
Information: Bratislava Information Service – tel: (++421)(0)7-54433715,
   07-54434370, 07-54434325; fax: 07-54432708; City Information Center –
   07-54433078, 07-52495906, 07-52495904, fax: 07-54433109,
   e-mail: bis@isnet.sk, web: www.isnet/bis

Bratislava, the capital of Slovakia, lies on both banks of the Danube River, a major European waterway, and on the foothills of the Little Carpathian Mountains, which form the beginning of the huge Carpathian Arc. The Little Carpathians recede to the Danube lowlands on the southeast, and to the Záhorská lowlands on the northwest. Both the Austrian and Hungarian borders are just "a stone's throw" from the city centre.

Most of Bratislava has a warm and moderate dry lowland climate with average temperatures ranging from –1°C to –4° C in January and from 19.5 °C to 20.5 °C in July; annual rainfall varies from 530 to 650 mm. In the Little Carpathians, the climate changes to a moderately warm and humid mountain climate, with lower temperatures and heavier rainfalls. Bratislava ranks among the warmest places in Slovakia, and strong winds help to remove excessive air pollution and to improve the air quality.

Bratislava, the largest and the most important Slovak city, has a rich history. From its beginnings and throughout its historical development it has ranked among the most prominent cities of central Europe. It has played an important role in the spheres of economic, politic, administrative, cultural, national, and social transformations, and in decisive historical events. Its strategic position on

the commercial and cultural crossroads in the very heart of the Central Danube area contributed to its development. The geographically advantageous location attracted people to settle here from the Early Stone Age. Its long history of inhabitation and transformation has left us countless artifacts, which may be found in museums, and also many monuments of the past. Archaeological finds turn attention to the fact that the present historical centre of the city and castle cliff are textbook examples of the development of European culture and civilization. Almost all historical epochs which mankind has experienced are reflected in relics and fragments of their existence in Bratislava.

Primeval settlements left few traces, as they did not possess a permanent character. During the early historical era, the territory – which was later to become a town-constituted a part of the system of Celtic *oppida* along the Danube, and it also played an important role in the Roman period.

The concentration of inhabitants in the Early Middle Ages – the pre-Great-Moravian period – culminated in C19 when a large fortified settlement was organized on a hill above the river with a palace, Great-Moravian basilica, burial ground and minor dwellings on the precincts within the walls. The refortified settlement continued its existence here also in the post-Great-Moravian

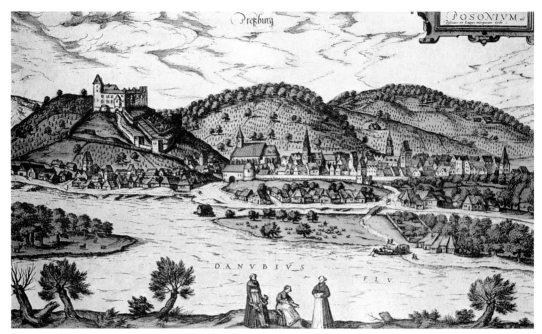

F. Hogenberg: Bratislava, a copper engraving after a German drawer, 1593.

period. A C11 source evidences a county castle with a priory and the Church of Saint Saviour built on the site of a Great-Moravian sacral construction. The settlement situated below the eastern slope of the castle hill developed into the earliest centre of the medieval town.

At the turn of the CC10 and 11, simultaneous with the beginning of the multinational Hungarian state, the settlement below the castle hill and the castle itself obtained immediate significance. As it comprised a canons' cloister, Stephen I (1000 – 1038), the first Hungarian king, made the town a county seat. Thus, the Great-Moravian fort developed into a county castle. For this reason it began to fulfill a variety of functions it was a garrison fortress as well as an administrative and religious centre. In the second half of C11, it became a residence of Hungarian King Solomon for a short time. In 1189, the Roman Emperor, Frederick Barbarossa, stayed at the castle.

In the vicinity of the castle hill separate settlements were founded; the one situated directly below the castle transformed later into a town and a bustling trading centre. Merchants from abroad came here to pursue commerce; many of them settled here and augmented their own, as well as the municipality's, wealth. During the rule of Stephen I, silver coins were stamped here, as evidenced by a unique discovery unearthed on the Swedish island of Gotland in 1939: the first known Árpáds' coin – the Hungarian denarius of Stephan I, dating from

the end of C10 and beginning of C11 with the inscription "/P/ RESSLAVVA CIV" on its reverse side.

A relatively large and compact settlement thrived in the first half of C12. The dwellings changed slowly from subterranean and semi-subterranean ones to log or timber houses with stone underpinning; later they were transformed into permanent stone tower houses. Examples of such constructions are to be found in today's Panská Street (No. 19) and around the Main Square (Hlavné námestie).

The precincts of the castle underwent essential rebuilding. The Slavonic hillfort surrounded by earthen banks was re-fortified, but this time with stone walls with bastions, which had a square ground-plan. A Romanesque stone palace with a large hall and compound windows was built on the hilltop in CC12 – 13. The earlier Great-Moravian church standing here, together with a priory and a circular charnel house until 1221, was renovated. Under the pope's permission it was moved to the area below the castle.

The first known settlers of the site below the castle are from the second half of C12 and the first half of C13. In 1213 Knight Čukár of the Bratislava castle was known to have lived there; his descendants significantly contributed to the development of the settlements around the castle. Later, a Knight Woch from the village of Grabes became a commander of the castle garrison. King

An aerial view of Bratislava and the castle.

Béla IV (1235 – 1270) raised him in the position of "royal guest" to the Bratislava castle. Knight Woch made Bratislava his permanent residence and became a founder of the oldest and best-known burghers' family of Bratislava. An important role at the process of Bratislava's constitution as an urban centre was played by the Jakubs – a family who arrived from Germany after an appeal by the Hungarian king. The members of the family were given their name after Jakub (James), the most distinguished one.

Jakub I became a magistrate of the settlement in 1279. Bratislava owes to the Jakubs the most valuable of its secular buildings – their house. Today it is incorporated into the structure of the City Hall. This patrician house, with its own defensive tower, represents a type of residential house in which traditional elements were combined with newer ones – German influences. Other examples may be seen in market and trading towns of Germany, such as Regensburg, Passau, Nuremberg, etc.

In mid-C13 construction activity indirectly influenced by the Tartar invasion (1241) took place both in the castle precincts and in the surrounding settlement. A new living quarter – the palace – in the form of a keep was built within the castle walls, as the castle was a royal county seat from the beginning of C11. The settlement around the castle expanded eastwards. In the second half of C13 the Franciscans built their monastery on its edge, on the site of an earlier secular building. Around the central square, patrician tower houses were erected. Their cores have been preserved in reconstructed town houses.

The culmination of the centuries-long creation of the city was in the construction of the city walls. The beginnings of the construction of the medieval fortifications date to the end of C13, but evidence from historical sources shows that the settlement began to be fortified earlier, immediately after it had been founded. The fortifications were being built during the entire CC14 and 15, when it was basically completed.

The skyline of the castle and the city from the north.

A view of the city from the castle.

The city and its famous dominant monuments – the castle and cathedral of St. Martin.

A contemporary view of the castle, the Danube, and the New Bridge.

The cathedral of St. Martin.

A view into the presbytery across the nave of the cathedral of St. Martin's.

During C14 the Gothic city developed into a well-fortified urban centre whose character was preserved in this form until the demolition of the defensive walls in the second half of C18. The hub of the Gothic town was the central square, with its quadratic ground-plan. At the corners, where the streets opened into the square, fortified towered houses stood. In the second half of C14 they assumed their final appearance. As ascertained by research, other plots were built up with similar houses. Only two free-standing houses built in C14 have been preserved today as parts of later ones: one near the cathedral of St. Martin, and a house in Kapitulská Street (No. 18). The troubled C15 did not bring any slowdown in construction; on the contrary, it became more intensive. Michalská Street was completed by a row of new houses; Panská Street grew along the walls; and constructions such as the City Hall, the castle, as well as churches, and especially the cathedral of St. Martin, were reconstructed. The settlements beyond the city grew considerably. In the first half of C15, the outer wall of the city fortifications was erected around those on the northern and eastern sides, composed partly of wooden palisades and partly of earthen mounds or brick walls.

G. R. Donner: An equestrian sculpture of St. George, the interior of the cathedral of St. Martin's.

The Good Shephard's House.

An interesting composition of the city's dominant buildings.

The adornments of the exteriors and interiors of both secular and sacred buildings became more intrinsic, and renown masters and masons' lodges were commissioned to execute them. The castle stonemasons' lodge headed by Konrad of Ehrling, as well as St. Martin's masons' lodge headed by Hans Puchspaum, the mason of Vienna's cathedral, exerted strong influence upon stonemasons in the city in mid-C15. Similarly, decoration of interiors was commissioned to such outstanding painters as Hans Maler, Hans Tiergarten and Hans mit dem Mittermal. Less known is the sculpture of the tombstone of Prior J. Schomberg, cut in the Vienna workshop of Nicolaus Gerhaert of Leyden in 1470.

During the reign of King Matthias Corvinus, a university known as Academia Istropolitana was founded in Bratislava in 1465. Well-reputed scholars such as astronomer Johan Müller, called Regiomontanus, and other professors well-known in the scholastic world of Europe started teaching here in autumn of the year 1467. Academia Istropolitana ceased to exist after the death of Matthias Corvinus in 1490.

During Matthias Corvinus' reign, Bratislava was one of the wealthiest cities in Hungary. Later, as

a result of the advance of the Turks northwardly and their victory over the Hungarian army at Mohácz in 1526, the Hungarian king declared Bratislava the capital of Hungary (1536), the seat of the Diet, the Hungarian Chamber, and the Palatine's Council. From 1563 to 1830, Bratislava was the coronation town of the Hungarian kingdom. The first king crowned in the Cathedral of Saint Martin was King Maximilian. The central administrative offices and religious institutions as well as the Royal Treasury and various valuable objects from the Buda cathedral were moved from there to Bratislava. The Primate of the country, the Archbishop of Esztergom, and the Royal Hungarian Chamber also moved to the city. Though the Turks laid to waste areas surrounding Bratislava, they never penetrated to the city itself.

As the Turks constantly harassed the country, military fortification engineer J. Priami was commissioned in 1663 to draw up a plan for the defence of the city and the castle. The building programme of the defensive systems following the Italian model – i. e., a fortress with triangular projections forming a star – was started but never finished. The last rebuilding of the city defences took place in 1670.

Wars against the Turks for almost two hundred years exhausted not only the Royal Treasury but also the treasuries of the royal towns. The increasing demands of the king aroused doubts in the aristocracy as to whether their decision to appoint a member of the Habsburg House as their ruler had really been to their of advantage. The

Michalská Gatehouse, from C14, renovated in C16.

The Old City Hall and its tower, a view across the Primatial Square.

situation was also aggravated after Protestantism penetrated into Hungary. Later, religious wars burst out, to be followed by the Counter-Reformation and re-Catholicization.

Because of unfavorable political situation of this period, when open warfare waged against the Habsburgs set the whole of Hungary aflame, and when wars and pillages devastated the country, Bratislava's economy stagnated. The troubles culminated in 1683 when the city was occupied by Thököly's troops and the Turkish armies were dangerously close to the town, moving toward Vienna. In Vienna the Turks suffered defeat. This event initiated the victorious march of the Christian armies. After the Peace of Szatu Mare was signed in 1711, the situation improved remarkably. Bratislava was on the way to a new prosperity. After the long wars, uprisings, and the Turkish occupations of Central Europe, a peaceful productive period started at the beginning of C18. It also "opened the door" for the Baroque, the new style coming from Italy and Germany. In Vienna, the Royal residence of the Habsburgs, the transformation from a Gothic city into a Baroque metropolis can be best seen thanks to the concentrated and strong support and patronage of

Entrance to the Old City Hall from the Main Square (Hlavné námestie), the end of C15.

The Gothic Church of the Clarists, C14.

Primatial Palace, 1778 – 1781.

the royal court, the aristocracy, and the church. The nearness of Bratislava to Vienna acquired key importance for the artistic production in the city at the end of C17 and throughout C18. Many Austrian and Italian architects (e. g., F. A. Pilgram, M. Hefele, M. Walch, F. A. Hillebrandt, M. Pacassi and others), painters and sculptors (G. R. Donner, C. F. Sambach, A. Galli-da-Bibiena, P. Troger, G. B. Rosso, G. Petrucii, F. A. Maulbertsch, J. Kohl just to name a few) worked in Bratislava.

The end of C18 brought about an essential change to the urban structure of Bratislava. The municipality began to demolish fortifications, and after the ditches had been filled in, the city united with the suburbs, which became equal in status to the historical centre. Other new neighbourhoods, streets, and burghers' houses developed, and in this way the ground-ares of the town spread extensively. Construction activity also provided incentive for the foundation of the Civilian Engineering Office at the Hungarian Court Chamber, which designed construction projects financed by the State, such as granaries, garrison barracks, etc. A portion of the city was designed by architect F. A. Hillebrandt.

Owing to the historical importance of Bratislava's being the principal coronation city,

and its proximity to Imperial Vienna, many palaces of the aristocracy were built here, changing the appearance of the inner city. At the expensively reconstructed castle, and in the new, noble residences in artfully conceived parks on the outskirts of the historical centre, annual cultural events and festivals took place; musical and the atrical events prevailed. A special theatre building appeared in Bratislava in 1776. The sway of religious architecture was closely connected with the liberation of the country from the Osmans Turks and with the strong Counter-Reformation. The building of splendid, vast monasteries and churches, exquisitely ornamented and furnished, flourished.

The C18 contributed to the beauty of Bratislava, with a large number of palaces and vast Baroque monasteries and monastic churches being built. The first workshops, inns, hotels, and representative gardens within the premises of palaces arose. Frequent visits of the Royal Court to Bratislava animated and added splendor to the social life here. In addition, renown European scientists and artists worked here. In 1782, the population of Bratislava exceeded 33,000 inhabitants, and it became the second largest city in Hungary.

St. George's Fountain in the courtyard of the Primatial Palace.

Mirbach's Palace, 1768 – 1770.

In the second half of C19 the growth of the town speeded up. Many new terrace appartment houses were built, after the models provided by Viennese and Budapestian houses in the Art-Nouveau style. In the first third of C20, architecture and urban patterns introduced "revival" styles here; later, construction activity concentred on the modern functionalism of public buildings and villas built on the slopes around Bratislava, which until quite recently had been covered by vineyards. Architectural production inspired by the International Modern style continued until the end of World War II, and died out after then. The period after the War and until the 1980s brought the most important urbanistic changes, when large housing estates consisting of pre-fabricated concrete blocks of flats encircled the historical city as well as the older historical suburbs. The most detrimental effect upon the historical centre was the construction of the New Bridge when whole portions of the settlement around the castle and a suburb were demolished, and the city's appearance was dramatically changed.

The most interesting part of Bratislava consists of palaces with sumptuously ornamentated exteriors and interiors, picturesque lanes, narrow streets, and squares surrounded by town-houses and churches. The historical city core was declared an Urban Conservation Area in 1954. The most significant structure dominating the skyline of the city is the castle.

1 The Castle Complex:

A National Cultural Monument; the earliest habitation of the castle hill dates to the Eneolithic Age. In the Iron Age, the castle hill became the acropolis of a large settlement discovered in the western portion of the historical centre of the city.

More extensive habitation of the castle hill can be dated to Early Proto-History, when the acropolis of a Celtic oppidum was situated on the hilltop.

Traces of Roman building activity discovered within the precincts of today's castle presuppose the existence of significant constructions from the Roman period.

In the vicinity of Bratislava the pre-Great-Moravian period culminated in mid-C9, when the Great-Moravian "hradisko," a fortified settlement covering an area of 5.5 hectares with defensive earthen banks strengthened by means of timber, was built. Within the area of the settlement, evidences of stone constructions dating from the second half of C9 were found, consisting of building materials from a Roman construction with ashlars, stones with inscriptions, and bricks bearing stamps of the XIVth Legion.

On the southern side on top of the castle hill, on the site of the present-day central courtyard, traces of a minor one-storeyed palace with two rooms were discovered, surrounded probably by log dwellings. On the eastern edge of the stone cliff, on the terrace outside the eastern wing of the castle, a three-nave basilica was discovered, and is the largest known Great-Moravian construction in today's Slovakia.

The excavation of this masonry architecture situated on the eastern side of the castle hill, next to the principal palace, points to the existence of a large secular and ecclesiastical administrative centre there. Its significant position was earlier indicated by passages in the Salzburg Annals concerning the Battle of Brezalauspurch in 907, which caused the political

destruction of Great Moravia in the course of C10. This Great-Moravian administrative centre was incorporated into the organizational structure of the Hungarian kingdom in C11, a fact testified to by the existence of the county castle with a priory, and the shift of the Church of Saint Saviour to the area below the castle in 1221.

Continuous habitation at the castle site is also proven by the utilization of the acropolis for the building of a new two-spatial palace with compounded Romanesque windows in C12, which not only respected the previous Great-Moravian palace, but also added a small courtyard with a cistern. A large Romanesque keep was built on the site of the palaces in the second half of C13. From this period, the Coronation Tower has been preserved as a part of the inner fortification.

In CC11 and 12 the defences of the fort were of the same type and extent as that of the Great-Moravian stronghold. In spite of various later renovations, the Slavonic earthen mound formed the outer defences of the castle until the first third of C15, when the mound was replaced by continuous walls. The most important modification of the Great-Moravian mound was its completion by masonry towers in the second half of C13.

In the 1420s – 1430s King Sigismund of Luxemburg reconstructed the castle in the Late-Gothic style, which influenced its present-day appearance.

In mid-C16 the Gothic castle was rebuilt into a four-wing Renaissance palace. During the next reconstruction in 1635 – 1649, the castle was given its present-day appearance. It was raised by one storey, and two corner-towers were added; simultaneously, the southern and western fortifications were made stronger by the addition of bastions.

During the magnificent Baroque Theresian reconstruction in the

second third of C18, which was carried out according to the plans of French architect J. N. Jadot, the castle acquired the appearance of an emperor's residence. In 1768 the Building of the Theresiana was joined to the eastern side of the castle; a valuable art collection – the basis for today's Albertine art collection in Vienna – was housed here. Only the foundation of this building remains.

In 1783 the palace was adapted for the purposes of the General Seminary, in which outstanding personalities of the Slovak National Revival studied and worked. After the Seminary was abolished, a garrison was placed there and the castle was employed as army barracks from 1802 until the great fire of 1811, when the castle burnt down. Within, the castle was reduced to ruin, and only the outside walls remained as a shell.

Years-lomg efforts to rescue the building culminated in 1954, when the total restoration of the castle began. In the reconstructed rooms of the castle, which today house the Slovak National Museum the Constitutional Law of the Czechoslovak Federation was signed in 1968. On the occasion of the 20th anniversary of this event, an exposition was opened to the public entitled „The lewels of the Slovak Ancient Past," where the most valuable findings of the Primieval, Proto-History and the Middle Ages in Slovakia are displayed.

2 The Cathedral of Saint Martin:

A National Cultural Monument. Today's cathedral is located on the site of a Romanesque church, which was altered after the canons' cloister and the priory had been moved from the castle in 1221; the reconstruction work became more intensive in the first third of C14 when a new shrine was built. The Swabian mason's lodge worked on the church in the second half of C14. From this period the northern entrance portal with a relief of the Holy Trinity has been preserved.

Former summer palace of the Archbishop of Esztergom, today the Executive Offices of the Government of the Slovak Republic, located on Námestie slobody (Freedom Square).

Towards the end of C14 a building guild from Vienna continued the work. After a short break, the work on the three-nave construction and the vaulting went on. The Late-Gothic reticulated vaulting in St. Martin's, built in 1443 – 1448, was inspired by Hans Puchspaum, a member of St. Stephen's Cathedral mason's lodge in Vienna. The nave of St. Martin's consists of five sections of reticulated vaulting, and the aisles boast five sections of star vaults. In 1467 – 1484 the predecessor of the shrine was demolished and a new one, much larger, and with exquisite reticulated vaulting appeared. In mid-C15 the Chapel of St. Ann was added to the northern entrance. The southern antechapel from early 1500s belongs to the last of the medieval works of architecture. The church belonged to the Lutherans from 1619 to 1621. From 1729 to 1732 the old Gothic sacristy was demolished and the Baroque chapel of St. John the Almonder arose instead, built most likely after the design of L. Hildebrandt. The sculpture in the interior is by Georg Raphael Donner. An equestrian sculpture of St. Martin in the main altar – originally flanked by bowing angels – was also by him. Today, the sculpture is situated in the southeastern part of the nave. In C19 the church was transformed into the neo-Gothic style. After a fire in 1833 the tower

was restored and a gilded model of the Hungarian Royal Crown was placed on top of the spire. In the second half of C19, when the Gothic was rediscovered, the original interior furnishings were replaced by new ones to correspond with the then fashionable neo-Gothic style. Epitaphs of distinguished personalities and of church dignitaries from C15 to C17 are to be found inside the church. The tombstone of prior Juraj Schomberg, made by Nicolas' of Leyden Viennese guild, is from the second half of C15.

The church treasury contains liturgical artifacts, representing works of goldsmiths and silversmiths from C15 to C18; among them there are chalices, monstrances, reliquaries, etc.

3 The Franciscan Church of the Annunciation of the Virgin Mary and the Monastery: Hungarian King Andrew (Endré) III and the highest church and secular dignitaries took part in its consecration in 1297. Of the Early-Gothic one-nave church only the outer walls of the nave and the polygonal-ended presbytery with the original rib vaulting remain today. At the northern wall of the church, the Gothic Chapel of St. John from the second half of C14 stands. The two-storeyed chapel with the crypt of Magistrate Jakub's family was built after the

model – of Sainte Chapelle, the royal chapel in Paris. This chapel is a brilliant example and a masterpiece of Gothic architecture in Slovakia. In C14 a new Gothic monastery was added to the southern side of the church on the site of the previous one. Earthquakes in the second half of C16 damaged both the church and the monastery, and the original Gothic vaulting in the central nave collapsed. In 1613 – 1616 the present day Renaissance vaults were built, resting on massive pillars.

In C18 the interiors and exteriors were renovated in the Baroque style. In 1745 – 1746 the architect Luca de Schramm refaced the church in the Baroque style. In the interior are the high altar and the side altars from C18, the pulpit from 1756, the Stations of the Cross, and other sculptural and historically precious works of arts. The epitaphs of secular lords and church dignitaries date from C16 to C18. In the church treasury, medieval, Renaissance, and Baroque liturgical objects may be found. The monastery is a four-wing, three-storeyed construction with a cloister around the courtyard and comprise of some Gothic elements from C14. The monastery was renovated several times during C17, throughout CC18 and 19, and in C20.

4 The Church of the Exaltation of the Holy Cross: Originally the Order of St. Clara Church. The members of Clare' order came to Bratislava in 1297; a one-nave church was built for them in the first half of C14. In the second half of C14 the church nave was elongated and a new presbytery was built. The interior was vaulted with cross-rib vaults. After 1400 a five-sided stone tower, which is a very rare phenomenon for the Gothic, was erected on the southwest corner. In 1515 and in 1590 the church and monastery were damaged by fires. In 1700 they were damaged by an earthquake. At that time a part of

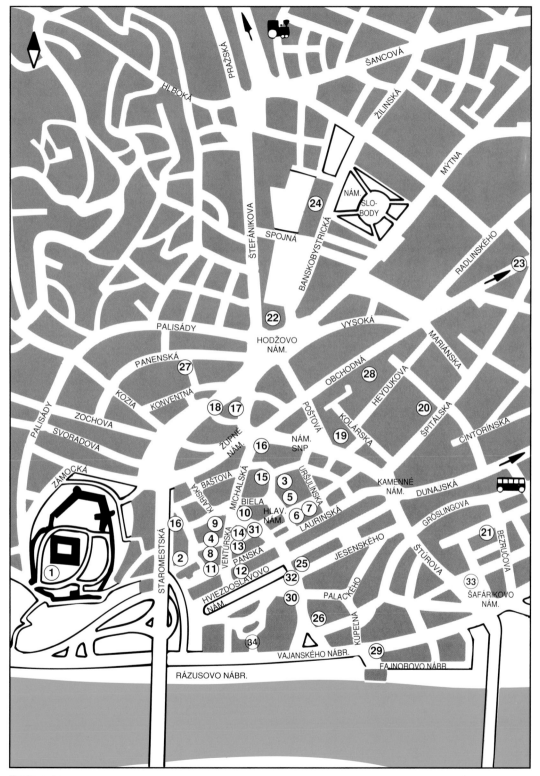

The town plan.

Baroque palaces, Panská Street.

The native house of composer John Nepomuk Hummel, Klobučnícka Street.

the damaged stone tower was replaced by a Baroque onion dome. Emperor Joseph II abolished the order in 1782 and the Poor Clares left Bratislava for Trnava. In 1783 – 1784 the building of the monastery was reconstructed according to the design of J. Thaller, to be used as a Royal Academy and a Gymnasium. The Law Academy occupied the building until 1851 and the gymnasium until 1908. In 1914 the municipality bought the church as well as the monastery to use them as a library. During the years 1964 – 1973 the church was transformed into a concert hall.

5 The Church of the St. Saviour: a Jesuitical Church. The church was built by German Lutherans on the site of older houses in 1636 – 1638. It is situated next to the City Hall. According to the Emperor's decree it could not have a tower and a presbytery, and the entry could not face a public area. In spite of the decree, the entrance faces the square. The Master-Builder violated the decree for a second time by clipping the presbytery into the last section of the central nave. In 1672 the church was taken from the Lutherans and transferred to

the Jesuits who dedicated it to the St. Saviour. The interior was embellished with lavish Late-Baroque furnishings.

The Late-Renaissance, three-nave hall construction, originally a Protestant church with tribunes, has barrel vaults with lunettes in the central nave, and cross vaults in the aisles. One of the most beautiful Rococo pulpits in Slovakia is to be found here. The pulpit was executed in 1753 by Ľudovít Gode, who was trained in G. R. Donner's workshop. Liturgical objects in the church are comprized of valuable goldsmith works from C18 and C19, such as ciboria and chalices, etc.

6 The City Hall: The most significant secular construction in the city. The corner tower from the end of C13, forming a section of the residence of Magistrate Jakub II, is the oldest part of the building. After mid-C14 a galleried one-storeyed wing with crenellations was added. In the first quarter of C15 the building became the property of the city, and was transformed for use as the City Hall. By the 1430s it had been so damaged that it had to be essentially rebuilt. The present day carriage-way with Late-Gothic

vaulting originated in 1457. Above it was a Gothic chapel, and next to the chapel was a new council hall. These spaces were also remodelled several times. In mid-C15 the walls of the chapel were covered by Gothic wall paintings. The apse of the chapel has been reconstructed from preserved original architectural elements. The adjacent Court of Justice hall appears as it did in the second half of C17, including a ceiling fresco of the Last Judgement by J. Drentvetta from 1695. Towards the end of C15 the municipality again renovated the City Hall, whereby an oriel was added above its entrance portal.

The building was used as the City Hall until the 1860s. At that time a new council hall was built and in some rooms of the City Hall the City Museum was introduced.

The City Hall Tower was renovated to its present form in 1733. In 1910 – 1912 the rear parts of the building were demolished and a neo-Renaissance wing was built towards Primaciálne námestie (Primatial Square) according to the design of Eugene Hübner. The former City Hall now houses the City Museum exposition.

7 The Primaciálny palác (Primatial Palace): This palace from 1777 – 1781 is built on the site of a medieval building which was the residence of the Archbishop of Esztergome during his visits to the town. The medieval building also contained the Gothic Chapel of Saint Ladislas. At the beginning of C18 it was rebuilt at great expense. As its construction did not satisfy the needs of Cardinal Batthyány, the Archbishop of Esztergom, who became its owner, had the old palace demolished and built a magnificent new palace in the classical style according to the project of Melchior Hefele. The palace faces a minor square where a market place used to exist. The building consists of four wings with a central courtyard and a chapel consecrated to St. Ladislas. A trompe l'oeil wall painting on the vaulting depicts the miracle of Saint Ladislas; the painting is by E. A. Maulbertsch. The entire first floor contains reception rooms. The sculpture of St. George and the Dragon from C17 is a part of the sculptural decoration which once embellished the park surrounding the Archbishop's summer Palace.

A ceremonial columned entrance room, hall and a monumental stairway originally decorated by statues ascends to the piano nobile (representative spaces) inclunding ceremonial Mirror Hall. The Peace of Pressburg between Austrian Emperor Francis I and Napoleon was signed in the Mirror Hall in 1805.

In 1903 the palace was bought by the magistrate and became a part of the City Hall. The Mirror Hall was employed by the City Council and the City Representatives for its sessions; significant state visitors were received here; later various festivals, celebrations, and weddings took place here as well.

During renovations of the City Hall in 1903, very precious early Baroque tapestries were discovered in the palace, woven in

The Slovak National Theatre (1886), Hviezdoslav Square.

V. Tilgner: Ganymedes Fountain, in front of the Slovak National Theatre.

approximately 1630 in the English royal workshops in Mortlake, London. They illustrate the antique legend of Leandros and Héró.

8 The Academia Istropolitana: A cluster of buildings which belonged to Magistrate Š. Gmaitl in mid-C15; at that time the royal manor house was located to the west of here. In 1465 King Matthias Corvinus founded the first university in the town, Academia Istropolitana. Its premises were the royal manor house and Gmaitl's houses. Academia Istropolitana ceased to exist after Matthias's death. The buildings then remained inhabited until the 1960s. After reconstructions and modernization they became the home of the School of Dramatic Arts.

9 The Hungarian Royal Chamber in Michalská Street (No. 1): It was built according to the design of Italian master G. B. Martinelli, on the site of older town houses in 1753 – 1756. In 1772 the building was extended and another house from Ventúrska Street was added to it. The renovations were directed by Bratislava builder K. F. Römisch according to the project of F. A. Hillebrandt. After the seat of the Royal Chamber moved to Buda, the Hungarian Diet sat here from 1802 to 1848. In mid-C20 it was reconstructed to meet the needs of the University Library. This unit is the finest example of Baroque palace architecture in Bratislava.

Town Houses and Palaces in the Old Town

Though the architectural and creative expression of Baroque became typical for the residential houses of Bratislava, highly developed forms of Renaissance architecture were preserved in C17. The most significant example may be found in the town house known as Segner's manor house, located in Michalská Street. At the same time, a period of superb Baroque palace architectural production was heralded by the buildings of the Bratislava bourgeoisie. Having started with transformations of Gothic and Renaissance houses to the style of the day, they embarked on building splendid palaces in the course of C18. They changed completely the appearance of the street line, which consisted originally of narrow Gothic and Renaissance façades. The wide, horizontally-spread façades of several-storeyed palaces were created by reconstructing and joining older houses, of which existing beams and posts were employed. The Baroque palaces copied Viennese patterns, and were built according to designs by J. L. Hildebrandt, M. Hefele, M. Walch, and others.

10 Jeszenák's Palace: Located in Michalská Street (No. 3), this palace was built in 1730 under the influence of the work of J. L. Hildebrandt; however, it incorporated classicist elements. It is a representative composition on the site of a medieval house, with a separate keep in the western portion of the yard. In the second half of C16 the keep was vaulted with Renaissance vaults resting on central pillars. The Baroque façade features a portal with pilasters on either side.

The church of Our lady and monastery, of Baroque buildings in Hviezdoslav Square, C18.

Academia Istropolitana – a complex of Gothic buildings, Ventúrska Street.

11 J. Eszterházy's Palace: Located in Panská Street (No. 13). This three-storeyed palace from 1743 was influenced by Viennese architect J. E. Fischer of Erlach. Its U-shaped ground-plan was conceived in a magnificient way. The four-storeyed high façade with stone portal entrance is decorated by Atlantes supporting the entablature with cornices; on the

sides there are vases, and a shell on the top. This façade is assigned to A. Hüter.

12 Pálffy's Palace: Located in Panská Street (No. 19-21) this palace from mid-C19 arose when three medieval houses were connected, portions of which have been preserved in the basement, in the passageway on the ground-floor, in the stairway, as well as on the first floor. After complex renovation, the palace houses the City Gallery of Bratislava.

13 Pálffy's Palace: Located in Ventúrska Street (No. 10), this palace was built in 1747 on several medieval lots. Gothic portals and medieval masonry have been preserved in the basement. This large palace consists of four wings and two courtyards with galleries running around them. Its dominant element is the lavishly decorated entrance portal on which trophies prevail; the wooden gate is decorated with carvings. In the palace various cultural and social events are organized at the present.

14 L. de Pauli's Palace: This palace in Ventúrska Street (No. 11) was built in 1775 – 1776. Its owner was the principal administrator of the emperor's estates in Hungary. The construction plans were most likely drawn by F. A. Hillebrandt. The palace originated on the site of several Gothic houses. A large garden, of which a Rococo music pavilion has been preserved, belonged to the palace. The four-wing construction has a central courtyard with galleries supported by decorative stone brackets.

15 Mirbach's Palace: Located at Františkánske námestie (Franciscan Square) (No. 11), this palace was built during the years 1768 to 1770 by M. Höllrigl on the site of a medieval house, whose masonry has been preserved in the basement and partially up to the second storey. The palace is a four-wing building with a central courtyard, surrounded by galleries with Rococo railing. The palace houses the City Gallery of Bratislava.

16 The Town Fortifications: The beginnings of the town fortifications go back to C13 when King Andrew (Endré) granted rights to the town in 1291. The inhabitants of Bratislava built a high crenellated wall made of bricks. Loopholes were accessible by means of the parapet, enlarged with a wooden construction resting on stone brackets. The entrance to the city was protected by three

The church of St. Elizabeth, known as the Blue Church and dating from 1907 – 1913, is located on Bezruč Street.

main gates: on the north, by Michalská Gatehouse; on the west, by Vydrická Gatehouse, and on the east, by Laurinská Gatehouse. Besides the main gatehouses there were also postern gates, one of which (the southern gate) made access to the river possible. Later it was rebuilt into the Rybárska Gatehouse. The defensive power of the walls was enhanced after they were reinforced by semi-cylindrical bations, and with the additional an outer wall with a rampart and a ditch running

along it. In the space between the walls, right-angle barbicans and drawbridges were built in front of the Michalská and Laurinská Gatehouses. In the first third of C15, when the Hussite troops threatened Bratislava, King Sigismund of Luxemburg issued a warrant for reconstruction of the city into a fortress. Huge barbicans were built in front of the Michalská Gatehouse in 1445, and in front of the Laurinská Gatehouse in 1433. The Vydrická Gatehouse was rebuilt, and on the southern side of

The castle. Sigismund's Gate.

huge barbican. The original medieval fabric of the Gatehouse reaches the third storey. In 1529 – 1534 it was raised by an octagonal superstructure above the gallery. It gained its final form in mid-C18 when it was surmounted by an imposing Baroque helmet with a lantern topped with a statue of Saint Michael slaying the Dragon. Two bells from 1589 and 1679 have been preserved in the Bell Tower. A stone tablet with three coats-of-arms of Hungary and the Jagiello House is situated above the passageway on the outer side of the gatehouse; also a metal cartouche with an inscription. A City Museum exposition of arms and fortifications are housed in the tower. On the outer side of the gatehouse, portions of the huge barbican's original stone cladding has been preserved. A Baroque bridge with two statues – Saint Michael and Saint John of Nepomuk – dating from 1727, leads to the gateway over the moat. In C18, houses were attached to the walls from the inside, yet the original route, at right-angles and turning northwest, was preserved. In house No. 26 is the Pharmaceutical Museum.

Historical Architecture in Greater Old Town

The architectural development of C18 Bratislava is typified by monasteries and palaces with large and beautiful gardens built beyond the walls of the city which had lost their defensive significance.

17 The Church of St. John of Matha: A church of the Trinitarians, of St. John of Matha was built on the site of the former parish church of Saint Michael. The order of the Trinitarians, who redempted captives out of Turkish captivity, was invited to Bratislava by Archbishop Leopold Kollonich around 1695. The foundation stone of their church was laid in 1717, and building was completed in 1725. It was designed according to

the fortifications the Rybárska Gatehouse was expanded. The original number of bastions was augmented by further high bastions with an elongated semi-circular ground plan. Defence of the area in front of the walls was strengthened by semi-circular bastions. In the suburbs, four gatehouses with palisades were built, protecting the town on the south and east. Apart from minute adjustments, the defensive system was built during CC14 and 15. Its development and the type of construction may be studied owing to the preserved

remains of the west wall, located to the north of the cathedral.
A continuous wall with three reconstructed semi-cylindrical bastions and one square tower is to be seen. The Powder Bastion, with an adjoining section of the wall, is situated to the east of the Michalská Gatehouse, in Zámočnícka Street (No. 11).

One of the most impressive dominating features of the historical centre, and the most significant preserved element of the city fortification system, is the Michalská Gatehouse, with its

the Church of St. Peter in Vienna, which was by the Viennese architect L. Hildebrandt. The church in Bratislava differs from the church in Vienna by its more simply conceived façade which was unfinished. The towers of the church, which originally carried spires, are topped with simple low pyramidal structures.

The ground-plan of the church consists of an oval nave with a segment-ending presbytery and an antechapel flanked by the towers. The central oval is domed. The church interior is adorned with Baroque splendour; trompe l'oeil frescoes on the vault of the presbytery and on the dome are by master-painter A. Galli-da-Bibiena, who painted them two years after the dome was built in 1742. The interior furnishings are from mid-C17; the painting on the main altar was created by F. X. Palko.

Fortifications of the castle on the southern side.

18 Former County Hall: Located in Župné námestie (County Square), this former Baroque convent of the Trinitarians was rebuilt after designs by J. Hild and I. Feigler Sn., under the influence of classical architecture. The four-wing construction arranged around a courtyard is entered through a vestibule comprized of three rooms. Today it is the seat of the Slovak Parliament.

19 The Church of Our Lady and the Monastery of the Mercedarians: Built at the turn of CC17 and 18, the cloister clearly shows the model which it copies: the Viennese Monastery of Mercedarians. The designer of Bratislava's spatially complex composition respected local conditions and created a cluster of buildings beyond the city walls. They were erected in Early-Baroque style. The horizontally-spread façade of the monastery and the hospital overlook a square. This ecclesiastical structure is dominated by a quandrangular tower – a centrepiece of the façade.

The decoration of the façade of the church and monastery developed gradually, during the end of C17 and the first third of C18.

The interior of the church is a variation of the Gesù type. The nave with a presbytery is accompanied by side chapels. Its longitudinal emphasis is perceived in the arrangement of the church along the major axis. The main altar dominates the church and its columned architecture fills the entire presbytery. Today, the monastery is employed as a hospital.

20 The Church of St. Elizabeth of Hungary and a Convent of St. Elizabeth's Order: In 1739 – 1743 the four-wing building of the convent of St. Elizabeth's Order, together with a hospital and one-nave church dedicated to St. Elizabeth of Hungary, were built thanks to care of Archbishop of Esztergom. This composition was designed by Viennese architect F. A. Pilgram. A large garden formed a part of the premises of the convent and the hospital; a cemetery was not far from them. The Baroque church is one-nave; the entrance and the presbytery are nothing more than

mere hints. The façade of the church with a central concave bay is executed in the High-Baroque style. Its interior, strictly articulated with an indication of a transept, is conceived in the classic Baroque style. The interior excels in its outstanding furnishings and paintings. Baroque painter P. I. Troger achieved the spatial extremes; he seems to have broken the boundary between reality and illusion through his illusive paintings on the vaults; he succeeded in creating an impression of enormous heights opening to heavenly vastness. In the convent is a hospital.

21 The Second Church of Saint Elizabeth of Hungary: Also known as the Blue Church, this Art Nouveau church was built in 1907 – 1913 according to the design of Budapest architect Ödön Lechner. The church is part of a complex which also consists of a high school and rectory. The church has one nave and a cylindrical tower. Its interior and exterior decoration is typical of the Hungarian Art Nouveau national style. The exterior walls are decorated with exquisite blue majolica tiles, set into rows in the exterior facade. Together with

The Slovak National Gallery, the courtyard.

the blue glazed tiles on the roof they were the inspiration for the church's name: The Blue Church.

22 The A. Grassalkovich Palace: This palace with a French style park was built sometime after 1765 in two rapidly successive stages as a summer residence by Earl Anton Grassalkovich. The original building featured a ground plan in the shape of a cross with two short wings. Originally, the Chapel of St. Barbara stood apart from the main structure. It was consecrated in 1769. The space between the chapel and the palace's west wing probably served as a passageway for carriages. Until recently, it was thought that A. Mayerhoffer was the palace's architect, but there are indications that the author could have also been F. A. Hillebrand in collaboration with the investor. Grassalkovich's son Anton II inherited the palace and enlarged it in 1771, resulting in the building as it appears today. M. Walch was the architect of this renovation project. The palace is a two-storey rectangular structure with three bays and exhibits the typical features of elegant aristocratic architecture, including a monumental staircase and central salon on the upper floor. Viennese painter Joseph von Pichler created the chapel's frescos. On August 10, 1775, Maria Theresa visited the newly renovated palace during a celebration in the garden. In 1897, Archduke Friedrich purchased the building and restored it. In the succeeding decades, it

underwent further renovations (the most recent in 1996 with revisions of the garden taking place in 1999) but the building remained essentially unchanged. Today the palace is the official residence of the President of the Slovak Republic.

23 J. G. Aspremont's Palace: Built in 1770 according to the plans of J. J. Thaller, this beautiful palace is an impressive example of a pure classical style. Together with a large park, it creates a significant complex urban composition in Bratislava. The two-storeyed diagonal wings of the building and the central oval bay with a balcony optically enlarge the courtyard opening to the park. The oval bay contains a large ballroom accessed by a wide staircase. The original park is open to the public and is known as the Medical Garden because the palace now belongs to the Faculty of Medicine, Comenius University.

24 The Former Summer Palace of the Archbishop: Presently the residence of the Slovak Government, this palace was created by reconstructing an older palace from the C17. To the palace an orchard and an ornamental garden belonged, called Lipay's Garden, known throughout the whole of Hungary. Archbishop F. Barkóczy ordered the last renovation which was completed in 1761 – 1765. The two-storeyed palace with a dominating central bay and side wings encompasses the cour d'honneur with its ornamental garden. There are several

stylistic elements reminiscent of Hillebrandt's style of architectural creation. In the palace there is a chapel containing wall paintings executed in 1740 by Italian painter A. Galli-da-Bibiena.

25 The Slovak National Theatre: Situated in Hviezdoslav Square, the theatre was built in 1886 on the site of its predecessor. The new theatre building was constructed in the neo-Renaissance style according to the designs of F. Fellner and H. Helmer. The rectangular ground--plan is filled by a horse shoe shaped auditorium with three storeys of balconies and boxes displaying sumptuous sculptural and ornamental adonments. The main facade featuring a balcony is ornamented by allegorical statues by V. Tilgner. The theatre was completely reconstructed and modernized in the 1980s.

26 The Reduta: Located in Mostová Street, the Reduta, i. e. the Ballroom, was built in 1913 – 1918 on the site of an original theresian granary. The two-storeyed representative building according the designs of architects Komora and Jakob is a composition based on neo--Renaissance and neo-Baroque elements. The representative entrance staircases and vestibules connect two halls – the larger one – a concert hall, and the smaller one – a theatre hall. On the ground-floor and in the basement a café and a restaurant are to be found. Today the Reduta is the seat of the Slovak Philharmonic Orchestra.

27 Old Evangelical Lycée, Major and Minor Evangelical Church: These three buildings form a complex in Konventná and Panenská Streets. The Lycée and the Major Evangelical Church were built according to the design of M. Walch in 1783 and 1776. The Minor Evangelical Church was built in 1778 according to the design by F. Romisch. The Late Baroque churches, both without a presbytery or a tower, feature rectangular ground-plans and galleries. The altars and other interior furnishings date from the last quarter of the C18. During the C19, famous representatives of the Slovak National Revival studied at the Lycée, whose valuable historical library has been preserved. The Lycée has also been listed as a National Cultural Monument.

28 The Synagogue: Located in Heyduk Street, the synagogue was built after the plans of A. Slatinský. The interior features an arcaded tribune resting on columns.

29 The Slovak National Museum: Situated on Vajanský Embankment, the building was constructed by M. M. Harminec in 1928. In front of it is a pylon surmounted by a sculpture of a lion, which was part of a monument to General M. R. Štefánik created by B. Kafka in the period after the 1930s.

30 The Carlton-Savoy Hotel: This compact block standing on Hviezdoslav Square, built according the plans of M. M. Harminec, replaced its predecessor, the U Zeleného stromu Hotel (The Green Three Hotel). Together with the buildings of the National Theatre and the Reduta, these three structures were the most prominent pieces of architecture of the former promenade.

Parks and fountains as effective elements have contributed to the atmosphere of Bratislava. The Maximilian (Roland) Fountain and the Ganymedes Fountain are two of the best known of the many others which adorn the squares and courtyards of palaces in the historical quarters of the town.

31 The Maximilian (Roland) Fountain: Located in Main Square, this stone fountain from 1572 represents the Knight Roland – the legendary protector of the city. The designer of the fountain is A. Luttringer.

32 The Ganymedes Fountain: Located in front of the Slovak National Theatre, this fountain is made of marble with a bronze statue of Ganymedes sitting astride an eagle. Other sculptures

The interior of the church with a convent of St. Elizabeth's Order, Špitál Street.

complement the centrepiece, and all of these adornments gush water. The fountain was dedicated to the city by the Bratislava First Savings Bank in 1880. The designer of the fountain is V. Tilgner.

33 The Goose Fountain: Located in Šafárik Square and the work of Bratislava sculptor R. Kuhmayer in 1914, the fountain is a poetic sculptural creation inspired by an old legend. In the center of the round pool is a pile of small boulders on top of which a boy is cavorting and chasing a gaggle of frightened geese, water streaming out of their bills. Thanks to the

natural elements and composition of this piece, each vantage point around the fountain affords a different perspective of the work.

34 Slovak National Gallery: Located on Dunajské nábrežie (the Danube Embankment), the avenue along the north bank of the Danube River, this Baroque building was the former army „Water Barracks" which underwent extensive renovations in 1949 – 1951 for use by the newly-instituted National Gallery. The modern wing of the building, featuring the controversial architecture of architect V. Dedeček, was opened in 1979.

City walls with three towers and a gate have been used as Bratislava's emblem since mid-C13. The tinctures (colours) may be seen in the letters patent dating from 1436. Bratislava is the only city which, in fear of loss or damage, had letters patent issued in two exemplars. The first one is dated 8th July and the second, 9th July, 1436. They are both considered as examples of the most precious heraldry. They were produced in a Viennese miniaturists' workshop by a painter Michal.

Bratislava has always been an enthusiastic supporter and advocate of music, drama, science and education. Bratislava opened its gates to many outstanding personalities who made it their home. One of them was M. Bel, the polyhistor and author of the first study of the history and geography of Upper Hungary, what is today Slovakia. Other noted personalities were: S. Mikovíni (a mathematician, cartographer and astronomer); J. M. Korabinský (a geographer and historian); L. Raisch (an astronomer); J. Lippay (a botanist and the founder of the famous Lippay's Garden); J. A. Segner (a physicist and mathematician, and the inventor of the so-called Segner's wheel); W. Kempelen (a builder, and creater of a chess automaton, a pump, and a pontoon bridge over the Danube); G. R. Donner and F. X. Messerschmidt (sculptors); J. Fadrusz, A. Rigele (painters), and J. N. Hummel (musical composer and piano virtuoso and pedagogue); W. A. Mozart, F. Liszt, A. Zimmermann, J. Haydn, K. Ditters von Dittersdorf, and others who conducted orchestras or gave concerts here.

In walking through the picturesque lanes, streets, and squares of the oldest part of the city, and with visits to museums and galleries, visitors may partake in the delights of the capital of Slovakia. Not only those who come from far and wide to admire the wealth of architectural beauties but also the inhabitants of Bratislava often follow the route – rich in historical associations – that runs from Michalská Gatehouse through Main Square and to the Rybárska Gatehouse towards the Danube. From the Main Square they may continue through Panská Street to Rybné square, and then through Sigismund Gatehouse come to the Castle. A visit to the Castle offers not only the attractive collections of the Slovak National Museum, but also a fine panoramic view of the whole city including the new housing estates situated beyond the Danube and the suburbs lying to the east.

Bratislava is among the few cities which have excellent recreational facilities directly in the city or close by. The semi-natural forest in Bratislava consists of three parts. The first one spreads westwardly from Bratislava and runs from Karlova Ves and Dúbravka through Devínska Kobyla up to Devínska Nová Ves. The second part covers the southern and southeastern slopes of the Little Carpathian Mountains and extends to the west as far as Košarisko, Borinka, Stupava, Marianka, Lamač, through Kačín, Železná studienka, Kamzík, and continues to Spariská, Biely kríž, and Neštich. The third part includes the landscape area of Lužné lesy, the recreational area of Jarovecké rameno, Rusovce, Čunovo, and the recreational area known as Na pieskoch near Podunajské Biskupice.

Horský park, as if being representative of the Little Carpathian Mountains, creates a natural background to houses located on the hillslopes above the castle. Bratislava and its residential quarters are ideal starting points for the numerous hiking paths which lead to nearly places in the Little Carpathian Mountains: Železná studienka, Kačín, Marianka, and Pajštún. Other attractive places within easy reach of the city are Rusovce and Devín with its majestic castle standing on a hill rising above the confluence of two rivers – the Danube and the Morava. The Devín Castle is a National Cultural Monument.

Archeological excavations have revealed surviving remains of a prehistoric settlement, then a Celtic oppidum, and a Roman army campsite. The Great-Moravian hillfort referred to in the Frankish Annals in 864 as Dowina, was a fortress of Prince Rastislav. In the Middle Ages a Gothic castle was built here, then was transformed into the Renaissance style in CC16 and 17. The Napoleonic troops advancing towards Bratislava destroyed it in 1809. Presently, the castle, which is open to the public, is still being reconstruscted.

In Bratislava there are several outdoor swimming pools – Tehelné pole, Matador, or Delfín, and the lakes in Zlaté piesky, Petržalka, and Rusovce, all of which provide a pleasant change to summer sightseeing tours. Bratislava also offers tourist cruises on the Danube. In the winter season, the slopes of Koliba, directly in the city, or the hillslopes of the Little Carpathian Mountains are ideal for skiing.

Beckov

Names: L – Blundus, **H** – Beckó
Latitude: 48° 48' N, **Longitude:** 17° 55' E
Elevation: average 190 m, **range:** 186 – 544 m
Population: 1400
Means of Access: By rail: 10 km from the railway station at Nové Mesto nad Váhom, route No. 120; By road: route No. 507 or 6 kilometers from the main road E 75 = 61 in Nové Mesto nad Váhom
Information: Town hall: tel: (++421)(0)834-987125, 0834-987116

This little town is situated on the left bank of the River Váh in the Beckovská brázda (Beckov Rift) leading out of the Váh Valley between the wooded slopes of mighty mountain ranges of the Považský Inovec and the Little and White Carpathians. The Beckov castle cliff, on the northeastern promontories of the Považský Inovec, is a 60-metre high remnant of a large limestone massif crowned with the castle ruins. The natural cliff formation combined with them formed a remarkably pleasant scenery. Beckov is located 105 kilometres to the northeast of Bratislava and 22 kilometres to the southwest of Trenčín. The climate is characterized as mostly warm and humid in the mountains, and as warm, mild, and dry in the lowlands. The temperatures range from –1.5 to –4 °C in January, and from 18.5 to 19.5 °C in July; the total rainfall varies from 650 to 700 mm a year and contributes to its mild climate.

At Beckov, natural conditions and architecture blend together to create a magnificent scenery. The beauty of the natural formation of a rocky cliff, which is essentially a coral cliff, shaped out of the alluvium of the River Váh; it was enhanced by masterpieces formed by human hands – the castle and the settlement below it. The fertile valley of the Váh with a vast inundation area offered favourable conditions for settlement already in the prehistoric

time. The habitation here is evidenced for the New Bronze Age, the late La Tène, and the Roman period. The finds of golden jewelry can be dated to C4.

The forboding appearance of the cliff and the impression of its impregnability attracted people to settle here and utilize its natural properties. Beckov Castle, as well as any other castle in the system of signal castles situated in the Váh Valley and having the defence function, was built at a strategically outstanding point. These castles guarded heavily a vast area and formed the protective system in the borderland between the Bohemian and the Hungarian kingdoms.

The earliest written record of a settlement called Blundix is from 1208. However, archaeological discoveries from this settlement indicate that it already existed in the early Middle Ages, in C9, throughout C10 and C12. Considering the location of the settlement, it is possible to assume that this place was advantageous for habitation owing to the existence of a ford across the Váh here. The charter from 1226, in which the settlement below the royal castle was also alluded to, conveys that Jakub (James), the Bishop of Nitra, gave one-fourth of his tithe of wine collected at the town of Beckov to the Benedictine monastery at Skalka, near Trenčín.

In the Middle Ages, there were two settlements

Beckov Castle, mid-C19.

situated below the castle. Both of them can be recognized at present when studying the plan of the village. The location of the former one, situated to the south of the castle hill, is delineated by the parish church of King Stephen the Saint. Though the first written records referring to it are only from 1424, the first allusion to the parsonage dates from 1332. This settlement lay aside the high road along the Váh, and therefore only a way to the castle passed through it. The owner of the castle, Stibor, gave the settlement to his castellan and his brother in 1396. According to a record from 1411 it was not fortified.

The latter settlement was located directly below the castle. It began to thrive only in 1388, when King Sigismund gave this originally royal demesne as a gift to Duke Stibor. In 1392 the new owner ensured application of the Trnava Law Code for the town. It was fortified with walls, a moat, and a gatehouse from 1398. However, the settlement did not develop into an important centre of crafts and trade; it remained an unfree town, dependent wholly on the castle. The town defences, which belong to the oldest ones in Slovakia, as well as the spacious market square, demonstrate an intention to change Beckov into an important economic centre. No pieces of architecture besides the town walls have been preserved from the time when the fortified settlement below the castle came to existence. The first houses were of timber or earthwork as those ones in the former settlement. Written sources say that the houses at Beckov were built after a pattern similar to that of manor houses which were often of timber. Only later, in C17, the manor houses were built of stone in a pattern which is familiar to us today.

The second oldest structure of the settlement below the castle, except for the town walls, is the building of the county orphanage. Most probably Stibor was the one who had it constructed. He also continued the constructions and reconstructions of the castle and the settlement below it. Throughout the whole C15 no construction works were continued apart the reconstructions of the castle. The C16 was marked by wars against the Turks, who approached also Beckov. The castle was besieged by them but never seized. The settlement around was most probably destroyed by the Turks. This idea is supported by the fact that all of the existing houses were built only after 1599.

The skyline of the castle and the town from the east.

The next stage of building activities and urban development of the small town below the castle can be studied in the preserved houses, which were built during C17, when gentry started settling here. They took over administration of the castle and the manor and ran them separately. After that the castle was slowly falling into disrepair and became uninhabitable. The small landed gentry also built simple manor houses, attached to the town walls from the inside. One of the earliest ones (now demolished) was that of the Mednyánsky family. During C17 the small town acquared the layout which is known today. Towards the end of C17 and first half of C18, the development of the town was completed; until mid-C20 no great changes took place. Not a long time ago some of the manor houses were demolished and new buildings took their places, destroying the character of the historic urban scheme.

Buildings built after 1600 represent a relatively simple type of a gentry's residence called *"kúria"* – manor house. Most of the manor houses were solitary dwellings, though some of them nearly touched each other. Predominantly they formed closed units possessing U-shaped ground plans. These isolated buildings stood on wide, but short building plots. They were directly attached to the castle walls and their courtyards opened towards the square. These manor houses had two storeys. The land registry map dating from C19 brings evidence that at that time there existed from 9 to 11 manor houses, a church, and a Franciscan monastery complex, an orphanage and a few minor houses, i. e., approximately 21 buildings altogether.

In the other parts of Beckov, types of solitary urban houses predominate, scattered along irregularly drawn roads, and dominated by the castle cliff.

The castle and the church tower of St. Joseph the Guardian and the Franciscan monastery from the north.

The castle, located in the southeast portion of the Trenčín valley; in the foreground is the church of St. Stephen the King.

The castle.

1 The Castle, a National Cultural Monument: The earliest enclosed settlement discovered on top of the cliff belongs to the transitory period which covers the span of time between the La Tène culture and the Roman period. Its range of size is considerable as it exceeds the present-day area within the castle walls. Another phase of habitation on this spot is documented by archaeological excavation from Great Moravia. The richness of excavated materials and the remarkably high level of craftsmanship of the objects provide evidence that this hillfort was permanently occupied and followed immediately by a settlement of the post-Great-Moravian period. The remains of constructions from that period were destroyed when the stone castle was being built.

For the first time the present-day castle is mentioned as "Castrum Blundus" by one of King Béla III's notaries, known as "Anonymus," in a Hungarian chronicle from the beginning of C13. Of particular interest is that in this chronicle were also used earlier records linked with events in C11. The notary's description glorifies the occupation of present-day Slovakia by the Old Magyars during the reign of Árpád. Among other castles, which they seized at that time, Beckov is recorded under various names such as Blonduch, Blondich, Bolondoch and Bolon-duch. It is accepted that the original name of Beckov, which is Blodinc or Bludinec, may be deduced from written sources comprising old Hungarian names. It was coined after the local topo-graphy and it reflects in an excellent way the enourmously difficult access to the castle. In the broad meandering valley of the Váh the route was very difficult to follow and people could have strayed very often.

Beckov belonged to the group of royal castles which guarded the western frontier of the Hungarian kingdom. The uppermost part of the castle is an elongated oval with a maximum length of 100 metres.

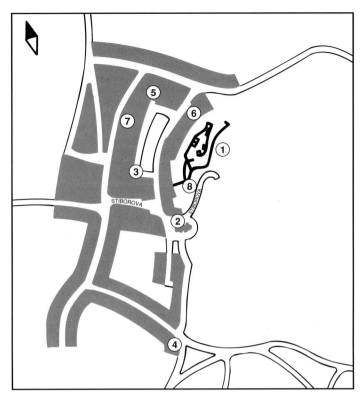

The town plan.

This part is approached only from the southern side where the hillside was only slightly falling down. During the construction works of the medieval castle, the slope was dressed to form a terrace with a drop of more than 15 metres. The difference in elevation was used by the masons who divided the whole area into the lower and the upper castle.

In the first half of C13, a palace was built on the northern, highest part of the cliff. The curtain walls, erected on the very edge of the cliff, were connected to the palace from both sides. On the most easily accessible southern side of the upper castle a quadrangular dungeon was built. The second palace was built at the southwestern part of the castle, just above the latter settlement site. This palace was essentially rebuilt in the Renaissance period. In C13 there was a water cistern in the spacious courtyard. It was cut

into the rock on which the castle stands.

Towards the end of C13, the first fortifications of the lower castle were built. However, they did not protect the entrance into the upper castle very effectively.

At the turn of CC14 and 15, the signal castle was rebuilt into a pompous fortified residence of a rich feudal nobleman, Duke Stibor of Stiborice. Fragments of Late-Gothic and Renaissance wall paintings, reticulated vaulting, which sprang from lavishly decorated brackets, and the window tracery have been preserved in the castle Gothic chapel. A most spectacular element of the castle architecture was the transverse Gothic palace accessible from the upper courtyard situated between the two earlier palaces and the chapel. It created the last line of defence of the living quarters, which were accessible through a corridor with sedilia. A cistern

The castle chapel and the ruins of the Renaissance palace.

The Renaissance inn in the square.

built of large hewn stones was located in the southeast corner of the courtyard between one of the palaces and the chapel. Subsidiary out-buildings, used by craftsmen and servants built in the lower courtyard of the upper castle, were moved to the newly-expanded lower castle in C16. At the same time a large battery tower was erected in this area. Characteristic features of the Renaissance reconstruction of the castle, which have been preserved up to now, are the high, arched gables crowning the palace and the chapel, and arched battlements and a stone gallery.

This not very large but elegant castle belonged to several successive owners: the Stibor, Bánffy, Mednyánsky, and Pongrác families. In C18 the castle had already been deserted and burnt out in 1804.

2 The Church of King the Stephen Saint: This Roman Catholic parish church is built into the fabric of the walls west of the town centre. A Gothic construction mentioned in 1424 was built on the site of a previous building. The preserved Gothic fragments date the church to an earlier period, approximately around 1400. During the first half of C17, the church belonged to the Protestants. In the interior a tribune was built roundabout the church and the Renaissance vaults were decorated with stuccoes. The façade was added a tower in 1770. The interior was predominantly in the Baroque style. The high altar dates from the end of C17 and is richly decorated with columns. The original stone floor has been preserved. The centrepice of the side altar of the Virgin Mary is a Late-Gothic sculpture of the Madonna from the end of C15. The side altar of the Piety, pews, and the sepulchre also date from C17; the organ dates from C18. Among very precious liturgical ornaments in the church are chalices from throughout CC17 and 18 and a monstrance from the second half of C18.

3 The Franciscan Monastery and the Church of St. Joseph the Guardian: Situated in the southern part of the square below the castle, this complex was built on earlier foundations in 1690 – 1692. The monastery is a two-storeyed, three-wing complex surrounding the cloister-garth. The church is one-nave; barrel vaults are decorated with stuccoes and lunettes. The interior decoration is in the Baroque and Rococo styles. The high altar is from the end of

C17, the organ is from the end of C18, and the altar in the sacristy dates from 1740. The sepulchre slab commemorates a monk – a saintly martyr.

4 The Evangelical (Lutheran – Augsburg Confession) Church: Built in 1791 – 1792 as a result of the Letter of Tolerance, the Evangelical church was later remodelled and renovated. In 1945 it was enlarged. The interior of one-spatial construction without a tower is treated in a modern style.

5 Manor Houses: Mostly two-storeyed, the manor houses Beckov have a U-shaped plan, with a courtyard facing the square. Oriel windows and vaulted rooms represented their characteristic features. The façades were transfored the Baroque and classical styles. An exhibition of the Trenčín Museum on the history of Beckov Castle, the town, and on famous natives is staged in the former manor house of the Ambro family.

6 The Inn: Located below the castle, it is a Renaissance building with a passageway. The inn was built in about mid-C17 as a road-side inn; it was remodelled in CC18 and 19.

7 The Town Fortifications: The town fortifications follow to the rocky cliff on the north, joining the fortification of the forecourt of the castle on the southern side, and closing off the simple plan of the town. Thus, they almost become a part of the castle fortifications as well. Trenčín has similar fortifications, but the Beckov ones are of an earlier date. They were built soon after Beckov received town privileges and liberties in 1392, based on the Trnava Law-Code.

The town walls are relatively high; their original height may be seen in several buildings which were later taken directly into the castle walls from the inside. An interior parapet ran along the walls

The silhouette of the castle from the entrance to the church of St. Stephen the King.

which were pierced with shooting slits; battlements were crenellated. Ramparts and a moat, which still can be seen in profile of the land arround the castle, are other characteristic features. To enter the town was possible through two gatehouses, on the southern and the northern sides of the walls, both probably equipped with drawbridges. These simple walled

fortifications are considered to be a traditional Gothic type of town fortification engineering.

8 The Cemetery: The cemetery at the foot of the castle cliff originally belonged to a Jewish religious community. Most of the grave-stones are from 1739 to 1845. They are Baroque and classical in style.

For over 400 years (from 1548), Beckov used the symbol of an elephant with a tower on its back in the municipal arms by mistake. The engraver who made a new seal for Beckov at that time did not comprehend the design dating from C15 which contained an engraving of a bull. But the bull was depicted with a cow-head. It was a mistake caused by the engraver from C15. Trying to correct it, the engraver in 1548 designed the head somewhat lower, creating thus the impression of an animal with a trunk. The presence of a bull in the Beckov arms is historically well-founded because a bull appears in the coat-of-arms of the local noble family – the Bánfies. Beckov became their property in 1434. Therefore, the correct symbol contained in the municipal arms is a bull, not an elephant.

Beckov is the birthplace of several celebrities, such as J. M. Hurban, a writer and politician; J. Ambro, a physician and gynecologist; D. Štúr, a geologist; L. Mednyánsky, a painter. Well-known writers and poets lived and worked in Beckov – e. g. H. Gavlovič, Š. Pilárik, and M. Mednyánsky.

This picturesque small town ranks among less pretentious tourist centres. The visitors will become familiar with it after a walk around the square, a visit to the museum and churches. If they climb the hill, they will reach the parish church, the Jewish cemetery, and the castle.
Beckov is also the starting point of the Považký Inovec mountain range. Hiking paths lead to the top of Inovec, Panská javorina, and Bezovec.
The recreational area of Zelená voda, near Beckov, offers lodging in summer; situated to the south of Beckov is Bezovec, another recreational area, which offers round-the-year lodging. It is popular especially in winter because of the ski lifts and the artificial skiing slope in the vicinity.

Komárno

Names: L – Comaromium, **N** – Komorn, **H** – Komárom
Latitude: 47° 55' N, **Longitude:** 18° 08' E
Elevation: average 112 m
Population: 37 941
Suburbs: Čerhát, Ďulov Dvor, Hadovce, Kava, Lándor, Malá Iža, Nová Osada, Nová Stráž, Pavel, Veľký Harčáš
Means of Access: By rail: routes No. 371, 373, 374; Bus service, local mass transportation, water transport on the Danube, and by road. Komárno has road, railroad and river border crossings to Hungary
Accommodations: Hotels: Danubius, Centrál, Čajka, Európa, Panoráma, Delta, Spoločenský dom; Hostels: ATC and CHO Natura, Nová Stráž
Information: CK Slovakotour, CK Tatratour, Information Center

Komárno lies in the Danube lowlands where the River Váh joins the River Danube. The western part of the town is in the eastern extremity of Žitný ostrov (Rye Island) between the Danube and the Váh. This territory is tectonically active; earthquakes occurred here in 1763 and 1783. On the island rare bird species nest: sea eagles, purple heron, ashy heron, and cormorant. Near the Danube is a wintering place for northern species of wild goose and duck. To the northwest of Komárno where the River Nitra joins the Váh is a State Nature Reserve where the nesting places of water fowl may be found in the swampy forests. The Reserve was established in 1954 on Apáli Island.

Komárno enjoys a dry climate. The average annual temperature is 9.7°C, i. e. in January –1.6°C, and in July 20.3°C. The average annual rainfall varies between 244 and 555 mm.

For centuries the rulers paid special attention to the junction of the Váh and the Danube and built here the defences. This spot was one of the most important strategic points of the defensive system of the whole Hungarian kingdom. Probably the first to build a fortress here were the Romans; other discoveries furnish clear traces of communities of the Avars, Slavs, and the Old Magyars. The first written piece of information about the construction of a fortress is from the period of the reign of King

Béla IV. An author, so-called Anonymus, wrote about a town and a castle named Komárom which were founded according to him in about mid-C10. On the site of the previous castle, a stone medieval castle was built in the second half of C13. In C15 the castle acquired the character of a comfortable royal residence for relaxation where King Matthias Corvinus liked to stay.

Further early information about the residence is from 1075, when Géza II granted three yokes of land and fishing rights in the Danube, which this settlement had enjoyed, to the Monastery of St. Benedict. The settlement was promoted to the rank of a town by Charles Robert of Anjou in 1331. The privileges granted in this year were later confirmed several times and in 1745 Komárno was declared a Free Royal Town.

The town grew from the old communities settled nearby the castle. The building activities bustled in the town especially during the reign of King Matthias Corvinus. In C16, after the Turks won a battle over the Christian rulers at Mohács in 1526, King Ferdinand I realized it was vital to organize defence of the realm, especially at the crossing-points on the Danube. Thus Komárno was converted into the most significant stronghold prepared to meet the Turkish raids. Italian fortification engineers invited by the King built

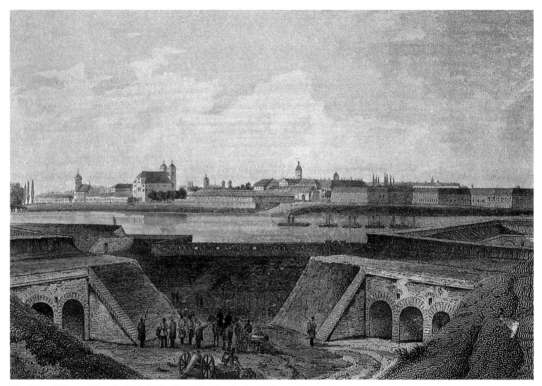

Komárno. A litographic print by G. Heïs after a drawing by L. Rohbock; the end of C19.

a Renaissance fortress on the site of once-existing Gothic castle in 1546 – 1557; this mighty fortress was the masterpiece of fortification engineering on the territory of today's Slovakia. The fortress was erected at a carefully chosen spot due to its peculiar geographical position in the tip of the junction of the Váh and the Danube. The configuration of the landforms marked its ground-plan, which is an elongated pentagon. When the building work was in progress the medieval town-plan scheme of the most important fanwise-arranged streets, which ran from the castle's gateway, was damaged. Later on, during the new construction stage of the fortress, the eastern portion of the town suffered damages again as the whole urban structure moved westwards. In C16 the town reached the Old Fortress and was enveloped by a curtain wall with towers and gatehouses.

In 1594 the town was completely destroyed by the fire which burst out when the Turks lay in siege outside the walls.

In 1663 King Leopold I issued a warrant for construction of a new fortress. This new fortress

The town charter granted by the Queen Maria Theresa.

The entrance to the Old Fortress, mid-C16.

The entrance to the New Fortress, from C18.

royal demesne as a gift to the town. In 1784 the individual buildings of the fortress, with the exception of the fortification system, were sold out at an auction.

The threat of Napoleon's military expedition against European feudal states prompted a new wave of building and modernizing the fortification systems in Europe at the turn of CC18 – 19. The attention of the Emperor's Court in Vienna turned to Komárno again; according to the decision of Emperor Francis I, Komárno was to be transformed into the mightiest fortress in the monarchy. In 1809 star-shaped earthen mounds with bastions and terraces were erected. The access into this new fortress was through two gateways. The new curtain wall enclosing the whole town was joined with the fabric of the fortress.

The urban structure of the historic centre has a ground-plan with a fanwise-arranged street network converging to the central space provided by the minor square, which creates C17 centre of the town. The eastern part of the town ceased to exist when the new fortress was erected. The actual street plan is of radial type and is orientated towards the main entrance into the New Fortress. The scheme of the streets has been completely preserved in the historic centre together with some other most significant historic buildings and spaces.

copied the shape of the older one and from which it was separated by a moat. The bridge connecting the town with the opposite bank of the Danube was closed by a projecting star-shaped outwork. The building development of the town was constantly subordinated to reconstructions of the fortress, and therefore the town was also constantly moving more and more westwards.

A highly animated building activity burst out in the town in C17. The Town Hall was finished, the Church of St. Andrew (Endré) was repaired, the Evangelical church and school were built, as well as the Calvinist and the Orthodox churches and the Jesuitical College.

Komárno acquired the privileges of a Free Royal Town in 1745. Having approximately ten thousand inhabitans, the town was the fifth largest in Hungary.

During C18 the growth of the town was disturbed by repeated earthquakes in 1763, 1765, and 1783, which destroyed not only the town houses but also the fortress to such an extent that Emperor Joseph II demobilized the garrison from there and gave this

The Town Hall, from 1875.

1 The Church of St. Andrew (Endré): This Late-Baroque church, built in 1748 – 1756, was renovated after the great fire in 1848. Its predecessor, together with the settlement, was destroyed by the Turks in 1594.

The one-nave church has side chapels above which are tribunes connected by a passage and an oval presbytery; the interior is vaulted with a flat vaulted ceiling. The two-tower concave façade is ended in the central part by a neo-Baroque balustraded attic. The interior furnishings are from C19. The hight altar of St. Andrew from the second half of C19 is made of marble and the painting on the altar depicts St. Andrew; there are also twelve neo-classical candle-sticks.

2 The Orthodox Church: This Late-Baroque church from 1754 was renovated after 1848. It is situated on the site of an earlier Gothic church from 1511, which was demolished when the New Fortress was being built. It is a one-nave structure with a straight end and a tower applied on the façade with a gable. The nave is vaulted with a flatvaulted ceiling.

The Rococo iconostasis (altar screen) dating from about 1770 is two-tiered and features a semi-circular „Tsar's gate". The pulpit is Rococo; the Baroque „stallae" (stalls) and pews are sumptuously carved. The pews and stallae are from the former Camaldulian monastery in Majk, Hungary.

The liturgical objects are of an earlier date, from the Late-Gothic style. The tomb-stones from CC18 – 19 are placed outside on the wall of the church.

3 The Former Garrison Church: This Late-Baroque edifice, originally a Franciscan monastic church, was built in 1769 on the site of an original church and monastery dating from 1677, which collapsed during the great earthquake in 1763.

The one-nave construction is vaulted with Baroque vaults; the furnishings are from CC19 – 20.

4 The Church of the Reformed Confession: It was built without a tower in 1788 after the Religious Reform Charter was issued; later on, the tower was added in 1832 and at that time the whole church was refaced. The hall construction with a flat ceiling has columned tribunes on three sides. The monumentally designed classical three-axial façade displays sumptuous architectural ornamentation.

The interior furnishings are in Rococo and classical Revival style. The pulpit dating from the second half of C18 is decorated with rocaille wood-carving. The organ in the style of Louis XVI is of 1788 and liturgical objects are from C17.

5 The Evangelical (Lutheran – Augsburg Confession) Church: This classical church from 1796, with a tower added in 1899, is a hall-church with a semi-circular apse. The façades were rebuilt in the neo-classical style after the tower was added. A Roman sarcophagus is built into the outer wall of the church.

The interior furnishings are from the period of the first construction stage of the church. The columned

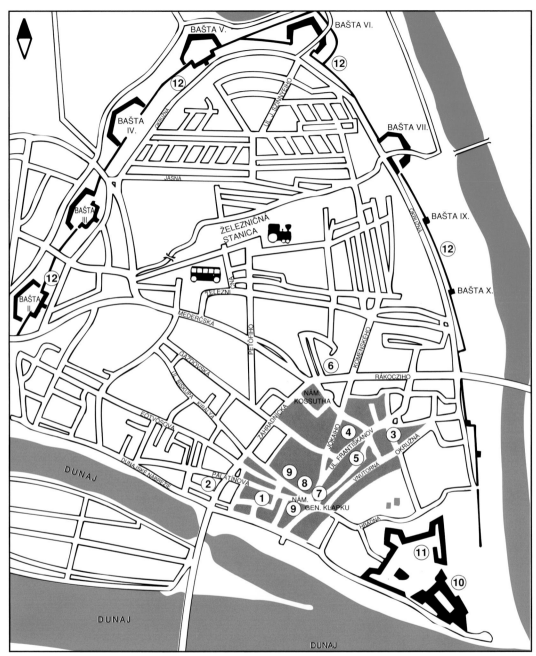

The town plan.

altar contains a painting of the Crucifixion.

6 The St. Rosalie Church: This neo-classical church was built in 1848 in the market place. The central construction is dominated by a lantern dome over the oval ground-plan. The main façade is decorated with four huge pilasters and is ended by a balustraded attic.

The interior furnishings are classical, dating from the period of the construction of the church. The high altar with the statue of St. Rosalie is also classical. The side altars of the Holy Cross and the Piety are from mid-C19.

7 The Town Hall: Built in 1875 on the foundations of an earlier

The buildings of the Danubian Region Museum from 1891.

The classical Church of St. Rosalie, from 1848.

The Serbian Orthodox church.

construction, this three-storeyed corner building possesses a tower situated in the central axis of the main façade. The neo-Renaissance façade is ended by a balustraded attic. On the first floor there are reception rooms.

8 The Former County Hall: A Late-Baroque construction dating from mid-C18, this Hall is classical in style. At the end of C19, it was elevated by another storey and it was refaced. The main façade of the three-storeyed building features bands of rustication.

9 Burghers' and Craftsmen's Houses: Mostly ground-floor three-axial houses are in Baroque, classical, and Art-Nouveau styles, and arranged in rows they flank the streets. They were not built in the usual pattern – on previous houses' foundations, as it is common in other historic centres – but were built from scratch on new plots when the town moved westwards in order to free space for the new fortifications.

10 The Old Fortress: Also known as the Anti-Turkish, this fortress was built in 1546 – 1557. It was designed by the Italian fortification engineer, Pietro Ferrabosco. At that time the fortress with its modern bastion system and excellent strategic position

No. 3 Tržničné (Market) Square

The icon Blessing Christ from the iconostasis of the Orthodox church.

The Baroque Holy Trinity column.

represented the superb point in the anti-Turkish defences on the today's Slovak territory. The fortress was erected in the tip of junction of the Váh and the Danube. This mighty fortification system with an earthen mound stregthened by brick cladding and a bastion, jutting out its acute angle, was orientated eastwards; the western portion overlooking the town was streghtened by two polygonal corner bastions; in-between them was the gatehouse with the so-called Ferdinand's Gate, accessible only over the moat. The defence of the northern and southern portions was secured by right-angle projections.

11 The New Fortress: This structure was begun in 1663. The fortress was the materialization of an older concept of strengthening the defensive power of the Old Fortress. Its construction was finished in 1673 according to the design of Franz Wymes, who employed here the latest experiences of French and Italian fortification engineers. The pentagonal fortress is situated to the west of the Old Fortress, from which it was separated by a widened and deepened moat. Its builder turned three polygonal bastions towards the town and clipped Leopold's Gate between the southwest and central bastions.

Two minor bastions protecting the northern and southern flanks were placed on the spots where the fortress is situated closest to the Old Fortress. When Napoleon marched through Europe, the existing fortress was modernized to hold off assaults upon the town; it became the centrepiece of other fortification constructions. In 1810 large army barracks were built here, and in 1815 the office-building of the head-quarters was built in the courtyard of the New Fortress.

The anti-Turkish double-fortress of Komárno resisted all military attacks and fulfilled all the hopes imposed upon it expressed in an inscription written below a statue in the northwest bastion of the New Fortress which reads: NEC ARTE NEC MARTE – "Neither by stratagem nor by power." The New Fortress is used by the army at present, while the Old fortress is being renovated and gradually made accessible to the visitors. Both of the fortresses are National Cultural Monuments.

12 The Town Fortifications:
A National Cultural Monument, during Napoleon's military campaign at the turn of CC18 and 19, this new protective line was begun to enclose the whole town. The fortresses were modernized and neo-classical fortifications were constructed according to designs by architect P. Nobile. On the western edge of the town, a continuous curtain wall, called the Palatine Line, was built. This line leads from the left bank of the Danube up to the Váh where Apáli Island lies. In mid-C19 along the Váh another line consisting of two bastions and four batteries was erected. This fortification line was punctured by several gates. Among Komárno's famous natives are writer Mór Jókai and composer Franz Lehár.

The town walls with towers and a gate are most typical of many medieval towns. Komárno accepted this motif in C15. To distinguish its own arms from other municipalities employing symbols with town walled fortifications, Komárno placed two starlets above the towers. These simple arms existed continuously until mid-C18. Maria Theresa issued a charter on the municipal arms of Komárno in 1745. From then onwards, the original simple and beautiful design was added those town fortifications, which are situated on the junction of the Danube and the Váh. Such an approach to the enriching of the original arms was common in C18. Besides, it is also a typical display of the deterioration of the heraldic production quality. The addition of the sod and rivers was not the result of an initiative of the Empress or the Court; certainly it was employed at the request of the municipality. The colour as well as the variety of heraldic elements agreed to the fashion of C18.

The visitors to Komárno may enjoy the exhibitions of the Danube Museum, or artifacts of sacral art in the Orthodox Church; the literature and music lovers will be attracted by the Mór Jókai Literary Memorial and the Franz Lehár Music and Literary Exhibition. Access to the State Nature Reserve is limited.

Komárno is a wonderful centre for summer sports, especially facilities for bathing and water sports.

Modra

Names: L – Modorinum, **G** – Modern, **H** – Modor
Latitude: 48° 20' N, **Longitude:** 17° 18' E
Elevation: average 175 m, **range:** 144 – 709 m
Population: 8 500
Suburbs: Harmónia, Piesok
Means of access: By rail: station in Pezinok – 9 km distant, route No. 120 in
    Šenkvice – 5 km distant; By road: routes No. 502, 503 and 504
Accommodations: Hotels: Modra; in Harmónia and Piesok – Haffner, Press,
    Zochova Chata, Chata Pod lipou, Pod Lesom – Narcis
Information: Malokarpatská (Small Carpathians) Tourism Information Office:
    tel: (++421)(0)704-6474302, fax:(0)704-6474662, e-mail: tik@post.sk, www.tik.sk

The town of Modra is situated in the wine-district on the southeastern foothills of the Little Carpathian Mountains and the Podunajská pahorkatina (the Danubian Dowers), 25 km northeast of Bratislava. The Little Carpathians are a nature Conservancy Area. Their geological basis is created by crystallized slate, lime-stone, dolomite, and karst. Large forests, which form a natural setting for the town, consist predominantly of deciduous species, providing good conditions for hunting.

Modra has a warm, dry, and mild lowlands climate with average January temperatures varying from –1 °C to 4 °C, average July temperatures varying from 19.5 °C to 20.5 °C. The annual rainfall fluctuates between 530 and 650 mm.

The first evidence of human activity in the vicinity of Modra may be dated back to 3000 BC. Bronze objects dating from the Roman period were discovered in its surroundings. The first Slavs settled here during the era of migrations of peoples. Evidence of their presence was proven by arch aeological excavations of a burial ground from 800 to 950, situated directly in Modra, and a fortified settlement site at Harmonia dated from the early Great-Moravian period; it is similar to the settlement near Svätý Jur.

In the first half of C12, Modra was permanently settled by royal subjects as documented in a charter dating from 1158. In 1241 the settlement was plundered by the Tartars. Modra belonged to the community of five west-Slovakia towns called *Pentapolitana,* consisting of Bratislava, Trnava, Pezinok, and Svätý Jur.

The economy of Modra was based on highly successful wine-growing, which had already been well-developed by C13. In the first half of C14, the economic prosperity of Modra increased, which was the reason for granting it town privileges in 1361. In spite of their attainment, Modra remained an unfree town. After 1428 the Hussites damaged the town several times. In 1437 King Sigismund gave Modra as a gift of royal demesne to a feudal noblemam, Michal Országh de Guth. It remained in possession of his family for more than 130 years. In this period the town flourished. The economic prosperity encouraged the inhabitants in their efforts to achieve political independence. They were successful in 1569 when King Maximilian II declared Modra a Free Town dependent only on the Crown. In 1607 it was promoted to the position of a Free Royal Town. One of the most precious privileges was to errect the town walls. They were begun after 1610 and completed in 1646.

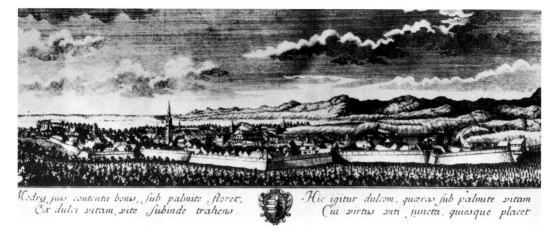

Modra jus contenta bonis, sub palmite floret,
Ex dulci vitam, vite subinde trahens.

Hic igitur dulcem, quæras sub palmite vitam
Cui virtus viti juncta, quiasque placet.

Modra, a coper engraving etching by A. Kaltschmied after a drawing by S. Mikovíny from 1736.

In C17 the growth and decline of the town's fortunes alternated. In 1702 Modra was set on fire by the emperor's soldiers and two thirds of the town burnt down. Another fire destroyed the town in 1705. In spite of these disasters, the inhabitants of the town kept on renewing their houses. The renewal was speeded up by prosperous viticulture, trade and crafts – the traditional manufacturing of cloth and pottery. Later on industry was introduced to Modra.

The local cultural and social life rose and fell in dependence on the rise and fall of the town's economy. In 1674 Benedictines settled in Modra, overtaking an already existing grammar school, churches, and several other buildings. In the second half of the 16th century, the spirit of Reformation began to diffuse among the burghers of Modra, encouraged by trade contacts with German towns. In 1714 – 1715 the Lutherans completed two churches. They also supported schools, which boasted high academic standards. In 1729 during another great fire, all churches, schools, and sacral buildings were grieviously damaged; they were renewed in 1730. In 1777 Emperess Maria Theresa abolished the Benedictine Gymnasium in Modra, thus leaving here only elementary schools.

The Evangelical, or Lutheran, elementary school existed parallel to the Benedictine Gymnasium and after its abolition it was added higher classes in order to preserve higher educational establishment in Modra. Karol Štúr was its rector from 1839 to 1846, followed by Ján Kalinčiak until 1858. The school was abolished in 1870; then a public school and teachers' training school were established here.

According to the town plan, Modra developed along the broadened road which was the axis of the plan. Its oldest part is the Romanesque settlement situated around the church of St. John the Baptist and the churchyard in Dolná Street. The town grew northwards to create the present plan. It consists of a narrow elongated square orientated north-south and broadened in the central part. Around this square, burghers' and craftsmen's town houses were built; one-storeyed houses at either end of the square, and two-storeyed ones in the middle. In C19 a new parish church was built in the middle of the western side of the square, stretched along the road to Bratislava. The town developed along this road, thus creating an irregular town plan. When Modra was walled in, between 1610 and 1646, the Pezinská brána (Pezinok Gatehouse) was built in this street. Other two gatehouses guarded the High Street – the Dolná and Horná brána (Lower and Upper Gatehouses); the Upper Gatehouse still has survived. The Lower Gatehouse was demolished in 1874, Pezinok Gatehouse in 1882. Outside each gatehouse, a suburb developed, bearing its name. The Lower suburb was the most important. In 1719 three hundred and thirty houses existed in Modra and the suburbs altogether.

In CC19 and 20 the town spread mainly westwards – towards Pezinok and Bratislava, and in this area tenant houses were built; some manufactures were established to the south of the town. In the second half of C19 Modra's economy was falling down as being distant from the backbone of industry – the railway. In C20, wine-growing remained prosperous as the main occupation in Modra, but the decay of crafts

The town from the south.

Evangelical churches: the so-called German and Slovak.

The square: the parish church.

The square: the Memorial to Ľ. Štúr.

The Upper Gatehouse, the northern part of the town:
a part of the town walled fortifications.

Circular bastion in the town fortifications, built in
1610 –1646.

Examples of the Modra majolica.

occurred. Only pottery-making flourished. Its
quality and fame has surpassed regional boundaries.
Today, wine-growing is the major economic basis
of the town, gradually crafts and local industries are
reviving. The majolica of Modra, famous for its
painted decoration, has preserved traditional
patterns and high standards. In addition, several
artists – potters – live in the town and manufacture
ceramics and majolica.

The most important buildings, both from the
architectural and artistic point of view, are situated
in the square, leading to Lower Street.

1 The Church of King St. Stephen: This parish church in the square was built between 1873 and 1876. The historicizing style of its architecture is inspired by Renaissance style. The tower is attached to the façade ended in a gable. Interior furnishings are from the end of C19; on the side altars of St. Ladislas and St. Barbara, paintings executed by K. Jakaby in 1874 are placed.

2 Evangelical (Lutheran – – Augsburg Confession) Churches: These two churches are located in Dolná Street and behind the former Lower Gatehouse. In 1682 the local Evangelical congregation received permission from the emperor to build two houses of prayer for its Slovak and German believers. It is not known when the construction of the churches began, but the German Evangelical Church was finished in 1714, its Slovak counterpart in 1715. These newly-built churches were destroyed by the great fire of 1729. In 1730 they were renewed; later, in C19, their façades were altered. The German church has a one-nave interior space with a polygonal apse and side tribunes. The interior furnishings are dating from mid-C19. The Slovak church is aisleless, and with flat vaulted ceiling. It was restored in 1921. The interior furnishings date from the first half of C19. The stone baptismal font is from C17, the candelabra with sculptures of angels are from the end of C18.

3 Church of St. John the Baptist: Located next to the churchyard in Lower Street, this church is originally a Gothic building from the second half of C14. It was altered in the second half of C15 by the same mason's lodge building the Church of Saint Martin in Bratislava. In the first half of C18 the church was enlarged. The one-nave church possesses cross ridge-rib vaults; the presbytery has a polygonal ending. The nave features tribunes,

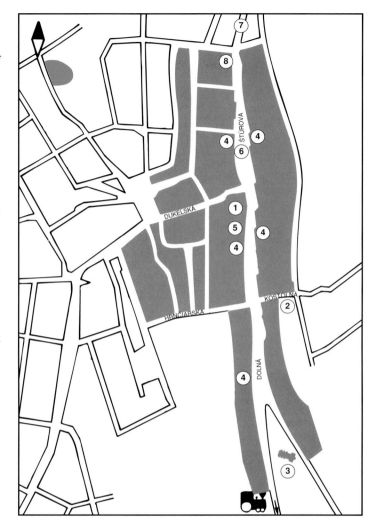

The town plan.

or lofts, and on the southern side, a Gothic stone portal has been preserved. In the presbytery are wall-paintings dating from C18. The high altar, the side altar, and the interior furnishings are from mid-C18.

Next to the church is the churchyard where several eminent personalities, including Ľudovít Štúr, are buried.

4 The Burgher's Town Houses: Situated in the square and Dolná Street, these houses create a complex of relatively

architecturally simple vintners' and craftsmen's houses. Most are one-storeyed, and only at the broader part of the square are two-storeyed ones with three- or four-axial classical façades. During frequent fires the houses burnt down completely and only temporal timber structures were constructed in their places; they lasted till new stone houses were built. Therefore, their oldest horizontal and vertical structural elements date only from C17. Façades used to be renewed to the architectural style popular at the time of renovation. The houses have a passageway and out-buildings in the backyards where large wine-press sheds and wine-cellars are situated. Architectural elements – portals, window-jambs, and vaults – mainly Renaissance ones – have been preserved in the interiors of the houses. Bay windows, very popular among the house owners and originally typical of Modra, have been only rarely preserved.

5 The Ľudovít Štúr Museum in Dolná ulica (Lower Street) is dedicated to the adherents and followers of Štúr, called *štúrovci*, and the history of Modra and its surroundings. A specialized exhibition of the Modra majolica has been staged here.

6 The Ľudovít Štúr Memorial: Situated in the square as a memorial to the author of the modern literary Slovak language, the sculptural group was made of white marble executed by F. Motoška in 1938.

7 The Mansion: Located behind the Upper Gatehouse, the mansion is built on the site of an earlier building, probably a castle. It was altered in C19, and in 1957 it was converted to house the Secondary School of Horticulture and Viticulture. The one-storeyed, four-wing building arranged around the central courtyard has rooms with Renaissance ridge-rib vaults on the ground-floor. Façades are plain, with a bay window located on the southern corner. The courtyard features a loggia seated on Tuscan columns, and in the niche is a statue of Saint Urbain, the patron saint of wine-growers. An ornamental garden, originally a Baroque park, with preserved stone works of art, spreads next to the mansion. A minor exhibition on viticulture is housed here. A visitor may taste wine from grapes grown in school vineyards. The Little Carpathian House of Wines is a part of the mansion.

8 The Town Fortifications: This system built between 1610 and 1646 has the character of a Renaissance fortress with earthen banks. Because it was necessary to use it immediately as a strategically important element of the anti-Turkish defensive system built at the foothills of the Little Carpathians, the town walls would not encircle the whole town, but only the northern part. The entrances to the town were guarded by three main gatehouses: the Dolná brána (Lower Gatehouse) on the south, the Horná brána (Upper Gatehouse) on the north, and Pezinská brána (Pezinok Gatehouse) on the west. The Upper Gatehouse, which has been preserved, has four storeys and a square ground-plan; above the passageway, on the side facing the town, the municipal arms are placed . The round sentry tower with key-shaped loopholes has survived on the western elevated part. A part of the stone cladding of the rampart has been preserved on the eastern elevation; in some other places, the moulding and parapet built of brick with loopholes remain.

Modra is among those few towns which already by C14 used a professional motif as its symbol – a branch of grape-vine with three bunches of grape. The turning point in evolution of the arms is the year 1607. Emperor Rudolf II declared Modra a Free Royal Town. By the charter , he added an element of the Hungarian coat-of-arms to this original symbol: the shield parted into red and silver halfs. The miniature painting which is contained in the charter is the obligatory pattern for the present arms, because it expresses the highest position of the town in the past.

A visit to Modra may start on its western side – along the road to Bratislava – where the remainders of the fortifications with round bastion still exist. Continuing to the square, the visitors reach the Upper Gatehouse and the mansion. When touring the town, a visit to the parish church, the Evangelical churches, and the Ľ. Štúr Museum should not be omitted. The sepulchre slabs in the churchyard remind the visitors of eminent natives and great personalities who once lived and worked in Modra.
A visit to Modra should be enriched by a tour of the Manufacture of Slovak Folk Majolica. The most valuable artifacts are on display in the showroom, where jugs, plates, and other products may be purchased.
   More ambitious tourists may be enticed by a hike to the Zoch's tourist Cottage and to Harmónia. Both of them are recreational areas which offer good facilities for swimming and skiing. Hiking paths lead from Modra to the Little Carpathians, Pezinok, as well as to the Červený Kameň Castle, a National Cultural Monument, or to "Štúr's Bench" at Holovnická dolina. In September the traditional wine festival takes place in the town, organized in turns by Modra, Pezinok, Rača (one of Bratislava's suburbs), and Svätý Jur.

Nitra

Names: L – Nitra, **G** – Neutra, **H** – Nyitra, **first historic name:** Nitrava
Latitude: 48° 15' N, **Longitude:** 18° 05' E
Elevation: average 151 m, **range:** 132 – 588 m
Population: 87 500
Suburbs: Čermáň, Diely, Dolné Kŕškany, Drážovce, Horné Kŕškany, Chrenová, Janíkovce, Klokočina, Kynek, Mlynárce, Párovské Háje, Staré mesto, Štitáre, Zobor
Means of Access: By rail: route No. 140; By road: routes No.
E 571, 65, 64, 61; By air: airport at Janíkovce
Accommodations: Hotels: Ax, Agroinštitút, Nitra, Olympia, Zobor, Športhotel, Trans-Motel, Tenis Hotel; Pensions U grófa & Zlatý kľúčik; tourist hostels; bed-and-breakfast
Information: NISYS – City Information Center – tel: (++421)(0)87-16186, 410906, fax: 087-410907, e-mail: nisys@nr.sanet.sk, www.nitra.sk

Nitra is located at the base of Zobor hill, at the foothills of the Tríbeč mountain range, in the Danube downs on the River Nitra, which winds around the prominent Nitra landmark, the castle, perched on a massive hill. From this site is a spectacular wide view of Nitra and the surrounding hills. Although the best-known of them is Zobor (588 m), it is just one of those which provide a beautiful scenery for the town. In the countryside around Nitra, there are several nature reserves: the Lubka Nature Reserve, the Zobor Woodland and Steppe, and the Nitra Dolomite Quarry Nature Reserve.

The climate of Nitra is warm and generally dry. Average temperatures range between –1.5°C and 4 °C in January, and between 18.5 °C and 19.5 °C in July. The annual rainfall fluctuates from 650 to 700 mm.

The beginnings of Nitra were in a site on an important crossroads of long-distance trade routes close to a major ford across the River Nitra. Finds from the region confirm continuous, long-term settlement of the area. Slavs are considered to be the most important settlers in terms of the history of Slovakia. Archaeological discoveries indicate that this ethnic group arrived in Nitra as early as C6. Sporadic allusions to Nitra in written sources can be dated to Great Moravia.

The earliest records about Nitra are due to the existence of a large hillfort with permanent buildings. About this enclosed settlement one fact is well-known: Prince Pribina, who was of Slavonic stock, invited Archbishop of Salzburg so that he would consecrate a church in Nitrava somewhere between 826 and 828. The stone foundations of this one-nave little church have survived at the foothill of Zobor – on Martin Hill; it is considered to be the last remnant of ecclesiastical architecture of this type in the region.

After Prince Pribina was expelled from Nitra, Prince Rastislav was invested a non-ruling prince. In 846, when Rastislav became the ruler of the Great-Moravian empire, Rastislav's nephew Svätopluk took over his position in Nitra. In 863 Rastislav invited a Byzantine Christian mission to Great Moravia. Cyrillus (Constantine) and Methodius, two brothers who arrived here, contributed significantly to the advancement of Slavs by translating the Bible into the Old Slavonic language, thereby standardizing its literary usage. At the time, when the Great-Moravian empire reached its climax, Nitra functioned as a significant centre. This is claimed due to large resident population in several walled settlements, e. g. at Vŕšok; the site coinciding with the grounds of the present-day castle: Borinka; Zobor, and Lupka.

Nitra. An etching by V. Hollar after a drawing by G. Hoefnagl, 1657.

After the death of Prince Svätopluk in 894, a period of intense internal strife followed. It was ended by the invasion of the Old Magyars/Hungarians and Bavarians at the beginning of C10. Nitra's development and strategic importance, however, were not diminished even after the fall of the Great-Moravian empire. Archaeological discoveries yielded a wealth of information on this period. Excavations confirm that the settlement continued to exist and even thrived, being only gradually affected by the influences exerted by the Hungarian conquerors. Other important site from this time referred to as standing out beside the fort, is a Benedictine Monastery of St. Hippolytus located atop Zobor. Although it was mentioned only in 1111, it must have been founded much earlier.

After the disintegration of Great Moravia, the newly created and strategically even more important Nitra duchy on the frontier with Moravia was administered from the castle enclosure by a succession of Árpád dukes – Béla, Géza, and Ladislas. The duchy ceased to exist at the end of C11. Nitra, a seat of the Bishop of Nitra and an administrative centre of a Hungarian *comitatus* (county/district), achieved new significance. The seats of both the bishop and the official of the county were probably located in the heavily

fortified castle. A horseshoe-shaped apse of St. Emeram's Church, which was founded at that time, is located on the castle hill. The settlement around the castle and in its close neighbourhood is well evidenced by archaeological finds. Further evidence was also yielded by a written record from Parovce, which once used to be a well-known merchant village. In CC11 and 12 a pre-Romanesque church of St. Stephan originally stood in its centre.

Nitra's further development was facilitated with a charter issued by Béla IV on the 2nd September 1248, which granted the guests (hostes /colonists) and local burgesses – the defenders of the castle against the Tartars – new liberties and privileges. However, their full advantage could not be enjoyed because of wars between the Bohemian and Hungarian kingdoms over territories under disputes. Nitra was plundered by Přemysl Otakar II and shortly after, it lost its status of a free royal town. From 1288 onwards, Nitra, owned by the Bishops of Nitra, lost its self-administration and sank to the rank of an unfree town. For a short time due to the Bishop's support, the town was usurped by Matúš Čák, the great Slovak magnate. The occupation lasted until his death in 1321. At his command, the Nitra burghers' property was plundered and the inhabitants relocated according to his own needs.

The panorama of the town.

There are only a few records dating from that period describing either the architecture of the town or the actual town plan. The agricultural character of its economy determined the style and size of many dwellings. In addition, the size of stone cellars, or their parts at least, which have been preserved in the Upper Town, confirm that viticulture used to be very important and traditional main occupation in Nitra; it also brought the town enormous profits. According to later analogies, most of the secular houses seem to have been built of mud brick and had thatched roofs.

At the beginning of C14, Nitra was divided into six independent sections; the Upper and Lower towns were separated from each other by a branch of the River Nitra – the Nitrička. The fortifications, which were constructed after a warrant by King Sigismund at the beginning of C15, consisted of several isolated parts. The most important one was the castle located on the hill above the meanders of the River Nitra. Below the castle, spread across its slopes, was the Upper Town, which was fortified by three types of defences. The third part of the fortifications consisting of mounds with palisades and ditches was built around the Lower Town. Muddy banks of the river were effectively employed as part of the fortification system.

From CC15 to 17, the advancement of the town was hindered by a series of wars; all military expeditions of greater importance passed through Nitra. The sequence of disasters started after Nitra had been taken by Stibor. Then it was besieged by the Hussites in 1431. In 1440 the town was conquered by Jiskra's troops, called Jiskrovci, and at the end of C15 by the troops of the Polish King Casimir. Later on, Bethlen's troops seized Nitra and in 1663 the Turks, whose occupation of the town lasted for one year. This long period of warfare, destruction, plundering, and fires left marks on the town. In mid-C17, there remained only forty-four houses in the Upper Town. The Upper Town as well as the Lower Town was set on fire by the withdrawing Turks. Born of strategic reasons, a decree was passed limiting the height of all new constructions in the Old Town to one storey. This decree remained in force until 1700.

At the end of C17, both the church and the castle were fortified and reconstructed, but the peace which Nitra enjoyed was very short-lived. At the beginning of C18, Nitra was again captured. Rákoczy's forces seized the town and beheld it for five years till 1708, when they surrendered. They left the town completely in ruins. Nitra had to recover from all the disasters: the houses were repaired and many new significant buildings were built only after 1710. The castle and cathedral

The skyline of Nitra from the Calvary.

The Nitra Castle – a national cultural monument.

The Upper Church of the bishop's cathedral. A view of the Baroque western tribune.

The altar of the Descent from the Cross in the Lower Church by J. Pernegger, in 1622.

church were rebuilt; the pilgrimage church of the Mother of God was restored; the buildings of the Piaristic monastic complex were being finished. However, many new and magnificent architectural structures appeared, whose examples are the Greater and Lesser Seminaries, the Provost's Palace in the Upper Town, and the essentially reconstructed Franciscan church. Other examples of this extensive rebuilding are the stone bridge in front of the gateway to the castle and the Plague Column erected in the open space outside the entrance to the castle.

At the beginning of C19, the Empire and classical styles shaped Nitra's appearance. Strong national revival movement impacted life in the town where many revivalists lived and exerted great influence upon cultural activities. A good illustration of this new development was the establishment of a publishing house in Nitra in 1836. Furthermore, the ornate County House located at the foot of the castle hill was reconstructed during the second half of C19. In 1882 it was followed by a noteworty classical theatre in the square. At the same time several town

The castle with church tower.

The southern part of the Early-Baroque fortifications with a carriage-passage and a postern for pedestrians. The stone sculptures on the bridge date from C18.

The Immaculata by the Austrian sculptor, M. Vogerle is a reminiscent of the plague epidemic.

houses in the eclectic style extended the range of design used in Nitra. Industrial development was notable; factories working agricultural products and producing foodstuffs which arose on the outskirts of the town must be mentioned.

However, World War II brought destruction. After the air-raids many buildings of considerable value were laid in rains not only in the Lower Town but also in other of Nitra. In the post-war period much of the Lower Town was gradually demolished to meet the needs for housing the growing population of the town.

Nitra, as a regional and county seat, is the economic center of the region along the Nitra River. It is the center of agricultural education and research in Slovakia (the Slovak Agricultural University is located there.) Other educational institutions include the University of Constantine the Philosopher and the Seminary of St. Gorazd. The national agricultural exposition is held annually at the Agrokomplex exhibition area, as are other international expositions and marketplaces including the well-known Nitra Autosalon.

In 1987 the Upper Town together with the castle was declared an Urban Conservation Area. In addition, the whole Lower Town is now the Urban Conservation Area.

Pribina Square in the Upper Town.

The buildings of the seminaries.

The former County House: a historicizing Art Nouveau building, the end of C19.

1 The Castle: (National Cultural Monument): This is the most impressive and characteristic building complex in the town. Its core is formed by the cathedral and the Bishop's palace. The oldest standing parts of the cathedral are the remnants of the basilica of St. Emeram: an apse of horseshoe plan dating from the period between C12 to C13 and an adjacent older cemetery. The oldest discovered castle fortifications belonged originally to the cathedral. The upper, originally Gothic cathedral church was built from 1333 to 1355. After its completion, the older Romanesque church served as a "locus credibilis," i. e. a place where authenticity of charters, legal agreements was established and where administrative warrants were verified. During the early Baroque reconstructions from 1622 to 1642, the Gothic cathedral church was extended by the Lower Church connected with the Upper Church by a broad stairway. The Viennese architect D. Martinelli, who is the designer of the decorations, collaborated with the painter G. A. Galliarti, who painted the frescoes.

The interior ornaments of both churches originated from 1732 to 1780s. The altar in the Lower Church depicting the scene of the *"Removal from the Cross"* is by the sculptor L. Y. Pernegger. It is a unique work executed after an engraving by Daniel da Voltera. The tower, erected in C17, was originally lower; the present-day dimensions resulted from the Baroque reconstruction which included the addition of a monumental entrance stairway with balusters surmounted with vases and statues. The Bishop's Palace, standing on the top of the castle hill, represents another addition to the sacral buildings on the western side. Its appearance resulted from the Late-Baroque renovations between 1732 and 1739. A window above the rocky cliff on the northern side has been preserved from the original Gothic structure. The state rooms on the first floor were arranged and

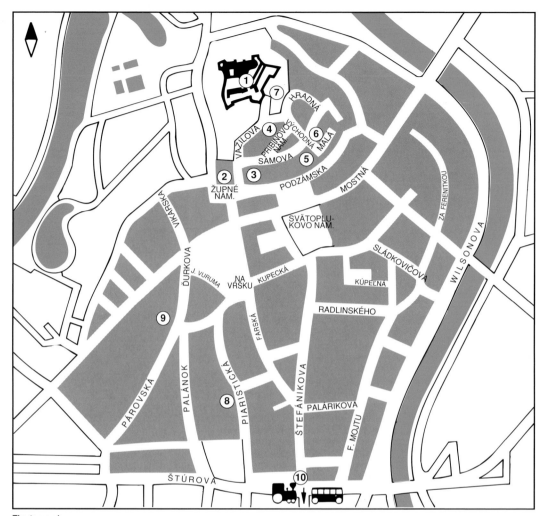

The town plan.

furnished in the Empire style at the beginning of C19.

A Renaissance entrance structure located between the outer wall and the cathedral buildings was constructed in mid-C16. It is approched through a gateway on the ground floor; it has a richly decorated portico on the eastern side. To the south of the Bishop's Palace is a subsiding out – building which was added to the castle fortifications as their extension during CC16 and 17. A part of the medieval town wall and rectangular Vazil's Tower with an almost square ground-plan have been well-preserved. The northeast

and south of the castle grounds are bordered by fortifications with bastions and casemates erected in the Early-Baroque style.
A passageway and a postern are on the southern side. The stone statues on the bridge over the castle moat date from C18. At present, the castle is the seat of the Bishops of Nitra.

The Upper Town was originally an isolated enclosed settlement consisting mainly of sacral buildings, e. g. a church with a monastery, seminaries, canons houses, and houses of wealthy burghers. The main communicational axis leads along

the street which starts at the passageway of the County Hall and runs towards the castle, and which is flanked with the most important buildings of the town.

2 The Former County Hall: This building was constructed in the Art Nouveau style at the end of C19. An older building was reconstructed after design of the architect O. Dümmerling. The result was a four-wing building with an irregular ground-plan developed around the central courtyard. Its south front has two storeys and faces the Lower Town. The passageway used for entering

The Piarist church and monastery in the Lower Town, a Baroque complex, from 1701 – 1763.

4 The Lesser Seminary: This late-classical structure of palatial type was constructed as a superstructure on the foundations of an older building according to the plans of the architect K. Mayer in the second half of C19. The palace stands in a row of houses; it has retained its copious façade facing the south. The entrance recedes into the façade, creating thus a tiny entry space with niches. This two-storeyed, two-wing building has a central courtyard whose northern part is ended by a wall supporting a balustrade.

5 The Greater Seminary: Located in the southern part of the Upper Town, this large state palatial construction dates from the second half of C18. It consists of three portions. Firstly, there is a one-storeyed Baroque building of the great seminary built from 1767 to 1770 by Bishop Y. Gustíny, who was also an *ispán*, a royal official representing the King's authority. In 1779 two wings projecting to the south were started on the western side of the building. Secondly, there is a neo-classical, two-storeyed structure facing the Lower Town built by Bishop A. Roskoványi in 1877. In this part of the Greater Seminary is a chapel in the neo-Renaissance style. The neoclassical diocesan library, built in 1878 – 1879 according to desings of two Viennese architects F. Schmidt and J. Lippert, is an exact copy of the Szécsenyi National Library in Budapest. In the Seminary Chapel is a wall painting by the same painter who painted the fresco of St. Cecilia in the cathedral. The rear wing of the Greater Seminary was also designed by F. Schmidt and constructed by the Archbishop's architect J. Lippert between 1877 and 1878. The library of the bishopric is a National Cultural Monument.

the Upper Town is part of it. The County Hall also houses the František Studený Gallery and a museum.

3 The Franciscan Church and Monastery: The church was built in C17 on the site of an older building destroyed by fire. The building may be dated back to the second half of C15. The one-nave structure with a polygonal sanctuary and side chapels imitates the ground-plan of the Gesù in Rome, but it possesses a projecting tower. Both the interior ornaments and furniture date from C18. The statues and stallae reliefs are by F. X. Seegen. On the western and northern façades are fragments of a Renaissance relief preserved from the former building. The church and the monastery were destroyed during the Turkish occupation between 1663 and 1664 and remained in ruins until the beginning of C18 In mid-C18 the monastery built on the site of the C17 building was restored. This two-storeyed structure attached to the northern side of the church envelops the courtyard; a cloister connects it with the eastern side of the church.

6 The House of Bishop Kluch: This two-storeyed corner edifice in the Empire style was built by Bishop J. Kluch in 1818 – 1821. J. Kluch was a supporter of the Bernoláks in Nitra. The Bernoláks were the adherents and followers of A. Bernolák, a linguist who attempted to describe and standardize the grammar of the Slovak language. The statue of Atlantean, popularly called *Corgoň*, stands on the corner of the house. This statue and the reliefs above the gate were created by V. Dunajský.

7 The Statue of the Immaculata: This monument is located in front of the castle entrance. The statue of the Immaculata which surmounts it was designed by the Austrian sculptor M. Vogerl in 1750. It commemorates all those who died during the Plague. On the cornices of the stepped four-axial pedestal are statues of the Saints-Adalbert, Stephan, Ladislas, and Emeric. The sculptural group is adorned by vases, putti, and other ornaments. The statue of the Virgin Mary – the Immaculata – stands atop the column. A convexo-concave balustrade forms a fence around the column. The iconography of this column resembles the one in the square in Hainburg, Austria.

The vast area of the Lower Town was separated from the Upper Town by a branch of the River Nitra – the Nitrička. Its fortifications were formed by earthen banks with palisades. The Lower Town was completely destroyed by natural disasters and wars. The remaining built-up area of great historic value consists especially of houses dating from C19, except for the churches. The most important edifices in this part of the town are also its most prominent landmarks.

The synagogue.

8 The Monastery and Church of the Piarists: The construction of this Baroque complex was begun in 1701 with the building of the college. Its first phase was completed in 1720. After the fire in 1723, the damaged buildings were restored; in 1742 the church was begun. Taking the height of the church into consideration, it was decided to add the second storey to the monastery, canons' cloister and school in 1759. The two towers were constructed between 1759 and 1763, and reconstructed at the end of C19. The interior decorations of the church were designed by Piarist artists J. Jaroš, L. Hradický, and H. Preissinger. After World War II, the church was restored and added further elements by E. Massányi. The interior furnishings of the church date from the second half of C18. The sculpture is by M. Vogerl.

9 The Church of St. Stephan in Párovce (a village adjacent to the Lower Town): This church is one of the earliest architectural structures in Nitra. It dates from C12, but its foundations are even older. This one–nave church had originally a flat ceiling with a conch above the semi-circular apse. During reconstruction at the beginning of C18 it was vaulted with the Baroque domical vault and a tower was added. Inside, next to the thriumphal arch, fragments of Romanesque frescoes and a Romanesque cornice have been preserved. The altar dates from C18.

10 The Calvary: Originally, a Gothic church stood at the foothill. It was renovated in C17. During the construction of the monastery of the Nazarenes in the second half of C18, the church was transformed; in 1878, it received a neo-Romanesque façade.

The Calvary consists of fourteen chapels lining the Stations of the Cross, which date from C19. All of them set in picturesque surroundings on the apex of hill create an impressive complex unique in Slovakia.

The oldest example of Nitra's town seal dates from C15. It shows an arm grasping a banner with a double horizontal cross. The banner indicates that the seal originated much earlier. The development of banners reveals in general that they were originally fastened to a fess and the applied heraldic figuration was shown in its usual vertical position. In C13, banners were fastened to a pole, so that the design on the banner was oriented horizontally. Analyzing Nitra's town seal, it is possible to conclude that it pictures the original Hungarian state standard. Then, owing to this fact, Nitra's seal is probably datable to a period before 1301, when the very first town privileges and liberties were granted.

During the long historical development of Nitra, a great number of important personalities settled in the town. Eminent among them were the painter and graphic artist E. Massányi; the poet Š. Krčméry; the Hussite professor of Charles University J. Vavrincov of Račice; J. Jesenský, a poet and writer.

The tour of the town may start at the southern part of the former Lower Town, continue along Štefánik Street, and then along Podzámska Street which is slightly ascending. A stairway will take the visitors to the little square of the former Upper Town. The route leads over the bridge and through the gateway into the castle courtyard and then up the monumental stairway to the church. It is also possible to pass over to Vazil's Tower and Pribina's Chapel in the eastern part. From there one must appreciate the spectacular view of Nitra and Zobor. A road leads westwards of the castle down to the Lower Town, with all its museums and churches. The Slovak Agricultural Museum, which is in the open air, is adjoining the "Agrokomplex," which is in Chrenová – a residential area of the town. In the museum are agricultural equipments and buildings from all parts of Slovakia, e. g. hay-lofts, borns, and even a narrow-gauge railway. In the very centre of the town in Svätopluk Square is a large, modern, and many-purpose theatre building in which various cultural and social events take place. It also encompasses a cinema, restaurants, and cafés. The town centre offers restaurants, coffee bars, and many other cultural and public facilities. To reach the summit of Zobor, which has an excellent position above the town, the visitors may take a chairlift or go on foot.

The parkland and the instructional pathways offer further pleasant walks. At the foot of Zobor, the "Ponitrianska Magistrála," a hiking trail through the Tríbeč mountains, begins.

Nitra, with its excellent attractions for lovers of sport, culture, and first-class entertainment, and wonderful nature and the open country-side which is within easy reach of the town, is an ideal centre of both summer and winter recreations.

Pezinok

Names: L – Basinium, **G** – Bösing, **H** – Bazin
Latitude: 48° 22' N, **Longitude:** 17° 15' E
Elevation: average 156 m, **range:** 138 – 752 m
Population: 22 000
Suburb: Grinava
Means of Access: By rail: route No. 120; By road: routes No. 502 and 503
Accommodations: Hotels: Jeleň, Penzión U leva; Motels: Slimáčka and Na vrchu
  Baba; Hostels: Pezinčan, lodging facilities of the Malokarpatské Wood Works and
  Investment and Development Bank (IRB); Recreational facilities: Domica, Tehliar,
  Kamzík and Rokyta
Information: Pezinok and Small Carpathians Regional Information Center –
  tel: (++421)(0)704-6412963; City Hall – tel: 0704-6412014, fax: 0704-6412303

Pezinok ranks among the most significant towns belonging to the group of the west-Slovakia Little Carpathians' towns whose inhabitants' main occupation is wine-growing. It is situated on the border between the Danube Lowlands and the foothills of the Little Carpathians, a Nature Conservancy Area. The Little Carpathians contain many karst and other interesting natural formations. The mixed deciduous forest complexes, consisting predominantly of oak, beech, and hornbeam, create a pleasant setting for this picturesque town.

The town of Pezinok's climate varies from a warm and dry to moderately dry lowlands climate with average temperatures ranging from –1 to –4°C in January and from 19.5°C to 20.5°C in July; the rainfall is of 530 to 650 mm a year. In the Little Carpathians, the climate changes into a moderately warm mountain climate.

The area where Pezinok is now located has been settled sporadically since prehistoric times, proven by the latest archaeological finds which date from the Neolithic and Eneolithic Ages, as well as the Bronze Age and the La Tene period. These finds were uncovered within the present town limits together with a cache of silver Celtic coins.

The earliest written record of the town dates from a manuscript dating to 1208; it is referred to as „terra Bozyn". Originally the property of the

Bratislava castle, Pezinok and other small towns became the property of the Nitra magistrate Tomáš of the Hunt-Poznan aristocratic family and remained so until their lineage died out in 1543.

In 1376 the town was granted the first of many privileges to follow – „market privileges" – from King Ľudovít I. Economic activity centered around viniculture. This fact was documented in writing as early as the C13. Further economic privileges were granted in 1466 and confirmed later by King Ferdinand I who expanded them to include an exemption for Pezinok residents from paying tolls anywhere in the entire territory of the Hungarian Empire.

After the death of the Earl of Pezinok, the town became indentured to Gašpar Seredy and other feudal lords until Štefan Illéházy acquired the entire Pezinok landholdings in 1580 and who refused to acknowledge the town's privileges. In 1615 Pezinok became independent of its owner and earned the right to build fortifications thanks to the charter granted by King Matthias II. In 1647 the town was declared an Independent Royal Town by King Ferdinand II and therefore gained the right to send representatives to Parliament. These privileges were proof of the economic importance of the town, influenced mainly by viniculture and crafts.

Pezinok. A woodcarving on the heading of a certificate of apprenticeship of a farriers' guild, around 1810.

The urban development advanced rapidly. The original street plan was orientated towards the castle; as a result of additional privileges and the increase in the town's significance, its inhabitants decided to create a square proper. The economic growth was reflected in the construction of a parallel street towards an earlier monastery. The construction of richly decorated churches documentates the wealth of the town in the past. A street-network was developed on the basis of an older settlement at the beginning of C17; at the same time the town walls enclosed the central part. There were a few settled areas in their close proximity, but they remained unprotected.

Of the earlier settlement dating from the Middle Ages only the rhythmic sequence of building plots in the centre of the settlement and the church with a cemetery have remained. Pezinok was expanded by new living quarters to the south, west, and east, which thus created an almost symmetric network with two main axes in the elongated plan of the town. Based on this new plan, a much more highly-developed fortification system was established in comparison with other wine-growing towns. It consisted of large bastions and high walls with parapets and embrasures.

In the first half of C17, as a result of the town's growing independence, the construction of burghers' houses began to predominate. From the end of the 15th till mid-C17, an enormous building activity took place, directed at building houses for the townpeople. On the whole, Pezinok's town-plan from the end of C16 did not differ from those of neighbouring towns. The siting of buildings at right angles to the axis of the road was a style already used during C13; it also created the organic structure of the building plots. This system was also used in the Renaissance buildings which were built at the end of C16, and which are now the oldest preserved monuments in the town.

The impact of Reformation in throughout CC16 – 17 and the arrival of German colonists called "guests" caused rapid advancement of cultural and social life, and extensive building activities. The Protestants built churches and founded schools which, together with those already existing, enhanced the level of the town's culture.

In 1753 a Jesuit mission and middle school were founded in Pezinok, and the students performed theatre in the form of Jesuit „school plays". This was the beginning of the town's theatrical tradition which lasted until the middle of the C20.

Along with the prosperity based on the thriving viniculture, the crafts industries also developed to the point that guilds and workshops were founded. Pezinok had a fulling-mill, papermill, brewery (from the end of the C18), and at the beginning of the C19 well-known brickworks and a glue factory were founded here. Gold was mined locally until the middle of the C18. Pezinok continued to grow in the C19, especially after the construction of the railroad line which ran through the town and connected Bratislava with Trnava.

The original urban structure and architecture were preserved until the middle of the C20 when changes began to leave their marks on the town. Modern buildings were constructed in the center of the old town, disturbing the local historic character. Large

The rows of winegrowers' house containing large winepress sheds and wine cellars.

A Renaissance burghers' house.

concrete-panel apartment buildings were built surrounding the center, obscuring the town's historic silhouette which includes many church towers.

Today Pezinok is well-known for its wine--making. The Small Carpathian Wine Festival is organized every other year, alternating with the towns of Modra and Rača.

The most significant buildings and cultural and social facilities of the town are situated in the main square, known as the Radničné námestie (Town Hall Square), and in M. R. Štefánik and Holuby Streets. A mansion stands in the park at the northern edge of the town.

The Gothic church of the Assumption of the Virgin Mary, in mid-C14.

The Late-Renaissance Catholic church of the Transfiguration, the so-called lower, from 1655 – 1659.

1 The Manor House: Reconstructed from the original lowlands fortress dating from the C13, the manor house is situated just outside of the original line of the town walls in the northern section of the town center. The Illésházy family began the reconstruction in 1609, building in the Renaissance style and using the foundations of the original fortress. In the first half of the C17 the Pezinok landholdings were transferred to the ownership of the Pálffy family and Pezinok became their headquarters. In 1718 the Renaissance manor house was renovated in the Baroque style, and the building's ground plan was transformed to a horse shoe shape, completely obliterating traces of its original „fortress" character. The present interior features a fireplace preserved from earlier times, clad in majolica tiles from Italy. The manor house was restored in the C19 and in 1938 adapted to a new use. Wine storage in the extensive vaulted cellars, a stylish Castle wine cellar restaurant, and administrative offices of the former wine-works are now located on the site. The garden and English park encompasses the manor house, featuring preserved old trees and shrubs.

2 Church of the Ascension of the Virgin Mary: The Roman-Catholic parish church is situated between the two main streets and was built in the mid-1400s. It was reconstructed in the latter part of the C15, with further interior and exterior changes taking place in the C16, C17 and C18. The three--nave main church contains an elongated presbytery and a minor chapel on the south side. The church's ceilings are vaulted with cross-ribs, and feature geometric patterns in the main nave and star vaults which spring from decorative stone brackets in the presbytery. The tower addition was transformed to the Baroque style and features corner quoins. Baroque interior furnishings date primarily from the C18. An Early-Renaissance stone baptismal font dating from 1573 is richly decorated with reliefs. The gravestone of Š. Illésházy dates from 1609; older gravestones are preserved behind the main altar, as is a tomb from 1467.

3 The Church of the Transfiguration of Our Lord:

Situated on the square and known as the „Lower Church", this Roman-Catholic church was originally built as a Lutheran church in the Renaissance style (1655 – 1659). The original main hall with its pillared balcony on three sides was rebuilt into a three-nave church with a polygonal presbytery. The main nave features a barrel-vaulted ceiling and lunettes. Well-known masons worked on the Baroque reconstruction of the interior and exterior, including J. Fidler who worked there in 1876. The main Baroque altar with its columned upper level dates from the C17.

4 Evangelical (Lutheran) Church of the Augsburg Confession:

Built in 1873, this single-nave church with its balconies, square-ended presbytery, and flat ceiling was reconstructed and enlarged in 1858; the tower is built in the Historical style. The Classicist altar from the end of the C18 is the most valuable furnishing in the church and features „The Lamentation over Christ's Death" painting which is attributed to the painter J. Kupecký. The pulpit and baptismal font date from 1784.

5 The Monastery and Church of the Most Holy Trinity:

This Baroque complex of the Capuchin Order, dating from 1718, is located on Holuby Street in the proximity of the parish church. Restored in the second half of the C19, the towerless single-nave monastery church features a square-ended presbytery and a barrel-vaulted ceiling with lunettes. The monastery was built onto the west side of the church and has a central courtyard and garden which is bordered on the north and south sides by the town walls. The interior Baroque

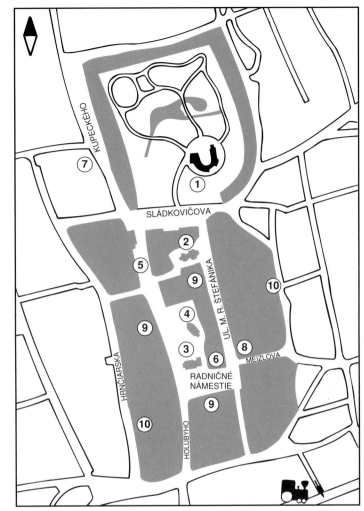

The town plan.

furnishings includes the tripartite main altar with columned upper level and central painting of the Holy Trinity dating from 1728.

6 The Town Hall:

This two-storey building featuring four wings is located on Radničné (Town Hall) Square. It has regular ground plan with a center courtyard. Built around 1600, it was reconstructed near the end of the C17 and again in the middle of the C18. The Town Hall, dominating the square, is one of the best examples of the earliest

architecture still remaining in Pezinok. The large, eleven-bay facade features cylindrical corner oriels which are oriented to the square. The courtyard wings contain blind arcades on the ground floor. The rooms of the Town Hall feature cross-ribbed vaults.

The Baroque church of the Holy Trinity, from 1718.

9 Town Houses: Typologically unique houses have a U-shaped ground-plans formed by two originally free-standing housing units which were joined by means of a common passageway. The two houses face each other and are entered from the inneryard which is surrounded by them. This way a functional arrangement of a new unit was achieved, while each wing preserved its basic functions; and the inner lay-out of an isolated hose as it had existed before was not altered. Both building plots are extended by workshops or various service-buildings, i. e. the wine-press sheds and cellars. Very often they can be found spread under the whole building. This type of vintners' houses remained unchanged until the end of C19; a few of them have preserved their original appearance up to now.

Façades of many town houses in Pezinok are characterized by an oriel seated on brackets, located above the main gateway or flanking it, or on the corners of the house. The best examples of the Renaissance pieces of architecture include the Town Hall. The same structural device was applied on the façade of the building which is on the corner of Kollár Street and the Town Hall Square (Radničné námestie). The regular rhythm of the first-floor windows with profiled jambs and moulding give the mass of the building taste of delicacy. The pediment and the oriel on the corner are further examples of the sophisticated attitude to Renaissance architecture in southwest Slovakia. The first floors of the houses overlooking the yard possess galleries, resting on corbels, or open arcades.

7 The Birthplace of Ján Kupecký: Located at 39 Kupecký Street this one-floor house with three openings (bays) on the facade dates from the C17 and features a memorial room dedicated to this well-known portrait artist of European renown.

8 The Small Carpathian Vineyard Museum: This museum, situated on M. R. Štefánik Street, is set in a typical burgess-vintner house dating from about 1600 with later renovations. The museum exposition focuses on the history of the city, viniculture, and fine arts, with a section of displays dedicated to the botanist-naturalist J. Ľ. Holuby.

10 The Town Fortifications: Built between 1615 and 1643, the town defences follow the pattern of Renaissance walled fortifications consisting of bastions and earthworks. Pezinok with its well-developed defences was strategically the most important member of the anti-Turkish fortification system built in the first half of C17 at the foothills of the Little Carpathians. Its ground-plan was of a relatively regular oblong shape with a longitudinal axis running north-south. The polygonal towers projected outwards of the curtain walls and were spaced at regular intervals. The towers cladded with stone featured moulding made of bricks above which were the shooting galleries with loopholes. The entrance to the town was heavily guarded by two gatehouses, most likely quadrangular towers with a gateway on the ground floor the vineyards were entered through postern gates in the town walls. The stone-cladded bastions and the curtain wall have been best preserved in the western part of the town, and only partially in northern and eastern.

Schaubmar's Mill: Dating from the year 1767, this technical and cultural monument is located in the so-called Cajla part of town, close to the center. The mill, which still contains its restored machinery, is home to the Gallery of Naive Art, the first and only gallery of primitive art in Slovakia, with almost 100 paintings and sculptures by famous foreign and domestic artists.

This original symbol of wine-making and viniculture was removed in the 1990s from the square in front of the former town hall and near the Evangelical (Lutheran) church.

The town walled fortifications erected in 1615 – 1643. In the background the tower of the town's firehouse.

Since the 15th century at the latest, Pezinok had used the symbol of the Immaculata standing on a half-moon and surrounded by the Holy Light as its town seal. In 1647 when King Ferdinand III promoted Pezinok to the rank of a town and chartered the use of its ancient symbol, the Saint Immaculata was declared to be Saint Anne; however, the attributes of the Immaculata (the half-moon and the Holy Light) were retained. After 1948 Pezinok attempted to combine the historical emblem with a motif of viticulture in its arms. In 1979 the town started searching for a convenient heraldic design containing just the viticultural motif. In 1990 the town returned to its earliest symbol heraldically stylized.

Several well-known personalities lived and worked in Pezinok; among the most famous are the portrait painter J. Kupecký, naturalist J. Ľ. Holuby, composer E. Suchoň, and conductor Ľ. Rajter. Painters Š. Polkoráb and F. Moravčík, sculptor Š. Prokop, graphic artist J. Baláž, and historian F. Bokes also worked in the town.

Aside from visiting the museums, a tour of the town would not be complete without stopping at the manor house's wine cellar and a walk through the park, the square, and the historic center. The sacred buildings offer the visitor the opportunity to familiarize himself with the Renaissance and Baroque architecture of the town. Energetic tourists can access the surrounding hills of the Small Carpathians on numerous footpaths which lead to Zochová chata (cottage), Červený Kameň Castle, or to the nearby towns of Limbach and Modra. The surrounding countryside of Pezinok, with its recreational area in Slnečné údolie (Sunny Valley) near Limbach or the Baba and Stupy peaks allow for hikes and recreation in both summer and winter.

Svätý Jur

Names: L – Danum Sancti Georgii, **G** – Sanct Georgen, **H** – Szentgyörgy
Latitude: 48° 15' N, **Longitude:** 17° 12' E
Elevation: average 165 m, **range:** 129 – 593 m
Population: 4 650
Means of Access: By rail: route No. 120; By road: route No. 502
Information: Town hall – tel: (+421)(0)7-4497321, 07-4497320

Svätý Jur is a picturesque little town in the wine district in southwest Slovakia, at the foothills of the Little Carpathian Mountains. It is situated in the Danubian Plain and is only 14 km of Bratislava. Forests, which crown the top of the mountains, have yielded to vineyards covering their lower slopes. Just below the town is an afforested area of 370 hectares, interesting both for tourists and botanists. It is the National Nature Reserve of Šúr, where rare flora and fauna occur in a swampy alder forest with a peat-bog. A thin oak-elm forest with preserved rare xerothermal vegetation is to be found in the area called Pannonian Grove.

Svätý Jur has a warm and mildly dry lowlands climate, with average temperatures ranging from –1° C to –4° C in January and from 19.5°C to 20.5°C in July. The average annual rainfall varies from 530 to 650 mm. The chain of the mountains features a mild and humid climate.

Svätý Jur is the smallest of the so-called west Slovakia Pentapolitana consisting of five important wine-growing centres: Bratislava, Trnava, Modra, Pezinok and Svätý Jur. The town has a rich history, which is also narrated by its art-historical and architectural monuments closely connected with the man-made landscape. The town was being formed for more than one thousand years, and countless generations whose main occupation was wine-growing had their most important share in this proccess.

The earliest settlements consisted of a La Tène settlement followed by Hallstatt and Slavonic fortified settlements from C9, which featured massive earthern banks. In C13 the Biely Kameň Castle, the residence of the Counts of Svätý Jur, now in ruins, arose above Neštich. In 1209 Šebuš, the founder of the dynasty of Counts of Svätý Jur and Pezinok, was given the settlement of Svätý Jur as a gift. During C13 Svätý Jur changed from a centre of their military power into the centre the economic prosperity. At the beginning, it was a market village, but very soon wine-growing prevailed. Vineyards were referred to in 1270, but the winegrowing played an important economic role even earlier. However, crafts developed as well. In mid-C14 the town acquired its first market privileges granted by King Louis I of Hungary and at the beginning of C16, King Louis II exempted local merchants from paying tools all over the Hungarian kingdom. These privileges, together with economic progress based on wine-growing and wine-production, crafts, and commerce, were the resources of Svätý Jur's economic, social, and cultural upsurge.

A. Kaltschmied: Svätý Jur, 1736; a copper engraving and etching after a drawing by S. Mikovíny.

In 1609 the Svätý Jur demesne was established, including Svätý Jur as its centre, and more than twenty-one villages (ranging from Myslenice to Most na Ostrove). In 1615 the town freed its ties with the demesne and became independent of local lords.

Together with Pezinok, Svätý Jur became a Free Royal Town in 1647.

The year 1663 was extremely unfavourable for the town. It was burnt down and plundered by the Turks. The crisis, which occurred, precipitated the stagnation of local economy and building activity; in 1871 Svätý Jur lost its previous privileges and position. Yet ten guilds still existed here at the end of C17, and in 1828 116 craftsmen rand their prosperous workshops there.

Economic development facilitated the development of culture, building activity, and education. For example, a school existed in Svätý Jur in 1514; a parsonage and church are referred to in 1271; a roadside chapel dates from 1409. From C16 onwards, vintners' townhouses and manors were built. The largest building boom lasted during C17: in 1603 – 1654, the town-walls were erected; in 1609 the Renaissance church was built; and in 1651 – 1654 the Baroque church and the monastery of the Piarists were erected. The Piarists also established a grammar school – Gymnasium – in 1684, which existed until 1918. In this school, drama, music, and singing were cultivated. In 1783 the Evangelical (Lutheran) church was built. In 1790 one of the manors was converted into a synagogue.

Wine-growing imparted its individual and most remarkable character to this little town and its architecture. The vintners' houses feature high and spacial passageways which enabled to pull in fully loaded waggons, as close as possible the large

The town of Svätý Jur. A view from the parish church.

cellars and wine-press sheds located in the backyard. Wine-growing could have been introduced here in times of intensive contacts with the Roman empire, whose border at the beginning of the first millenium was running near today's Svätý Jur. The large scale wine-growing is also connected with the arrival of German colonists here who were attracted by the application of German emphyteusis, i. e. the German law. The strongest influx of colonists was evident after the Tartar invasion in the second half of C13. German incomers led the wine-growing in the Little Carpathians to prosperity. By the end of C13 vineyards were divided among individual families. Such divisions created the characteristic scenery of Svätý Jur, which was then preserved until mid-C20. As a centrepiece of this man-made landscape, Svätý Jur stretches its triangular town plan on a mighty alluvial cone of the Starý Potok (Old Brook),

surrounded by a swampy plain and Pannonian Grove.

The town core is formed by a slighthy ascending Prostredná ulica (Middle Street), whose central portion is spindle-shaped. Originally, markets were held here. At the highest point of the town core stands the parish church of St. George, dominating its surroundings. Lower, at the end of the square, the Pálffy Mansion is located. The main crossroads features other historically important buildings: the former Piarist monastery and church; the Segner manor, later changed into an Evangelical church; the Old Town-Hall; the Zichy manor, which houses the Town Hall today; the Kautz House; and other rich burghers' town houses built mostly in throughout CC16 – 17 in the Renaissance style.

In 1990, Svätý Jur was declared an Urban Conservation Area, whose beauty is enhanced by the surrounding man-made landscape.

The Early-Gothic parish church of St. George, the parsonage and the former house of the bell-ringer.

The church of the Piarists, 1651 – 1654.

The parish church. The high altar of St. George, stone altar architecture, 1514 – 1520.

The bell-tower next to the parish church.

1 The Parish Church of St. George: An Early-Gothic building from the last quarter of C13, with aisled interior and a polygonal presbytery; the Late-Gothic Trinity Chapel (1465) was annexed to its southern side. The Gothic vaults were introduced in the first third of C15. The Renaissance alterations and the western tribune date from 1585 to 1590. On the place of the bell-tower (which burnt in 1663) a new separate wood bell-tower was erected. The wall paintings are from C15. A very precious and unique Early-Renaissance stone altar of St. George, carved in 1517, was carried out by a master from the workshop of the Austrian sculptor, A. Pilgram. The tomb of Count Juraj of Svätý Jur and Pezinok, with a relief of the deceased in full armour, dates from 1467; other tombs and epitaphs found in the church are from CC16 – 17.

2 The Piarist Monastery and Church: The church erected in 1654 as an Evangelical church of the preaching hall – church type with a gallery, came into the possession of the Piarists in 1686, who rebuilt it to the Baroque style. After the fire of 1708, the church was repaired. The monastery, featuring a regular four-wing plan, was built on the site of former vintners' houses. Another renovation of the church and monastery in 1754 was precipitated by another fire. In 1763 the grammar school building was added. The church has one nave which is elevated by a gallery supported by pillars. The side chapel of St. John was added in 1734. The interior is Baroque in style, from the end of CC17 and 18.

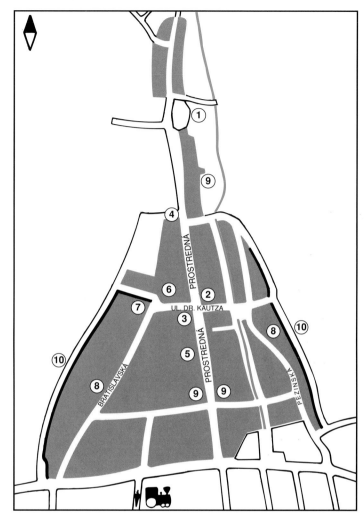

The town plan.

3 Evangelical (Lutheran – Augsburg Confession) Church: Built in 1783, this building was originally a Renaissance town house known as the Segner Manor, a part of which was converted into the church. It is located in Prostredná – Middle Street; the adjoining house in Dr. Kautz Street was remodelled for ecclesiastical purposes as well. There are Renaissance vaulted ceilings in its interior, but in the nave proper the ceiling is flat. A new belfry conceived in a very interesting architectural design was erected on the back end of the roof in the second quarter of C20. The most

peculiar artifacts from the interior furnishings are an altar paiting of Christ, after the Van Dyck school, and a Rococo pulpit.

4 The Pálffy Mansion: This late-Gothic building is located at the end of Prostredná – Middle Street. In 1609 it underwent a Renaissance reconstruction, in 1746 the Baroque one, and at the end of C19, it underwent adaptations under the influence of the Romantic movement. It is a free-standing building with a large courtyard, and large and deep Renaissance vaulted cellars. The

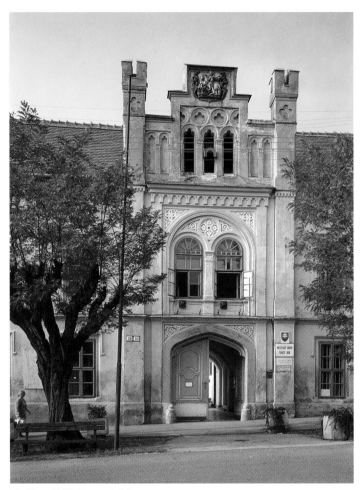

The Town Hall in Prostredná Street.

A view into the courtyard of the Renaissance Pálffy manor house.

Romantic architectural expression appears in the interconnecting representative rooms and the staircase as well as in the reception rooms on the first floor. The façade was altered in the spirit of the neo-Renaissance style.

5 The Town Hall: Originating in 1865 by the conversion of the former Zichy Manor in conjuction with two additional Renaissance manors. Renaissance vaulted ceilings have been preserved in several rooms. The façade is wholly neo-Gothic in style.

6 Vintners' Town Houses: Located in Dr. Kautz Street (No. 2), this originally Late-Gothic house was built in about 1500. It was rebuilt in mid-C17 and modified to the Baroque style in the second half of C18. The ground-floor burgher house is a typical representative of a vintner's house with wine-cellars. The wine-cellars are two-storeyed. The wine-press shed and the lower cellar possess Renaissance vaults which spring from the central pillar.

7 Vintner's Town House: When this Renaissance town house in Dr. Kautz Street (No. 1) was being built, walls of an earlier mid-C16 house were employed. It was renovated about the year 1600, and transformed to the Baroque style in the second half of C18. The house is approached through a large Renaissance gate which opens to the entrance hall with Renaissance ceilings. In the passageway, above the former portal, there is a coat-of--arms cut in stone and tablets with dates of 1547 and 1590. The inner yard wing of the house has large, two-storeyed cellars; the wine-making equipment dating from 1780 has been preserved there as well as the wine-press.

Prostredná Street. Winegrowers' houses typical of the town.

8 Vintners' Houses: Dating from throughout CC17 – 18, these houses possess typical L- or U-shaped plan. The common entrance to two or more flats and service-buildings is through a vaulted passageway. Cellars used for wine production are located under the houses.

9 Burgers' Town Houses: Mostly two-storeyed, Late-Renaissance houses situated on wider plots, whose ground-plans are similar to the one-storeyed vintners' houses. On the upper floor there were state living quarters. The façades were often divided by oriels. A typical example of this house is the Ambruster House on the corner of Dr. Kautz Street, containing preserved architectural details and a tablet dated of 1590.

10 The Town Walls: The fortification system was built during the years 1603 – 1647; after the invasion of Turks, it was being renovated until 1664 and Renaissance fortification engineering elements, common at that time, were applied. The stone curtain walls were strenghtened by five semi-circular and nine angular bastions, spaced at regular

Dr. Kautz Street. A Renaissance winegrower's house containing wine cellars and winepress-sheds.

distances. These bastions, filled with earth and not higher than the walls, were used for mounting cannons. Gunners were protected by merlons. Entrances to the town were guarded by four main rectangular gatehouses. The access to vineyards was made possible through several small postern gates in the town walls; one of them has been preserved on the eastern side. The most coherent sections of the preserved town walls, including bastions, have survived on the western side, and only partially on the eastern side. The town with its fortification system represented one of the strategically most important elements of the anti-Turkish defences which had been built at the foothill of the Little Carpathian Mountains in the first half of C17.

Svätý Jur has the speaking arms, i. e. the figuration pictured on the shield coincides with the name of the town. The symbol of Svätý Jur, St. George, is in full armour and mounted on horseback, and is depicted as slaying the dragon with a spear. These arms date back not only to June 14th, 1647, when the town was declared a Free Royal Town by Emperor Ferdinand III, but their beginnings are of a much earlier date when the town was still unfree. The earliest known records are represented by three charters from 1433, now reposited in the Bratislava City Record Office. Unfortunately, these seals have been only partially preserved.

From the historical point of view the town of Svätý Jur is also interesting as a wine-supplier to the royal court; its duty was to deliver more than 22,000 litres of good wine a year. It is also of interest because of its building development in relation to the wine-producing industry.

The visitors' tour of this picturesque little town is about to begin along the highroad from Bratislava to Pezinok. Walking along the slightly ascending square, they can visit the Piarist church, the museum of town history on the premises of the Town Hall or the Museum of P. Jilemnický, a well-known writer. Continuing to the area of the parish church with a churchyard, the beauty-searchers may enjoy the fine appearance of the town and the country spread along the Danube.

More energetic visitors may take the marked hiking path to get to the ruins of the Biely Kameň Castle, or to the fortified settlement of Neštich. In Jozefské údolie (Joseph Valley) are good conditions for skiing and swimming. Svätý Jur is the starting point for the ridge trail along the Little Carpathians.

Trenčín

Names: L – Trentschinium, **G** – Trentschin, **H** – Trencsén
Latitude: 48° 55' N, **Longitude:** 18° 03' E
Elevation: average 211 m, **range:** 202 – 700 m
Population: 59 100
Suburbs: Biskupice, Istebník, Kubrá, Kubrica, Opatová, Orechové, Záblatie, Zlatovce
Menans of Access: By rail: route No. 120; By road: routes No. D 61 = E 75, E 50
Accommodations: Hotels: Laugaricio, Tatra, Trenčan, Brezina; Pensions:
　Konštrukta industry, Evergreen, Svorad, Rimini, Ozeta, Extos; Cottages: Odevák,
　Opatová, pod Ostrým vrchom; Hostels: ATC Na ostrove; other hostels
Information: Cultural Information Center – tel: (++421)(0)831-16186,
　tel/fax: 0831-433505, e-mail: kic@trencin.sk

Trenčín is located on the boundary between the Trenčín and Ilava lowlands in the broad valley of River Váh. The town is surrounded by forested promontories of the Strážovské vrchy (Strážov Hills). The White Carpathian Mountains, the Nature Conservancy Area to the northwest of Trenčín, dominate the local topography. They are a flysch mountainous arc composed predominantly of rocky cliffs. Oak and hornbeam forests are found on the lower slopes of the mountains, and beech forests in deep valleys and on the mountain tops. Deer and wild boar have their home here, and in the western portion of the mountains lynx live. On the precincts of the town, the Trubárka National Nature Reserve, formed by a curious rock formation, may be found at the close of the Kubrická dolina (Kubrica Valley), and the Zamarovské jamy (Zamarovské Pits) – little water reservoirs which serve as habitats for marsh- and water-fowl.

Trenčín possesses a warm valley climate, which ranges from moderately dry to humid with average temperatures of –2.5 °C to –5 °C in January, and of 16 °C to 17 °C in July. The average annual rainfall varies from 600 to 700 mm.

Trenčín, the most significant town in the central part of the Váh Valley, was founded on the crossroads of ancient long-distance trade routes running from Moravia along the valley of the River Vlára, then across the River Váh Ford to enter the River Nitra valley.

Archaeological discoveries confirm settlement on the present site of the town in the Paleolithic, Neolithic and Eneolithic Ages, the Bronze Age, and the Hallstatt and La Tene periods. A Roman inscription cut into the rocky cliff below the castle in 179 A. D.; which is an epigraphic memorial whose significance extends beyond the borders of Slovakia. It documents the northern limit of the Roman army's expansion into Central Europe, a territory already extensively settled by Germanic tribes.

Slavonic settlements, dating from the transition of the Early Slavonic to the pre-Great Moravian period, were concentrated in the surroundings of present-day Trenčín. It is generally accepted that Trenčín has been an important center of the central Váh valley since the Early Slavonic period.

The concentration of archaeological finds from the Great Moravian period appears to be connected with the fortified complex, including a rotunda, which was discovered on the castle site. Although these finds date to the C11, there is written

Trenčín and the castle; a vista, C19.

material and indirect evidence which points to the beginnings of this complex or its predecessor sometime before this territory was annexed to the Hungarian Empire. Trenčín first became the administrative seat of the lands at the border of the Empire and later was the administrative center of the Royal County of Trenčín.

The castle complex, as well as the town which formed below it, was destined for a lengthy period of development, mainly because of its strategic location. The very beginnings of the town can be traced to the market settlement already referred to in 1111, located on the old road leading from the river ford at the foot of Brezina hill. A bishop's seat was also most likely a part of this larger settlement.

The oldest remnants of the settlement were found in the locality of the entry road to the castle on Matúš Čák Street and date from the Middle Ages, its buildings lining an old street which no longer exists.

The market settlement was formed along the old road which ran along the Váh River.

It gradually widened and formed the irregular rectangular square which from both ends leads to the castle's entry road. The disposition of the square has not changed since the Middle Ages, as research has shown that most of the homes located around it have Gothic origins.

The city's first privileges appear in a manuscript dating from 1324. Further privileges granted by King Zigmund in 1412 included Trenčín as one of the Independent Royal Towns. Evidence of Trenčín's key position exists in defending the Váh River valley during the period of the growing threat of attack from the west by the Hussites.

Newer privileges were connected with the annual market, emancipation from paying taxes for use of bridges in the entire country, jurisdiction of the court, as well as the right to build town fortifications. Later the city received the right to bear arms and warehousing rights.

In the C15 the Gothic city featured town walls with double town gates. The town walls were joined to the outer fortifications of the castle. In spite of the towns privileges, the feudal owners of the castle abused their position, and interfered unceasingly in the affairs of the town lying just below.

The silhouette of Trenčín Castle towering over the Váh.

In C13 essential transformation of the castle was begun due to the construction of the residential keep. It was followed by building extensive activity at the beginning of C14 when the oligarch Matúš Čák of Trenčín, the much feared "Master of the River Váh and the Tatras," and the mortal enemy of Charles Robert of Anjou, the King of Hungary, resided in the castle. During Čák's rule, a palace adjoining the castle keep was built, but it was demolished later. Military and domestic functions of the castle were multiplied also because it changed hands several times. The last recorded renovations were done after the Habsburg armies under General Katzianer had plundered the town and after the great fire of the town and castle in 1528. The parish church did not escape damage either; later, it was renovated to the Renaissance style under an Italian master, Sebastian, between 1553 and 1558. The burnt-out houses on the square were rebuilt and extended. A new building element – the ambulatory – was used, which appeared only sporadically in the High Middle Ages. The widespread use of arcades in the houses on the square occurred in the second half of CC16 – 17.

Unfortunately, most of them disappeared during the complex reconstructions which took place in C19 and at the beginning of C20.

In C16, the constant need of increasing the defensive force of the castle resulted in another building phase of fortifications, especially at the weakest section of the castle orientated towards Brezina. Additional outwork with two ditches was built. The defensive system of the town was strenghtened when the Upper Gatehouse was added a barbican on the front side; there was not enough space for fortifying the Lower Gatehouse.

In C17, the town became a centre of the Counter – Reformation in the northwest of the Hungarian kingdom. This new situation fostered further building activity in the town. Between the years 1653 and 1657, the Jesuits built a large complex here, comprising the church of Francis Xavier with a monastery on the site of several burghers' houses. This one-nave church with shallow chapels resembles the church of Francis Xavier in Vienna in type.

Entrance to the castle via the Parish Steps.

The turbulent CC17 and 18 left its marks on the fate of the city and the castle, in the form of the threat of Turkish invasion and the conflicts between the Emperor's court and rebels from the rank of the Hungarian aristocrats. An army unit of the Emperor, charged with securing the defense capability of the castle and city, moved into the castle together with its owner, the Illésházys, in 1670. In 1708 the city was besieged by a fire, and later the Black Plague and a flood. The Holy Trinity Column is a memorial to these events. Thanks to the Illésházys' patronage, the Jesuits restored the church and monastery.

Houses destroyed by the fire and war were gradually reconstructed to the Baroque style. The town defences lost their importance after the Peace Treaty of Satumár had been signed, and they started dilapidating. In 1761 the County-Hall was built on the site near the Lower Gatehouse, which was later demolished.

The year 1790 was another turning point in the history of the castle. János (John) Illésházy succeeded in expelling the German garrison from there and began organizing the reconstructions for the needs of his family. Unfortunately, a fire broke out in the town and spread over the castle. After this disaster, only several buildings outside the castle were reconstructed and the castle proper turned gradually into ruins.

During CC18 – 19, sections of the town outside the defences began to change. New streets and squares appeared outside the walls and gatehouses. New palaces were built, whose best representatives are found in Palacký Street. The town took on the neo-classical appearance.

Urban development of the historical centre towards the end of C19 and at the beginning of C20 was influenced especially by the construction of railway and was concentrated on industrial districts related to this new means of transport. The urban structure of the Gothic centre remained intact, though facades of most of the buildings were altered in C19.

The preserved historical, urbanistic, and architectural composition of the city with its castle compose a unique dominant complex in the countryside of the central Váh valley. The former county seat, now a regional capital, is one of the most important cities of Slovakia and a cultural, societal, and industrial center where the national fashion industry exposition (Trenčín – City of Fashion) takes place on a regular basis.

The finest examples of architecture are in the oldest and the most characteristic part of Trenčín arranged around the main square, which is overlooked by the castle on the cliff.

The town was declared an Urban Conservation Area in 1987 with the goal of preserving all the historic, artistic, and architectural values of the town intact.

The castle fortifications.

The castle at the sunset.

The entrance bastions and the castle tower.

The square with its typical city houses and the area of the Piarist monastery.

The view of the square with originally Renaissance and later rebuilt houses.

Mierové námestie (Peace Square).

1 Trenčín Castle: A National Cultural Monument, the castle belongs to the largest and the most majestic castles in Slovakia. It is also an impressive landmark to wering above the town. The picture of Trenčín without it would be incomplete. Foundations of the pre--Romanesque central building are proof of settlement in the period following the end of Great Moravian Empire. An older settlement transformed into a king's guard castle in the C11. The oldest part of the castle is the tower dating from the C11 with its fortifications; its present day appearance after reconstruction has its roots in an addition by Matúš Čák at the end of the C13.

After the death of this legendary oligarch, the castle was expanded by a new fortified palace under the reign of King Louis the Great of Hungary; a representative palace with a bay was added during the reign of Sigismund of Luxemburg. This palace was named after his second wife Barbora Celská. At the same time a new chapel was built near the keep, and most importantly, a gatehouse and a defensive tower were built to complement the fortifications.

At the end of C15 and at the beginning of C16, extensive reconstructions led by the owners of the castle, the Zápolya family, took place. The rebuilding continued especially in the older living quarters and soon, Zápolya's new palace appeared. During feverish preparations for war with the Turks, older fortifications were rebuilt and an additional fortification system in the shape of triple semi-circles including bastions and ditches was built to defend the most easily accessible point – forested Brezina. In charge of this work were Emperor's military fortification engineerings.

In 1600, the Illésházy family became owners of the castle. The castle burnt out in 1790. With them another stage in its renovation began. Large scale preservation work of the castle began at the end of the 1950's. Today, the castle is a part of the Trenčín Museum.

2 The Church of the Nativity of the Virgin Mary: This Roman Catholic parish church is a fortified structure on a slope called Marienberg, which is between the town and the castle. It stands on the site of a former little church. Only the polygonal presbytery of the original Gothic construction from C14 has been preserved, as the church was rebuilt to the Renaissance style and changed into a three-nave structure after the fire in 1528. In mid-C18, funerary chapels of the Illészházy family were built in the aisles. The exterior of the church was also renovated at the end of C19 when the roof was surmounted with a new helm. The parsonage and the charnel house, which is directly built into the fabric of the walls, formed a unit with the church. Originally, this two-storeyed chapel of quarried-stone had Gothic ribbed vaults. Late-Gothic tracery windows were later walled up. The charnel house lost its original function after 1560. In C17 it was changed into an armory. After the fire in 1790, the chapel was used as a granary and now it is restored and used as the museum premises.

3 The Parish Stairway: Built in 1568 as an important defensive communication connecting the medieval town with the fortified precints of the parish church and with the road to the castle. After the fire in C18, the stairway became a public communicational axis between the town and the castle and later, also with the forest park. It was restored in 1978-80.

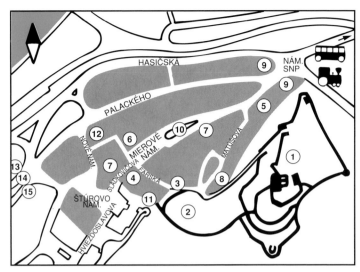

The town plan.

4 The Town Hall: The Town Hall was built on the site of an earlier construction according to a functionalist design of architect Šebor in 1929. It was altered in 1934.

5 The Trenčín Museum: The former County Administration Hall is a Late-Baroque construction of 1761 with an accentuated entrance. Meetings of county officials took place in the state rooms on the first floor.

6 The Piarist Monastery and the church of St. Francis Xavier: Originally a Jesuitical monastic complex, it was started in 1653 and consecrated in 1657. The Baroque one-nave church with side chapels and a tribune reminds of the medieval Jesuitical one-nave church as St. Michael's in Munich and St. Francis Xavier's in Vienna. The vaulted ceiling of the church features a trompe l'oeil painting which rises illusions of a dome. The two-tower façade is divided by corner pilasters with capitals on each storey and niches with Baroque sculptures of St. Peter and St. Paul. The interior was richly decorated by a disciple of Andreo del Pozzo, Krištof Tausch; the decorations are based on the legend of St. Francis Xavier. The fresco

was created after the fire, approximately in 1713, and it ranks among the most highly appreciated Baroque masterpieces in Slovakia. From the interior furnishings of the church, especially the high altar with its rich decoration by Trenčín painter J. Grimberg, attracts interest. A silver statue of the Madonna, a tabernacle and reliquaries date from 1710 to 1720. They were made by Vienna goldsmith I. A. Tobber. The side altars with rich sculptural decoration date from 1723 to 1735 and were created by B. Baumgartner. The pulpit, organ, and the pews belong to outstanding works of Baroque handicraft in Slovakia. Liturgic artifacts of the church, such as a chasuble of C15, chalices, censers, crozier, etc., create the church's treasure.

The monastery built simultaneously with the church was renovated after the fire in 1708. In 1776 the church and monastery became the property of the Piarists, who rebuilt the monastery. The vaults in the refectory and the former monastic pharmacy have copious stucco decoration which is said to have been by Italian masters. Today, the M. A. Bazovský Gallery is housed in the monastery.

The town walled fortifications: the Upper Gatehouse with a passageway on the ground-floor, the first half of C15.

walls on the site of an older one-storeyed inn called "U Červenej hviezdy" (Red Star Inn). The portion of the castle cliff with the Roman inscription can be seen only from inside of this hotel.

10 The Holy Trinity Column: Erected on the square in 1712, the column was donated by Miklós (Nicolas) Illésházy as a reminder of the flood, fire, and plague in the early 1700's.

11 The Town Fortifications: The town began to build a relatively simple fortification system in the first decades of C15 after the town was granted the privileges to do so. The system consisted of stone walls without bastions and towers and was connected to the castle cliff on the eastern side, and on the west it was attached to the castle fortifications. The entrance to the town was protected by two main gatehouses, the eastern Upper Gatehouse and western Lower Gatehouse, both originally quadrangular towers with a gate passage on the ground-floor. Other improvements of the fortifications were carried out at the beginning of C16 when another section of the curtain wall was built at the western side; at the same time the defensive force of the Lower Gatehouse was strengthened by a construction of a gateway and a drawbridge. During the final construction stage of the defences in mid-C16, huge barbicans were created: in front of the Lower Gatehouse a circular one and in front of the Upper Gatehouse a rectangular one with two corner bastions protecting the entrance to the castle. Only one continuous section of the curtain wall and the tower of the Lower Gatehouse have been preserved of the entire system of town fortifications. The continuous section of the castle wall has embrasures and a gallery built of brick. It connects the Lower Gatehouse and the castle fortification. The Tower of the Lower Gatehouse originated in the first half of C15, designed on a quadrangular base and with

7 Burghers Houses: The town houses standing on the Mierové námestie (Peace Square) are mostly of Gothic – Renaissance origin. They represent a type of a two-storeyed building with a passageway on the ground-floor. Most of the houses were rebuilt, refaced and redecorated in C18. During these renovations, the arcades, which were added in CC16 – 17, were removed. House No.1 is well worth attention because lozenge vaults dating from the turn of CC15 – 16 have been preserved on the ground-floor.

8 The Hangman's House: Originally a secular two-storeyed stone house in Matúš Street, it is situated on a steep slope in the town quarter known as Hôrka. The house, which originally featured a wooden balcony, was rebuilt in C18. Its present name may relate to the fact that at the end of the last century the town hangman lived there.

9 The Tatra Hotel: An Eclectic-Art Nouveau style building dating from 1901, the Tatra Hotel was built outside the medieval town

a passageway on the ground-floor. The upper floors of the tower have an octagonal ground plan and were built in the first quarter of C17. The barbican was demolished in mid-C19. The tower was restored in C20.

The built-up area outside the town walls is characterized by several buildings which, together with the residential houses, create the image of the town. The most interesting units are the synagogue, chapels, and two churches.

12 The Synagogue: Built most probably on the site of a wooden synagogue near a Jewish school from 1909 to 1912, the building is in the neo-Romantic style, but reflexes also Byzantine and Oriental influences and elements of post Art-Nouveau style. Today it is a stage of various cultural and social events.

13 Notre Dame Church: Dating from 1909 to 1924, the church is a fine example of neo-Romanesque sacral buildings where elements of Art Nouveau are applied. The wall paintings, the altar painting, and the Stations of the Cross are by P. J. Kern.

14 The Evangelical (Lutheran – Augsburg Confession) Church: This church, built after the Letter Patent of Tolerance was issued, is a classical construction dating from 1794. It contains a characteristic hall with a flat vaulted ceiling.

15 The Chapel of St. Anne: Baroque in style, the chapel was built in 1789 on the site of an original Gothic hospital church. The simple one-nave construction with a presbytery and a projecting tower is furnished in C18 style including altars, the pulpit, and the organ.

The former Jesuitical, later Piarist, Baroque church of St. Francis Xavier, 1653 – 1657.

The synagogue, 1911.

The Easter Lamb became the symbol of the town in the first half of C14; since then, Trenčín has been using this symbol almost without any change. The original town seal has not been preserved, but two other Gothic seals exist today, and are in the National Museum, Budapest. They were sent there before 1825 at the request of Palatine József (Joseph). The design is a symbol of St. John the Baptist. It is notable that the earliest seals show the lamb carrying a standard with a cross, but on later seals the standard is quartered. The present standard of Trenčín follows the tradition of the historic one.

The particularly rich history of the town was also influenced by many great personalities who lived here: astromonist and physicist M. Hell; Czech historian F. Palacký; poets M. Dohnány, Samuel Chalupka Sn., and M. Institoris; writer D. Krman; and painters T. Mousson, M. A. Bazovský, and others.

Many famous people are buried in Trenčín; for example, from the Štúr family, the mother of Ľudovít Štúr, his brother, and nephew are interred here, as are composer K. Pádivý and the head of the Piarists and writer J. Branecký, among others.

The best entrance to the town is the location of the former Upper Gate. A view of the square leads the eye to the castle perched on top of the rocky cliff. It is possible to see the Roman inscription on the cliff only from upper hallway of the Hotel Tatra. A tour of the town, the square, and its important buildings and museums are best ended by entrance to the castle, from which there is a beautiful view of this part of the Váh valley. A protected park in the in the suburb of Záblatie is also worth a visit.

After the sightseeing tour of the town, the visitors can have a swim in the outdoor swimming pool in summer, and in winter they can go skating to the skating rink. All the year round many fine walks are in the park forest of Brezina. Marked paths in the Strážov Hills and the White Carpathians are for more ambitious hikers who like to take longer hikes. Holiday-makers may find ideal and pleasant recreational facilities at Krásna, Opatová, Kubrica, and Drietoma Valleys, which are not far from the town.

Visitors may plan a special trip to Trenčianske Teplice, which is a spa located 16 km northeast of Trenčín. Diseases of the locomotor and nervous systems are treated there. A thermal swimming pool, tennis courts, and a ski-lift are provided for the public.

Trnava

Names: L – Tyrna via, **G** – Tyrnau, **H** – Nagyszombat
Latitude: 48° 22' N, **Longitude:** 17° 36' E
Elevation: average 147 m, **range:** 137 – 174 m
Population: 73 000
Suburbs: Modranka, Trnava
Means of Access: By rail: routes No. 120, 116, 133; By road: routes No.
    D 61 = E 75, 61 and 51
Accommodations: Hotels: Budovateľ, Koliba, Kriváň, Trnavan, Skloplast, Slávia,
    Nukleón; Pensions: Oáza, Tulipán
Information: Trnava Information Service – tel: (++421)(0)805-16186, 0805-511022,
    fax: 0805-501455

Trnava is situated in the Danube lowlands on the Trnavská tabuľa (Trnava table), bordered by the Little Carpathian Mountains on the northwest. The town is 50 km east of Bratislava. Near Trnava flows the longest Slovak river, the Váh, with its tributaries – the Dudváh, the Parná, and the Trnávka. There are several facilities nearby the town, which offer bathing in the open-air, for instance, including Štrky and Kamenný mlyn. To the south of Kamenný mlyn lies the Nature Reserve of the Trnavské rybníky (Trnava Ponds), a significant ornithological locality where rare species of water-fowl can be found.

The town enjoys a warm and moderately dry lowlands climate with average temperatures of –4 °C to –1 °C in January and of 19.5 °C to 20.5 °C in July; the annual rainfall is varying between 530 and 650 mm.

Trnava belongs among the most ancient towns in Slovakia. It grew on the foundations of a previous settlement dating from the early Middle Ages, but many archaeological findings which can be dated to the Neolithic Age testify to a long and more complicated history of the site. The continuous habitation of the region could have started after the arrival of Slavs. The surroundings of Trnava were attractive because of very rich soil and favourable conditions for sedentary life and farming. The existence of the medieval settlement is documented in several written sources of CC12 – 13. The earliest allusion to Trnava is dating from 1211 with a reference back to the year 1205. In a charter of Archbishop Jánosz (John) of Esztergom Trnava was mentioned for a portion of revenues of the church of St. Nicholas was donated to the Cathedral and canons' cloister of Esztergom.

Especially precious is the charter of 1238 giving Trnava the town rights; this document is the oldest preserved charter of this type in Slovakia. According to it, King Béla IV made Trnava dependent directly on the Crown. These rights enabled then a very rapid development. Owing to the royal support, Trnava, after its promotion to the rank of a town, acquired all the qualities of a medieval town. Farming as the original occupation of most inhabitants of Trnava was gradually left to be overtaken by crafts and trade, which changed profoundly its character. In the second half of C13 the inhabitants erected town walls against harassing raids and to protect their wealth and their rights. The town was enclosed in earthen banks, topped by wooden palisades and girt with a moat. Later on, the moat was filled with water, and a high brick wall with bastions and four

Trnava, coloured copper engraving of J. Ch. Leopold by F. B. Werner, mid-C18.

gatehouses was built. The whole fortification system was completed by the architect-engineer Pietro Ferrabosco in the first half of C16.

The town privileges attracted German colonists called "guests" to Trnava, especially after the Tartar invasion. In the second half of C13 the settlement spread to create a new section. The town-plan of Trnava shows the earliest centre on the site of the original Romanesque church of St. Nicolas, which is easily distinguishable from the later centre established nearby a former brook. In the first decades of Trnava's existence as a town, the Hospitallers of St. John of God followed by the Dominicans settled within the town walls; the Benedictines settled in the western section and so did the Poor Clares and the Franciscans after them. From the location of these early monasteries and the convent, it is possible to determine the size of the area of the pre-Tartar town including its minor domestic architecture.

At the turn of CC13 – 14 the town almost completely burnt down and it had to be rebuilt; at that time it spread westwards. In the centre of the new section a square developed, being the core of the bustling town. The diagonal axis ran then to the parish church, the centre of the former settlement. On its opposite end a Franciscan monastery was founded.

Trnava acquired an extraordinary position in C16. In 1563 Bratislava was promoted to the rank of a coronation town, and Trnava took the role of the spiritual and cultural leader of the Hungarian state. The functions of Esztergom's religious centre were bestowed upon Trnava. The canons were the first to move here and after them the Bishop-Primate arrived in the town in 1543. At that time the synods and sessions of the Hungarian Diet also took place in Trnava.

The most glorious period in the town's history is connected with C17. The first complete Hungarian university was established here by Cardinal-Primate Peter Pázmány in 1635. Its four faculties, which existed 142 years, grouped themselves according to academic disciplines – theology, arts, law, and medicine; they exerted great influence upon the spread of education all over Hungary. The university also became famous for the astronomical observatory established by Maximilian Hell, a library, gardens, and a theatre. The appearance of the town was impacted by new university buildings which were designed, constructed, and decorated by Italian artists. The dominant buildings of the Jesuitical university church added a new element to the town. Being the leading religious centre of Hungary from C17 onwards, Trnava drew other religious orders that settled here besides the

Silhouttes of Trnava church towers behind the town walled fortification from C 14.

The town tower and burghers' houses in the Holy Trinity Square.

Dominicans, Franciscans, and the Poor Clares. Their building activity brought further changes of appearance of the town, especially of its skyline, so often depicted by contemporary artists in their pieces of graphic art. The original university premises were a core around which new university buildings developed. During time of Maria Theresa's reign, new colleges were built in 1750 – 1777 which enhanced the beauty of the town. The range of magnificient forms and details in the Baroque style which were universally used here placed Trnava in the acceptance of new designs far ahead of other towns. The wide variety of patterns set here was taken over and emulated by others. Owing partly to this fact and partly to the town's being a spiritual and religious centre of the Hungarian kingdom, Trnava was often compared to Rome. Henceforth, its denomination Slovak Rome could have originated both in this context and in this period. In 1770 the University of Trnava was nationalized, and in 1773 the Jesuitical Order was abolished. The university was transferred to Buda, and later to Pest. Trnava was deprived of its prominent position and all of Upper Hungary lost its own spiritual centre. Nevertheless, the traditions of the cultural and spiritual life were retained here. In the second half of C18, the deeper interest in studying the Slovak language was connected with

The theatre building in the Holy Trinity Square from 1831.

The Franciscan church of St. James from 1633 – 1640 behind the Bernolák's Gate, originally a Gothic one.

The town hall in High Street. Present appearance from 1683.

the awakening of the national consciousness. The efforts of Anton Bernolák to write the Grammar of Slovak as a literary language were successful: its literary usage was codified in 1787. The Trnava printing house also promoted the diffusion of the language, and also raised the level of the Slovak literary culture.

With the gradual expansion of the town, new patterns in architecture appeared not only in the centre but also in the suburbs. In C19, when the railway reached the town, the building activity was accelerated and economic life advanced rapidly forwards. Then, several factories were founded on the outskirts and the town changed into an

industrial centre. Trnava has always striven to preserve the high cultural and social standards which were attained in the bygone past.

In the period of the first Czechoslovak Republic the importance of the town grew, sparking the creation of many businesses, services, and banks; Trnava became an important center in western Slovakia. Famous Slovak architects worked here, including Belluš, whose work is represented by an apartment house, storage building, mill, and water works. Architect M. M. Harminc designed the Roľnícka banka (Farmer's Bank), Roľnícka vzájomná pokladnica (Farmers' Mutual Fund), Slovenská hospodárska banka (Slovak Economic Bank), and several residential areas. Still in existence are buildings which were designed by other well-known architects: F. Florians, G. Schreiber, and F. Weinwurm, among others.

Among the most valuable town buildings are the constructions and complexes of sacral architecture complemented with the buidings dated from CC17 – 19. The extensive urban structure and originally almost regular plan of the town were created on a basic system of three principal streets: the first one was connecting the Holy Trinity Square with Svätopluk Square and the remaining two were the original north-south oriented streets between the gatehouses on the south and the north – Staromestská (Old Town Street) and the Hlavná (the High Street), nowadays used as pedestrian zones.

The preserved medieval urban and architectural „wholeness" of the town with a large number of excellent monuments was the reason for declaring Trnava an Urban Conservation Area in 1987.

The Church of St. Nicolas.

The University basilica of St. John the Baptist, an Early-Baroque building from 1629 – 1637.

Trnava's main dominance – parish church of St. Nicolas.

The interior of the University church with the main altar.

1 The Church of St. Nicolas: This Roman Catholic parish church in Svätopluk Square dominates the town by its towers. It is situated on the place of a former Romanesque church dating from 1380. To construct it lasted quite a long time and it was finished only in 1440. The vaulting of its nave goes back to mid-C15. Its essential characteristics sounds: a nave with aisles of a basilica-type in the Late-Gothic style. In 1629 the church was expanded by side chapels, and a year later the northern tower was rebuilt. The extensive Baroque transformation in 1618 – 1630 changed the entire exterior appearance and partially the interior of the church. In 1739 – 1741 an octagonal Baroque chapel was added on the northern side, bearing all signs of the architectural style of the well-known Viennese architect L. Hildebrandt. The dominant part of the very rare interior furnishings is a Gothic panel painting of the Trnava Virgin Mary complementing the canopied altar. The major part of the interior is dating from C18, including the high altar with a painting by J. Zanussi of 1798 and the side altar of All Saints of 1659. The interior is furnishing with stalls of 1741, a pulpit, an organ, and Rococo pews. Tombstones of church dignitaries dating from the Middle Ages and following periods are located in the side chapels.

2 University Basilica of St. John the Baptist: This Roman Catholic metropolitan cathedral of Slovakia in University Square was built in the Early-Baroque style by architects P. and A. Spazzos in 1629 – 1637. The church is situated on the site of a former Dominican monastery and church which had existed here from C13 to the beginning of C17. The one-nave building with side chapels and straight-ended presbytery is a variation of the Gesù in Rome. Over several decades, many Italian, Viennese, and Slovak sculptors,

The Church of St. Helen in High Street from the first quarter of C14.

wood-carvers, stuccoers, painters, and gilders participated in the decorating of the church. The most valuable artifact of the interior is the high altar of 1640 by B. Knilling and V. Stadler. The paintings and stuccoes in the church interior are by renown Italian artists G. B. Rosso, G. Tornini, and P. Conti. A part of the ceiling paintings is by the Viennese painter J. Gruber dating from about 1700. Interior furnishings include altars in the side chapels, and other ornaments date mostly from C17: a pulpit, a platform, pews, mortuaries, etc. In the general history of the basilica its spiritual functions prevailed; however, it was also a scene where theological disputes took place. Since recently, graduation ceremonies of Trnava University when Baccalaureate and Doctorate degrees are awarded have been organized here.

3 The Monastery and Church of the Holy Trinity: Located in Štefánik Street, this Roman Catholic church was built in 1710 – 1729 by the Trinitarians who came to Trnava at the beginning of C18. The church nave with aisles is designed in the High Baroque style with half-lowered side chapels, two towers and

a richly articulated façade. The dominant of the interior Rococo furnishings is the painting on the high altar by F. A. Maulbertsch of 1758. The complex of buildings also comprised a four-wing, two-storeyed monastery where a Royal Gymnasium was established in 1784 after the abolishment of the Jesuitical Order. Nowadays, this building houses the National District Record Office with many rare collections of documents dating from C13 up to C20.

4 The Church of St. James: A Franciscan church located near the Bernolák Gate, and monastic complex in Františkánska ulica (Franciscan Street) built in 1633 – 1640 on the site of an earlier Gothic church with a churchyard and monastery. It is a one-nave church with a polygonal presbytery and a tower projecting from the front; the interior spaces are vaulted and decorated with stuccoes. The high altar with a painting by J. Zanussi is dating from the end of C18. Side altars date back to CC17 – 18; the pulpit is of C18; Baroque sculptures of saints and en epitaph are of 1691. The monastery was built on the site of a medieval building in 1619 – 1749. In the refectory, cross vaults, stuccoed cartouches, and portals have been preserved. In the 1950's the monastery was adapted for various social occassions.

5 The Church of St. Helen: Built in the first quarter of C14 this Roman Catholic church in the Hlavná ulica (the High Street) is the oldest church in the town. The nave vaulting is from C17; the side chapels date from C18. In the wall of the sanctuary there is a Gothic pastophory dating from C14, and in the nave there are remains of Gothic wall paintings. The interior furnishings date from CC17 – 19. The high altar dates from the end of C19, and side altars date back mostly to C18. The Renaissance side altar "Vir dolorum" with two Gothic side panels dates from the first half of C17. The pulpit and sculptures of the saints date from C18. In the vicinity of the church, the town hospital and poorhouse were originally located.

6 The Church of St. Joseph: This Roman Catholic Paulist church in Paulínska ulica (Paulist Street) was originally built as a Protestant church without a tower, but in 1671 it was appropriated by Paulists who complemented it according to the needs of their order. This church represents a Protestant hall-type church with a three-storeyed gabled façade. The architectural conception of the church is of German-Silesia Renaissance. The high altar dates from the end of C17, the side altars date from the beginning of C18, and the pulpit dates from 1905. The monastery dating from 1719, an original part of the church complex, was converted into apartments in 1946 – 1947.

7 The Church of St. Anna: A Roman Catholic church located in Hviezdoslavova ulica (Hviezdoslav Street), it was built in 1730 – 1776 in the High-Baroque style together with the convent of the Ursulines. The convent was transformed into a school building in 1857 and then in 1942.

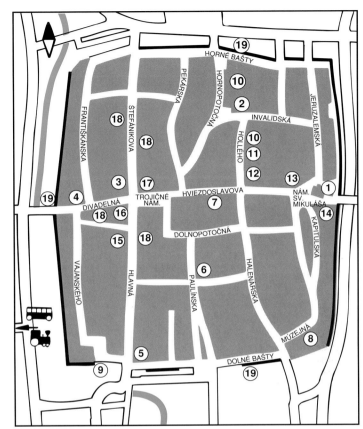

The town plan.

The church has a central oval nave which carries a low dome. Originaly two pavillions of monastery buildings were connected to the church. The western one was demolished in 1942 and on its site a new school building was constructed. The interior furnishings of the church date from CC18 – 19; the high altar with a painting of St. Anna by J. Zanussi is of 1789; the side altars date from CC18 – 19.

8 The Church and Convent of the Clarists: Located in Múzejná ulica (Museum Street), the church was probably a Romanesque building dating from C13, but it was rebuilt to the Gothic style in mid-C14. In 1683 the complex partially burnt down. The building of a new church and convent began in 1690 and continued until 1718.

The side wings enclosing two atrium courtyards were added. The Baroque two-tower church has a vaulted nave with lunettes featuring plant and figural ornaments dating from 1690. The original tower projecting from the front receded into the building when the church was added the extension of a Baroque monastery. After the abolition of St. Clare's Order, the monastic complex was changed into a hospital. Since 1954 the West-Slovakia Museum is housed here. Among the original furnishings is the high altar dating from the first half of C18; three side altars and C18 pews have been preserved. In the museum exposition are interesting collections of Slovak and Haban pottery, folk-art artifacts, and documents on the history of the town and the university.

The Baroque column of St. Joseph from 1731.

The complex of convict buildings of the Roman-Catholic parish from 1768 and a oollegiate church at the corner of the Svätopluk Square.

9 The Evangelical (Lutheran – Augsburg Confession) Church: Located in Žarnov Street in the southern part of the town behind the Lower Bastion, the church was built in 1923 – 1924 according to a design by the architect J. Marek. The masonry building has a reinforced concrete ceiling, an amphitheater ground-plan and diagonally situated side towers. After cracks appeared due to a statics failure of the church and after renovations in 1974, the simple interior was added a suspended ceiling.

10 The University: The premises of the university comprise nine buildings; the largest of them is connected to the university church. The construction of this complex began in 1643 when the right wing was started; later, in 1678 – 1688, the three-storeyed wing was built. The typical long western wing was added in 1700 – 1718. It contained lecture-halls, offices, and also the academic theatre. The northern wing contained a library consisting of about 15,000 volumes. Its interiors were decorated with the paintings by Italian master G. Giorgiolli. In the northwest corner of the university complex the printing house was located, where books in many languages

have been printed since 1644. The university premises also included an astronomical observatory. When the medical faculty was established, another building was erected in 1770 – 1773 according to a project by F. A. Hillebrandt. Nowadays, it is used as the Military Record Office.

Near the university church in J. Hollý Street there are other spectacular pieces of architecture representing the once-famous university colleges; the most exquisite buildings are arranged around University Square and in Hollý Street.

11 The Building of "Albertinum": Located in Hollý Street, it was built by Cardinal-Primate Peter Pázmány in 1623 as a seminary for students of socially lower-classes. It was reconstructed around 1710, then again in C19; it was transformed into a school in C20 where the first town library and museum were located. The former college is now used by the military forces.

12 The Aristocratic Seminary: Located in Hollý Street, it was built in 1747 – 1754 by Maria Theresa. An unknown architect designed the stately four-wing building in the Viennese

High-Baroque style. It contains a chapel with a trompe l'oeil painting of the Apocalypsis by V. Mussinger dating from 1758. Nowadays it is employed by the military forces.

13 Olah's Seminary: Situated in St. Nicolas Square, this is the earliest part of the university complex. It was built in 1567 as a seminary, and renovated in 1590. Extensive reconstruction was executed in the 1970's when it was adapted to the needs of the West-Slovakia Museum. An exhibition of literature and history of book-printing is staged here.

14 The Archbishop's Palace: Located in St. Nicolas Square, this palace was built on earlier Gothic foundations; it is a Renaissance two-storeyed building dating from 1562. Two stone coats-of-arms showing the years 1561 and 1691 adorn the façade. In the northern wing projecting into the square were the library and the printing house of 1639. This palace is the seat of Archbishop-Metropolitan of Slovakia.

15 The Town Hall: Today's Town Hall in Hlavná (High) Street emerged in the process of reconstructions of the previous Gothic town hall (destroyed in 1683) when several medieval houses were joined together. Its present-day appearance was acquired in 1683. The surrounding area is composed of buildings from throughout CC16 – 19. The principal building of the Town Hall is classical in style with High-Baroque features. The chapel in the courtyard is from the beginning of C19.

16 The Theatre: This building in the Holy Trinity Square was built in 1831 according to a design by the architect Grünn and ranks among the most majestic and impressive town buildings. This original Empire building with a seating capacity of 548 seats was the sixth stone theatre in the Hungarian kingdom. The theatre had a *reduta* (ballroom) and an inn. The interior of the theatre dates from 1959.

17 The Town Tower: Shooting up from the Holy Trinity Square and being originally a watch-tower, it was begun in 1574. It was rebuilt in 1666 and 1683 when it was surmounted by a dome. In 1739 a two-metre high statue of the Immaculata was placed on the top of the tower.

18 The Town Houses: Built at the end of C16 and in the first half of C17, many of these houses stand on Gothic foundations. After the great fire in 1666, the houses were reconstructed or new ones were erected. When the university was established, some of the town houses were incorporated into its premises; some of the canons' houses appeared on the university ground as well. The town houses are mostly two-storeyed with a passageway, and they have three or more axes and classical façades. The most valuable of them are situated in the High Street, Štefánik Street, Staromestská

The Evangelical (Lutheran – Augsburg Confession) Church from 1923 – 1924.

The Clarissian cloister area, today a museum.

(Old Town) Street and Divadelná (Theatre) Street. They boast preserved groud-plans medieval and Renaissance vaulting, portals and stuccoes.

19 The Town Fortifications: Belonging to the most extensive and the best preserved brick-wall fortification systems in Slovakia, the defences were being erected from the last third of C13 to C14 as a superstructure on earlier foundations. The high curtain wall was strengthened by rectangular bastions, four massive gatehouses, and two posterns. On the southern and northern sides were two gateways through which Bratislava Road and so-called Bohemian Road passed. The town walls were surrounded by a moat. The modifications of this system in 1435 and in 1553 – 1556 enhanced its defensive power. The transformations in C16 were carried out under the military ortification engineer P. Ferrabosco. At that time, barbicans were constructed on Bratislava Road in front of the Lower Bastion; a part of it was rebuilt in order to mount cannons there. At the end of C18 the walls lost their significance and they were gradually demolished in C19; all gatehouses were removed and only the postern in the western part was widened to create the Bernolák Gate. The postern near the Church of St. Nicolas was not altered and it preserved its Empire style from the first half of C19. In that period minor domestic houses started to be built attached to the walls; their windows were punctured directly into them. Large scale reconstructions of the fortifications started in the 1970's; and all later additions were removed from the preserved portion of the Lower Bastion and the western part of the wall, so that the masonry of the walls could be shown to the observers. The parts of the moat on the western and southern sides were changed into parks; on the eastern side the scarp remained unchanged.

The original symbol of Trnava dating from the beginning of C14 was a six-spoke wheel with the head of Christ in the middle. In the space between the spokes were the letters "alpha" and "omega," then scales, a crescent, and a star. Of this C15 symbol only Christ's head in the wheel has remained. In 1420 Trnava began to use a municipal seal. In the middle of the seal an engraved shield containing only a wheel appeared. Nowadays the wheel is supposed to conceals initials of the name of Christ: the Greek letters iota and chí, i. e. I and X – Iesos Christos. Today Trnava's arm contains a wheel in a shield dating from the first third of C15.

With Trnava, a town of considerable importance, many famous personalities are associated. In 1328 Louis I of Anjou, Hungarian and Polish King and the patron of the town, died here. Among those who made Trnava famous through their work were Mikuláš Telegdy, a founder of the first printing house in Trnava; Johann Sambucus, a humanist, philologist, historian, and an editor of antique authors, court historian to King Ferdinand I, as well as to royal officials; M. Oláh, a humanist, scholar, and high church dignitary. From 1562 onwards, Cardinal-Primate and Palatine P. Pázmány, an imperial governor of Hungary, politician, high church dignitary, and patron of the town lived here. Trnava attracted writers of modern times – J. Fándly, J. Hollý, F. Urbánek; composers – Z. Kodály, M. Schneider-Trnavský, and many other accomplished artists. The outstanding Slovak linguist A. Bernolák studied and then worked in the town.

Visitors to Trnava will be delighted with walks down the pedestrian zone in the centre of the town. Innumerable lovely places, especially churches, as the parish church and the church of St. Helen, and the noble buildings of the university, all of them provoke to think of the eventful history of the town. The exhibitions of the West-Slovakia Museum in the Clarist convent, Oláh's seminary containing the Mikuláš Schneider-Trnavský Memorial, the theatre, and the district art-gallery tempt the curious to come in. The side streets running along the restored parts of the town walls will offer an unusual view of a most interesting defensive system.

Trnava's surroundings with several fine places offering bathing in the openair, e. g. at Kamenný mlyn, Štrky, and in the suburban recreational area Jahodníky, bring another pleasant way of spending free time. The health resort Modranka, the indoor swimming pool, and the artificial ice skating rink are other attractive facilities attended in winter.

Better-trained hikers will go and admire other charming places as the Driny cave at the foothill of the Little Carpathians, 25 km distant of Trnava, or the forest park around Smolenice Castle, the water reservoir of Boleráz, and the impressive Červený Kameň Castle.

Central
Slovakia

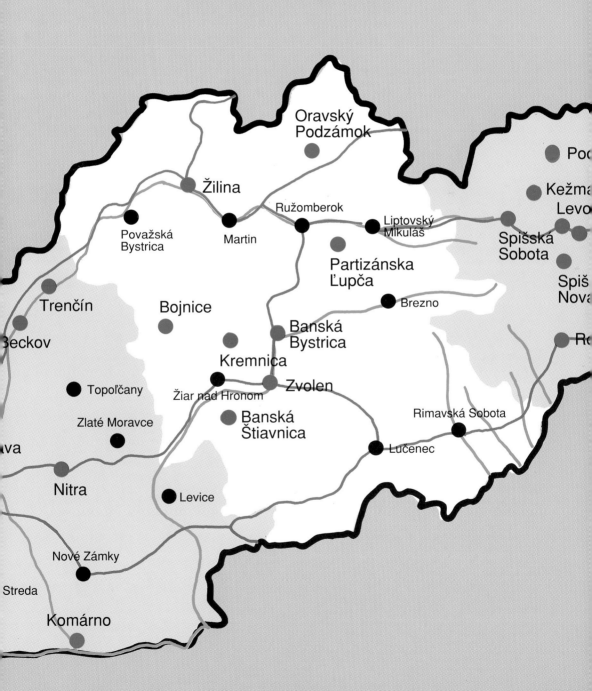

Oravský
Podzámok

Po

Žilina

Kežma

Levo

Ružomberok

Liptovský
Mikuláš

Spišská
Sobota

Považská
Bystrica

Martin

Spiš
Nova

Partizánska
Ľupča

Trenčín

Bojnice

Brezno

Ro

Beckov

Kremnica

Banská
Bystrica

Topoľčany

Žiar nad Hronom

Zvolen

Zlaté Moravce

Banská
Štiavnica

Rimavská Sobota

va

Nitra

Levice

Lučenec

Nové Zámky

Streda

Komárno

Central Slovakia, the most mountainous part of Slovakia, covers almost 18,000 square kilometres. Its longitude ranges from 18° 04' E to 20° 28' E, the latitude ranges from 48° 03' N to 49° 35' N.

Natural beauties of this region are unusually rich and diversified. It is also well endowed with organic and inorganic natural resources. Natural beauties, rare cultural-historical monuments, and the charming folk architecture, all help to create the pleasant appearance of the region. Scores of precious historical objects are located in the central-Slovakia towns.

The Fatra and Tatra Mountains, as components of the Inner West Carpathian arc, determine the appearance of the region. The volcanic mountains of the Slovak Stredohorie mountain range and the Slovak Ore Mountains, which contained rich deposits of ores, chiefly gold and silver, are connected to the Tatras and Fatras from the south. In the northwest, the region is bordered by the Outer West Carpathians. The rivers flow through hollows and basins, connecting them to one another: the basins of the Liptov and Žilina regions are connected by the Váh River and the Upper Hron basin and the Žiar hollow are connected by the Hron River. The Turiec River rushes along the Turčianska hollow, the Orava River flows through the Orava basin, the Nitra River flows through the Upper Nitra basin, and the southern Slovakia hollows are interconnected by the Ipeľ River. The main roads run along the rivers and connect larger central-Slovakia towns. The thermal mineral water spas are very popular places for relaxation. The woods, which cover mainly mountain slopes, are home to many kinds of wild animals.

The majority of the Protected Areas, portions of the High Tatras and Low Tatras National Parks, and the Little Fatra Mountains National Park are located in central Slovakia. Further protected areas in the region include the Greater Fatra Mountains, the hills of Poľana, Kysuce, Upper Orava, the Štiavnické vrchy, the Strážovské vrchy, highlands of the Cerová vrchovina, a portion of the Nitra basin, and a portion of the plateau of Muránska planina (Muráň Plateau). In general, the territory enjoys a cold and humid mountain climate; the river basins feature a warmer climate and the southern parts of the territory belong to the moderately warm zone.

The first settlement of the central Slovakia region goes back to the period of the Middle Paleolithic. This period is represented by cave and open-air settlements – the campsites of Neanderthal man, which were discovered close to the thermal water springs of the Upper Nitra district – Bojnice, Prievidza, in the Liptov region, at Bešeňová and other places in the southern Slovakia lowlands.

In the Upper Paleolithic, the campsites of the hunters covered rather extensive areas of rolling lowlands and hollows of the Lučenecká, Rimavská and Ipeľská kotlina (Lučenec, Rimava and Ipeľ hollows).

The Neolithic settlements of the Danubian culture typical of the use of linear pottery (Bandkeramik) were concentrated in the southern lowlands of central Slovakia. The settlements sites established in single waves appeared in the northern, mountainous portion of the region, much later – in the Eneolithic or Bronze Age (1900 – 700 BC).

The cultures existing in the earlier periods of the Bronze Age influenced the lowland portions of central Slovakia only partially. In the later Bronze Age period, the development was influenced by the rapid emergence of the Kyjatice culture and by the fast growth of a dense network of settlements. In the later Bronze Age the dynamic development of the Lusatian culture was evidenced by archeological excavations in the northern portion of central Slovakia. The centres of bronze industry were found in Liptov, the Upper Nitra region, Turiec, Orava, the Štiavnica Hills, as well as in the Zvolen Hollow. The Lusatian culture was also influenced by the eastern Hallstatt culture, which underwent development of its own and survived in the closed-off mountain areas until the end of the Hallstatt period (700 – 400 BC). The distinctive development during the late Bronze Age and Hallstatt period was connected with the people of the Lusatian culture, typical of urnfields; they settled in the north in an enclosed enclave in Orava and survived until the beginning of the Púchov culture in the La Tène period.

From the southern lowlands of central Slovakia the peoples of Thracian culture penetrated up to the foothills of the mountains at the final stage of the Hallstatt. Similarly the Thracians, or their branch – the Alföld-Tisza-Slovak group, settled in the southwest.

The character of the settlements in central Slovakia was not essentially changed at the beginning of the La Tène period. The isolated finds of Celtic origin were discovered only accidentally. The Celts penetrated to the lowlands in south-central Slovakia until the middle of La Tène (300 – 100 BC) and later; they might have been pushed by the Dacians up along the river valleys to the sub-mountain districts.

In the Roman period, the northern portion of central Slovakia was settled by peoples of the Púchov culture, representing various ethnic groups settled in central Slovakia. South-central Slovakia, mainly the mountainous districts rich in ores, were most probably under the influence of this culture. At the end of the Roman period the region appeared under the influence of the Quadi.

The Great Migration of Peoples occurred when masses of tribes had left their long established settlement sites; in the final phase of this mass migration to the west also the first Slavs reached what is today Slovakia.

The Slavs arrived in central-Slovakia from two directions. Approximately since C5 – C6, the first Slavic tribes had pressed at very irregular intervals through the Orava passes, coming from beyond the Carpathians. The inhabitation of south-central Slovakia in C7 is closely connected with the gradual arrival of the main wave of incomers from the southeast. The scanty early-Slavic settlements of the Žilina, Turiec and Liptov hollows grew dense at the end of C8, and especially during C9. This movement directed outwards from the southern overpopulated territories was also connected with the effort to exploit the mineral resources (metal ores) for the needs of the Great-Moravian state.

The continuity of the Slavic habitation of central Slovakia in CC9 – 12 testifies to the gradual territorial expansion of the Old Magyars in the early stages of the Hungarian kingdom. Moreover, this process was characterized by the appropriation of the existing social structure and administration of the state. The continuous development of the older central-Slovakia settlements was interrupted by the Tartar invasion in 1241 – 1242, during which the regions along the Central Váh and the Hron were greviously devastated. After the Tartars had withdrawn, the administration and organizational structure of the Hungarian state was transformed; Royal counties (*comitates* – administrative units) were gradually replaced by aristocratic counties: the County of Gemer including Malohont, then the Counties of Hont, Liptov, Novohrad, Orava, Turiec and Zvolen came into being.

In C13 several important communities were granted town rights, e. g. Babiná, Banská Štiavnica, Banská Bystrica, Dobrá Niva, Hybe, Rimavská Baňa, Krupina, Nemecká (Partizánska) Ľupča, and Zvolen. Banská Štiavnica, the oldest town on this list, having a long history as a place of habitation, was first documented only in CC11 – 12; nevertheless ore prospecting activity started there much earlier. These privileged settlements became centres of economic, social and cultural life, where building activity began to develop on a large scale. After the situation was made stable in this region, the county castles and castles of feudal overlords in Orava, Liptov, Turiec, Zvolen, Budatín, and Hričov were built or rebuilt. Hronský Beňadik and Liptovská Mara became „loci credibile,“ i.e. they enjoyed special privileges to attest the authenticity of written documents.

The C14 was a period of remarkable growth of towns and villages; more towns were chartered, or older town rights and privileges were confirmed. At that time well-known towns as Kremnica, Žilina, Nová Baňa and Pukanec received their charters. Especially the towns and former villages located in the oremining area, where precious metals (gold and silver) were exploited, enjoyed privileged positions. The central Slovakia as an ore-mining area held a completely specific position in Central Europe. This district was the ore-mining base of the entire Hungarian kingdom and the towns of Banská Bystrica, Banská Štiavnica and Kremnica formed its backbone. The mint which was established in Kremnica in 1329 has been operating continually until the present day.

During CC14 and 15, other central Slovakia communities in Brezno, Ľubietová, Ružomberok, Martin, Prievidza, and Kysucké Nové Mesto were given their charters of town rights. The towns and the settlements patterns of the whole region were definitely formed at that time. At about the same period, the Slovak nationality started to develop, this fact proven by the Letters Pattent *"Privilegium Pro Slavis"*, issued in Žilina in 1380.

The towns and villages created the basic settlement pattern of the whole central Slovakia in C15. Gold and silver extraction in the ore mining areas increased; the Kremnica gold ducat became extraordinarily well-accepted in all of Europe. The copper mines in

the Banská Bystrica district were also known all over Europe. Central Slovakia did not stand aside the conflicts during the period when the Hussites attemted to expand their ideas. The troops of Hussite commander Jiskra came to the south of central Slovakia and occupied several localities.

The architecture and character of the central-Slovakia towns reflected also the social structure of their inhabitants. On the whole, the development of the urban settlements was determined by the mountainous terrain, the presence of ore, easy access, as well as the technical equipment of the mining enterprises. The most generally repeated pattern of central-Slovakia towns in the C15 was that the houses of the rich burghers and patricians were built around the square – the market place. At the beginning, in CC13 – 15, the towerhouses or houses shaped as compact blocks used to be placed in the middle of the building plot with ground provided around it; in the mining-towns the houses stood just at or over the entrances to the mining galleries (Banská Štiavnica). In the Late-Gothic period, the ground-plans of the houses gradually expanded. The houses with passageways and hall type houses developed; their ground-plans depended on the terrain. The alignment of the houses in a row, as seen nowadays, started to form in C15. Colours applied on the façades made them more conspicuous as well as rustication on the corners. Painted edges of the richly profiled stone jambs of the windows, doorways and many various details also contributed to the aesthetic qualities of the facades. In the interiors the elements of stone and carved ceilings in the "piano nobile" – stately rooms on the first floor – were treated in colours. Exquisite Late-Gothic lierne vaults appeared in a ground-floor hallway in Kremnica, in contrast to the more typically employed plain barrel vaults. Public town-buildings, most often the parish church and the town hall, were located in the centre of the urban structure. The houses built at the base of the hills were inhabited by craftsmen and miners, and the town-poor lived in cottages on the hillsides. Where the terrain allowed, a regular Late-Gothic square arose adjacent to the older, original settlement. By the Romanesque period it had already been traditional that a monumental church became the central building of the so-called town-castles, which were very well-fortified and standing in the centre of a medieval town; they fulfilled the function of inner defences of the town. Typically this complex was also the seat of the Chamberlain, the high royal administrator, the representative of the king, responsible for the control of revenues from mining and coin-stamping. Of all the components of the castle precincts, especially the town hall and a splendidly furnished church, where the divine services took place, cannot be omitted. These unique town-castles, that had been fortresses, administrative and spiritual centres in one, existed in Kremnica from C14, and in Banská Bystrica a century later.

The development of the other towns in central Slovakia, where the inhabitants pursued trade and crafts, was similar to the building development in all other regions of Slovakia, but especially similar to the situation in western Slovakia.

The C16 was marked by feudal expansiveness and the revolts of the serfs towards the efforts of nobility. In consequence of the growing tension, there were riots and rebellions, the most severe were the open revolts in mining districts. The miners rose in Banská Bystrica (1527) and Banská Štiavnica. The general economic situation was turned worse also because of the imminent Turkish invasion. These turbulent events culminated in the defeat of the Hungarian troops at Mohácz in 1526. Central Slovakia appeared among the territories which got into close neighbourhood with the Osman Empire. The Turks penetrated to Hronský Beňadik and conquered Fiľakovo in 1554, and as a result, the Fiľakovo sanjak (a part of a Turkish province – vilayet) was consequently established. The towns as well as the castles, forts and manor houses, had to build or rebuild their walls, according to the principles of Renaissance military fortification engineering.

Uniqueness of the defence system of Banská Štiavnica deserves description in greater details. Banská Bystrica and Kremnica could use the generally applied model of modern artillery defence; in Banská Štiavnica the Italian engineers designed a distinctive system: taking into account the highly varying terrain of the town. Remnants of the anti-Turkish fortification system have been preserved in most of the towns which stood in the way of the Turkish invasions. The preserved remnants in Pukanec, south of Banská Štiavnica, are the evidence of these historic events.

The new architectural style reshaped, too, the appearance of the town structure. Especially the squares changed. An eminently characteristic element was used to create a new type of a house: a broad, horizontally spread façade joined and connected up several original buildings into one unit, whose horizontal lines were also emphasized by the parapets at the roof line. The façades as well as the interior spaces were enriched by new elements. The paintings and sgraffitoes rhythmicized the façades, which were often adorned with inscriptions, emphasizing the civic virtues and town rights. Banská Štiavnica serves as an exellent example. The ground-plans of the houses were usually added a vaulted entrance-hall or a broadened passageway; the stately upper floor – the *"piano nobile"* – was decorated with struccoes and cartouches filled in with allegories painted on the vaults. The columned arcades in the courtyard became very popular as they helped to achieve the feeling of intimity of the inner spaces.

In 1540 Slovakia became a component of the Habsburg monarchy. The advance of Reformation caused a conflict between the Protestant Estates and the Catholic Habsburg court. In C17 it burst into open warfare and a sequence of uprisings of Hungarian Protestant Estates. In 1610, under the patronage of Palatine J. Thurzo, the first organization of the Evangelical church in the Hungarian Kingdom was founded at a Synod of Žilina. Of great significance was the development in south-central Slovakia, which was constantly raided by the Turks in the course of C17.

After the defeat of Turkish armies at the Battle of Vienna in 1683, a period of gradual economic and social stabilization allowed the process of recovery of a country so heavily damaged by wars and rebellions.

In C18, mainly during the rule of Maria Theresa, the overall economic, social, educational and cultural situation in the Austro-Hungarian monarchy improved. Central Slovakia prospered, the towns and villages were rebuilt in the spirit of the new style of those times, the Baroque. The fortifications gradually lost their importance as there was no need for their original functions and the towns spread beyond their original town walls. Crafts and manufacturing industry thrived, creating the basis of economic, social and cultural prosperity. In this period and in this context the Slovak national consciousness awoke fully: the literary usage of the Slovak language was codified for the first time in 1781.

The Baroque style, the characteristic artistic expression of Counter-Reformation, had a considerable effect on the appearance of the town when new, magnificent monasteries and splendid churches were built, overdecorated with works of art exuberating in colours and a wide variety of applied materials. Other representatives of this style – minor sacral buildings such as chapels, calvaries, sculptures of saints, and mainly votive sculptures – the intricate sculptural compositions, such as the Plague Columns in Banská Štiavnica and Kremnica, overhelmed the space in which they were located.

The Baroque used all means to increase grandiosity, splendour and stately character of architectural production. The expensive reconstructions of aristocratic residences and patrician houses influenced other buildings in the towns; the newly built and remodelled parish churches, and administrative buildings, especially the county halls are characterized by delight in Baroque forms. The typical Baroque skyline of a town laid stress on emphasizing the dominants by ingenious arrangements of onion-shaped roofs. The soft roof lines were also used in the details, for example in the oriel windows; thus well thought-out minor details affected the general appearance of the whole town.

With regard to the political and economic situation and technical progress, the end of C18 and beginning of the C 19 were a period of revolutionary changes. Serfdom was abolished in 1785; many changes also occured in towns, which spread beyond the original medieval defences. The revolution of 1848–1849 fostered the process of awaking Slovak national consciousness. The rise of the Slovak nation was supported by the first Slovak patronage gymnasia established in Martin, Kláštor pod Znievom and Revúca. In 1861 the National Assembly convened in Martin and accepted the "Memorandum of the Slovak Nation" there. Martin became centre of the Slovak social and cultural life; the *Matica slovenská* (the Slovak National Foundation), established there in 1863, became centre of the above-mentioned social and cultural processes.

From the mid-C19 to the beginning of C20 the towns and villages passed through another important phase of development which was heralded by many new types of buildings such as railway stations, theatres, blocks of flats, and especially factories.

World War I ended the era of the multi-national Austro-Hungarian monarchy. The Czechoslovak Republic originated in 1918. In 1944 central Slovakia became a centre of resistance against fascism and Banská Bystrica became headquarters of the Slovak National Uprising. To crash the national resistance of the Slovaks, Fascists used merciless methods: they burnt down the villages of Kalište and Nemecká. During the fights other towns suffered grevious damages. For instance, a part of the historical settlement site around the castle in Kremnica was destroyed. After the war the towns were renewed; the subsequent political and economic transformation caused changes in the appearance of the majority of them. New trends were demonstrated in radically rebuilt Prievidza, Liptovský Mikuláš and others. In central Slovakia several towns have preserved their ancient historic character and those represented in this book belong to the most compact and historically most valuable.

There are fourty-one other towns in central Slovakia besides those which have been selected and described in this book; the district towns of Čadca, Dolný Kubín, Liptovský Mikuláš, Lučenec, Martin, Považská Bystrica, Prievidza, Rimavská Sobota, Veľký Krtíš and Žiar nad Hronom are economic, social and cultural centres of central Slovakia.

From the list of important towns, it is necessary to mention Martin, which is known as the centre of the national revival movement. The first building of the Matica slovenská originating from 1869 – 1875 and the Slovak Gymnasium from 1866 rank among National Cultural Monuments. Many outstanding Slovaks found their last reposing place in the Martin National Cemetery, which is also a National Cultural Monument. Liptovský Mikuláš was a seat of Liptov County; several period houses have been preserved from that time. The legendary folk hero Juro Jánošík of Terchová was executed in Liptovský Mikuláš in 1713. In the town there is a unique museum of Slovak Karst. Brezno and Ružomberok are also historically significant towns.

Brezno was declared a town in 1380 and its development in the course of centuries has been connected with mining and craft production. Several preserved historical buildings are located in the town centre. The town tower, town hall and parish church are the most important among them. The skiing and sporting facilities at Jamy, Diele and Mazorík remain an atraction both in winter and summer.

The town of Ružomberok boasts many memorials from C14. The most important is the National Cultural Monument which is located in its suburb of Černová. Ružomberok is a starting point for hikes to the Veľká Fatra Mountains, Choč Hills and the Low Tatras.

The beauty of mountainous central Slovakia is multiplied by plentiful castle ruins. Strečno Castle is a National Cultural Monument; other castles – Liptovský hrádok, Likava, Lietava, Hričov, Považský hrad, Vršatec, and Súľov – were strongholds guarding the road along the Váh River. Other remarkable ruins of once famous castles – Šášov and Revište – are in the region of Turiec; attention is turned to the castles of Blatnica, Sklabiňa, and Zniev; in south-central Slovakia, there are castles of Čabraď, Fiľakovo, and Modrý Kameň. The Primeval fortified settlement site of Havránok, a National Cultural Monument, which was reconstructed in outlines, is located next to Liptovská Mara (an artificial lake with a hydro-electric power plant).

The sacral monuments in central Slovakia are represented by old churches and monasteries. Hronský Beňadik is a Benedictine abbey dating from C11; during the centuries it was constantly modified and rebuilt until C19. It is a National Cultural Monument. The church and the monastery in Okoličné dates from C15. The wall paintings in the churches of Čerín, Ludrová, Liptovský Ondrej, Kraskovo, Kyjatice, Ľuborečie, Martin, Necpaly, Rimavská Baňa, Rimavské Brezové, Poruba, Smrečany, and Zolná have been declared National Cultural Monuments. The wooden church of Palúdza was moved to Galovany, otherwise it would have been buried in the waters of the reservoir.

Many charming country seats, manor houses and mansions are scattered over central Slovakia. The Baroque country seat at Antol as well as the Renaissance wedding palace at Bytča have been declared National Cultural Monuments. Country seats and mansions at Diviaky, Divín, Dubnica, Jaseňová, Krasňany, Kunerád, Lednica, Necpaly, Orlové, Teplička nad Váhom, Turčianska Štiavnička and at some other places are a feast for the eye. The manor houses stand mainly in Turiec, but also in Liptov; Liptovský Ján is of great interest since several of them have been preserved here together with a few mansions and a medieval church of St. John the Baptist.

Exceptional opportunies to admire the beauties of folk architecture, art and customs are offered in several localities. Museums of folk architecture in Martin-Jahodníky, Pribylina and Vychylovka show how people of this region lived in the past. Among the constructions moved to the open-air museum in Pribylina are churches from Liptovská Mara and Liptovská Sielnica, and a mansion from Palúdza, which "stood in the way" of the artificial lake of Liptovská Mara. Vychylovka is a museum of the Kysuce village; it was founded in the open-air at the same time when a narrow-gauge forest railway line was revided after it had fallen to disuse. A similar technical memorial – a forest narrow-gauge railway line – is in Oravská Lesná: it commutes between and Chmúrna-Tanečník. It is included on the list of National Cultural Monuments. The Folk Architecture Preservation Areas are in Podbiel, Čičmany, Ružomberok-Vlkolínec, Sebechleby and Špania Dolina. They are famous and deserve special attention as localities with original folk buildings preserved on the site.

The patterns of pottery produced in central Slovakia may be easily discerned from others because of the designs typical of jugs and dishes. In Heľpa, Detva, Očová, Polomka, Terchová and Sliače local traditions of wearing folk costumes have survived and are part of everyday life. Preparation of well-known and typical local dishes of "kapustnica," or sauerkraut soup, "bryndzové halušky," gnocchi with brindza cheese (cheese made of sheep milk), and the making of other sorts of cheese of sheep's milk – "oštiepok" and "parenica" – are also part of local traditions. Festivals of folk songs and dances take place in Detva and Východná every summer.

Central Slovakia is also famous for its spas where many kinds of diseases are treated. Rheumatism, arthritis and other diseases of locomotor and nervous system are treated in Dudince, Rajecké Teplice, Bojnice, Kováčová, Sklené Teplice and Číž. Diseases of the digestive and respiratory systems as well as occupational diseases are treated in Nimnica and Korytnica. In Lúčky women's diseases are treated; diseases of lymphatic and locomotor systems are treated in Turčianske Teplice. Sliač is famous for treating diseases of heart and the circulatory system. This region also offers several brands of mineral water: Fatra, Budišská, Maštiná and Korytnica.

Central Slovakia is interesting not only with regard to its record in history and preserved historical heritage, but also because of its natural environment and the richness of landscape variety. Wonderful nature, and mainly exceptional mountain scenery, create a fascinating background of the towns and villages. Recreational centres are located in very attractive places.

Central Slovakia is particularly attractive for excellent recreational centres which cater to the visitors. There are water reservoirs and rivers for water sports lovers. Besides the water reservoir of Liptovská Mara, which is of relatively recent date, there are other dams Oravská, Kurinec, and Ružín. Especially interesting are mining water reservoirs "tajchy" – the artificial lakes around Banská Štiavnica in the Štiavnica Hills. There are also thermal open-air swimming pools in Bojnice, Kremnica, Mošovce and Liptovský Ján.

The mountains of central Slovakia offer many possibilities for spending pleasant moments in the open-air in winter. A lot of snow covers hill slopes which offer excellent skiing conditions even for extremely demanding skiers. The most famous skiing centres are in the Low Tatras: Jasná, Bystrianska Valley, Donovaly, and Čertovica; Terchová-Vrátna is in the Lesser Fatra; Kubínska hoľa, another skiing centre, is in Orava. Good conditions are also on Veľká Rača in Kysuce and on the Martinské hole mountains in Turiec.

In summer the mountains of central Slovakia offer a great variety of forest fruits, such as bilberries, cranberries, raspberries as well as mushrooms, which are much sought-after. This region is also a good place for fishing and hunting. Trout-fishing as well as bear, wild-boars and deer hunting are most attractive.

A pleasant alternative to these activities may be seen in visits to beautiful caves, e. g. the Demänovská stalactite and stalagnite and ice caves, and also other stalactite caves at Bystré, Harmanec and Važec; all of them offer visitors rich and exciting experiences.

Banská Bystrica

Names: L – Neosolium, Neosolim, **G** – Neusohl, **H** – Besztercebánya
Latitude: 48° 43' N, **Longitude:** 19° 07' E
Elevation: average 350 m, **range:** 304 – 1265 m
Population: 85 100
Suburbs: Iliaš, Jakub, Kostiviarska, Kráľová, Kremnička, Majer, Podlavice, Radvaň, Rakytovce, Rudlová, Sásová, Senica, Skubín, Šalková, Uľanska
Means of Access: By rail: routes No. 170 and 172; By road: routes No. E 77 and 59, 66, 69; By bus
Accommodations: Hotels: Arcade, Lux, Passage Urpín; Motels: Uľanka – Vesel, Madona; Hostels: Turist ATC, Šachtička Mountain Hotel, Bocian Manor House
Information: Cultural and Information Center – tel: (++421)(0)88-16186, 088-4155085, fax: 088-4152914, e-mail: pkobb@isternet.sk, www.isternet.sk/pkobb

Banská Bystrica owes much to its wonderful natural background which makes it one of most attractively situated towns in Slovakia. It lies in the very heart of the country, spread along the Hron in the Zvolenská kotlina (Zvolen Hollow). It is surrounded on all sides by mountains: the forested Low Tatras, the Kremnické pohorie (Kremnica Hills) and the Bystrická vrchovina (Bystrica Highland). The intact natural beauties of several Nature Reserves, e.g. the Greater Fatra Mountains, Poľana Mountain, the Štiavnica Hills, the River Nitra Valley, and the Low Tatras National Park, are all within easy reach of the town. The River Hron flows through Banská Bystrica and winds like a blue thread through the territory of Slovakia, collecting water from the mountains. The town is strang along the river and the foot of Urpín Mountain.

Banská Bystrica features a moderately cold and humid climate with heavy temperature inversions; the average January temperature fluctuates from –3.5 °C to –6 °C, and the average July temperature from 16 °C to 17 °C; an average annual rainfall varies from 600 to 850 mm. A cold mountain climate prevails in the northern parts of the region; in winter it creates excellent conditions for winter

sports. The surroundings offer excellent conditions for both winter and summer sports.

The settlement of the Banská Bystrica region, similar in many ways to most Slovak towns, can be traced to ancient times, as shown by the finds from the Bronze Age and later periods. There is also evidence of the early extraction of copper on a vast area along the River Hron.

As the crossroads of trading routes running along the Hron, and those running to the Liptov region and farther to the north, the place was extremely attractive for habitation. The first written record of the existence of Banská Bystrica dates from 1255, when King Béla IV issued a charter granting rights to German "guests" (colonists) to mine gold, silver, and other metals; they were also granted the township. The immigrant Saxon miners settled close to an already existing Slavonic community, whose location has not been determined yet, and they named their settlement "Novisolium". The rich deposits found in its vicinity, and especially of copper ore, made Banská Bystrica world-renown in the Middle Ages. The ore was exported to the north to Poland, and from the end of C14 was exported to Venice, Austria and to southern Germany.

The oldest existing building is the originally

Banská Bystrica, mid-C18.

Romanesque aisled church of the Virgin Mary; the original churchyard no longer exists. This church is situated on the knoll above the confluence of the Hron and Bystrica River, and is the core of the later-constructed town castle. The settlement spread to the south and to the east of the church.

The town spital with a Gothic chapel of St. Elizabeth was built at the lower end of the settlement in 1303. This structure determined the town's south-east boundary in that period along its major urban axis, which ran along the road to Zvolen. In C13 it was called the "Via Magna". This road may have later expanded to a spindle shape in the north-east direction. Thus a market place arose, extending towards the castle.

At the end of C14 the building lots around the square were only sparsely built up with stone tower houses or one-storeyed, three-spatial ones, which were rebuilt later in C15.

During the High Middle Ages Banská Bystrica, then a rich mining town, became a member of the Union of Seven Central Slovakian Mining Towns. The Union played an important role in the unification movement against their internal and external enemies.

At the begining of the second half of C15, there was a stagnation and crisis in the mining industry, caused by technical difficulties in the deep-mining of ore. After many miners and mine entrepreneurs had gone bankrupt, a successful entrepreneur from Cracow, Juraj Thurzo, advanced to the head of the entrepreneurial Union of Central Slovakian Mining Towns. At the turn or throughout CC15 – 16 he became a member of the family of the Augsburg banker Fugger through marriage. Both families owned houses in Bystrica. Then he established the *Ungarisches Handel* Corporation, which brought both him and the town large profits. This fact is confirmed by the intensive building activity at the end of C15. The precincts of the town castle, used for religious purposes and as the seat of the town council, underwent extensive renovations. The Chamberlain representing the Crown, who supervised the mining activity and controlled revenues of the mines, also had his seat there. Buildings which were built or renovated for common fortification purposes served different functions; among them were: the King Matthias House; a rectory located by the Rectory Bastion; the Mining Bastion and the Pisár Bastion (no longer

Panorama of the town from the west.

existing); galleries with an adjacent construction; the Town Hall; and the Church of Holy Cross. At the same time, the Roman Catholic parish church was rebuilt in a very impressive Late-Gothic style.

The urban area became denser as the older buildings were rebuilt and interconnected. The façades received new artistic expression, and their exteriors were adorned by sgrafittos. The wealth of the town was reflected in the pretentious interiorsdecoration of buildings; as in, for example, the Green Room of the Thurzo house. The Thurzo-Fugger Corporation disputed with the burghers over the privilege to supply the miners, besides this the Thurzos and Fuggers defrauded the money of the mining guild – the Brotherhood of the Corpus Christi. The conflict between the town's interests and the corporation's interests finally caused the miners uprising in Banská Bystrica in 1525. It spread quickly to the entire central Slovakia mining area, but it was suppressed in the next year. This discontent with the feudal authorities was connected with the ideas of Reformation which spread from Germany, where the mining towns had intensive contacts. These ideas were mediated by merchants, as well as the

students returning from the German universities. The ideas of Reformation met with a wide acceptance by the middle and lower classes very quickly. Therefore after 1539, all churches in Banská Bystrica belonged to the Evangelicals, or Lutherans. After 1620 with the advent of the Counter-Reformation, the churches changed hands several times; they passed over to the Catholics, only to pass over to the Protestants again.

During the first third of C16, owing to the expected Turkish invasion after the battle at Mohácz, the town castle began to be rebuilt into a fortress against the Turks. The Italian fortification builders were commissioned to complete the castle defensive system according to the latest developments in fortification engineering. The town hall, a part of the castle area, rebuilt at the same time, received an arcaded loggia and a Renaissance gable. The town gatehouses (Dolná (Lower), Horná (Upper), Strieborná (Silver) and Hronská) were built around mid-C16; the construction of town walls began during the 1580s. The walls' sophisticated layout respected the existing urban structure. The fortification system was completed at the beginning of C17. The building activities

The northern portion of the square with burghers' houses.

continued in the town and included the Renaissance clock tower, added to the town weighing house, and the Renaissance transformation of the town-houses, not only in the square but also in the streets. The façades ended in gables. Especially for the houses in the side streets, their owners sought to emulate the style, both exterior and interior of their wealthier neighbours' residences which were developing in the square. The vast amount of unique architectural details proves the exceptional workmanship of the builders. Among them, several generations of the di Pauli family, of Italian origin, reached unprecedented prominence.

The first Baroque building in Banská Bystrica, the St. Francis Xavier Church, was started soon after the arrival of the Jesuits. The Jesuits also modified the second castle church, the Church of the Holy Cross, in mid-C18.

The clock tower, the town hall, the churches, the town-houses and especially the Church of the Virgin Mary were destroyed by fire in 1761. After the vaults over the nave of the parish church had been restored, the nave was decorated with frescoes by the Baroque painter Anton Schmidt, who

worked in the central Slovakia mining area. Town houses were renovated, receiving a new layout; they were extended inwards to the depths of their lots. Additional stories elevated the street façades. New rooms with vaulted ceilings were another novelty. Interiors were adorned by modern tiled (Dutch) stoves and often the vaulted ceilings were embellished adorned with decorative plaster work.

The establishment of the Bishopric in Banská Bystrica was another important event in the religious history of the town. One of the town houses was rebuilt in the Late-Baroque style for the needs of the new church institution.

Two other older buildings were rebuilt to create the county administration hall, after the county offices of Zvolen County were moved to Banská Bystrica at the end of C18. The Church of St. Francis Xavier standing in the square was emodelled in the 1840s.

After the decline in mining production, which had been the decisive source of the town's economy, manufactural and craft production during C18 enabled Banská Bystrica to recover its economic growth.

The southern portion of the square.

The façades of the town houses were modernized in the Eclectic style in the second half of C19. Many of them got additional storeys, necessitated by the need to house the steadily growing population.

The town walls and gatehouses hindered the urban development of the town, and also took up valuable space for building; therefore, they were gradually demolished. In their place, large new buildings arose at the beginning of C20: National House, a branch of the National Bank, and blocks of flats. Suburbs and factories spread out along the highway towards the country. The Art Nouveau produced several remarkable residential houses near the Creek Bystrica and in the eastern portion of the town.

Banská Bystrica became a centre of the Slovak National Uprising during World War II. Several national historical monuments have been preserved from this period. The new building of the Museum of the Slovak National Uprising (SNP) is a highly remarkable and imposing piece of architecture dedicated to this event.

After World War II, Banská Bystrica became a seat of the District Administration Offices, which brought enormous changes in the appearance of its urban architecture. Poor quarters vanished, concurrently being replaced by large office buildings and extensive high-rise pre-fabricated concrete blocks of flats.

The most important and interesting buildings surround mainly the extensive central square, whose northeast portion also features the original area of the castle.

The medieval historical centre was declared an Urban Conservation Area in 1955 after reconstructed individual buildings were opened to the public.

View of the main square with the Church of St. Francis Xavier and the city clock tower.

1 The Town Castle Area:

A National Cultural Monument, the castle is composed of a group of buildings situated around the central parish church, originally surrounded by walls in C15. Approximately three-quarters of the walls were demolished, and so was the bastion, in order to make way for the new post office building in 1948.

a) The Church of the Virgin Mary: This Roman Catholic parish church, the oldest building in the town, dates from 1255 and was built in the Romanesque style. The tower with its Romanesque windows and the north wall of the nave are remain from the original structure. The sacristy was added in the early C14; during the Late-Gothic modification taking place from 1473 to 1516, the ground-plan was expanded with several chapels, dedicated to Saint Andrew, the Corpus Christi, St. Anthony, St. Barbara, and St. John of Charity, and an oratory was built over the sacristy. The reticulated vaulting in the north chapel of Saint Barbara is supported by figural cantilevers of the saints. The church was subsequently elongated; after fire in 1761, when the vaulted ceiling collapsed, the last extensive reconstruction was performed and the building was fitted with barrel vaults and flat-vault ceilings.

The Altar of St. Barbara, the work of the Master Pavol of Levoča and dating from 1509, is a remnant of the once richly-furnished interior that was created after the Late-Gothic renovation of the church. Also preserved is the altar of Mary Magdalene, located in the southern chapel, and dating from the end of C15. The highly prized bronze baptismal font from 1475 is the work of Master Jodok.

"Christ on the Mount of Olives" is the best extensive sculptural work from the beginning of C16. It is situated in a niche with reticulated vaulting on the southern side in the Church's exterior.

Anton Schmidt extented the paintings (1770) on the Baroque vaults. The main altar contains two paintings, the Assumption of the Virgin Mary and the Holy Trinity, both created by J. L. Kracker in 1774.

b) The Church of the Holy Cross: This Roman Catholic church was originally a one-nave building annexed to the castle wall. In one earlier renovation, in 1492, it was elongated to reach the Matthew House. The portal has a depressed arch, which bears the incorrect date of 1452. The Evangelicals, who owned the building in C17, unified all the interior spaces by demolishing the partition wall. The Jesuits modified the exterior of the building in the spirit of the Baroque, in 1742 – 1747. The church was damaged by a fire in 1782 and its interior furnishings were destroyed. The present furnishings date mainly from C19.

c) The Matthias House: The seat of the Royal Administrator, this house came into existence either as a part of the castle fortification, or was built into the fabric of the Miner's Bastion in 1479. It is a narrow five-storeyed construction with a high pitched gable ending projecting above the town wall. King Matthias' coat-of-arms with the date 1479 is located on the south façade.

d) The Town Hall: Called Pretórium, is the seat of the Town Council. This three-storeyed Late-Gothic structure, built after 1500, was donated by the mine owner and later Zvolen County Administrator, V. Mühlstein. Arcaded galleries were added in 1564 – 1565 to three exterior walls. In C18 the façade was redone in the Baroque style.

e) The Shooting Gallery: This most important fortification construction of the town castle took on its present appearance after the fire in 1761. The original gatehouse, whose defensive strength was enhanced by an outwards projecting shooting gallery, was built in 1512. The sole original entrance was over a moat. The passage in the gatehouse was defended by the usual machicolations or "murder holes", through which the inmates could pour or hurl things. In the passageway of the gatehouse a star vault has been preserved.

2 The Church of St. Francis Xavier: Built in 1615 – 1729, this Roman Catholic church, also known as the Kapitulský (Cloister) Church, dominates the square. It is a Baroque building, later transformed into the classical style. It was built on the site of the house

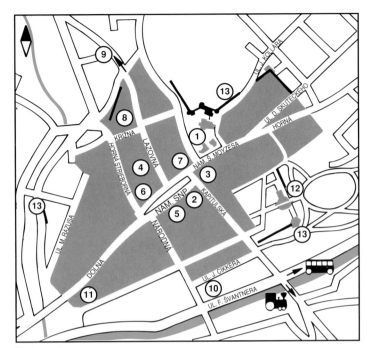

The town plan.

called the Burgher Königsberger Oberhaus, and in which the Jesuits situated the chapel of St. John the Baptist after their arrival. In 1695 they started building the church, simultaneously with a college, according to the design of J. Häffels, which was conceived after Vignola's architectural plan for "Il Gesú". After the establishment of the Bystrica Bishopric, the church was promoted to the cathedral church in 1776. The dominant twin-towers were built during the renovations in 1844. The church was elongated after the sacristy had been abolished. The balustrade around the towers dates from the Romantic remodelling of the end C19.

The church's interior furnishings from the first half of C19 consist of the Empire main altar, the side altars, and the pulpit. The liturgical objects, such as the ciboria and the monstrance, date from the end of C19. The former Jesuit college

from 1695 belongs to the church, and was rebuilt in the classical style in 1806; it underwent further remodelling in C20.

3 The Clock Tower: Standing in the upper part of the square since 1552, the tower with its clock and basement torture-chamber was a part of the town weighing house (1506). The tower, known as the Weighing or Green Tower, was remodelled several times, receiving a new stone gallery in 1665 and a new Baroque polygonal upper floor with a helm roof in 1782-1784.

4 The Bishop's Palace: House No. 19 was built in 1783 in the classical style on the site of two Late-Gothic houses. After the fire in 1787, the palace was renovated by *comes* Berchtold. Bishop Štefan Moyzes resided in this palace in the middle of C19.

The Town Hall, the so called Pretórium.

The town castle, a view from the south.

The interior of the parish church of the Virgin Mary.

5 The Thurzo House (No. 4): Also known as Mittelhaus, the administration office of the Thurzo-Fugger Corporation had its seat here during the years 1492 – 1540. It originated when two older Gothic buildings were connected by means of a unifying sgrafitto decoration of the facades into one unit. The Green Hall has been recently restored. It is adorned with sumptuous plant and figural ornamentation. Upper storeys were added in 1530, and at the same time the neighbouring lane was built up. The façade was transformed in 1660, when its corners were rusticated.

6 The Benický House (No. 16): Its present form appeared after 1660, with two repeated reconstructions and the interconnection of two originally free-standing Gothic houses; the loggia which opens to the square, is from the same period. Two fires and frequent changes of proprietors influenced the present appearance of the façade, which displays the most important phases in construction of the house. During the last renovation, the sgraffitos and wall paintings from throughout CC16 – 18 were restored. A portion of the house serves as an exibition hall, employed by artists from the region for art shows; it is also used for other social events.

7 The Ebner House (No. 22): Originating when two Gothic houses were interconnected in the first third of C16, this building has a passageway and a sumptuously decorated Renaissance oriel (1636), the work of the Master Ján Weinhardt from Spišské Vlachy.

8 The former County Administration Office Building: Situated at No. 9 Lazovná Street, the present-day house developed from two older houses during the Baroque renovation in 1764 – 1768. An original Renaissance loggia overlooks the courtyard.

The altar of St. Barbara by Master Pavol of Levoča.

9 The Evangelical (Lutheran – Augsburg Confession) Church: Located in Lazovná Street, the church was built in 1803 – 1807 and is situated behind the original town walls on the site of an older timber church, similar to the old Evangelical church in Kežmarok. The central church is built in the classical-Empire style. The painting on the main altar is by Prussian painter Daege. The pulpit originates from 1853 and the bronze baptismal font dates from

1803. The liturgical objects include chalices from C17, a tankard with original Renaissance ornaments from C17, and the ciborium, are the work of Master-Goldsmith Libay from 1897.

10 The National House: Located at Národná (National) Street No. 11, this National Cultural Monument is a hotel built according to the designs of Academician E. Belluš in 1924 – 1929. A memorial tablet dedicated to the first Board of Chairmen of Matica Slovenská (the Slovak National Foundation) and its Banská Bystrica members is to be seen in the vestibule.

11 The Spital Church of St. Elizabeth: A Roman Catholic church located on Dolná (Lower) Street, it was built on the west edge of the town as the first Gothic building in approximately 1303. The church, originally a part of the hospital, had a polygonally closed sanctuary with cross-ribbed vaulted ceilings. After 1750 the church was rebuilt in the Baroque style. The Gothic sanctuary thus became the side chapel of St. Anna. At the end of C19, the church was remodelled by F. Storno in the Romantic Historicizing style. The main altar as well as the other interior furnishings are from the end of C19, replacing the original

A panel painting on the altar of St. Barbara.

Matthias House, a part of the castle complex, Gothic, finished in 1479.

A Renaissance, so called Benický House in the square.

A bastion of the town walled fortification.

Baroque furnishings. The original hospital building burned down in 1605, but in 1618 a new one was built which was subsequently renovated several times.

12 Monument of the Slovak National Uprising:

This National Cultural Monument is a monolithic reinforced concrete block built in 1965 in the southeastern part of the historical centre near the eastern town wall, according to the project of Professor D. Kuzma. Weapons and technical equipment from the Slovak National Uprising are on display in the park surrounding the monument.

13 The Town Fortifications:

Beside simple defences consisting of earthen banks with palisades, fortifications built of stones or bricks served the townspeople until the end of C14. The stone walls proper began to be built only in C16. At first the town gatehouses were built: the Dolná (Lower) or Kremnická Gate; the Strieborná (Silver) Gate located to the north of the square; the Lazovná Gate situated to the northeast of the Silver Gatehouse; the Upper Gatehouse, guarding the road towards Ružomberok on the east border of the town; and the Hronská Gatehouse to the south. The irregular layout of the town and the varying landscape made such extensive works necessary in 1593, and in 1613 – 1614 they were not yet finished. The town walls on the south were doubled after 1590. Until their demolition at the end of C19 and the beginning of C20, the walls, which were several times reconstructed, had retained their original character. At present only a portion of the walls exists – in the southeast the Mäsiarska (Butcher) Bastion, and in the north the Čižmárska (Bootmakers) Bastion.

The interior of the Evangelical church.

Monument of the Slovak National Uprising.

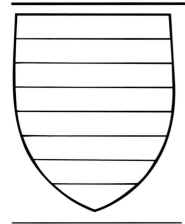

The simplicity of the Banská Bystrica arms indicates that they were adopted in the deep past. Their content is derived from the earlier state coat-of-arms from the period of the Árpáds. The heraldic shield representing the Arms of the sovereign is divided by bars displayed in gules and argent; the Banská Bystrica shield is also divided by bars, but displayed in argent and gules. These arms were created before the Árpád family died out in 1301; i. e., sometime during the last two decades of C13.

Banská Bystrica as the hub of the central Slovakia region was the home town of many celebrities; poets and writers M. Braxatoris-Sládkovičov, J. Kollár, S. H. Vajanský, J. G. Tajovský, B. S. Timrava, and M. Rázus; painters F. Motoška, V. Ruttkay-Nedecký, D. Skutecký; and Matej Bel, the famous polyhistor of C18, also called the "Pride of Hungary". The Matej Bel University in Banská Bystrica was named in his honour.

Sightseeing tours enable the visitor to get acquainted with the historical development of the town as well as its present-day life. The heart of the modern town is the central square. The castle, the Central-Slovakia Museum in the Thurzo House, and the Regional Gallery are especially popular sights for tourists. Past the Clock Tower is the Church of Saint Francis Xavier, which is especially worth visiting. Another place of interest is the park containing technical and army equipment dating from World War II, which surrounds the monumental Museum of the Slovak National Uprising. The town walls and several bastions are accessible from this part of the town. A nice view of the new housing estates of Banská Bystrica and the surrounding mountains, dominated by Urpín, may be had from the stairway of the Slovak National Uprising Museum. A pleasant evening can be spent at the J. G. Tajovský Theatre, watching an opera or other performance.

Banská Bystrica and its surroundings are an ideal starting point for tours to the southern part of the Low Tatras, the Kremnica Hills, and Poľana Mountain.

Hiking paths lead up into the mountains, as well as to the Vartovka, a look-out tower located above the town. Banská Bystrica and its surroundings are an exceptionally ideal centre for both winter and summer vacations, with swimming pools, an ice-skating rink, and good skiing areas with ski-tows a ski-lifts, all within easy reach of Banská Bystrica.

Banská Štiavnica

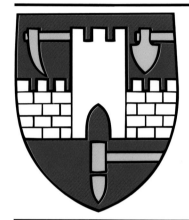

Names: L – Schebnyzbana, Bana, **G** – Schemnitz, **H** – Selmeczbánya
Latitude: 48° 26' N, **Longitude:** 18° 56' E
Elevation: Average 600 m, **range:** 375 – 938 m
Population: 10 600
Suburbs: Banská Štiavnica, Počúvadlianske jazero, Sitnianka, Štefultov
Means of Access: By rail: route No. 154; By road: routes No. 525, 524
Accommodations: Hotels: Grand, Salamander, Bristol, Matej Pension, Pod
   Klopačkou, Na kopci, Tomino, Kami; Cottages: Bačíkstav, Dinas; Hostel ATC
   Počúvadlianske jazero; other hostels
Information: City Tourist Information Center – tel: (++421)(0)859-16186,
   fax: 0859-691859, e-mail: tik.bs@spark.sk

The oldest mining town in Slovakia, Banská Štiavnica is located in southcentral Slovakia. Individual parts of the town spread upwards from a picturesque valley to the terraced slopes of Glanzenberg, Paradajs, Šobov, and Kalvária, which form a part of the volcanic Štiavnica Hills. Man-made lakes dating from the 1600's dot the hills surrounding the town. Lakes Klinger, Štiavnica, Hodruša, Belian, and others were built for use in the mining industry. The Štiavnica Hills have been designated a Nature Conservancy Area; they are one of the largest ranges of mountains of volcanic origin of the West Carpathians, and contain different types of volcanic minerals. The insect realm is well-represented, especially by the butterfly family; 120 species of birds and more than 40 species of mammals are found in the region. Several species of bats live in abandoned mines.

Banská Štiavnica enjoys a humid temperate mountainous climate with average temperatures ranging from –3.5 °C to –6 °C in January, and from 17 °C to 17.5 °C in July. The average annual rainfall is 650 – 800 mm.

The main attraction for the settlement of this relatively inhospitable mountainous area was the presence of precious metals, mainly silver and gold. The term „terra banensium" (land of miners) was used to describe the region as early as 1156,

referring to a grouping of settlements connected with the mining of several kinds of ore, mostly silver. Further illustrating this fact is the use of the name "ARGENTIFODINA" to identify this region in CC12 and 13.

Banská Štiavnica achieved its leading position among surrounding mining settlements at the turn of C12 and 13.
Its development was localized to the south of the parish church, where the main road runs through the present-day town. The town's upsurge was connected with the increased intensity of mining activities, as well as the arrival of Tyrolian colonists. The protection of the surrounding mining district and settlement was secured by the fortress built on the top of Glanzenberg.

Banská Štiavnica achieved its legal status as a town in 1255 (but possibly as early as 1237), during the period when the first town charters were being granted in the Hungarian kingdom. Its town charter was used as a model for other mining towns, as for example, Banská Bystrica (1255).

The town had already grown to a considerable size by the 1230s, as demonstrated by the existence of two, three-naved churches located 500 metres distant from each other. These are skillfully and artistically constructed buildings in the late Romanesque style, in which a strong influence of

Banská Štiavnica – A Rohbock's engraving from C19.

C12 Cistercian architecture from Lower Austria is evident. The parish church of the Virgin Mary, later transformed into the anti-Turkish "Old Castle" and containing a two-storeyed charnel-house, or ossuary, is located above the town at the foot of Paradajs. The location of St. Nicholas', or Dominican, church – today's parish church – was to be in the southern section of the town. In fear of the threat of Tartar expansion into the immediate area, the Dominicans postponed the construction of their monastery for 30 years.

The existence of buildings dispersed along the main road is evidenced by the discovery of ground plans for single-room, compact block buildings and workshops. These constructions were either demolished or incorporated into Gothic and Renaissance houses in later periods of the town's development.

At that time, there was only one fortified area in the vast ore district – the castle which was located on top of Glanzenberg. This castle represented the king's enclave – the Mining Chamber – controlling the revenues flowing from the mines.

The prosperity of the gold and silver mines and the town's promotion to the level of an Independent Royal Town influenced the later building-up of the town and its architecture. The older sacral buildings were rebuilt in the Gothic style, and the town spread to both sides of what became Holy Trinity Square. This building and rebuilding activity incorporated only recently abandoned entrances to mine galleries into the new structures.

The town spread along the main road to the south towards Ilija and Antol, which is evidenced by the building of the Špitálsky church of St. Elizabeth (in approximately 1310) in the so-called "poor quarter". The chapel of St. Mary of the Snows was constructed on the west edge of the town along the road to Levice. The building of new houses greatly increased when industrial and mining activity was pushed farther away from the town centre. During C15 the homes of the rich burgesses – "waldbürger" – were extended and modified to incorporate large vestibules. The mining settlements spread both to the steep hillsides along the roads and to the close proximity of the mines and manufacturing facilities.

During 1442 – 1443, the town, including churches, burghers' houses, castles, and mining works, suffered damage from the struggle for the Hungarian throne, as well as from an earthquake. These events gave cause for the renovation of burghers' houses and sacral buildings, as well as for the construction of new ones, including the

Panorama of the mining town of Banská Štiavnica.

town hall, town fortifications, and a new parish church, among others.

The one-nave St. Catherine's Church, with its late Gothic reticulated vaulting, was built by the burghers in the centre of the town in 1488 – 1491. Following the construction of St. Catherine's, the middle of the C16th gave rise to the large-scale project of the building of the houses around the main square (Holy Trinity Square), located below the parish church. The church itself was rebuilt to a Late-Gothic hall during the years 1497 – 1515.

At the end of 15 and the beginning of C16, respectively, mining production began to stagnate in the Banská Štavnica ore district, even though the yields from the mines were still considerable. The cause was a combination of the not-yet solved problem of water pumping, and the decrease of gold and other precious metal prices on the European market. Social unrest within the Central-Slovakia ore districts, in response to the worsening economic situation and unsatisfactory working conditions, culminated in the miners' revolt of 1525 – 1526.

At the same time, Turkish armies defeated the Hungarian army near Mohacs, and began to turn their sights on conquering the central-Slovakia mining towns.

During the extensive building activity of C16,

plans for the construction of Trinity Square and the reconstruction of the town became less important than the need to fortify the town against the Turkish armies. The older burgers' houses were reconstructed and extended, new grand Renaissance palaces arose, and the offices of the Mining Chamber and its head – the Chamberlain – the High Royal Administrator were built. The houses built in the main square, typically, had richly embellished interiors and highly decorated façades. The houses flanking the main road in the town began to take on a new form – that of the terraced town house. The municipality built an extensive sewage system, the main lines of which have been preserved.

The former parish church was rebuilt into a fortress for defense against the Turks. In the western part of the town the New Castle was built as a watch tower. The town walls did not represent typical lines of defence; they were built in two lines by connecting and reinforcing the outside walls of houses. The main roads were closed off by the Antol, Belian, Kammerhof, Piarg, and Roxer gates.

At that time the contacts of Banská Štiavnica with other European mining centres were orientated towards searching for and inviting specialists both on water pumping and water treating for ore

Old Castle, rebuilt to a Renaissance town castle in mid-C16.

Detailed view of the Old Castle.

New Castle, a Renaissance building constructed in 1564 – 1571.

Calvary above the Town.

Holy Trinity Square with the sculptural grouping of the Holy Trinity, by sculptor D. Stanetti (1756 – 1764).

Piarg Gate, originating from 1554, and rebuilt to its present Baroque appearance.

preparation. Owing to the concentration of extraordinarily gifted inventors, such as M. K. Hell, S. Mikovíni, J. K. Hell and others, various inventions such as the highly effective water reservoir and canal system, and machinery for water-pumping, helped to revitalize the production of ore and to advance the standard of mining in Banská Štiavnica. At the same time the importance of the town as a promoter and supporter of technical achievements increased. In addition, it gained new prominence as the most important centre of precious metal mining in the Habsburg monarchy. This fact is confirmed by the

St. Catherine's Church; the tower of the Old Castle may be seen in the background.

Andrej Kmeť Street, a busy commercial street lined with burghers' houses built in the Renaissance style.

establishment of the first mining school in Hungary in Banská Štiavnica (1735), which was subsequently promoted to the Mining Academy

in 1762, as a result of its being the best-known centre of mining science and technology in Europe at that time.

This new period of economic prosperity incited the growth of the town, and influenced its appearance. The older dominant buildings and palaces obtained Baroque features, the interiors were redone, and the facades became nearly uniform.

During C18, Banská Štiavnica was the third largest town in Hungary. By this time, the town boasted a water supply system, roads were paved, and new Baroque and classicist monumental buildings appeared in the town. To the east of the town, the grandiose Baroque complex of Calvary (Stations of the Cross) was constructed on the dormant volcano, Scharfenberg. The town centre was completed by the addition of the classical Lutheran church. The imposing Baroque plague column executed by Italian sculptor Stanetti features the Holy Trinity. It also gave the name to the main town square where it stands: Holy Trinity Square.

Once again, ore production in the Banská Štiavnica ore districts decreased toward the end of C19, and the main interest of the town shifted from mining to education. Owing to this change, campus buildings for the Mining and Forestry Academy, surrounded by the Botanical Garden, were constructed to the east of the town centre between 1892 and 1912. As a result of the disintegration of the Austro-Hungarian monarchy after WWI, the Mining Academy was moved from Banská Štiavnica. The gradual and constant decline of the importance of the town began, in spite of the building of new factories on the southern edge of the town; they did little to slow down the economic deterioration which consequently resulted in lower and lower numbers of inhabitants.

Ironically, due to the overwhelming economic stagnation of the town, its scheme and the magnificent architecture of the town centre have remained intact, without any interference of further building activities. The present appearance of this historical town is the result of continuous development, reflecting political and economic conditions and cultural changes in the region.

In 1950, Banská Štiavnica was declared one of the first Urban Conservation Areas in Slovakia. The most important edifices contributing to this designation are the sacral buildings, the burghers' houses, and the buildings connected with mining activities, education, and the town fortifications.

Banská Štiavnica and the technical monuments in its environs were inscribed on the UNESCO World Heritage List in 1993.

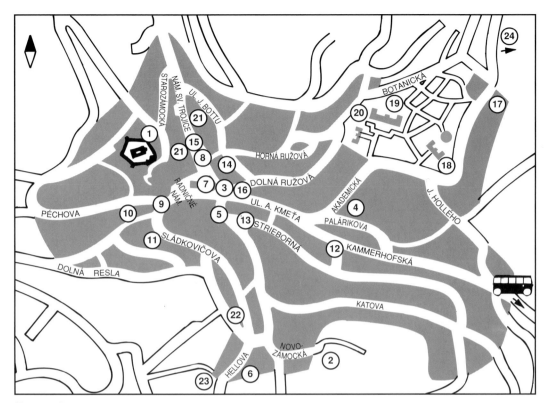

The town plan.

1 Old Castle: A National Cultural Monument, the Old Castle is located on the edge of a raised terrace in the west part of the town at the foot of Paradajs Hill. Various renovations since C13 have altered the original appearance of the building to create that one that stands today. The oldest portion of the Old Castle, the former parish church of the Virgin Mary built in the first third of C13, was originally a three-nave Romanesque basilica with a rectangularly closed presbytery in the axis of the main nave. The aisles were probably closed with semi-circular apses. The tower was located on the west side of the basilica in the axis of the main nave. Simultaneously, the fortification system was strengthened by the annex of an irregular hexagonal gunners' bastion to the ossuary. On the north side there was a squared sacristy with cross-ribbed vaulting. A two-storeyed charnel-house, or

ossuary, dedicated to St. Michael, was built at the same time as the basilica. The vaults of the ossuary were supported by a large central, squared pillar. The basilica itself was reconstructed (1497 – 1516) to a Gothic cathedral with an extended, polygonal presbytery terminating the axis of the main nave. At this time the castle walls were constructed, incorporating two square, Early-Gothic towers. The threat of Turkish invasion precipitated the further rebuilding of the church into a sentry fortress in mid-C16. The vaulting was demolished, and the arcades between the nave and aisles as well as the triumphal arch were walled up. The reconstruction resulted in the current three-storeyed, four-wing building, around the central courtyard. Renovations in the Baroque style were expressed by a remodelling of the gateway tower, originally Gothic.

Within the wall of the Old Castle, administered today by the

Slovak Mining Museum, many valuable pieces of fine art and castellated architecture may be found, which illustrate each stage in the castle's construction.

2 New Castle: A Renaissance stronghold used as a look-out post and built between 1564 and 1571 as a part of the fortification system against the Turks the New Castle is a massive six-storeyed, squared-off edifice with four circular corner bastions. It was connected to the town walls on two sides. The curtain walls were pierced with loopholes. The ground floor, which has two rooms, is approached through a semicircular portal. The larger space is vaulted over by groined vaults resting on central pillars. The other floors have wooden ceilings, except for the bastions, which have vaulted ones.

The building has a steeple roof with a lantern which is surmounted by a helm. Its name "Virgin Castle" is of more recent origin,

Former Dominican church; at the present parish church.

4 Former Dominican church with remains of a monastery:

The Church of the Ascension of the Virgin Mary, the today's parish church, also knowns as "German Church", was built originally as a three-nave Romanesque basilica of St. Nicholas. It consists of a transept with a tower projecting into the ground-plan, semi-circular apses terminating the aisles, and a straight-ended presbytery. This building from the 1230's was rebuilt several times, and in 1806 modified to the Empire style. The classicist interior of the church is from CC18 and 19, and so are the side altars. The main altar dates from 1811; the pulpit from the second half of C18; the stallum is from approximately 1800; the patron's stall is from the end of C18; pews from the second half of C18; and the organ from the beginning of C19.

Liturgical ornaments, such as the monstrances, reliquaries, candelabra, thuribles, ciboria, etc., are from CC17 and 19.

5 Evangelical (Lutheran – Augsburg Confession) Church:

This classicist central building was built in 1794 – 1796 according to the design of J. J. Thaller. Its ellipsoid nave is expanded by three-storeyed galleries. The church is actually a terraced house, and its façade is well integrated with the neighbouring houses. Interior ornaments – the organ, altar, pulpit, etc. – originated in the period when the church was built. The liturgical items – chalices, candlesticks, vessels, ciboria, etc., date from C16 to C19.

6 Church of the Virgin Mary of the Snows:

Also known as the Frauenberg Church, and originally built as a Gothic chapel by the High Royal Administrator, the Chamberlain Erasmus Roessl, in 1512. It was renovated in the C18, and later in the 1950's and 1970's. The church is used today as a funerary chapel.

7 The Town Hall:

Originally a one-storeyed Gothic house which was extended at the beginning of C16. At the same time the brick annex – the chapel of St. Anna – was added to it. It underwent

and a coincidence may be noted with the name of the nearby church and the hill where the castle is constructed. Today the castle is used by the Slovak Mining Museum. The exposition staged here illustrates the history of wars in Slovakia against the Turks.

3 St. Catherine Church:

The so-called "Slovak church", St. Catherine's has a one-nave construction with low side chapels, and a sacristy with Late-Gothic reticulated vaulting which spreads towards the end of the presbytery without a triumphal arch. Built in 1488 – 1491, it was consecrated in 1500. The building was renovated in 1692. In 1776 an annex to the presbytery – the Chapel of St. John of Nepomuk – was added. At the end of C19 the interior was rebuilt in the neo-Gothic style. The ribs and bands of the vaulting over the choir are seated on figural brackets, whose motifs are repeated on the upper corners of the main partico situated on the west side of the church, and overlapped by a vestibule of a later date. The county and municipal

arms are painted above it, with the year "1555" commemorating the promotion of St. Catherine's to a parish church. Below the church a crypt is located, where magistrates and wealthy burghers were buried. At present the crypt is inaccessible. The main altar, from 1727, is executed in the Baroque style, and features pillars and s steeple superstructure. A picture of the engagement of St. Catherine adorns the altar. The side altars in historical revival styles originated at the beginning of this century.

The Late-Gothic stone baptismal font dates from the beginning of C16, as do the wooden chest for chasubles and vestments, and the sculpture of the Madonna. The Madonna is a polychromed, carved wood statue dating from 1506 assigned to Master MS. This statue and the statues of St. Catherine and St. Barbara stood most probably on the original Late-Gothic high winged altar. From 1580 to 1672, the church belonged to the Protestants. The name "Slovak Church" originated in 1658, when services began to be held in the Slovak language.

renovations in C17, and in the 18th century it was given its present day appearance. In this free-standing building, with an oblong ground plan and a turret on the south-east corner; the Renaissance ridge vaults have been preserved, as well as the Baroque ceiling painting, "The Apotheosis of Justice", which is in the ceremonial hall. The building houses the Municipal Council.

8 The Holy Trinity Plague Column: Erected on the square to which the column gave its name, from 1759 – 1767, was built after the design of Italian sculptor D. Stanetti to commemorate the victims of the Black Plague. The architectural elements of the column were created by K. Hobznecht, one of the best stone-masons in central Europe of that time.

9 The Marian Column – the Immaculata: The column, standing close to the town hall, dates from 1748 and is the work of sculptor F. Rössner.

The Town Hall, originally a Gothic house modified to its present appearance in C18.

10 Pecha Street No. 5: Originally a Renaissance building from the second half of C16, rebuilt in 1778. From 1861 lecturing theatres, a library, and a collection of models of the Mining Academy were housed in one part of the building, and the town hospital and court of justice in the other.

11 Belházy House: Sládkovič Street No. 11: This free-standing compound burghers' house located in the western part of the historical town centre saw a very complicated architectural and historic development. Decisive for its current appearance was the rebuilding in the Renaissance style in 1616, when two solitary two-storeyed Gothic buildings were joined together by means of an oriel and loggia. In the second half of C 17 the south-western portion of the building was raised to the third floor. After 1756, when the house was owned by the magistrate J. Belházy, its renovation in the Baroque style took place. A colonnade was added to the north section, and new living spaces to the east section.

During this rebuilding, the spaciousness of the large reception halls was lost, as they were divided into smaller rooms. The spaces between the windows on the façade were decorated with wall-paintings of St. Catherine, the Immaculata, and St. Florian.

Between 1770 and 1912, after the chemical faculty and the laboratories of the Mining Academy had been moved into this building, modifications connected with its new use were executed. The stately spaces remained unchanged.

12 Chamber Court, Kammerhof: Kammerhof Street No. 2: Today this building is the home of the Slovak Mining Museum. The complex originated as the seat of the Mining Chamber in the mid-C16 after the rebuilding and joining together of Gothic and even older buildings. Since the Chamberlain also held the position of Director of the Mining Academy until 1864, the Kammerhof also served as the centre of the Academy's administrative offices. Under one arch of the loggia in the

upper courtyard a stone tablet with an engraved line denoting the Štiavnica Meridian may be seen.

13 Kretschmáry House: Andrej Kmeť Street No. 19: Today an apartment house with shops on the ground floor, this building consisted originally of two isolated Gothic and Renaissance style buildings which were joined in the Baroque period. In 1764 the first professor of the Mining Academy, Mikuláš J. Jacquin, lectured here.

14 Former Mining Court of Justice, Hellenbach House, Holy Trinity Square No. 6: Today housing exhibitions of the Slovak Mining Museum, this was likely a minor Gothic building renovated in the Renaissance style in C16. In C18 it underwent reconstructions in the Baroque style. From 1859 it was used by the Mining and Forestry Academy. The entrance to the St. Michael mining gallery (76 m long) is preserved in the rear wing of the building on the ground-floor.

Burghers' House; Holy Trinity Square.

Paintings on the façade of a burghers' house; Holy Trinity Square.

15 Žemberovský House, Holy Trinity Square No. 1: Also known as the Maršalek House, this building has been recently renovated and now houses administrative offices of the Town Magistrate and a cinema. The building originated in C16 when two Gothic houses were joined together. In 1803 it underwent a radical reconstruction. From 1809 onwards, the first professor of forestry at the Mining Academy, Dr. H. D. Wilckens, held lectures here.

16 Fritz House, Town Hall Square No. 6: The house has been recently restored, it is used by the State Central Mining Record Office. In 1891, the original building in Gothic and Renaissance styles was extended and reconstructed in neo-Renaissance style in order to house the administration office of the Mining and Forestry Academy. It also housed Academy collections, drawing studios, and its library.

17 Geramb House, Academy Street No. 25: This building, also known as the "Fortuna", was built in the classicist style at the beginning of C19. The forestry department of the Academy was located here in the middle of the C19; presently it is a residential house. A fresco with the Goddess Fortuna adorns a ground-floor room.

The Mining and Forestry Academy campus consisted of eleven isolated buildings. Some of them were modified burghers' houses, and others were constructed for the Academy's purposes. Some of them were declared National Cultural Monuments. The Mining and Forestry Academy was established in 1846 on the bases of two earlier institutions, the Mining Academy (1762) and the Forestry Academy (1808). This educational institution existed here until 1919, when it was moved to Sopron, Hungary.

18 Academy Street No. 16: Built in 1892 after the drawings by E. Cserei of Banská Bystrica, it was the first new building constructed exclusively for the

The "Klopačka" (Clapper).

needs of the Academy, and housed the forestry faculty. It is surrounded by the Botanical Garden, founded in the mid-C19. The three-storeyed building is in the neo-Renaissance style. Its ground plan was expanded by means of three wards creating wings and a central, elevated pavilion. Today the building houses the Forestry Secondary School.

19 Academy Street No. 13: Between 1898 and 1900, on the site of several earlier residential houses, another building for mining and metallurgical faculties of the Academy was constructed. It is also significant for its spreading ground-plan, and the main entrance in the central part. Today it is the seat of the Chemical Secondary School.

20 Academy Street No. 12: This three-storeyed eclectic neo-Renaissance building was constructed in 1911, in order to house laboratories of the Mining and Forestry Academy. Its ground-plan was expanded by means of three wards creating wings. Its central part is elevated and surmounted by a gable and square turrets.

The buildings of the former Mining and Metallurgical and Forestry Academy, together with the Botanical Garden, create an integrated campus area which is used today by the Forestry and Chemistry Secondary Schools.

21 Burghers' Houses on Holy Trinity Square: Burghers' houses were mostly located in the town centre in Trinity Square. Houses from No. 1 to No. 12 belonged to the most highly respected burgesses – the waldbürgers.

They are mostly one-, two-, or three-storeyed state houses of the *Máshaus* type, and included a tavern or a tap-room in the Gothic and Renaissance styles. Houses from No. 197 to No. 199 are being reconstructed into guest houses. Other residential houses in the historical centre date from C17 to C19, and later were mostly changed to one-family houses.

22 Klopačka: Located in the Dolná Resla part of the town, this Baroque tower-shaped building was built in 1681. It contained the "clapper", a kind of alarm which was used for summoning the miners up by means of its sound. The sound was produced by clapping together two resonant wooden boards. The original rectangular oblong two-spatial unit consisted of a two-storeyed living area with a gateway, above which the four-storeyed tower with the clapper was built. In C19 another living area, attached to the rear side of the tower was added to the structure. The gateway on the ground floor of the tower contains barrel vaults with lunettes while the rooms on other floors have flat vaulted ceilings. A steeple shingle roof with a high lantern carrying miners' insignia on its very top covers the tower. Today the building, an exhibition of the evolution of mining technology and equipment is housed.

23 Town Fortifications: The character of the urban scheme of Banská Štiavnica was growing in accordance with the highly varied relief of the terrain; this fact, together with widely dispersed dwellings, prevented the town from being contained within the town walls soon and prevented the rapid construction of the defensive fortification system. Nevertheles, the defence of the town was secured by double town walls, after external walls of isolated houses had been connected. The access to the town was guarded, and was possible only from the main roads through the corresponding gatehouses: Roxer, Piarg, Belian, Kammerhof, and Antol. Even the older castellated fortress on Glanzenberg was incorporated into a later arrangment of the fortification system, after a moat and earthern banks had been added to it.

24 Calvary: Calvary consists of a complex of sacral Baroque buildings located to the northeast of the Urban Conservation Area, on a steep hill named Scharfenberg. It was built during the years 1744 – 1751. The lower church has an oval ground-plan with towers on two sides; behind the church is a cross with a grouping of statues. The Holy Stairs lead upwards to the isolated chapel "Ecce homo" built below the top. The centrally planned church on the top of the hill consists of an open oval nave with two squared towers on either end. Behind the church is the Holy Sepulchre. Chapels demonstrating the Stations of the Cross flank the paths winding up from the lower church to the upper one. The interiors of both churches are adorned by Baroque wall paintings and stone sculptures. Scenes describing the Stations of the Cross are executed in wood reliefs.

The arms of Banská Štiavnica were the oldest granted to a municipality in the Hungarian kingdom. It was already designed in the first half of C13. Among heraldic symbols it enjoys an exceptional position, not only because of its age, but because of its subject matter. The first Štiavnica seal is also the oldest representation of town's fortifications which is a pre-heraldic topographic symbol, and with mining implements (an occupational motif) set into the Arms. All other towns used fortification motifs without Arms, during the whole of C14.

Many famous scientists worked and lived in Banská Štiavnica, active mostly in the fields of mining and forestry. Among them were the mining equipment designers and inventors J. C. Hell, M. K. Hell, and M. Hell; physicist J. J. Hoflinger; chemist and botanist J. Jacquin; astronomer and cartographer S. Mikovíni; physician Dr. J. G. Hellenbach; and also A. Divaldi and S. Daxner, to name just a few.

The location of the town in the highly varied surrounding landscape makes it one of the most picturesque towns in Slovakia. In Banská Štiavnica it is possible to admire the artistic and architectural styles of several periods in the sacral buildings. Though technical expositions staged at the Slovak Mining Museum, the Klopačka, and the Old and New Castles as well as other places of interest, one may learn about the history of the town and the mining and forestry industries. One of the most attractive parts of the Slovak Mining Museum's instructional exposition is the Skanzen, or Open Air Mining Museum, which features an actual mine shaft and tunnel, with mining accessory buildings on the surface all of which were once actively employed.

Adding to Banská Štiavnica's attractiveness is its surrounding scenery, which draws hikers to nearby mountains and lakes. In winter skiing conditions are good. Recreational areas near Lake Klinger, Sitno Mountain, and Lake Počúvadlianske jazero offer visitors enjoyable holidays both in winter and summer.

Bojnice

Names: L – Boymuch, **G** – Weinitz, **H** – Bajmóc
Latitude: 48° 52' N, **Longitude:** 18° 35' E
Elevation: average 296 m, **range:** 257 – 825 m
Population: 5 100
Suburbs: Bojnice-kúpele, Dubnica, Kúty
Means of Access: By rail: route No. 140; By road: routes No. 50, 64, E 572 in
   Prievidza
Accommodations: Hotels: Regia, Tatra Hroznár, Lipa-Tarčík, Strážov, Športcentrum,
   U Filipa; Pensions: Družba, Jánošík, Mado, Alena, Bojník, Rybničky; Hostels: ATC
   Kopálková Silvia, Recreational Center Tatra Hroznár, Elitex, Devín Cottage, spa
   facilities; bed-and-breakfast
Information: Prievidza – tel: (++421)(0)862-16186, fax: 0862-5423135

The spa town of Bojnice is located two kilometres to the west of Prievidza where the Upper Nitra Valley meets the promontories of the Strážovské vrchy (Strážov Hills). From here, it is only a short distance to the Lesser, and Greater Fatra Mountains, and the Vtáčnik Mountain. The Prepoštská Cave, Nature Preserve is to be found within the town as a part of the Bojnice karst. It is a huge travertine dome containing a cave eleven metres long and eight metres wide, datable to the Paleolithic Age. Evidences of the prehistoric settlement of the Upper Nitra region were found here. Above the cave is a castle surrounded by a forest park, which blends with the Strážov Hills.

The town has a warm climate, varying from slightly dry to humid climate, with average temperatures ranging from –2 °C to –4 °C in January, and from 18.5 °C to 20 °C in July. The annual precipitation runs from 600 to 700 mm.

The earliest settlements in this area reach back as far as prehistory. The oldest findings date back to the last interglacial period, which, according to geological chronology, began 135,000 years ago. The mineral water springs and travertine caves attracted Paleolithic people to station themselves in this environment. The people of the Lengyel culture arrived in what is now Bojnice at the end of the New Stone Age – approximately 2600 B. C. The Bošáca culture people settled here later. The people of the Luzatian culture appeared in this locality at the end of the Bronze Age and at the beginning of the Iron Age (700 B. C). These people inhabited the today's castle precincts and the square which both were built much later. After the Luzatian culture had faded, the people of the Púchov culture occupied the site and founded a fortified settlement here. This place of habitation was exploited later by Slavs, who built their subterranean and semi-subterranean dwellings there. Ceramic shards, quernstones, and various iron products testify to a busy life of these people. Highly developed crafts in the 9th and 10th centuries are evidenced by discoveries of iron and blacksmiths' workshops as well as a tar-melting furnace.

Bojnice and its surrounding area developed into an important centre in the Upper Nitra region owing to two major factors: first, the considerable advances of crafts producing an astounding amount of goods; second, the cultivation of fertile soil along the Nitra. The surplus products of crafts and agriculture allowed these people to run barter trade and to contact other settlers in the neighbouring regions.

The existence of a settlement round the castle was mentioned in 1113 in a charter of the Abbot of Zobor; it confirmed indirectly its being a property

Bojnice on the painting by J. Ledentu from 1641 – 1642.

of the Benedictine monastery located on Zobor Mountain near Nitra. Owing to this information we may conclude that the castle had already existed before. Most probably it was constructed of timber. From 1299 till 1321, the settlement belonged to the lands of Matúš Čák. In 1366 this settlement was granted its town charter derived from the Krupina Law Code. In C15 it was created a market town. In 1530 and again in 1599, the town suffered grievously from the ravages of wars with Turks. The threat of further raids made the inhabitants start constructing town fortifications, which were completed in 1663. At the end of C17 and at the beginning of C18, the town was plundered by the insurgent armies of Thököly and F. Rákóczi who revolted against the Habsburgs. Bojnice developed into a prosperous town which owed its upsurge to trades, agriculture and markets. Mills and a brewery were built here in C19.

The presence of mineral springs, already known in C16, was the reason for building baths here which gradually grew into a health resort. Palatine Thurzo, Count Pálffy and J. Baťa among were its owners. This pleasant health and holiday resort attracts more and more people every year.

The town gradually grew from the settlement spread round the castle. An elongated, slightly widened square surrounded by one-storeyed two- and three-axial houses constructed on narrow building plots was created here. Some of the houses were aligned in a row; several of them were free-standing ones with enough free space around. The preserved C17 vistas show, therefore, a large market square surrounded by narrow houses with high gable roofs on one side, and small houses with gambrel roofs on the other.

The square is closed up by two dominant structures – the castle and the St. Martin's Church, and is encircled by town walls containing two main gateways. The town-plan, which is still in existence today, was created after the original central axis, set by the high street, had been shifted southwardly to its current location. The houses from the earlier settlements have not been preserved; they were, like the castle, made of timber. They were simple rural houses without that sumptuous decoration which

View of the castle, rectory, and church.

View of the Castle.

The Romantic castle with a partially original Gothic and Renaissance castle.

was so typical of the burghers' houses in other towns at that time. However, several more imposing houses with Baroque illusory paintings on their façades have survived. The health resort itself is located in a park in the northwest area of the town.

The most important structure in Bojnice is the castle, which, together with the zoological garden and park, belongs to the most frequently visited places of interest in Slovakia.

The entrace gate to courtyard.

A corner of the castle garden with its small lake and stone belvedere.

1 The Castle: a National Cultural Monument: In the long and remarkable history of Bojnice castle several stages in the construction stand out. The contemporary romantic outlook of the castle is the result of an extensive rebuilding at the turn of CC19 – 20. The existence of the castle and the settlement around it was mentioned in 1113 for the first time. During C13, the wooden structure was transformed into a stone one. It was raised upon a rocky apex of a travertine mound, in the middle of which there is a deep crater containing a mineral spring. The crater was later adapted into a castle well, twenty-seven metres deep. The well is to be found in a deep, round cave twenty metres wide and six metres high. Around the edge of the cave there are several little pools nine metres deep. In C13, the core of the castle was girt by hude walled fortifications, which followed the uneven rocky terrain, thereby creating an irregular, oval ground-plan. Most probably, a round keep had already stood on the eastern side of the mound at that time. At the end of C13, when Bojnice was seized by Matúš Čák, the lower courtyard, encircled by a ditch, spread at the foot of the castle core. After 1527, the Thurzo family undertook the transformation of the castle core into a majestic, stately and comfortable residence. The massive defences, which had been erected at the end of C15, were considered to be massive enough; therefore the Thurzos could turn their attention to the old keep. The original Gothic castle took on a Renaissance appearance with its lofty palaces arranged round the inner courtyard. This stage in the construction of the castle was finished in 1568 or 1569.

At the turn of CC16 – 17, the upper castle was rebuilt; this step was followed by the construction of new living quarters situated in wings built in the Baroque style on the periphery of the fortifications in mid-C17. The courtyard in front of the entrance gateway was surrounded by new out-buildings, including large barns, and several residential buildings. In 1662 a chapel was built, it contained decorative stuccoes and painted vaulted ceilings.

In 1852, after a longer period of stagnation and the decline of the Bojnice domain, Ján F. Pálffy inherited the castle. After 1888 he began large-scale reconstructions. Being a great admirer of the Gothic architecture of central and southern France, especially of the castles along the River Loire, and the Renaissance architecture of northern Italy, he decided to transform the castle completely into a stately, massive yet romantic residence where his rich collections of fine arts could also be housed. The Budapest architect J. Hubert was commissioned to work out the project of the rebuilding but Pálffy himself corrected the plans and directed the work.

The first phase of the reconstruction was begun in the oldest inner part of the castle between 1890 and 1895. The old round keep was rebuilt, and on the western corner a new, huge tower was erected, forming the contemporary skyline of the castle. In the next stage the courtyard and the interiors were renovated. The interior decoration was treated in the Late-Tyrolian Gothic style; many of the details for the doors, windows, and decorative wall paintings were worked out by Pálffy himself. There is little doubt that the Gothic interiors and ornamental decoration of the Tyrolean castles of Merano, Kreusenstein and several others were the source of inspiration for his designs. The interiors were furnished with antiques that he bought at auctions all over Europe. The wall paneling in the „Turkish

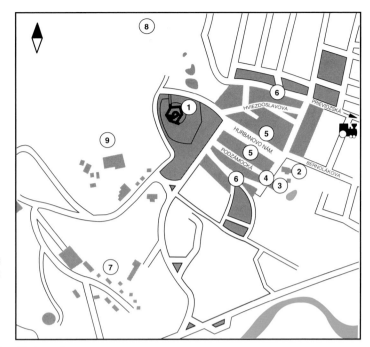

The town plan.

Hall" was imported from Serbia and dates from the C17. The chapel features an Italian Gothic altar from the mid-to-late C14. It is the work of Nardo di Cione, the brother of Andrea di Cione, and who is known under the pseudonym of Orcanga. A portrait of the owner appears in the center of the carved ceiling of the „Golden Hall". Several sculptures by W. Th. Story are included in the castle's collections.

When Ján Pálffy died in Wienna in 1908, the range of construction works at Bojnice Castle was significantly reduced. Much of the overall concepts and details of Pálffy's plans as well were never realized, and most of the art collections were sold off. Restoration works of the interiors and the entire architectural complex are in progress now. In the castle precincts, an exhibition of natural history, ethnography and works of fine arts is staged. Besides, there is also a gallery of visual arts. In the Golden Hall wedding ceremonies are held. The beauty of the environment and

attractiveness of the castle are multiplied by the adjacent park, in which huge trees several hundred years old, including Matthew's Lime Tree, grow; in the park a zoo is also located.

2 Parish Church of St. Martin:
This Roman Catholic church located in Sládkovič Street was built in the Gothic style during the second half of C14 on the site of an earlier church referred to in 1244. Renovated several times in C15, then sometime after 1530, after it in 1640, and finally in C18, the church has one nave, a polygonally closed presbytery, a side chapel,

Interior of the „Golden Hall".

3 The Rectory of St. Martin's Church: A two-storeyed Baroque edifice constructed between 1730 and 1746 on the site of an older building, it was reconstructed in the first half of C19. A block-like structure with a rectangular oblong ground plan whose southern façade features a bay with a loggia on the first floor. The rooms contain Baroque vaulting.

4 The Chapel of St. John of Nepomuk: Located next to the parish church, this chapel was built in 1732 in the Baroque style on the site of a gateway in the defensive walls protecting the church. The chapel features a rectangular oblong ground-plan; on the ground--floor there are flat vaulted ceilings with stuccoes. The interior on the first floor possesses a dome decorated with an illusory painting giving an illusion of reality.

5 Burghers' Houses: The houses lining the square in Bojnice have a rather provincial and rustic appearance and contrast with the castle overlooking the town. Most of them are one-storeyed; several houses have two storeys and are built on narrow, long building plots; the alignment of rooms respects their spatial requirements. Built in throughout CC17 – 18, they contain Renaissance and Baroque vaults and stonejambed windows and doors. The houses are plain, confirming the fact that their owners, mostly craftsmen, did not have enough money either to build or emulate the luxurious burghers' houses. Unfortunately, some of the historical buildings in the square have been demolished in this century.

and a tower projecting from the front of the building. The chapel of St. Anthony, on the southern side, has Gothic groin ribbed vaulting. The chapel was founded by the Onofries in the second third of C15. High walls connected to the town fortifications surrounded the church. After they had been demolished, the chapel of St. John of Nepomuk was added to the church on the north. The interior dates predominantly from the end of C17, including the prominent wooden organ choir, carved by an unknown folk master, and the Baroque high altar and pulpit; the baptismal font dates from the beginning of C18. Liturgical objects ornaments dating from C15 up to C18 include a Late-Gothic monstrance and a chalice; the chasuble and the bell date from C18.

6 Town Fortifications: Built in mid-C17 as defences against Turks, the fortifications had two main gateways; the eastern one was pulled down in 1948. In addition to the main gateways, there existed postern gates which have been preserved partially near the rectory of St. Martin's Church. On the western side a postern dating from the early 17th century has remained too.

7 Baths: The presence of hot springs in the area was recorded in 1113, but the construction of the baths was undertaken only in C16. The core of the original building from throughout CC16 – 17, transformed in throughout CC18 and 19 received its today's appearance in mid-C20. "John's Bath" was built in 1939 by A. Cugliš. The baths are set in a pleasant park in which a 600 year-old lime tree grows. Diseases of nervous and locomotive systems are treated here.

8 Zoological Garden: Located adjacent to the castle in Bojnice, the zoo was established in 1955 on a 42-hectare site. Among the numerous animals typically found in a zoo, 39 endangered species from the IUCN Red Book and 31 endangered Slovak species are also protected here. The oldest zoo in Slovakia, it specializes in the raising of ostriches, European lynxes, and mountain goats.

The „Turkish Hall".

Spa Hotel „Baník".

Already in C14, fortifications appeared as the symbol of Bojnice; heraldically, its most distinctive form dates from C16, and is of interest from both the historical and artistic points of view. The central monumental building with double crenellated battlements symbolizes the castle with the side postern gate, which cannot be seen. Between the upper and lower battlements the existence of a courtyard has to be envisaged. The cluster of turrets represents the bastions as located at various distances from the castle; these elements projected onto the flat surface of the arms contributed to its unique appearance.

A visit to this picturesque town, its squares, and the baths provides a pleasant walk, enriched with a visit to the church and a tour of the remains of the town fortifications. Of all the places of interest, the most attractive and impressive by far is the castle whose architecture evokes illusions of Italian or French Renaissance architecture. The museum collections and the picture gallery as well as the Golden Hall enhance its attractiveness. This unique monument also offers a wonderful view of the Upper Nitra Valley. In summer-time, holidaymakers may have a swim in the thermal swimming pool called Čajka, it also provides a wonderful and romantic view of the castle. Hiking paths lead from the town to the zoo, to Malá Magura mountain range, to the Strážov Hills, and to the Lesser Fatras.

Kremnica

Names: L – Cremnicium, **G** – Kremnitz, **H** – Körmöcbánya
Latitude: 48° 41' N, **Longitude:** 18° 44' E
Elevation: average 550 m, **range:** 250 – 1265 m
Population: 5 940
Means of Access: By rail: route No. 431; By bus; By road: route No. 65
Accommodations: City of Kremnica – Veterník Hotel, Gluck auf, Soler Pensions,
    Toliar and Termál, Recreational Facilities, Hostel ATC, bed-and-breakfast;
    Skalka – Minciar, Fortuna, Skalka Hotels; Limba and Elba Cottages
Information: Information Center – tel: (++421)(0)857-742856; INFOTEL – 0857-186

Kremnica, also known as "Golden Kremnica", was one of the most important gold mining towns in the Middle Ages. It lies on terraces in the central portion of the Kremnické vrchy (Kremnica Hills), the northernmost mountains of volcanic origin in Slovakia. The highest Flochová hill rises with its 1318 metres above the surrounding countryside. The Kremnica Hills are surrounded by several hollows of Zvolen, Pliešovce, Žiar, Horná Nitra, and Turiec. Not far from Kremnica are the Greater Fatra Mountains, the Štiavnické vrchy (Štiavnica Hills) and Mount Vtáčnik; Kremnica is 16 km far from Žiar nad Hronom, the district seat. To the east of Kremnica is Kremnica Peak (1 008 m) with steep rocky cliffs orientated towards the River Rudnica Valley. It is a famous vantage point which affords a wonderful view of the town. The andesite cliffs of "Kremnica Štós", the State Nature Reserve, are on the western side of Kremnica Shield.

Kremnica has a temperate mountain climate; the average temperatures in January range from –3.5 °C to –6 °C, and in July from 17 °C to 17.5 °C; annual rainfall varies between 650 and 850 mm. The highest parts of the surrounding mountains have a slightly cold climate.

The highly varying landscape relief, picturesque woods, and mountain meadows in Kremnica's hinterland create, together with the historic buildings of the town, a unique complex of a former free royal town.

Favourable natural conditions – especially the presence of ores rich in precious metals, then the driving power of precipitous streams and abundance of wood in the forests – accelerated the process of concentration of settlements and the subsequent dynamic development of Kremnica. The pre-urban settlements were probably preceded by solitary timber houses freely scattered in the valley stretching southwards to the Bystrica hollow along the foot of Revolta Mountain. The earliest written records proving the existence of Kremnica, date only from the first third of C14. In 1328 King Charles Robert of Anjou granted the "guests" – the coin minters from Kutná Hora concentrated in Kremnica special privileges which supported intensive development of the settlement. At those times Kutná Hora (Kuttenberg) was not only the centre of gold and silver mining but also the seat of the Royal Mint of the Bohemian kingdom. Shortly after their arrival, they began minting coins – the Hungarian *groschen* in 1329. Eight years later, gold florens enlarged this production. They became well-known as Kremnica ducats.

Kremnica, C17.

The core of the medieval town – the *"Ring"*, obtained its shape at that time. The relatively large and irregularly shaped space of the market place was located to the south of the site where an older settlement was supposed to have existed. Later this portion of the town was named *"Im alden Kammerhof"*, or The Old Chamber Court. Because of the sloping terrain, it was not possible to give the square an ideal level and regular shape. Even the building plots adjacent to the square do not follow the same pattern of other newly founded Gothic towns featuring narrow, elongated lots. What is most specific about Kremnica is the highly limited central area of the fortified town, tightly squeezed by walls which hindered the development of the street plan. Only three roads lead from the square through gateways in the town walls. Along the northern road which passed through the Upper Gatehouse, fields of the miners stretched on the slopes of hills could be approached. Later on this road connected Kremnica with the Turiec region. The southern road led through the Lower Gatehouse, following the stream running towards the River Hron. The Bystrica Gatehouse standing on the highest point to the east of the square was reached along a steeply ascending path from the square. The third road which passed through it

continued along a stream where crushers and stamper battery were located, it is alluded to in charters dating from C14.

The most ancient built-up area, which developed around the square, consisted of stone, one-spatial, free-standing houses which were situated in the rear division of plots. However, their parts facing the square are supposed to have been of wood; only later they were replaced by masonry structures.

The constructing of the town coincided with the building of the castle. Some parts of it, e. g. the charnel-house, bastions and the first walled fortifications, seem to have existed before Kremnica received its town charter; they served not only as the religious centre for the local people, but probably also as a refuge in times of wars.

The town fortifications built approximately between 1405 and 1426, were connected with the fortified castle area. The area within the castle walls took shape gradually during C15: the two-nave church of St. Catherine and the charnel-house were built. The Town Hall, the clock tower and the entrance tower as well as the polygonal bastion date from throughout CC13 – 14. The dominant position of the castle over the town affords an assumption that the first residence of the Chamberlain, the high royal administrator and the representative of the

A view of the historical core of the town.

Crown, was most probably just within the castle walls.

The town's prosperity in C14 is documented by its rapid expansion. The approximate extent of the medieval settlement southwardly can be easily identified. The town stretched to the spital (hospital) Church of St. Elizabeth built in 1382 – 1393 in Dolná (Lower) Street. The northern border of the town was marked by the so-called *Wetterkreutz,* which was a lamp-column dating from C15. On approaching Kremnica along the road from Šášov, one could see another Gothic lamp-column, known as *Fernkreutz,* it was alluded to in 1464 for the first time.

When prosperity of the town in the High Middle Ages reached its climax, the houses of the mine owners, arranged around the square, underwent profound alterations. The original free-standing stone houses were of two types: first, those with a one-wing ground-plan which featured three rooms lined up one after the other and second, those with two wings, which possessed an entrance hall and a cellar accessible through an individual entrance leading from the square. These two types of houses grew gradually into one compact building. A great number of preserved stone details and fragments of paitings in both interiors and exteriors, document the sumptuous and very impressive appearance of these Gothic burghers' town houses. The mint, which consists of a cluster of buildings situated next the Upper Gatehouse, was also incorporated into the central part of the town.

The unsatisfactory situation caused by poor economic output due to the decline of mining activity, followed by social riots, and the thread of Turkish invasion were worsened by a huge fire in 1560. During the fire not only the castle but also one-third of the town burnt down. A part of rich archives was also destroyed in this disaster. The Town Hall, which had been housed in the castle precincts up to that time, was moved to the town centre.

Even in the last third of C16, the burghers had their houses reconstructed, and the walled fortifications were reinforced when barbicans were added to the Upper and The Lower Gatehouses.

The relentless counter-Reformation policy of the Habsburgs was clearly visible in Kremnica: the second largest building complex was constructed within the fortifications opposite the mint. In 1653 – 1660 a Baroque Franciscan monastery and church were erected on the site of demolished town houses, on the western side of the square. The parish church, standing separately on the square, was

A view of the castle. In the background the Kremnica hills can be seen.

Silouhette of the city with the castle.

Lamp-column.

remodelled into the Baroque style; in the second half of C18 a monumental plague column was erected in front of it, replacing the original, more simple column, which is standing in Horná Ves now.

The typical Baroque tendency to give some architectural work a dominant position in the surrounding landscape was manifested through the construction of a small church of the Calvary built on a hill above the town, and simple chapels along

A vien across the square at the castle church, C15 and the burgers' houses.

A restored Renaissance house in the square.

The town house No. 48 in the square.

The upper portion of Kremnica's main square featuring the town hall.

the road of access. Nevertheless, the imposition of magnificent Baroque architecture did not revive the grandeur once enjoyed by the renown "Golden Kremnica" in the Middle Ages. Similarly to other mining towns of Upper Hungary, its importance gradually declined and the once busy centre became a provincial town.

The essentially medieval character of the town could be preserved, ironically enough, due to the long-lasting economic stagnation. Besides sporadic repairs of the houses, which usually obtained only new façades, no other major building activity

The lown town gate.

The sculptural group of the Holy Trinity. In the background the Franciscan monastery can be seen.

thrived there. Only an Evangelical Lutheran Church was built in the southern portion of town outside the town walls in C19. Economic life of the town revived and was accelerated when the railway line connecting the River Hron valley to Turiec had been built. Kremnica thrived again; new streets stretched up the hill to reach the railway station, which was built there, high above the town. Larger public buildings, connected with the rapid growth of cultural and social life, were built in the southern portion of the town after Kremnica became the county seat in 1876.

During the earthquake in 1880, the parish church in the square was seriously damaged and then it collapsed. The burgesses of Kremnica subsequently turned their attention to the castle church of St. Catherine, which was to replace the previous parish church; they renovated it into the Gothic-Revival style.

Apart from burghers' town-house architecture, also miners' houses characteristic of Kremnica deserve great attention. Several of them have been preserved in the Bystrica Valley. These huge two-storeyed wooden houses with galleries on the second floor were originally occupied by two up to four families. They are presently used as recreational cottages.

The compactly built-up area of the square was damaged by fire at the end of World War II. After the fire, houses on the whole northern side and on one third of the eastern had to be replaced by new buildings; fortunately, these do not considerably interfere with the historical environment. Though the growth of Kremnica after the war left the oldest parts of the town core nearly intact, the parts lying behind saw many essential alterations.

The fortified part of the town with the historical center was named a City Historical District in 1950.

1 The Town Castle; a National Cultural Monument. The area of the castle is formed by a group of constructions surrounded by a partially preserved double curtain wall, which is connected to the town walls. The entrance tower, which is linked to the *karner* (charnel house), is located on the northern side of the fortifications. This quadrangular fortified medieval tower features partially preserved machicollations (stone spouts through which hot pitch was poured on the attackers trying to penetrate through the passageway) and the outer part of the passageway was originally protected by a drawbridge. The two-storeyed charnel-house attached to the tower features Romanesque rib vaults of rectangular profiles in the basement. The space on the ground level has Late-Renaissance vaults. The wall paintings and crosses originated at the beginning of C15. The Mining Bastion, open to the courtyard, possesses a semicircular ground-plan and a polygonal enclosure on one end. Crescent-shaped shafts have been preserved in its interior.

Another building built into the fabric of the fortifications is the former Town Hall, which originally had four storeys, of which only two have survived; the other two, because of their cracked structures, were demolished at the end of C18. Little lattice windows still exist in the basement; a Gothic portal with a pointed arch is to be found on the ground-floor. The entrance stairway and the southern tower served as an interconnection of the castle with the town. The stairway leads towards the church of St. Catherine. It suggests the idea that one of the main reasons for its construction was to facilitate the municipal officials the access to the church.

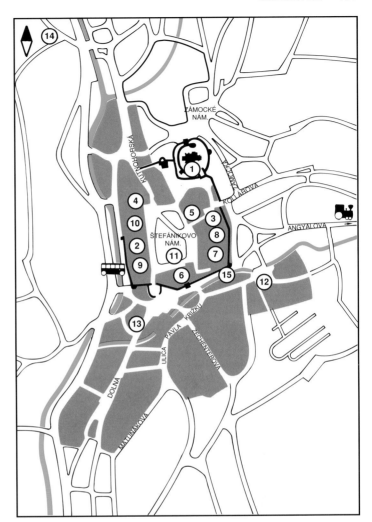

The town plan.

The last building within the castle walls, which served as a part of the fortification system, is the clock tower, or *Türl*. Its core is supposed to be the most ancient construction not only here but also in the town. The church dedicated to St. Catherine, the patron saint of miners, is an aisled hall church which dates from 1488, according to the date inscribed in the portal. The church tower, rebuilt after the fire in 1560, shows an inscribed date "1576 – 1578". The shape of the roof as well as the whole interior resulted from an extensive renovation into the Gothic-Revival style executed by F. Storno at the end of C19. The castle fortifications, built gradually since the Middle Ages, do not entirely copy the curtain wall of the older castle, whose traces were found on this site. Its current height and appearance, including crenellated parapet walls, are also the result of this gothicizing reconstruction.

A view of the presbyterium of St. Catherine's Church at the castle.

2 The Monastery and Church of the Franciscans: After their arrival in Kremnica in 1649, the Franciscans settled in the Pizetár House in the south-western corner of the square. Of this house only cellars have remained. Having bought two town-houses on the western side of the square, they began building a monastic complex with a church on the site of the demolished houses, in 1653. They finished them in 1660. The one-nave church of St. Francis was consecrated in 1715. After 1758 the Loreto Chapel, which is accessible from the church through a cloister, was built on the site of another demolished town house. The interior furnishings of the church originated in mid-C18, and the Rococo interior of the Loreto Chapel dates from the second half of C18. The monastery was originally a two-storeyed building with four wings developed around an arcaded courtyard. In 1732 another wing was added to the monastery and connected to the castle walls. The monastery, church and chapel have a common frontage. The central axis is accentuated by a portal with a tympanum, pilasters and a high tower. On the left is the non-articulated two-storeyed façade of the monastery; on the right is the façade of the church with three high windows on the second floor; a portal is in the central axis of the ground-floor. The chapel next the church has a one-axial façade with a portal on the ground-floor and a window on the second floor. The furnishings of the church originated at the beginning of C18.

3 The Town Hall: Originally a Gothic house having an entrance hall dating from mid-C15, this building was renovated in 1738 to be used as a Town Hall. During this renovation its exterior was altered; a huge mansard roof and a four-axial façade divided by pilasters and accentuated by a balcony gave this administration building splendour and dignity. The lateral façade shows several well-preserved architectonic details and Late-Gothic exterior ornamentation, typical of the early Kremnica houses. An originally free-standing house located close to the Bystrica Gatehouse also creates a part of the Town Hall. It was built in C15 and joined to the Town Hall in C18. In the former passageway original Gothic sedilia have been preserved, as well as an oriel on the façade of the house and an original polychrome painting.

4 The Mint: Located on the north-west corner of the square and built before 1434, the present-day mint's predecessor stood to the north of the present one, on the site called "The Old Crusher". The originally Gothic buildings of the mint were radically rebuilt and expanded in C16. At that time the mint was a solitary fortress with its own armoury. During the process of modernization of the mint's technology in 1882 – 1889, a new coinage hall was built. The oldest portion of the mint – the southeast wing – is composed of several one-wing buildings, arranged around the central courtyard. Here is also the former treasury which possesses ribs springing from a Renaissance central column. The façade of the building was renovated to the classical style in the first half of C19.

5 The J. L. Bella's Native House: The birthplace of the composer J. L. Bella, this house was originally built in the Gothic style as a one-space building located in the centre of the building plot. A fresco of the Nativity scene has been preserved on its lateral façade. The roof and the façade were restored to their original style according to the results of the research carried out in the 1980s.

6 The Museum of Coins and Medals: The Museum is located in a two-storeyed town-house, with an entrance hall dating from the end of C14. From a two-storeyed cellar cut into the rock beneath the edifice, a corridor led directly to the mine-galleries, which are inaccessible today. The museum exhibition presents the history of almost seven centuries of coin- and medal stamping in Kremnica. Several other museum exhibitions are situated in Kollár Street in an original town house consisting of several buildings dating from throughout CC15 – 16. A Gothic portal in the passageway, C16 lierne vaults on the second floor, and original polychrome Gothic paintings and outlets for smoke on the façade may be included in the preserved details of the house.

7 House No. 7-9: In the courtyard of this house located in the square, is a small ground-floor house dating from C15. It boasts many preserved architectural details including outlets for smoke on the façade and two-partite and three-partite Gothic windows. The entrance hall on the ground level leading to the courtyard has intricate lierne vaults which are scarce in this area and indicate contacts with southern Moravia and Bohemia.

The castle church of St. Catherine; the vault over the presbytery, 1488.

8 The Parsonage: Originally a Gothic free-standing house dating from the end of C14, it was rebuilt to a parsonage in the third quarter of C18. The classical façade dates from C18. The building underwent reconstructions after 1945, but the Gothic basement rooms, the stairway and portals have been preserved. The entrance hall features a Baroque staircase adorned with sculptures.

9 House No. 48: Originally a Gothic house with a passageway, house No. 48 was renovated in 1527 and 1624. In mid-C18, it was remodelled into the Baroque style, and another floor was added. The wall paintings of the vaulting continue freely out of the so-called green rooms – state spaces embellished with green plant

motifs painted during the reconstructions in C16. Gothic portals and stone jambs of windows and doorways have been preserved on the ground-floor and in the basement. Decorative plaster cavetto vaults with paintings date from C17. The façade is Baroque in style and has an oriel supported by Tuscan columns; in niches on the façade, Baroque sculptures can be found. The Gothic main entrance portal is flanked by small rectangular windows.

The Mint.

10 House No. 38: Representing a typical Gothic town house, this building is situated on a narrow building plot, it was remodelled in throughout C17 – 18. The decorative plaster vaults on the second floor, the façade, and a part of the staircase balustrade date from C17. In the building the skiert's Museum is housed.

11 The Holy Trinity Plague Column: Built in the Baroque style by Dionýz Stanetti between the years 1756 and 1772, the column stands on the site of an earlier column dating from 1711 which was relocated to Horná Ves. Sculptures of patron saints of miners and of protectors against plague stand on a two-stepped, three-sided pedestal. The sculptural group of the Holy Trinity surmounts the column; the stone fence surrounding it dates from 1905.

12 The Evangelical (Lutheran – Augsburg Confession) Church: The original timber church was built outside the fortifications in 1688. In 1824 – 1826, it was built in stone; the project is ascribed to the architect M. Pollack. The central church is domed. The interior furnishings from dating C19 are enriched by a wooden baroque baptismal font dating from C18. The front of the building features a central projecting bay with a semicircular portal receding to the building.

13 The Dolná Street Town Houses: The burghers' town houses flanking the road which leads to the Lower Gatehouse possess cores dating from the Renaissance. Their ground-plans corresponded to the needs of their owners and reflected their occupation. Their minor size and more modest appearance point to the marked difference between the middle classes of the town and the "Ringbürgers", who occupied the imposing houses in the fortified centre of Kremnica.

The town walled fortifications, the Red Bastion, built in the first half of C15.

14 The "Klopačka" (Clapper):
The one storey block-like tower with the façade articulated by splicing is situated behind the fortified part of the town in Mining Road. It has a huge gable roof with an ornamental ending; it is surmounted by a turret. Once, a clock used to be placed on its eastern side. The clapping sound produced by clapping two wooden boards against each other was to summon miners to work, or, to announce accidents.

15 The Town Fortifications:
The town walls with bastions and gatehouses were connected with the castle precincts in the northeast part of the town. The fortifications began to be built at the turn of throughout C14 and C15. Three gatehouses, the Lower Gatehouse on the southern side, the Upper Gatehouse on the northern side and the Bystrica Gatehouse on the eastern side guarded the main entrances to the town. Ramparts and a moat made the whole fortification system more effective. The Lower and the Upper Gatehouses were strengthened by barbicans fortifying entrances in 1539. The walls of the fortifications were raised in C17 and in C18 hornworks were added to protect the gatehouses. In the second half of C19 the walls were gradually demolished, but only Bystrica and the Upper Gatehouses with the barbicans were removed. The remaining parts of the fortifications have been almost completely preserved. The Lower Gatehouse with the barbican, the Red and Black Bastions, and other ones border the most important parts of the town.

Miner's Houses: Scattered around the historic center, these examples of folk architecture were built from the end of the C16 through the middle of the C17. The houses are of two storeys in height and most feature a wooden balcony. One of the oldest homes has the date of 1593 carved into its cellar portal; only a few homes of this type still remain.

A miners' house No. 40.

The "Klopačka" (Clapper).

The oldest town seal dates from 1331 and depicts St. Catherine kneeling in front of a cogged-wheel, and a minute shield with the coat-of-arms of the Angevines behind her. But this was not the arms of Kremnica yet, because neither the figurations nor their composition responded to the rules of heraldic production. The first attempt to create the municipal arms may be seen on a signet-ring dating from 1432. Only the attribute of St. Catherine – a half-moon wheel – is shown on it; it is set in the shield with the capital letter "C" (denoting "Cremnicia") placed above it. The current arms were created in 1567. The shield is parted per fess. The upper part shows the town symbols and the lower part represents the coat-of-arms of the sovereign – the House of the Angevines.

Several famous people are associated with Kremnica: the physician and writer G. K. Zechenter-Laskomerský; the historian and journalist P. Križko; the painters G. and V. Angyals, who pictured Kremnica; the writer J. C. Hronský; historian M. Matunák; the composer J. L. Bella; and poet J. Kollár, just to mention a few.

A visit to „Golden Kremnica" usually begins at the Lower Gate. The view up the sloping square with its Holy Trinity Plague Column and the Baroque fountain serves as a visual corridor leading one's eye to the monumental dominance of the castle. Kremnica's museums and the interior of the Franciscan Church located on the square enrich the visitor's understanding of the history and cultural heritage of the city. The castle is approached by ascending the hill, passing through the site where the Bystrica Gate once stood. Having undergone extensive reconstruction, the castle offers visitors the chance to explore its many corners as well as the prepared exhibitions. The clock tower affords an unforgettable panorama of the town and surrounding mountains. From the castle one descends a steep side street and through the site of former Upper Gate (behind the mint) on the way back to the square. Kremnica is the starting point for hiking trips to the surrounding mountains where the ski centers at Krahule, Šibeničný Hill and Skalka Mountain, all equipped with ski lifts, are well-known for cross-country as well as downhill skiing. In summer visitors can swim in the thermal open-air pool. The town and its surroundings provide many possibilities for recreation all the year round.

Oravský Podzámok

Names: L – Sub-arx, **H** – Árvaváralja
Latitude: 49° 15' N, **Longitude:** 19° 15' E
Elevation: average 520 m, **range:** 495 – 1224 m
Population: 1 300
Suburbs: Dolná Lehota, Oravský Podzámok, Široká
Means of Access: By rail: route No. 181; By road: routes No. E 77 = 59, 521
Accommodations: Oravan Hotel, Zámocká hostel, bed-and-breakfast
Information: Information Center – tel: (++421)(0)845-5800027; Municipal office – tel: 0845-5893107

Oravský Podzámok is situated on the right bank of the River Orava in the Oravská vrchovina (Orava Highlands) 11 km northeast of Dolný Kubín. It lies below a 112 m high rock which towers above the river. This curiously shaped rock formation is a Protected Geological Structure.

The climate of the little town is a moderately cool and moderately humid mountain climate with average temperatures of –4 °C to –6 °C in January and of 13.5 °C to 16 °C in July, the average annual rainfall varies from 800 to 1 100 mm.

Oravský Podzámok was founded at the foothill of a rock on which a majestic castle stands, and on an old long-distance trade and military route running from Hungary to Poland. The first written sources relating to the territory of Orava date back to the second half of C13; however, archeological excavations give evidence that the territory had been settled since the pre-historic era.

Orava was first mentioned in conjunction with the castle, built on an estate of the same name, in a charter from 1267. According to this source the origin of this castle goes back to the reign of Andrew (Endré) II, sometime before 1235. The castle originally served as a guarding post and later became a centre of political and social life of the

Orava region. The castle was also the Orava County seat, beginning from the second half of C14 onwards.

The Orava region belonged to the royal estate in C13. The strategically important Orava Castle represented a fortified point guarding this part of the borderland of the Hungarian kingdom.

In the second half of C14 Orava became a separate *comitat* (aristocratic Hungarian county); Orava County was governed by an *ispán,* the head of the county administration residing in Orava Castle. Until mid-C16 Orava was possessed by the Crown and administered by successive royal administrators. In 1556 Orava was bestowed on František Thurzo by the King. Thus Orava became a feudal domain of the Thurzo family; when the family died out on the spear-side in 1621, the Orava domain was owned jointly and non-divisibly by all of the heirs of Juraj Thurzo and their descendants. This trust existed even after the abolishment of serfdom in the form of a great forest estate, until its nationalization in 1945.

The settlement site below the castle hill had very limited possibilities for expansion and constant development. Additionally, the character of the houses which accommodated mostly people and

Oravský Podzámok, a copper engraving and etching by M. Griescher (around 1680).

livestock under one roof did not allow the transformation of the settlement into a town. Instead, it maintained the character of a little town. The first houses built below the rock were a farmstead and a customs station where the merchants had to declare their goods and pay their thirtieth part. In the year 1559 four farmsteads belonging to the Castle are referred to together with gardens, lofts, a pub, a customs station, a mill, a saw-mill, a brewery, a fulling-mill, a gun powder manufacturer, and a fish hatchery. A free-standing house is typical also of the later period, when the number of clerks and craftsmen increased. It was at this time that the castle began slowly losing its defensive and administrative functions. Towards the end of C17 and at the beginning of C18, the administrative offices moved to the settlement below the castle into newly built brickhouses. Most likely the older houses in the under-castle settlement were made of wood and therefore were not long-lasting and rotted; the preserved pieces of historic architecture are only from CC18 and 19.

The settlement was developed along a zigzagging road below the rock. It is necessary to note that the growth of the under-castle settlement was particularly restricted by the local topographic conditions: mountain range with steep slopes falling down to the River Orava, and the River Orava itself. The relatively irregular shape of the built-up area was caused by the scattered houses which grew around the rock without any special plan. Their composition created the historic core, which consists today of an irregular square which follows the terrain, sloping downwards on the west to the Račovský brook and to the River Orava.

Arriving by road or by rail from Tvrdošín and Dolný Kubín, you will immediately see the town's most famous landmark – Orava Castle. The situation of the castle grounds affords dazzling prospects of the surrounding countryside. The singular and unique configuration of the landscape with its dominating castle is the most characteristic feature of the Orava region.

Oravský Podzámok cannot be said to represent a typical urban settlement; nevertheless, its form which developed from the under-castle settlement creates, together with the castle, an impressive historical agglomeration. The street plan derived from the system of roads leading to the castle. The free spaces, which existed owing to no strict rules in town planning, were employed by generations of Renaissance and later builders who "filled" them

Orava Castle.

A view of Orava Castle.

Oravský Podzámok.

with remarkable structures of a profane character. These spontaneously, yet sensibly, sited houses, together with the monumental castle create an admirable complex all situated in the untouched natural environment. This aesthetically and historically highly valuable residential formation is incomparable to any other settlement in Slovakia.

The courtyard of the castle.

The interior of a room in the castle.

The interior of the castle chapel.

The epitaph of Juraj Thurzo.

1 The Castle: A National Cultural Monument, the castle was built in the second half of C13. It was erected on the site of an earlier settlement, dated most likely to the beginning of the Christian Era. Archaeological excavations also confirmed the existence of an earlier Great Moravian hillfort in C9. A stone construction is documented for the first time in a charter of 1267. The castle was built originally as a strategic point near the customs station in Tvrdošín. In 1370 it became a county castle, a seat of county administration offices. The complex of buildings of the upper, middle, and lower palaces was built gradually, beginning in the mid-C13 until the first third of C17. The earliest living quarters were in a spacious tower built into the walls and situated on the site of the present-day middle castle. Within the fortifications were located other residential quarters, the so-called Pálffy Palace, built during C14 to C15. In 1539 the castle was fortified with two horseshoe-shaped bastions. A citadel, in which a chapel was later located, was built in the upper keep. The halls of the lower palace, with fortifications and a bastion which stood on the site of the present-day chapel, were built in the Gothic style. The entrance gatehouse, with a drawbridge and a red-and-white sgrafitto on its façade, contains the coat of arms of Ján of Dubovec, dated to 1535. The building activity of the Thurzo family during the years 1556 – 1561 was concentrated on the renovation of the upper castle. The residential area was moved to the middle and lower palaces, where the palace of František Thurzo and a chapel were built. At that time the entrance gate was fortified with a bastion. The chapel, with its decorated stucco vaults, is remarkable because of a Renaissance triptych altar dating from 1611, and the epitaph of Juraj Thurzo (from 1616), created by the well-known sculptor, G. Menneler of Augsburg. Casemates were built under the entrance tunnel in 1606;

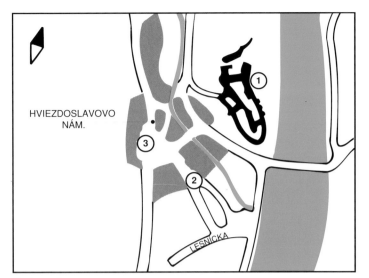

The town plan.

a new entrance gate, which still exists today, was built in the wall.

The interior furnishings of the chapel were baroquized in 1752.

After a fire in 1800, the buildings of the lower palace were reconstructed; in the upper keep and middle palace only the roofs were repaired. A museum was housed in the lower palace in 1868.

At the turn of CC19 and 20, serious structural failures began to endanger the whole castle. In response, a reconstruction to neo-Gothic style was carried out by the Pálffies in 1906; simultaneously, the constructions on the site of the third gatehouse, the terrace of the tunnel, and the palace in the middle castle were secured against further structural failures. The scheme for remodelling the palace included the decoration of walls with paintings by painter M. Mann of Munich. The palace was equipped with neo-Gothic furniture, including the dining-room, the library and the picture gallery containing portraits of the Orava counts.

In mid-C20 it was again neccessary to secure the whole castle against structural failures. Another complex reconstruction was carried out, during which many significant works of art were

discovered and restored; e. g., exterior and interior wall paintings, and stone architectural members from the Late-Gothic and Renaissance.

The Castle houses the Orava Museum, which was established to preserve precious artifacts from all of the region. The museum maintains and continues of the original castle collections.

2 The Church of St. John of Nepomuk: A Roman Catholic church, the first reference to it dates from 1637. Most probably only the nucleus of the original church was preserved, because the building of a new church and parsonage were mentioned in 1705. The parsonage was begun only in 1774. The church was again rebuilt in 1782, and burnt down in 1827. The present-day appearance of the church dates back to 1831. The simple one-nave church with a transept and a projecting front tower has interior furnishings from the period after 1880; the pulpit, confession booth and pews are from the beginning of C19 and are Empire in style.

3 The Former Prefectory: This Late-Baroque two-storeyed building from 1797 is a free-standing structure at the edge of the square. This characteristic piece of architecture dominates the site. The Baroque articulation of its façade and the gambrel roof are complemented with a wooden gallery resting on columned arcades and containing flat vaulted ceilings. The front façade has a slightly projecting three-axial bay terminated by a parapet carrying vases on either end and a sculpture representing Justica, which is in the middle of the roof line.

Other interesting buildings, built mostly in the classical style at the beginning of C19, housed mainly administrative offices after these had moved from the castle to the under-castle area. They lined the road and were arranged around the square.

To achieve self-government and to acquire municipal arms for this undercastle settlement was a long-lasting process accompanied with many setbacks. It was adopted only in the mid-C19. It was designed as a cluster of six castle stone buildings, symbolizing the monumental Orava Castle, above which floats the coat of arms of the Thurzo family. From the heraldic point of view this symbol was too complicated, and therefore the Budapestian archivist and student of heraldry, Altenburger, simplified the symbol in 1880. The walls with two towers and a gatehouse are a symbolic abbreviation of the upper keep and the lower palace of Orava Castle; the minor shield with a cross above the walls symbolizes the Templars, the alleged founders of the upper keep.

A tour of this picturesque and singular town begins near the River Orava, and leads through the square to the entrance gateway to the castle. Eight hundred and eight steps bring the visitor through several courtyards to the citadel, which is on the highest point of the castle. A magnificent view of the entire surrounding countryside and far-off mountains rewards visitors who climb and reach the top.

Oravský Podzámok and its vicinity offer many attractions for pleasant summer and winter holidays, especially in the recreational areas of Kubínska hoľa, the Orava water reservoir, and in nearby Dolný Kubín, Tvrdošín, and Trstená, which is on the border with Poland.

Partizánska Ľupča

Names: L – Lypche, Theutunicalis, **G** – Deutsche Lipsche, **H** – Némethlipcse
Latitude: 49° 04' N, **Longitude:** 19° 27' E
Elevation: average 560 m, **range:** 512 – 1950 m
Population: 1 300
Suburbs: Magurka, Železnô
Means of Access: By rail: Liptovská Teplá (route No. 180) – 4 km; By road: route
No. 18
Accommodations: Magurka Cottage or lodging in Liptovský Mikuláš.
Information: Municipal Office – tel: (++421)(0)849-5590331; Information Center,
City of Liptovský Mikuláš – tel: 0849-16186, 0849-5522418, fax: 0849-5514448,
e-mail: infolm@trynet.sk or aices@trynet.sk, www.info.sk/aices

Originally the oldest mining-town in the Liptov region, Partizánska Ľupča is situated in the valley of the Ľupčianka brook on the northern fringes of the Low Tatra Mountains, 15 km east of Ružomberok and 20 km west of Liptovský Mikuláš. The forests of the Low Tatras National Park create a natural background of this small town. To the east the water reservoir of Liptovská Mara is located on the River Váh; it covers 27 square kilometres.

Partizánska Ľupča has a moderately cool and humid climate typical of hollows, with average temperatures of –3.5 °C to –6 °C in January and of 14.5 °C to 17 °C in July, and rapid variations in temperatures; annual average rainfall is of 600 to 700 mm.

The beginnings of winning gold in the area, especially by washing gravel is supposed to have already started before the arrival of the German "guests" (colonists) sometime before mid-C13, when besides gold, and silver mines, also antimony mines were opened.

The mining settlement was originally colonized by the German Saxons after the Tartar invasions. The earliest record of a German community dates from 1252; their settlement was described as a well-developed urban structure. The first

municipal privileges were given to Partizánska Ľupča by King Béla IV in 1263; they also determined the boundaries of the town. In 1270 Stephen V confirmed and completed them by further ones; additional municipal privileges predestined the conversion of the small town into a flourishing mining town. King Andrew (Endré) III confirmed the charter dating from 1270. The actual development of the town resulted from the types of rights acquired: first, the right which allowed free exploration for gold, silver and copper; second, the right which allowed to hold markets; then among other rights the exemption of paying tolls all over Hungary. Apart from mining, the inhabitants were occupied in trading cloth and linen in markets in larger towns in the surroundings.

At the end of C14 Partizánska Ľupča became subject of the domain of the Starhrad castle in Liptov, where the officials of Liptov County resided until 1474. Subsequently in the last quarter of C15, the town belonged to Likavka castle domain. After 1677 Liptovský Mikuláš became the seat of Liptov County seat and the general convention. Until then, the general convention held sessions at various places, most often in Liptovská Mara and Partizánska Ľupča, documenting thus

A view of the town from the tower of the church of St. Matthew.

the significance of the town. The nobility began restricting vehemently municipal rights and their excessive demands hindered advancement of the town. In the second half of C17 the burghers made an agreement with the local gentry and paid themselves out of serfdom and forced labor. The end of throughout CC16 and 17 saw a period of rapid development of crafts and establishment of craft guilds; more then twenty of them operated here still at the beginning of C19. The years 1631 and 1856 brought disasters to Partizánska Ľupča: devastating fires ravaged here and destroyed almost the whole town. Recovery from these disasters was slow. In C19 due to the stagnation of the mining industry and after its abandonment, the town turned into a forgotten provincial agricultural town situated off the major roads and railway. However documents detailing the development of the urban structure dating back to the earliest times, chronicle both its advance as well as decay.

The years of advance and prosperity, and of bustling social life have left their impact on the town in the form of valuable cultural heritage. The town plan consists of a large rectangular square through which the Ľupčianka (brook) flows. Into the square, which is oriented north-south, two pairs of roads converge and fork again off when leaving the town. The urban structure submits evidence that the square was created in the period when the old original settlement was promoted to the rank of town. The square was formed near the then-existing settlement which appears to have been on the northern side of the present-day town. The freedom with which it was designed reflected the expectations of future prosperity based on the discovery of high-grade ore and on mining ventures. The town plan had already been established in C14 as documented by the location of the spital church. The town plan is characterized by rows of houses situated on long, narrow building plots, at the back of which various subsidiary out-buildings stood, occupying the entire width of the grounds. Fields were accessible through the walled-in plots in the eastern and western parts of

A look towards the town.

the town. To this compact historic ground-plan new housing estates were joined on both the southern and northern sides. Originally the main Liptov road intersected the square but it lost its importance when the new motorway from Ružomberok to Liptovský Mikuláš was built.

The town was not fortified. Instead of within defensive walls, the people sought for refuge in the fortified Gothic church of St. Matthew in times of danger. The out-buildings standing at the back of the grounds of individual houses could be partially employed as defences.

In spite of the economic stagnation in C19, a relatively busy cultural life thrived in Partizánska Ľupča. A pupils' amateur theatre was founded here in 1840. This theatre developed into a student one and later an adult amateur theatre whose tradition has been cultivated for a long time.

The most interesting building complexes of the town are situated around the original rectangular square.

The church of St. Matthew.

The Evangelical church, built in 1887 on the site of a former one.

A view at the built – up area; originally Renaissance houses refaced in C19.

1 St. Matthew's Church: This Roman Catholic parish church was built in the last third of C13 in the middle of the square. In 1320 the second nave was added, creating a two-nave ground-plan with a polygonal presbytery situated off line with the main axis. The presbytery and the sacristy were rebuilt in 1459 – 1479; they contain preserved Gothic architectural elements and Gothic iron lattices in the portal. The church was added a tower in 1554. More extensive renovations were executed in 1620 – 1630 when the church began to be fortified. At

that time the two-nave church was spanned with Renaissance vaults and the tower was added by a gallery, effectively making it into a watch-tower as well. The defensive wall with a gatehouse in the southern side has loopholes; the gatehouse has a Renaissance gable-end with swallow tails. On the front side of the tower is a portico with a niche containing a statue of St. John of Nepomuk dating from C16.

In the interior furnishings dating from CC18 and 19 prevail. Behind the present-day neo-Gothic high altar is the preserved high altar of

1620, donated by Illészházy. The original Gothic altar of about 1450 is deposited in the Slovak National Gallery in Bratislava. The painting in the presbytery is by J. B. Klemens and it dates from 1855; the pulpit dates from 1800; the paintings on the tribune are of 1620; the mortuary, dates from 1719. Liturgical ornaments – chalices and a reliquary – date from throughout CC18 – 19.

2 The Church of Our Lady of Sorrows: Surrounded by a churchyard, this Roman Catholic church was originally Gothic built approximately in 1263. In C17 it was extended by a Renaissance anteroom and it was fortified; in C18 it was vaulted and refaced in the Baroque style. It is a hall church with a polygonal presbytery. Numerous Gothic details have been preserved; the Gothic portal with the stone jambs is the most beautiful of them all. The Stations of the Cross were created in the second half of C18. The interior furnishings are neo-Gothic. A painting dating from 1861 by P. Bohúň is located on the side altar. The grave-stones of the burghers in the churchyard date back to the first half of C19.

3 The Evangelical (Lutheran – Augsburg Confession) Church: Built in 1887 on the site of an older church which ceased to exist in 1883, this church is an aisled nave with tribunes surrounding the central space and resting on cast-iron columns. The high classical columned altar contains a painting of the Crucifixion by P. Bohúň. The rest of the interior furnishings is neo-classical.

4 The Former Town Inn: The building of the former town inn situated in the square is a Late-Renaissance construction dating from mid-C17. The large two-storeyed, eight-axial building was refaced in approximately 1910 in the Art Nouveau style. Its rooms contain Renaissance vaults. The building is historically renown owing to the first performance given by the Slovak National Theatre; it took place in August 1841 and provided incentives for the rise of the theatre tradition in the town.

5 The Town Houses: The present-day appearance of the town houses reflects renovations the burghers' houses underwent after the great fire in 1856. A row of ground-level houses still exists in the town, but in the very centre near the churches two-storeyed houses are more common. They are typical burghers houses with a passageway and rooms possessing barrel vaults with lunettes, and occasionally flat vaulted ceilings. The ground level houses repeat the ground-plan common to folk architecture where each house comprises a suite of rooms. This type of houses is worth noticing as it shows certain architectural standard to regard of the arrangement of the rooms along the straight axis; the suite starts with living quarters and continues to the rear division of the building plot where subsiding out buildings developed in several phases. The plots are enclosed by out-buildings with timber-post and beam constructions filled in with quarried-stone masonry. They are attached to each other and form a continuous wall enveloping the historical core of the town as if there were a coherent protective wall around.

The burghers' houses have cellars featuring Renaissance vaults. The cores of the houses are medieval, and period architectural details have been preserved in vaults and portals. Other details were changed after the great fires. The façades of the houses are classical in style.

In the square stands an interesting group of buildings which formerly contained blacksmiths' forges; on the brook is an old mill with a water-driven equipment. The mill was built in the mid-C17 and modernized in C20.

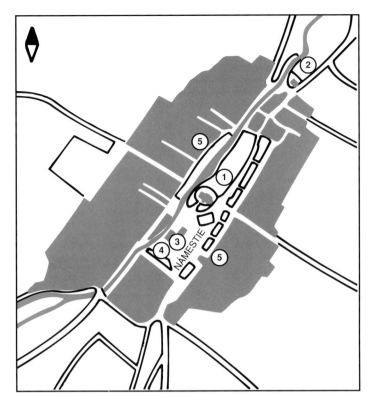

The town plan.

A Renaissance town house in the square.

It is a generally well-known fact that a round seal was used to be superseded by a shield. In the seal of Partizánska Ľupča, which dates from C14, the arms of the Angevines appear as a shield above which there are two starlets and a crescent, and with miner's tools as supporters on both sides. The students of heraldry suppose that the arms of Partizánska Ľupča were a transformed version of the Angevines coat of arms and that all other figurations are without any heraldic function. The miniature of the arms patent letter dating from 1604 convinces us about the uniqueness of the municipal arms. The transformed coat of arms of the Angevines currently used in the coat of arms in family heraldry and in arms of states. The town's symbols proper, which have been until now supposed to be additional figurations, form the contents of the back shield. The arms of Partizánska Ľupča were conceived already in C14 as compound ones and are unique in the sphere of municipal heraldry. Today the municipal arms include only part of the original compounded coat of arms.

The tradition of amateur theatre created framework for the activities of many educationalists, poets, ethnographers, collectors of folk songs and musicians who lived and worked in Partizánska Ľupča. Among them were D. Krman, M. Bohuš, J. Dvorský, A. Chalupka, K. Ruppeldt, A. Sokolík, and others.

Partizánska Ľupča is one of Slovakia's oldest, well-known historic towns which have preserved their historic spirit. Local churches welcome visitors who want to enrich their knowledge of medieval architecture. A road runs directly from the town to the Low Tatras National Park and the Magurka recreational area, which is an excellent centre for skiing; at Železné, a mineral spring and a sanatorium for children are to be found. The town is also a starting point to Ľupčianska Valley which links the Liptov region and the Revúca Valley.

Zvolen

Names: L – Vetersolium, **G** – Altsohl, **H** – Zólyom
Latitude: 48° 34' N, **Longitude:** 19° 08' E
Elevation: average 293 m, **range:** 275 – 887 m
Population: 45 500
Suburbs: Kráľová, Lukové, Môťová, Neresnica, Zolná, Zvolen
Means of Access: By rail: routes No. 150 and 171
Accommodations: City Hotel, Poľana, M Hotel na námestí (on the square),
   Pensions Almada, BE + KA, Modrá Lagúna, Quatro, Zolium, Hostel ATC
   Neresnica
Information: City Information Center – tel/fax: (++421)(0)855-26330,
   e-mail: icko@zv.psg.sk

Zvolen is one of the oldest towns in the central Slovakia region. It is located in the southwest of the Zvolenská kotlina (Zvolen Hollow) at the confluence of the rivers Slatina and Hron, and at the foot of the Javorina Mountains. The Kremnické pohorie (Kremnica Hills) are near the town to the west; the Štiavnické vrchy (Štiavnica Hills) lie behind the Pliešovská Depression to the southwest. Several Protected Areas are situated in the mountains surrounding the town – e. g., Boky, Čertova skala (Devil's Rock), and Borová Hill, which is a woodland reserve.

The urban climate of Zvolen ranges from moderately dry, to moderately humid with average temperatures of –2 °C to –4 °C in January and of 18.5 °C to 20 °C in July. The average annual rainfall varies from 600 to 700 mm.

The fertile terraces of the rivers Hron and Slatina have been permanently settled since the prehistoric times. The advantageous location, through which an old trade route crossed from the North to the South, and the vicinity of rich ore districts increased the importance of the area already in the Early Bronze Age. Archaeological studies show settlement by the Slavs from C7 continuously up to C12, evidenced by the Pustý hrad (The Deserted Castle),

the Priekopa fortified settlement and the town area proper.

Zvolen was most likely a part of the old Hont County in C11 and C12. In C12 Zvolen County was separated from Hont County. When it being a county seat, Turiec, Liptov and Orava were also administered by the Zvolen officials until C14. From the second half of C12 Tekov became a part of Zvolen County as well. A large part of the county was covered by the Zvolen Forest (*silva de Zolum*). The seat of the county was in the Starý hrad (Old Castle), called today the Pustý hrad; it is located southwest of the town. Originally, this castle area consisted of two castles datable roughly to C13 – 14.

The first Count of Zvolen, Detricus, was referred to in 1222. A warrant issued by King Andrew (Endré) II in 1232 and mentioning the royal estates in Zvolen ordered to pay the tithe to the canons' cloister of Esztergom.

The first reference to the settlement in Zvolen is evidenced in a charter from 1243, in which King Béla IV confirmed the privileges of the inhabitants of Zvolen which had been granted before the Tartar invasion in 1241 – 1242. These privileges exempted them from the county administration and entitled

ΛLTSOL, ò SWOLENA.

Zvolen; a copper engraving by G. Bouttats, from 1676.

them to vote freely their magistrate and a pharer. In 1254 further rights were granted upon the colonists. As early as 1326, Zvolen was referred to as a town.

Many dark places exist in the history of Zvolen and the two old castles standing above the town. They do not regard only chronology; many questions concerning the pre-urban settlement and the settlement around the Pustý hrad have not been answered yet. Both settlements might have appeared on the site of a former Slavonic settlement existing from C9 to C12. Neither the location of the church of St. Nicholas nor the parsonage mentioned in 1263 have been found yet. Information regarding Father Peter, a canon there in 1292, might also refer to the large sacral C13 building whose basilican ground-plan was unearthed in the courtyard of Zvolen Castle. This construction was mentioned in a charter from 1325 as a royal chapel associated with the royal estate.

Owing to the town plan, the town and castle were growing simultaneously. The castle stands on a hillock and closes off the elongated square on the south. The parish church, originally a fortified free-standing construction, is located in the northern part of an unusually spacious square. The original fortifications, of which only parts remain today, encircled the simple network of three short streets; which ran off to both sides of the square.

The plan and economic importance of the town had not changed until C18. In the 1840s, it was known for various cultural events and activities supporting the national revival movement. At that time the town was represented by Ľ. Štúr in the Hungarian Diet. In C19 the town revived, due to industrial entrepreneurship. A factory producing

tin plate was established besides a manufacture producing smoking pipes, a distillery and a sawmill. The railway built in 1871 contributed greatly to Zvolen's prosperity. As a result, Zvolen was converted into an important railway junction.

Under the influence of the castle, the town developed predominantly as an agricultural and craft centre. Starting in C17, important cattle markets were held in Zvolen, flourishing up to C20. Despite the markets organized in the town, Zvolen did not possess the air of a bustling economic centre, it remained in the shadow of nearby Banská Bystrica in the neighbourhood. Besides agriculture, which gained greater significance for the town, the merchants and craftsmen – tanners, shoe makers, tailors and potters – contributed to its growth. In 1635 – 1667, when the attacks of Turks got most intensive, the burghers of Zvolen built continuous protective walls, thereby determining the layout of the town.

The economic growth or decline of the town were reflected in the advancement of education and local culture. The first reference to a school appeared in 1401. During the Reformation, the school employed excellent teachers. Nevertheless, its existence depended on the fluctuating political and economic conditions.

During the first half of C20, more administrative, bank and school buildings were built in the town, e. g. the Court of Justice; district administration offices, the "Légia" Bank, etc. Zvolen was one of the centres of the Slovak National Uprising during World War II. Today district town of Zvolen is an administrative and economic centre with a highly developed wood-working industry. Zvolen has also

The square with the Evangelical church in the background.

A view of the square with burghers' houses.

become a well-known research and educational centre; a Forestry College and a Woodcrafts College have enhanced its importance; advanced technical university training in every branch of forestry, woodcraft, and also commercial subjects, have been long established here.

The Gothic church of St. Elizabeth the Widow, in 1381 – 1390, remodelled in 1500.

The Gothic castle, the last third of C14, rebuilt into the Renaissance style.

The Evangelical Church, in 1921 – 1923.

A bastion in the western portion of the walled fortifications.

1 The Castle: This National Cultural Monument which dominates the town and enhances its picturesque appearance was built by Louis the Great of Hungary in the last third of C14, most likely in 1370 – 1382. It was originally a two-storeyed Gothic hunting-lodge similar to Italian town castellos. The castle possesses a regular oblong ground-plan with four wings developed around the central courtyard. The main entrance is from the northern side, facing the town. In the western wing there are two towers receding to the ground-plan and a Gothic arcade, overlooking the courtyard. In southwest corner is a well. The reception rooms are situated in the northern wing. Located in the eastern wing is a two-storeyed chapel which is entered through richly decorated stone Gothic portals. The ground-floor rooms are vaulted; stone ribbed vaults and windows,

which are little more than incisions in the wall, have been preserved in them. The rooms on the first floor have timber ceilings and two- and three-partite windows with stone mullions and transoms. Wall paintings ornamented the hallways. The façades are decorated with quadratura, a regularly alternating pattern painted in red on the plaster to imitate ashlars. The stone window jambs are also painted in red.

The first extensive renovations of the castle took place in 1491 – 1510 when Ján Thurzo of Betlanovce was in possession of it. Simultaneously with the Late-Gothic remodelling, the exterior stone fortifications with four round bastions were built, in which all latest achievements of fortification engineering inspired by Italian quattrocento were employed. The fortified area was approached through a passage in a quadrangular tower in the

northeast corner. During the Renaissance rebuilding in 1548, the castle was elevated by one storey and little corner towers were added. The battlements were crenellated and had a penthouse roof. Instead of a typical Gothic gallery supported by brackets, arcades resting on stone pillars were built around the courtyard. At that time the whole castle was replastered and decorated with Renaissance sgrafittoes which covered the original Gothic decoration of the façades. G. Ferrari, who was commissioned to supervize the fortification works, erected also the western bastion in 1590.

From 1626 onwards, the Eszterházy family owned the castle. In C17 they had it renovated; in mid-C18 they added an extension which connected the northern wing with a gatehouse at the entrance tower.

The two-storeyed Gothic chapel

was rebuilt in C18. The high Baroque nave had a flat vaulted ceiling and a dome with lantern. Under the extended presbytery, which projected out of the original castle, a three-nave crypt was arranged.

A painted wood ceiling was installed in the great hall on the first floor of the west wing during Baroque renovations. This wood ceiling is divided into seventy-eight panels. Each of them shows a portrait of a Roman or a Habsburg emperor. The restoration of the castle for the needs of the Slovak National Gallery and the collections of ancient Slovak fine arts lasted from 1956 to 1969.

2 The Church of St. Elizabeth the Widow: This Roman Catholic parish church is situated in the middle of the square. Its original Gothic core was built from 1381 to 1390, and modified around 1500. The nave was covered by a Renaissance reticulated vaulting. The tribunes were built in the second half of C16. The structure is characterized by a Gothic one-nave with a polygonally ended presbytery and a projecting tower. A little Gothic chapel was added to the sacristy on the eastern side. Minor renovations and repairs of the façades and the interior furnishings were carried out from C18, through C19 and C20.

Several Gothic architectural details – portals and the pointed-arch windows – have been preserved. A one-nave chapel of the Pieta was added to the southern side of the church in 1650. Inside the chapel is a Baroque altar of the Pieta dating from 1693. The Renaissance epitaphs were created in C16 and C17. The interior ornaments date mainly from C17, C18 and C19.

3 Evangelical (Lutheran – Augsburg Confession) Church: Standing in a row of buildings on the western side of the square, this church was built in 1921 – 1923 in the neo-Gothic style on the site of

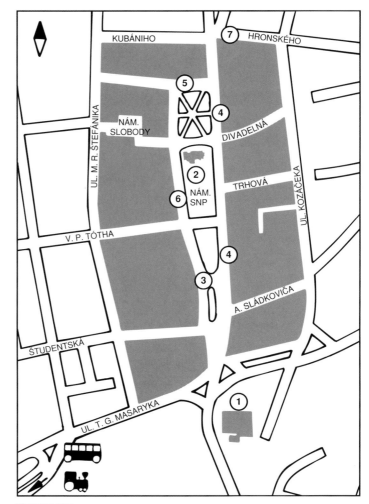

The town plan.

an older wooden church dating from C19. The three-nave church with a polygonal apse has a projecting tower dating from 1850, which projects from the façade line created by the other houses and which was incorporated into the new church building. The interior ornaments exhibit some Art Noveau style artifacts which date from the period when the church was being built.

4 The Town Houses: These two-storeyed houses in the square have two or three-axial façades and are situated on narrow, relatively short building plots,

which reach back as far as the former town fortifications. The houses have passage-ways and two courtyard wings. Built mostly in the second half of C17, some of them incorporated torsoes of Gothic architectural members and Gothic wall paintings. In some cases the original urban structures were replaced by administrative and commercial buildings in the second half of C20, and thus the original historical environment was damaged. Renaissance and Baroque vaults still exist in some of the original houses. Original ground-plans of some of the houses have also been preserved. Houses

No. 48 and No. 68 are fine examples of the original urban structures.

5 Little Mansion: This house is located on a corner on the northern side of the square and is a most impressive one. It was built in C17 and remodelled in the second half of the C18. The two-storeyed building has a seven-axial façade with a central bay, and a tympanum containing coats-of-arms. The halls on the ground--floor feature Renaissance vaulted ceilings.

6 The Local History and Geography Museum and the Fink Manor: Located in the square (Nos. 21 and 41), these buildings are situated in the original historical built-up area are further examples of architectural development of the town core. The exhibitions of ethnology and archaeology document the life of the town and its surroundings. One specialized exhibition shows the development of forestry and wood-working in Slovakia; another specialized exhibition is devoted to life and work of Ľudovít Štúr.

7 Town Fortifications: The original fortification system was formed by a wall with two bastions on the northern side, four gatehouses located on the access roads to the town, and smaller round bastions. The walled fortifications were begun in 1541 and finished in 1667. Existing today are only portions of the northern wall with the bastion, located behind the Evangelical Church; fragments of walls have survived in the gardens of town houses.

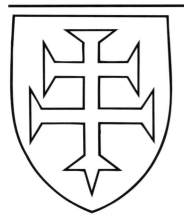

Zvolen's oldest town seal dates from C13. It is of triangular shape and belongs to the so-called shield seals. Its imprints belong among the most valuable Slovak memorabilia, evidencing the high level of heraldic and sphragistic production, whose quality is comparable with countries having the most advanced heraldic production. The intentional modification of the double cross in municipal arms is of great interest. No municipal arms could be identical with the double cross in the coat-of-arms of the Hungarian kingdom. For this reason the endings of arms of the double cross differ from the state coat of arms. The Zvolen arms as well as arms with double cross of other towns confirm the fact that the coat of arms with double cross was not only the original state symbol of the Hungarian kingdom, but since C13 is has also been used as the symbol of Slovakia.

Zvolen is the birthplace of several famous personalities, among them the poet V. Balassa, the journalist J. Ferienčík, the meteorologist S. Ferienčík, and the painter S. Oravec. Among others, Ľudovít Štúr also worked in Zvolen for some time.

After a walk around the square and visit to the museums and the churches, visitors will be drawn by to Zvolen Castle, where exhibits of the Slovak National Gallery are housed. On the western side of the castle, near the highway, an armoured train used during the Slovak National Uprising is shown.

A visit to the town may be enriched by hikes to the surrouding hills, as Zvolen is a starting point for many hiking trails which lead to the Zvolen Hollow, the Javorina Mountains, the Môťová water reservoir, the Štiavnica and Kremnica Hills, or to the Pustý Castle. At Zolná a Roman Catholic church of St. Matthew the Apostle with preserved Gothic elements and wall paintings, from C13. They are National Cultural Monuments.

Visitors may spend their time in the spas and recreational centres of Sliač, Neresnica, Kráľová and Kováčová, where they may take a swim in a swimming pool with thermal water. The Borová hora arboretum and the botanical garden are also of interest. Zvolen with its attractive surroundings offers excellent year-round recreations.

Žilina

Names: L – Zilna, Selinan, **G** – Sillein, **H** – Zsolna
Latitude: 49° 11' N, **Longitude:** 18° 42' E
Elevation: average 344 m, **range:** 323 – 769 m
Population: 83 900
Suburbs: Bánová, Bôrik, Brodno, Budatín, Bytčica, Celulózka, Centrum, Hájik, Hliny,
Mojšova Lúčka, Považský Chlmec, Solinky, Strážov, Rosinky, Trnové, Vranie,
Vlčice, Zádubnie, Zástranie, Závodie, Žilinská Lehota
Means of Access: By rail: routes No. 320, 380, 400, 402; Bus Service; Local Mass
Transportation; By road: routes No. E 50, E 75, E 422
Accommodations: Hotels: Astória, Casino, Polom, Slovakia, Slovan; Motels: Anita,
Šibenice; TU Makarana Hostel
Information: Selinan Travel Agency – tel: (++421)(0)89-5620789, fax: 089-5623171

Žilina's wonderful natural background is formed by several interesting goemorphologic formations. Three rivers, the Rajčianka, Kysuca and Váh, converge upon it. On the north of the Žilinská kotlina (Žilina Hollow) it is surrounded by promontories of the rocky Súľovské skaly Mountains, by the Kysucká vrchovina (Kysuce Highlands) and the Javorníky Hills. The Žilina Hollow is closed off from the south and east by the Lesser Fatra Mountains. Žilina's geographic position predestined it to develop into an important traffic junction.

The town has a warm to moderately cool climate typical of hollows with inversions of temperature. In January the average temperature fluctuates from –2.5 °C to –6 °C, and in July between 16 °C and 18.5 °C; the annual average rainfall varies from 600 to 850 mm. The northern parts of the foothills have a moderately cool mountain climate with temperatures ranging from –4 °C to –6 °C in January, and from 16 °C to 17 °C in July. The annual average rainfall varies between 800 and 900 mm.

This territory used to be only sporadically inhabited in the Paleolithic, Neolithic and Eneolithic Ages. Plentiful and rich archaeological discoveries from the Bronze Age, the La Tène, and Roman periods testify to the existence of a community which had organized here its technological and religious centre at the prehistoric times.

A hill-fort was located at Divinka on Veľký vrch (High Hill) in the C9 and served as a refuge for people from nearby settlements. It also was a part of the fortification system of the Great Moravian Empire. A Slavonic settlement existed on the site of present-day Žilina in the C10 and C11. At the same time another, more important settlement was located at Štefanica. The earliest written references to Žilina date from the C13. Written references to „terra da Selinan" appeared in 1208 and 1267; in 1312 it is mentioned as „civitas" or city.

The oldest preserved architecture in the area dates from the middle of the C13. The Church of Saint Stephen the King, located in Rudiny (near Závodie), is proof of the existence of an older settlement with indigenous inhabitants. German settlers from Těšín (Silesia) arrived at the end of the C13, establishing what is now the Medieval core of the town on a strategically-located hill above the Váh River. At the same time (the second half of the C13) the ancestors of the Balassovský family, who were owners of the nearby territory, built a castle on the site where a parish church was later built. It became an early type of „customs station" on a long-distance trade route where merchants

The vista of the town from mid-C19.

had to declare their goods and pay a fee equal to one-thirtieth of their value. Conflicts arose between the new German residents and the local citizens. In 1381 King Ľudovít I resolved the dispute through his decree known as „Privilegium Pro Slavis" which confirmed the right of the indigenous citizens to equal representation on the city council.

Žilina gained its city charter at the beginning of the C14. The so-called „Těšín law" was in force up until 1370, later replaced by the „Krupina" rule of law. The character of the first privileges granted to the city is not known, but in 1321 King Charles Robert of Anjou granted Žilina's citizens the exclusive right to fish within a mile of the city, exemption from payment of tolls, and probably the right to hold weekly markets on Mondays. Other „mile" rights were also granted, requiring craftsmen working within one mile of the city to secure the approval of city authorities.

The city was ruled by a mayor and 12 member council. They held judicial power and served as the intermediary for other cities which were founded on the principles of „Žilina law".

Žilina was among the most important cities in north-western Slovakia in the middle of the C14. The city was divided into 140 lots which formed a regular street network with a great square in the center. Irregularities in this street plan occurred only in the castle area where the lots were adapted to the terrain. This symmetrical plan has been preserved to the present day in the historic center and is evidence of the colonization which took place during the Romanesque period on the site of older Slavonic settlements – those which existed near the original hill fort and near the Church of Saint Stephen the King.

Similar to those in other cities at that time, houses on the square were built of wood and only a few fragments have been preserved. However, they point to the differences in location of houses in relation to the street compared with the present-day buildings located there. The large market square is surrounded by houses whose facades feature arcaded open passages on the ground floor, located in front of the craft workshops and stores. The Gothic tradition of these passages was respected when buildings underwent reconstruction until well into the C19.

Around the year 1400, the citizens built a new Gothic parish church dedicated to the Holy Trinity on the site of the old castle. It underwent several renovations, and was fortified against attack in 1540.

Zigmund of Luxembourg issued a decree in 1405 directing Žilina to begin building fortifications; a written reference to this construction exists from the year 1474. The walls were not a continuous masonry construction but a combination of wood--reinforced earthen banks with a trench; it is not certain if the trench was filled with water. The walls had two larger gates, an eastern gate in the direction of Turiec, Liptov, and Nitra and to the west, the Framborská Gate, leading towards Trenčín and Silesia. The third or postern gate was small and only for pedestrians.

Žilina experienced a temporary decline when Hussite armies invaded the city in 1429. But by the end of the C15 the city began to experience unprecedented rapid growth due to the development of commerce and crafts, and especially, the manufacture of cloth.

From Medieval times onward, Žilina became a center of trade and crafts whose constantly growing importance was thanks to its location on the long-

The parish church of the Holy Trinity and Burian's Tower.

The parish church's Calvary and its mosaic decoration.

-distance route between Košice and Silesia. Local merchants were thus able to take part in much broader circles of trade.

With the King's decision to give Žilina to Burian Svetlovlasý in 1526 as collateral for a loan, the city began to be considered as a part of the Strečno domain.

Sometime before mid-C16, Žilina became a centre of Protestantism in the Hungarian kingdom. In 1610, a synod took place here at which the first independent organization of the Evangelical Church in Slovakia was founded. General inclination towards the ideas of Reformation was connected with the Renaissance atmosphere, which was reflected also in the architecture of the town. The burghers' houses treated with arcades on the ground floors may be found around the square and also in the principal streets leading to the square. At the same time Burian's Tower was erected.

Violent incidents of the Thirty Years' War and revolts of the Hungarian Estates, especially Thököly's revolt against the Habsburgs caused damage to the town. Fires and plague epidemics, which followed immediately after the war, were the main causes of the decline of the town.

From the 1680s the Jesuits started their activities in the town under the patronage of the Eszterházy family. The Jesuits built a twin-tower church with a monastery in the main square, and established *the Gymnasium.* In spite of their enormous efforts to convert the Protestants to Catholicism, they were not successful. In a new wave of religious revolts and revolts of the Hungarian Estates against the Habsburgs, the burghers supported the Protestants and identified themselves again with Protestantism. Only after the revolts were crushed in 1708, the town was converted to Catholicism.

At the beginning of C18, the Franciscans, too, came to Žilina. They built a monastic complex with a one-nave church without a tower. Frequent fires in 1744 and 1756 caused boom in building activities as the people were made to rebuild their houses. Besides trade, crafts were the most important source of prosperity of the town. Even during the period of a deep economic decline of the town at the beginning of the second half of C18, there were more than 450 workshops retained. Craftsmen represented 90% of the population of 3000 at that time. The decline of crafts at the end C18 led to stagnation of Žilina.

City hall and the main square.

The burghers' houses with arcades.

The opposite side of the square.

The Jesuit Church of St. Paul.

The second half of the C19 saw a renewal of the city's growth. On the site of the former town walls and trenches, residential houses were built, approximately following the line of original fortifications. In the year 1872, transport on the Košice – Bohumín railway began, and in 1883 Žilina was connected by rail to Bratislava by means of the track which runs along the Váh River. This important connection was the impulse for another period of rapid development. This surge of growth was documented by the construction of major buildings flanking the street connecting the center of town and the railway station. After the turn of the C20, the gradual establishment of industries, banks, and branches of existing companies helped make Žilina into the center of industrial and cultural life in north-western Slovakia. Today the city is also home to Žilina University.

The declaration of Žilina an Urban Preservation Area in 1987 paved the way for saving and recovering the highly valuable urban structure and architecture which have survived here, in the metropolis of northwestern Slovakia.

The central part of the town has a regular street plan with a rectangular square in its very centre. It includes the best known burghers' houses and other notable buildings which are most typical of Žilina.

The interior of the Jesuitical church.

A view from under the arcades.

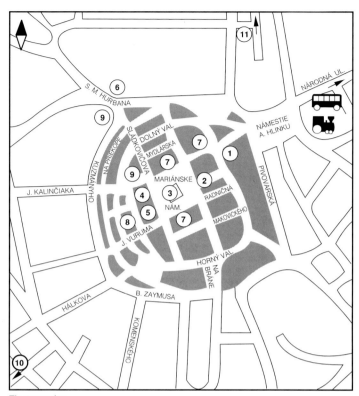

The town plan.

1 The Church of the Holy Trinity: This Roman Catholic parish church, and **Burian's Tower** are medieval constructions built after the year 1400 on the foundations of an earlier one. It was fortified in 1540. The Church of the Holy Trinity obtained its present appearance after considerable reconstructions which took place at the end of C16 and during C17, and several renovations after fires in 1848, 1869, 1888, and in 1942 – 1943. It is a three-nave basilican church with a polygonal presbytery. The spaces have barrel vaults with lunettes, cross ribs and ridge-ribs, and flat vaulted ceilings. The painting on the ceiling of the nave is from 1914. The high altar dates from before 1869 and is adorned with a painting of the Holy Trinity by J. B. Klemens, from 1870. The painting of the Virgin Mary placed on the altar of the Immaculata on the left side of the church, as well as the painting on the altar of Crucifixion on the right, and the altar of St. Anna, situated under the choir, are by the same author. The statue of Saint Anna is by F. Štefunko.

A detached bell-tower is situated next to the church; its position indicates that it may have belonged

to the original castle and only later was transformed into a bell-tower. Literary sources recorded it in 1550; later it was elevated, and during the last renovations in mid-C20, it was adapted to equate with the church tower. Outside the church, a stairway was built, and the whole area was fenced by ballustrades in 1942 – 1943.

2 City Hall: House No. 1 on the main square dates from the end of the C19 and its neo-Baroque facade was made compatible with those of the houses surrounding it. It is a two-storey corner building with a central bay covered with a steep roof.

3 The Statue of the Immaculata: This Baroque statue was placed in the square in 1738. It stands on a pedestal decorated with scrolls and bearing a relief depicting St. Florian.

4 The Jesuitical Monastery and the Church of St. Paul the Apostle: A Baroque complex founded in 1743; the one-nave church has a rectangular presbytery and a side chapel. The wall paintings are from the first half of C20. Its two-tower façade dominates the square. The interior of the church dates mostly from C 18. In the middle of the high altar from mid-C18 is a painting of the patron saint of the church by J. B. Klemens. The pulpit and other paintings are from C18; statues on the side altars date from C20. The monastery is a two-storey building which was consecrated in 1833. The simple, five-bay facade with its arcaded passageway is oriented to the square.

The church of St. Barbara and the Franciscan monastery.

5 The Former Manor House: Built on foundations of an earlier house, this Baroque corner house was created by joining together two Renaissance buildings. It is a seven-axial house with a passageway and a spacious courtyard. An original arcaded passage which was preserved during the Baroque reconstruction, faces the square. The basement contains medieval stone vaults. The manor house was originally used for various social events and gatherings.

6 The Franciscan Monastery and the Church of St. Barbora: Situated almost on the rim of medieval fortifications, the church was built simultaneously with the monastery from 1704 to 1730. The one-nave monastery church without a tower is a typical example of Franciscan churches; its interior spaces are vaulted by barrel vaults with lunettes. On the right side of the nave runs the cloister. On the same side is the cloister-garth. A Baroque statue of St. Barbara adorns the gable of the church façade. The interior furnishigs are mostly in the Baroque style. The high altar from the first half of C18 is lavishly ornamented and adorned with a painting of St. Barbara from 1891. The side altars, the organ, the pews and the pulpit are from C18. The Loreto Chapel is situated next to the church; the chapel and the Baroque interior furnishings date from mid-C18.

7 The Town Houses: These typical town houses form a compact built-up urban area around the large central square and in adjacent streets. They have become fine examples of the development of architectural styles and alterations made in the houses up to now since they were founded in the Middle Ages. Their original function has not been changed for centuries: the ground floors and basements have been used as shops or workshops, and cellars for storing material; the first floor was occupied by the owner of the house. The houses in the square, excepting No. 5, 21 and 27, have clearly visible medieval construction elements in their cellars. Nevertheless, the ground-plans of the present-day constructions are not identical with them because the front spaces of the cellars reach under the present square. Large scale reconstructions of the houses in CC16 and 17 shaped the basic layout of the rooms. At that time first arcades serving as comfortable covered passages containing shops developed around the whole square. They are best surviving examples of architectural structures closely linked with the commercial environment of Žilina. The arcades have been preserved up to now in spite of additional later reconstruction. They show many advantages for a town dependant mainly on trade and crafts.

The consistent style of the square was disturbed by a new element, the monastery and church of the Jesuits, which appeared in the square in C18. This building complex with twin-towers is a pendant to the towers of the parish church and the bell-tower. In C19 interesting architectural features developed in Žilina which became typical of the burghers' houses: spacious sky-lighted halls and magnificent colonnaded staircases. They were introduced because of practical needs: the houses were built side by side and elongated to the rear of the building plots and the need for natural lighting of the interiors became more urgent. But several fires completely destroyed these types of houses. The architecture of the square was then classicized. Gambrel and hipped roofs were replaced by shallow pitched roofs, which changed the proportions of the entire square. Additionally, the original semicircular or segmental arches of arcades were altered to flat arches during the last phase of historicizing adaptations of the façades. Houses built on the site of former mounds do not achieve the impressive appearance of houses in the square. They have remained as examples of one-storeyed, two- and three-room simple houses.

8 The Art Nouveau Chamber Orchestra Hall: Built in 1921 as a theater and movie house, it bore the name „Grand Bio Universum". The premier of the first Slovak film, „Jánošík", took place here. It was a 1921 production of the American--Slovak Tatra-Film Corp. of Chicago. Today's Fatra Art Center is home to concerts and other cultural events.

9 Synagogue: Built in 1933 – 1934 according to the design of Berlin professor P. Behrens (a leading modernist in European architecture), this corner building features a central dome. The use of colored plasters accents its horizontal architectural lines.

10 The Roman Catholic Church of St. Stephen the King: The oldest historic building in Žilina, this late Romanesque church dating from the middle of the C13 underwent reconstruction in the C16, C18, and C19. The original flat ceiling gave way to Baroque cross vaults and early C14 wall paintings in the presbytery depict Christ (as the Judge) and the apostles. A free--standing Renaissance chapel is located on the south side of the church. The walls surrounding the church feature a Renaissance entry portal and round bastion from the C17.

Budatín Castle.

The main building of Žilina University was originally a high school, dating from 1912.

11 The Castle at Budatín: Today's Považské Museum was originally a castle surrounded by a water moat. The central building of the castle complex is a Romanesque cylindrical tower. Written reference dating from 1323 mentions it as serving as a secure location for the collection of tolls. The Renaissance addition to the castle was built after 1545, and it underwent reconstruction in the C18. A fire in 1849 necessitated further restoration work, at which time another addition was built. At the end of the C19 the terrace around the castle was remodeled, and further renovations to the building took place between 1920 – 1923 and in the 1970s.

The museum houses an exhibition of tinkers' crafts and finkerware.

Among the most precious preserved literary monuments regarding the history of the town is a manuscript from 1378, the socalled „*Žilinská kniha*" (the Žilina Law Code), which is a survey of laws then in force. This book is considered to be one of the earliest literary records in the Slovak language, Another highly valuable literary monument is the „*Privilegium Pro Slavis*" from 1381, in which the king granted the Slavonic population equal rights with the German colonists.

The Žilina arms are one of the most remarkable and beautiful Slovak municipal arms. The earliest known document on its use is a charter dating from 1379. The double cross is also a part of the original Hungarian state coat of arms, it was promoted for the state coat of arms by the Árpád dynasty; for this reason the arms of Žilina seem to have originated during their reign – sometime before 1301. In the Middle Ages one emblem could not represent two different subjects. Therefore, Žilina modified its own arms using the state coat of arms as a model but the ground is displayed in vert instead of in gules, and the double cross is displayed in or instead argent. The figuration is also different – the double cross is with roots and two little stars are in or.

The town of Žilina is associated with many outstanding personalities such as, e. g., the historian J. Fischer-Piscatoris, the humanist writer J. Milochovský, the poet Hugolín Gavlovič, the writer M. Hollý Sn, the painter G. Szalay, the physician D. Makovický the personal physician of the Russian writer and philosopher, L. N. Tolstoy, and the founder of Slovak neurosurgery, J. Žucha.

A tour of the city usually starts from the train station; walking along one of the newest streets, one soon comes upon the parish church with its bell tower. Passing by the church and wandering through the symmetrical little streets, one reaches the main square where, walking through the arcades, it is possible to visit the Church of St. Paul.

Energetic visitors may go on foot or use public transport to see also the church in Závodie or the Považské Museum in Budatín Castle.

The surroundings of the town offer outstanding possibilities for mountain-walkers both in winter and summer. The hills Dubeň (613 m) and Straník (769 m), in the Kysuce Highlands, are famous vantage points providing a wonderful view of the area. Recreational resorts near the town are ideal places for pleasant holidays. The Hričovská water reservoir and skiing areas in the mountains within easy reach of Žilina are traditionally reputed for pleasant recreation all the year round.

Marked hiking paths lead to the Súľovské vrchy, Javorníky Mountains, Kysuce Highlands as well as to the Lesser Fatra Mountains.

In the little spa town of Rajecké Teplice in the valley of the Rajčianka brook below the promontories of the Súľovské vrchy, the diseases of the locomotor and the nervous systems are treated. A thermal swimming pool is available to public.

Eastern Slovakia

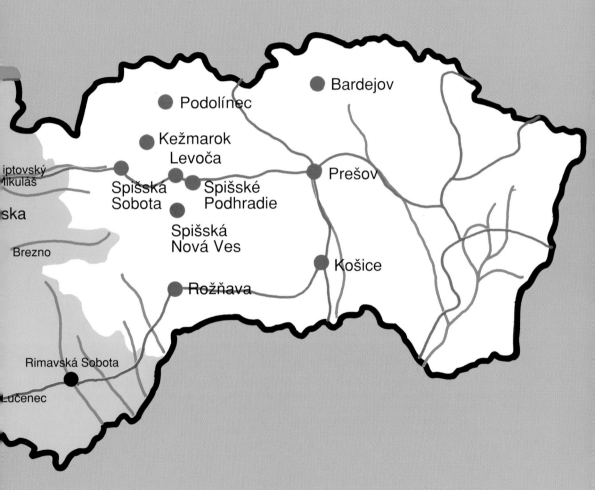

Bardejov

Podolínec

Kežmarok

Levoča

iptovský
Mikuláš

Spišská
Sobota

Spišské
Podhradie

Prešov

ska

Spišská
Nová Ves

Brezno

Košice

Rožňava

Rimavská Sobota

Lučenec

The diverse natural, cultural, and historical territory that is eastern Slovakia has an expanse of more than 16 000 km². Its western border approximates the longitude 19° 35' E and its eastern one the longitude 22° 30' E. Slovakia is situated approximately between the latitudes 48° 25' N and 49° 25' N. Perhaps none of the territories in Slovakia have such a fantastic mosaic of natural points of interest and tourist attractions. The topography of the territory is characterized by considerable differences in altitude. Including both the extensive East-Slovak Lowlands with rolling hills and high mountainous relief, this area offers a broad variety of landscape and breathtaking panoramas.

Both the highest point of Slovakia (Gerlach Shield 2655 m in the High Tatras) and the lowest one (the Bodrog River in Streda nad Bodrogom at 95 m) are to be seen in eastern Slovakia.

The varied configuration of the landscape and the natural riches contributed to the brilliant artistic achievements in architecture as well as in other fields of human activity performed here. The Gothic architecture of Spiš, the eastern Slovakia Renaissance, the timber-wood churches, and the castles hold an irreplaceable position within the world's cultural heritage. Eight historic towns in this territory were declared as Urban Preservation Areas. In addition, the largest number of National Cultural Monuments as well as other treasures of national heritage attract many visitors to eastern Slovakia.

The Carpathian Mountains tower above two-thirds of the area; three national parks (the Tatras National Park, Pieniny National Park, and Slovenský raj National Park) and five Protected Landscape Areas (Slovak Karst, Vihorlat, a part of the Muráň plateau, the Eastern Carpathian Mountains, and the Latorica). A world of exceptional beauty can be found in numerous caves.

Busy tourist centres have developed near the numerous water reservoirs. Due to the natural curative thermal and mineral properties of several of the water springs and the excellent climatic conditions, several spas and health resorts were built here.

The Tatra Mountains, a centre of summer and winter tourism, enjoy a moderately warm climate, and the East-Slovak Lowlands have a moderately dry lowland climate.

Advantageous natural and climatic conditions as well as the long-established long-distance trade routes running from the south, via Italy and Hungary to the north, to Poland and onwards to the Baltic sea, were the main reason for the permanent inhabitation of this part of Slovakia.

The oldest evidence of prehistoric occupation of eastern Slovakia is the remarkable discovery of the Lower Paleolithic Age fossil skull in Dreveník (a hill near Spišské Podhradie) believed to be Australopithecus – a human ancestor about 1.2 million years old. Another discovery of a fossil skull-cast from Gánovce dating to the Middle Paleolithic represents the earliest developmental type of Neanderthal man, who lived around 80 000 years BC.

The high density of settlement sites in eastern Slovakia in the Upper Paleolithic Age is documented by Aurignacian camp sites found in Košice-Barca, the Zemplín Hills, and in the valleys along the rivers Rožňava, Hornád, and Poprad; later, they were replaced by Gravettian camp sites which expanded to the eastern Slovakia lowlands, the Vihorlat mountain range, and the Ondava and Šariš Hills. The rather sparse inhabitation characteristic of the Mesolithic is confirmed by the excavation of a settlement site of the Tisza culture in Košice-Barca, characterized by the obsidian industry.

The development of Neolithic inhabitation in eastern Slovakia is centred on the river Tisza with which it created a single cultural and geographical unit. Characteristic for this culture is *Bandkeramik,* pottery, the with decoration of parallel lines forming various ornaments, often painted in black, or jabbed. More densely inhabited area is known to have existed also in the East-Slovak Lowlands, Košice Hollow, Slovak Karst, and the Šariš Hills. In the Middle Stone Age, this territory was occupied by the people of the *bukovohorská* (Beech-wood) culture; later they penetrated over the southern lowlands and highlands to central and western Slovakia. The people of this culture traded in obsidian and their camp sites consisted mainly of cave dwellings or clusters of huts. The Eneolithic Baden culture produced pottery with channelled decoration which became typical of the settlements over much of Slovakia except for the Kysuce, Orava, and Upper Hron regions. The expansion of this culture up to the hills is evidenced by the situation in the Spiš region: the castle hill of Spiš Castle, Spišské Tomášovce, and Dreveník with three hillforts. According to archaeological excavations, it was the most important centre of this culture in the region at that time.

The Early Bronze Age Košťany culture diffused in the areas of the Košice and Spiš Hollows as well as in the East-Slovak Lowland. This group, according to the level of technological advancement, was similar to the Nitra region. The peoples of the Otomani culture of Transylvania (northwestern part of Romania) reached the areas inhabited by people of the Košťany culture and gradually occupied Spiš and Rimavská kotlina (hollow). They brought the Mycenaean culture with them to eastern Slovakia. The influence of the Mediterranean civilization, mediated by the Otomani culture manifested in the building elements of the fortified sites, in construction of fortifications, and features of material culture. Unique remains of this legacy were found in Barca, Spišský Štvrtok, and Gánovce.

The peoples of the Pilin culture moved to the area between the basins of Košice and the Ipeľ and the Slovak Ore Mountains in the Middle and Later Bronze Age; the remnants of their settlement sites were also found in Spiš and in the river valleys of the Hornád, Torysa, and Topľa. Further changes are coupled with the influence of Gáva and Lusatian cultures, which penetrated deep to the north at the end of the Bronze Age.

During the Early Iron Age – Hallstatt – characteristic elements of the Thracian culture in southeastern Slovakia were found. These peoples flew

freely from their settlements in Ruthenia – eastern
Ukraine.

The next cultural stratum was formed by the Celts
who arrived in eastern Slovakia (mainly in the
southeast). However, the direct contacts with their
culture are documented only for the middle La Tène in
the Trebišov region. It created a separate group here.
In late La Tène, mixed settlements of Celts and
Dacians spread over the East-Slovak Lowlands, with
Zemplín as its centre.

During the Roman period the area of eastern
Slovakia was still inhabited by Celto-Dacian groups.
Regional development was simultaneously influenced
by other barbarian culture – Púchov or Przeworsk
cultures, and the Lipice culture in the Zemplín region.

In the first phase of the Great Migration, the vast
area became depopulated; it opened way for the
migrations and soon afterwards the first Slavs arrived
and inhabited the area around Prešov.

The first wave of Slavic settling migrants, who were
farmers, was concentrated in the Zemplín Basin;
the more intensive settlement of this northern region
developed only in C9.

Traits of the movement of the Avars to the north are
traced in eastern Slovakia only in C8, it is later than in
the southern and central Slovak lowlands. They
gradually penetrated to the Slavic environment, found
their new homes there and most probably fused with
these earlier settlers. Noteworthy features of their
coexistence are evidenced in the Avaro-Slavic burial
sites in Košice and Trebišov.

The mountainous areas were most probably separate
Slavic territories. A hypothesis of the uninterrupted
inhabitation is supported by fortified settlement sites
and hillforts which, survived according to their earliest
strata mast have reached much deeper to the past, and
formed the background for the immigrants.

The continuity of the Slavic settlement sites was
clearly evidenced for the Great-Moravian period up to
C12. The individual parts of eastern Slovakia became
gradually incorporated into the Hungarian state. The
regions of Zemplín and Michalovce might have been
the first ones which passed under the Hungarian
kingdom, followed by the Košice basin in C11; Spiš
and Šariš were incorporated much later.

The first settlements of urban character arose along
the important long-distance trade roads on the sites of
previous settlements. Their inhabitants dedicated
themselves to trade and crafts. The towns were
gradually given privileges by the rulers, thereby
assuring their advance. The development of urban
agglomeration was influenced by the German colonists
who emerged from the west. The level of urbanization
of the Spiš region was apparent and surprisingly high:
twenty-four urban centres with Levoča as the most
eminent one. The Tartar invasions interrupted the
process of inhabitation and economic, social, and
cultural development in eastern Slovakia as well as in
other parts of the country. The southern Šariš and Spiš
regions were the most grievously damaged. In the
second half of C12 the long-settled colonies revived;
the administrative division of whole eastern Slovakia
was altered: the county system was changed and

a sub-system of districts was established. The new
administrative units covered Spiš, Šariš, Turňa,
Gemer, Uh, and Zemplín. The most important and
ancient towns of the region became Bardejov,
Dobšiná, Gelnica, Kežmarok, Košice, Levoča,
Michalovce, Prešov, Rožňava, Sabinov, Spišská
Sobota, and Veľký Šariš. These towns were chartered
in the second half of C13 and in C14. Jasov, Leles, and
Spišská Kapitula were loci credibile, i. e. they were
entrusted with the privilege both to establish and
verify authenticity of various documents (charters,
agreements, warrants). The way of life in towns was
shaped by the main occupations of the townfolk
– trade and craft production. They also profited from
the long-distance trade and trade contacts with the
South and North of Europe. Long-distance roads
running from Hungary to Poland, to the Baltic and
Germany passed through the eastern-Slovakia towns.
Of the historical events at those times, it is necessary to
mention the Battle of Rozhanovce in 1312, where the
power of the aristocratic oligarchy was enhanced in
favour of the ruler, King Charles Robert of Anjou. The
social riots came to a head in eastern Slovakia in C15
much the same way as in other regions of Slovakia.
The German Emperor and Hungarian King, Sigismund
of Luxemburg pawned 16 towns to the Polish King
in order to obtain money to fight the Hussites (who
refused him as the King of Bohemia); these towns
were located mostly in northern Spiš – the borderland
with Poland.

The Lower-Spiš region was very important. Owing
to the deposits of ore it became the ore-mining centre
of the Hungarian Kingdom.

The medieval towns of eastern Slovakia
distinguished themselves from other Slovak towns
because of their wealth and remarkable appearance.
Arts flourished here and their achievements were not
confined exclusively to this area. Košice and Levoča
became centres of artistic activity in CC14 and 15.
Their significance and formative influence were much
greater than of ony other towns and were apparent
behind their boundaries. The building of the Košice
parish cathedral-church of St. Elizabeth, which was
conceived as a five-nave, took more than 100 years.
The high altar of Košice's St. Elizabeth's, originating
from 1474 to 1477, with its Late-Gothic remarkable
polyptych, shows the largest European collection of
panel-paintings contained in one altar (numbering 48);
they depict scenes from the legends of St. Elizabeth
and St. Mary and the Passion Cycle. A prominent
lodge of stone-cutters and sculpturers moved to
Košice, and during 1420 – 1440 created the most
precious portions of the cathedral – the three great
portals. The same lodge participated in the building of
the Franciscan Church. Several Gothic houses
located in the spacious square, such as Levoča House,
so-called Mikluš Prison and town fortifications
underlay the great architectural beauty and nearly
fabulous wealth of Košice.

Levoča, Kežmarok, Spišská Sobota, Bardejov,
Prešov, and many other medieval towns in the Spiš
and Šariš regions and the Košice Hollow, which are
much poorer today, demonstrate by the richness and

architectural style of the parish churches their extraordinary prosperity in the Middle Ages. The spacious Bardejov square with the Gothic-Renaissance Town Hall from the beginning of C16, the continuous rows of burghers houses, and the interior of the parish church of St. Aegidius with eleven triptych altars dating from C15 and the beginning of C16 are evidences of the high prosperity and very fine cultural standard of the town; today Bardejov's fortunes have changed, as it is bypassed by important traffic routes.

Several public buildings, the parish church of St. James, the Town Hall, with the shops on the ground floor, and the school have been preserved in the square in Levoča. Master Pavol of Levoča, who created the high Levoča altar and many others, continued at the beginning of C16 the artistic work begun by his predecessors. He himself became the founder of a sculpture-school and lodge which created many precious works of art in eastern and central Slovakia.

During C16 eastern Slovakia became a neighbour of the Osman Empire, and the Eger Bishopric was moved to Košice. This dangerous neighbourhood impacted the southern portions of Šariš and Spiš as the Turks plundered them at that time. The necessity to improve the town walls, fortify the castles and manor houses initiated new intensive building activity. Subsequent historical events in what is today Slovakia were the same as events in other parts of the Hungarian kingdom; after the defeat of the Turks at the end of C17, the damaged country began to revive. The C17 in eastern Slovakia was known as the period of East-Slovakia Renaissance, manifested by the specific treatment of the gables and roofs of the houses in Spiš and Šariš. Thurzo's Palaces in Levoča and Prešov, the church spire in Spišský Hrhov, the belfries in Strážky and Vrbovce, and the mansion house in Fričovce are the principal best-known examples of this architectural style.

Levoča represents a specific kind of Spiš Renaissance. The mid-C16 and the second third of C17 was the period of fast advance of the town, represented by great building and art activities. Wealthy patricians' and burghers' houses with various gable ends have been admired up to now. The façades are richly decorated by trompe d'oeil architectural paitings and by sculptural adornments. Painted figures on the Town Hall façade symbolize the town rights and bourgeoise virtues; in its interior are preserved the council chamber and the entrance hall. The inner courtyards with stone brackets supporting loggias and galleries are quite unique. Their appearance is enriched by a wide variety of details, windows, portals, stairways, railings, fireplaces, and cornices which are remarkably diverse. The collections of Renaissance epitaphs in the church have special significance for Slovak art-history.

In 1770 the period when the Spiš towns had been pledged came to an end. In CC18 and 19 they started expanding beyond the town walls and fortifications as these had lost their significance. Among other significant symptoms of the new oncoming era was the new mode of transportation – the railroad – and new types of specially designed buildings, such as railway stations, rental houses, theatres, and concert halls.

The relatively stable situation in the regions of eastern Slovakia at the end of C19 and beginning of C20 was impacted by World War I. This period was critical for eastern Slovakia regarding the fact that Ruthenia (the western part of present-day Ukraine) was incorporated into Czechoslovakia and thus became a part of eastern Slovakia. World War II, after 20 years of Czechoslovakia's existence as a Republic, had a great impact on this part of the country. The Battle of Dukla Pass was one of the most severe. Many towns and villages, for instance Prešov and Bardejov, were damaged.

After the war, the badly damaged towns and villages were rebuilt; most of them have preserved their original appealing appearance. The nine eastern Slovakia towns which are presented in this book rank among the most interesting and most important with regard to their atmosphere, architecture, and history.

Eastern Slovakia is highly interesting because of its unrivalled natural beauties; many towns and settlements are set in wonderful nature and offer pleasant conditions for rest and recreation. Besides the selected towns described in this book, there are thirty other towns here, in this region; the largest and most important ones are the district towns and administrative centres of Humenné, Michalovce, Svidník, Trebišov, and Vranov nad Topľou. Historically and architecturally excellent – Dobšiná, Gelnica, Jelšava, Rožňava, Sabinov, Spišská Belá, Štítnik, Stará Ľubovňa, and others – have preserved the period architecture unaffected. The exclusive historic town centres, splendid burghers' houses, dominant parish churches, and other precious buildings have survived in the above-mentioned towns.

In the mountains of eastern Slovakia are many castles. The castle of Krásna Hôrka from CC14 – 18 is a National Cultural Monument and today it houses a museum exposition. The castles of Hanigovce, Čičava, Jasenovce, Kapušany, Markušovce, Muráň, Plaveč, Parič, Slanec, Šariš, and Turňa once-famous and mighty, are only picturesque ruins today. The castle of Stará Ľubovňa is open to public and a Geography Museum is located in the reconstructed portion.

Churches and monasteries represent other kinds of monuments in eastern Slovakia; a historically significant sacral building is to be found in almost every village. The best surviving among them are two National Cultural Monuments – the churches in Štítnik and Žehra. The church in Žehra is interesting, with its shingle, onion ended tower and well-preserved medieval wall paintings; its beauty is enhanced by its situation in the village. The monastery complexes in Červený Kláštor and Jasov are also National Cultural Monuments. Červený Kláštor is a well-preserved complex of the former Carthusian monastery from CC14 – 18; today it houses a museum exposition. The monastery of Premonstratensians in Jasov, dating from C18, is unique owing to the church interior decorated with paintings created by J. L. Kracker. The churches in Batizovce, Bijacovce, Dravce, Čečejovce, Chyžné,

Koceľovce, Ochtiná, Plešivec, Rákoš pri Jelšave, Svinica, Švábovce, and Veľká Lomnica all display wall paintings; these paintings represent precious medieval collections, therefore they have been declared National Cultural Monuments. In Leles, Nižná Myšľa, and Nižná Šebastová, notable monastery complexes have survived.

The manor houses and mansions and country seats represent other remarkable archtectural types in this region. The country seat at Betliar (CC16 – 20) and another one with a church and bell tower on its precincts at Spišská Belá-Strážky are National Cultural Monuments as well. Other mansion houses located in Betlanovce, Borša, Brzotín, Fintice, Fričovce, Hertník, Demjata, Jelšava, Kluknava, Pribeník, Snina, Spišský Hrhov, Spišský Štiavnik, Streda nad Bodrogom, and Žehra-Hodkovce are pleasant pieces of architecture. The country seats and mansions in Humenné, Hanušovce nad Topľou, Michalovce, and Markušovce are used as museums with permanent exposition on natural-sciences, local history and geography and other specialized expositions. Well preserved examples of manor houses are in Markušovce, Rozhanovce, and Spišské Župčany.

Spectacular instances of folk architecture can be admired in 27 villages in the six districts of Bardejov, Humenné, Michalovce, Prešov, Stará Ľubovňa, and Svidník. Small wooden churches built in most of the villages still remain today, all together declared and representing a National Cultural Monument. The most interesting little wooden churches are situated in Bodružaľ, Hervartov, Ladomirová, Lukov-Venécia, Šemetkovce, Topoľa, and Tročany. Museums of folk architecture are located in Bardejov Spa, Humenné, and Stará Ľubovňa. Osturňa and Ždiar are Folk Architecture Preservation Areas. The performance of a village wedding is a show of marriage customs and forms a part of the general exibition of local customs and usages in Ždiar. The notable survivals of local costumes originating from Letanovce, Vernár, Rejdová, Zemplín, and Ždiar present the diversity of eastern Slovak folk clothing. The production of dark-brown pottery with white-and-green-and-ochre ornamentation is a tradition at Pozdišovce as well as in Bardejov. Easter eggs were painted in a traditional manner at Papín. Folk festivals are traditional occasions and take place every summer in Gombasek, Košice, and Svidník. The Marian liturgical celebration in Levoča is the most popular and most celebrated religious occasion in all of Slovakia. The pilgrimage at Levoča is attended by worshippers from far and wide.

Eastern Slovak spas and health resorts are among the most important medical centres in Slovakia. The climatic health resort in the High Tatras and the Bardejov thermal water spa are known all over Europe. Digestive system diseases, non-specific diseases of the respiratory system, and occupational diseases are treated in Bardejov. The High Tatra spas and health resorts are located in Štrbské Pleso, Smokovce, and Tatranská Lomnica, where treatments are given for the lungs, tuberculosis, asthma, and allergic diseases of the respiratory system. Nervous system diseases, high blood pressure, and some occupational diseases are treated in Vyšné Ružbachy. Štôs is a climatic health resort where diseases of the respiratory system and occupational diseases are treated. Mineral water is bottled as table water under the brands of Baldovská, Salvátor, and Cígeľka. The geyser in Herľany is a unique natural attraction in Slovakia.

Thermal waters, open air swimming pools, reservoirs, lakes, and rivers offer many possibilities for an enjoyable summer holiday. Thermal water pools are situated in Vrbové and Vyšné Ružbachy and a small bathing area is in Gánovce. The large water reservoirs of Domaša and Zemplínska Šírava are the most popular centres of summer sports. There are also other water reservoirs – Bukovec, Ružín, Palcmanská Maša, lakes in Košice and in Čaňa.

Eastern Slovakia features a landscape very convenient for skiing and other winter sports. Štrbské Pleso, Tatranská Lomnica, and Starý Smokovec are the best-known sport centres, and they offer good conditions for all kinds af skiing. The ski lifts, cross-country skiing trails, and ski-jumps offer skiing possibilities for the top and most experienced skiers. At Drienica-Lysá pri Sabinove, Kojšovská hoľa, Zlatá Idka, Jezersko, Bachledova dolina, and Ždiar are other centres for winter sports.

Fishermen, hunters and those who enjoy picking mushrooms and forest berries have a good opportunity to dedicate themselves completely to their pleasure in eastern Slovakia. This unique, fascinating and most diverse region affords a view of landscape from the lowlands with minimal relief to the highest mountains – attracts people for hiking through the valleys and mountains, providing soft woodland beauty in sharp contrast to tremendously dramatic rock scenery which is unforgettable. It would be unthinkable to visit eastern Slovakia without going to the most attractive parts of the region: the High Tatras, Belianske Tatras, Pieniny, and Slovenský raj. Visitors should turn their attention to the East-Slovak caves which offers a unique experience of the magnificent and dignified underground world of stalactite-stalagmite formations in the Belianska, Gombasecká, Jasovská, and Domica caves, and the fabulous masterpieces of Nature – the Dobšiná ice cave and Ochtinská aragonite cave.

Bardejov

Names: L – Bardfa, **G** – Bartfeld, **H** – Bártfa
Latitude: 49° 02' N, **Longitude:** 20° 35' E
Elevation: average 277 m, **range:** 250 – 550 m
Population: 33 200
Suburbs: Bardejov, Bardejovská Nová Ves, Bardejovské kúpele (spa), Bardejovská
  Zábava, Dlhá Lúka, Miháľov
Means of Access: By rail: route No. 194; By road: routes No. 68 and 545
Accommodations: Hotels: Baal Šport, Gemm, Republika, Topľa, F. Kopačka Pension,
  Kríže Cottage, Kamarát Recreational Center, Secondary Technical School
  (Stredné odborné učilište), Educational and Rehabilitation Facility JAS, hostels; at
  the Bardejov spa – Hotels Mier, Minerál, spa facility Ozón, Alžbeta, pensions
Information: Tourist Information Center – tel: (++421)(0)935-16186, 0935-4723013,
  0935-4726072, fax: 0935-4746979

Bardejov, the centre of the Upper Šariš region, is spread on the plain and low terrace of the River Topľa, and in the Ondavská vrchovina (Ondava Highlands) which are a part of the Low Beskydy Mountains. In the past the region of Upper Šariš was a part of the relatively large Šariš *comitatus* (a district or county). The town of Bardejov is situated in the centre of northeast Slovakia near the border with Poland. The mountain range of Busov is north of the town; to the west lies Čergov, which belongs to the Beskydy mountains. Because of their natural characteristic, they were declared a Nature Preserve. In the surroundings of Bardejov there are National Nature Reserves, including Stebnícka Magura and Zborovský hradný vrch; both of them feature educational nature trails.

Bardejov enjoys a moderately humid and warm climate typical of hollows with average temperatures of –2 °C to 6 °C in January, and of 17 °C to 18.5 °C in July. The average snow-cover lasts for 120 days a year; there are about forty summer days; the average annual rainfall is between 600 and 800 mm.

The natural background of the town is composed mainly of coniferous forests of the Ondava Highlands.

The existence of the first settlements in this part of Slovakia dates back to the prehistoric times. In the Eneolithic Age, they were represented by the East-Slovakia Tumulus culture, dating back to 1900 – 1800 BC. Isolated archaeological discoveries impart only a modest indication of the settlement structure of the region up to the early Middle Ages.

This territory is presumed to have been included in the early-feudal Hungarian state as a part of the Novum Castrum comitatus (a district or county) in the second half of C11. A separate administrative district of Šariš, having its administrative centre in Šariš Castle, was established at the end of C12.

The original core of Bardejov was most likely the Slavic settlement which was localized on the site of present-day Slovak Street, mentioned in tax registers of C15. The "terra Bardfa" ("Bardejov lands") including an extensive surrounding area is already mentioned in written sources in 1247. At that time the possessions of the Cistercians in Bardejov, who owned a monastery and a church of St. Aegidius as its patron saint, were settled by German colonits arriving from Prešov.

Earlier information dating back to 1241 recorded in the chronicle of the Ipatijev Monastery mentions

A vista of the town, from mid-C19.

"Bardujev" as a place through which passed a road from Hungary to Poland.

At the turn of CC13 and 14, new colonists from Silesia settled nearby an older colony planted along the road. In 1320 King Charles Robert of Anjou endowed their community with extensive privileges, which accelerated the development of the town. The inhabitants of Bardejov were involved mostly in trade, crafts, and agriculture. Some other privileges were given to the town in 1352 and 1355, and it also received a warrant to errect town walls. In 1376 Bardejov acquired the status of an Independent Royal Town enjoying the same privileges as Buda and Košice. The letters patent describes the town as standing within protective walls with towers and as having a relatively regular plan developed around the central rectangular square. On the northern side of the grandiously conceived square is the monumental parish church of St. Aegidius; the Town Hall was built on the site where a market hall had once existed.

In the second half of C14 and then during C15 the development of the town steadily continued; the burghers built their houses not only around the square. The right to store imported goods granted upon the town provided new opportunities for the Bardejov merchants who were permitted to trade throughout the entire kingdom without paying tolls.

Later a monopoly of packing linen encouraged further economic upsurge of the town which grew very rich and became an important centre. The burghers expanded the volume of their wealth by production of linen. For instance, in the 1430s approximately 250 000 ells were produced a year. In the first half of C15, the economic advancement of the town, which at that time had approximately 500 houses and 3000 inhabitants, reached its full climax. Commercial ventures, production, and trade in linen were the main economic activities of the town. Considering the number of craft and merchant guilds, only Bratislava, Košice, and Levoča surpassed Bardejov. Significant sacral buildings emphasized its religious importance: a monastery and a church of the Augustinians were built in the town. At the same time the urban structure had to absorb more and more houses. As the space within the town walls was very limited, expansion outwards began. Suburbs sprawled outside the town walls along the long-distance trade roads. The Holy Spirit Hospital with a poorhouse was erected on Vysoký rad; in present-day Šancová Street, southeast of the centre, potters had their workshops, as evidenced by the discovery of a potter's kiln which dates back to C15. During the Hussite movement, the town rebuilt its fortifications, which then ranked among the most ingenious town fortifications in Slovakia in the

The panorama of the town from the east.

Middle Ages. The town also reconstructed the parish church into an aisled nave, and the burghers refurbished their stately houses. The town was also an owner of mills, sawmills, a brick yard, a brewery, a town scale, a prison, a bath, a stock yard, and several buildings related to the weaving, bleaching, and selling of linen. The style of burghers' houses of that time was typical of high gables with throughs ended by wooden gargoyles.

The beginning of C16 brought a slight economic decline to the town but it did not hinder and set back its flourishing cultural life. Income obtained from the 13 surrounding towns which belonged to Bardejov pledged to the Polish king and were sold and substituted for the decreasing profits of linen production. Various building activities in the town continued. A new town hall, the first work of architecture in the Renaissance style in Slovakia, became the most splendid edifice in the town. Reconstruction works of the church and the Augustinian monastery, and also of the town fortifications continued. At that time the first Latin school in the town was opened. Soon it achieved a position of an important centre of education in northeast Hungary. It enjoyed an excellent reputation, especially when Leonard Stöckel, a disciple and follower of Martin Luther, also called "The Teacher of Hungary," was teaching here during the Reformation.

In this context, it is worth mentioning that the ideas of humanism and Reformation raised the cultural level and national consciousness of both the Slovak and German inhabitants of Bardejov. Under their influence, the Luther's "Catechism," the first book written in the biblical Czech language was printed in Gutfesall's printing house in 1581.

The following period of uprisings of the Hungarian Estates and riots in C17 and at the beginning of C18 caused heavy damage upon the economy as well as the finances and demographic situation of the town. The sack of the town and its surroundings, then payments of contributions, and the epidemic of Black Plague resulted in general poverty of the town.

Later on, in C18, the situation gradually improved; the town and the population grew because villagers started moving and settling there. The parish church was given back to the Catholics; the monastery of the Augustinians was taken over by the Franciscans. The town gradually achieved its previous economic importance, largely due to a large-scale building activity.

The national structure of the population changed; the number of Slovak inhabitants increased and Jewish merchants also settled here. On the western side of the town they built a synagogue in Mlynská (Mill) Street, which was later extended by a bath, a school, a communion hall, and a workshop.

A portion of the square with the new town hall.

Town houses on the western side of the square.

A cemetery belonged to this complex as well. The burghers' houses and many other buildings were rebuilt and modified to suit the spirit of the Baroque.

At the turn of CC18 and 19, the fortification systems in many Slovak towns became gradually dismantled. Bardejov was not an exception; the town plan definitively expanded outwards of the walled medieval core. People employed the moat and founded their gardens there just below the fortifications; on the north a promenade developed; further growth of Bardejov was then orientated towards the Topľa river.

In C19 several fine structures were built; the Evangelical Church of Augsburg Confession was finished in 1808; wooden bridges in front of the Lower and Western Gatehouses were replaced by stone ones and the complex of Calvary was built on the hill above the Lukavica river in 1868 – 1869.

A destructive fire in 1878 destined the extent of further reconstructions and renovations in the town. The parish church was rebuilt to the Gothic Revival style; the Franciscan church was also renovated; fifty-eight new houses were built and all the houses which remained in the town after the fire were remodelled.

The turn of CC19 and 20 was accompanied by building activities which began in the former suburbs. Several industrial and public buildings, such as the former public school

The eastern side of the square.

and the Graeco-Catholic church, which dates from 1901 up to 1902 and is treated in the Historical revival style with neo-Romanesque members, were built there. The railway station was built to the southeast outside the original town care in 1890. Bardejov was connected to Prešov by railway, thus being linked with other towns of the former Hungarian kingdom. In 1902 Bardejov was again damaged by fire; the houses on the square were subsequently covered by gable roofs, thereby they liquidated the picturesque gables with gargoyles disappeared.

During World War II several buildings of the town – the mill and sawmill, the Republika Hotel, the bridge on the Zborov road, and several houses were damaged. After the war the town recovered from destruction by fights and expanded and flourished again. Several new industries, such as shoemaking, food production, and wood-working were introduced here. Also large housing estates were built around the town.

The elongated rectangular central square is the most interesting part of the town; it is where the most notable and the most stately buildings have survived.

A Gothic town houses, remodelled to the Renessance style, with Baroque paintings on the façade.

The church of St. Aegidius, Gothic, from the beginning of C15.

Because of astounding urban, architectural, artistic, historic, and cultural values preserved in Bardejov, it was declared an Urban Preservation Area in 1950. A gradual long-term revitalization of the historical buildings has been continued in the town's historic core since it was declared an Urban Preservation Area. In 1986 Bardejov was awarded "The European Prize – Gold Medal" for preservation and restoration of cultural heritage; it was the first town in former Czechoslovakia to be honoured. Bardejov was therefore entered on the list of cities which rank among the most spectacular centres of European culture.

The church of St. Aegidius: the interior.

The statue of St. Florian.

The Town Hall.

The church of St. Aegidius: the altar of St. Anna.

The Town Hall: the oriel staircase.

The Council Hall: the Renaissance carved, painted panel ceiling.

1 The Parish Church of St. Aegidius:

This Romanesque Catholic church, a National Cultural Monument, is a three-nave basilica dating back to the beginning of C15. It was created through the reconstruction of a previous religious building dating from C14. This church stands most likely on the site of the Cistercian monastic complex which is referred to in a charter of 1247. In 1448 – 1458 Master Nicholas of Bardejov built the sanctuary and the sacristy, above which is a royal oratory, and the chapel of Saint Catherine, which was also used as a library. Though the reconstruction of the church was accomplished in 1464, cracks which appeared afterwards as well as the unprecedently daring design for the construction of vaults caused its collapse. Master Štefan embarked on its reconstruction; he also built new reticulated vaulting over the sanctuary; in 1465 he, too, completed the Gothic pastophory. In the second half of C15, the church was reconstructed anew and finished. A brilliant and spatially grandiouse new structure was created which exhibited particularly remarkable architectural details. The central nave received reticulated vaulting which was designed by Master Ján of Prešov in 1513 – 1518. At the end of C15, the interior of the

The Renaissance portal of the Town Hall.

cathedral began to be decorated. The church's impressive furnishings are represented by a unique complex of eleven triptych altars dating mostly from the years 1460 – 1520.

During the fire and earthquake in 1725 the tower collapsed but fortunately it could be repaired. Another fire in 1879 was the reason for the complete redesigning of the building, but in the spirit of the Gothic Revival style, which was flourishing at that time. The renovations were carried out by J. Steindl and F. Schulek in 1878 – 1899. The tower was

rebuilt, the façades were remodelled, and the bell-tower as well as the walls surrounding the church were abolished. The whole building received a new roof including the church tower over which was a spire with pinnacles. The most valuable elements of the church interior, the eleven Gothic triptych altars, are still in their original places; some older sculptures and paintings were installed on them over the years. There are side altars of the Nativity; Vir Dolorum; the Holy Cross; The Virgin Mary; St. Nicholas and St. Erasmus; St. Apollonia (St. Anna Mettercia); Our Lady of Sorrows; St. Barbora; St. Elizabeth the Widow; the Virgin Mary (Saint Anna); St. Andrew (All Saints) and the Virgin Mary. The high Gothic altar is dedicated to St. Aegidius the Bishop; it is a polyptych of 1878. In the church's interior there are several paintings, a Gothic pastophory and a baptismal font, a Gothic sculptural group depicting the Stations of the Cross in the triumphal arch, which dates from 1479 – 1485, and a road screen in front of the high altar. The tomb stones, stallae, pews, and liturgical ornaments form highly valuable interior furnishings of the church. Gothic paintings of C16 have survived on the exterior of the church, depicting St. Christopher and three Hungarian patron saints – Ss. Stephan, Ladislas, and Emeric.

2 The Former Town Hall:

A National Cultural Monument, this building is unique in Slovakia; it combined elements of the Early-Renaissance typical of areas north of the Alps with the fading out of Late-Gothic artistic and architectural details. The high stepped gables and pitched roofs, as well as the staircase oriels are unique and characterize the two-storeyed block-like building of the former Town Hall located in the middle of the square. Today the most valuable items of the Šariš Museum collections are on display in this building.

The Town Hall conceived as the counterpoint to counterbalance the parish church was the centre of business, social, and cultural life in the town. The building was begun in 1505 and completed in 1511 under Master-Masons Alexander and Alexius. The exterior paintings date from 1641. Later on, the Town Hall was renovated several times and the last reconstruction of the former Town Hall took place in 1988.

The most valuable members of the building are architectural details: the portals, sumptuously decorated gables, entrance bay, staircase, wall-paintings, timber ceiling in the Council Hall, painted signs, coats of arms and various inscriptions document the interrelation of the Late-Gothic forms with the Early-Renaissance elements. The Town Hall of Bardejov is the first Renaissance edifice in Slovakia.

3 Fountain and Statue of St. Florian: Situated in the center of the square, the statue was erected to commemorate the fire of 1774. The sculpture of the saint is representative of high-quality Late Baroque stone carving.

4 Gantzughof House (No. 13): Today the home of the Šariš Museum, this house was originally built in the Gothic style in a row of houses in the square. It was transformed into the Renaissance style in 1566. The Rococo façade dates from 1778. The building was restored in 1978.

5 The School Building – today's Town Hall: House No. 16, it is a two-storeyed row house which was composed of three neighbouring houses; they were built originally in the Gothic style, then transformed into the Renaissance style; in mid-C19 they were connected up with each other. It housed administrative offices and later a school was opened here. A richly decorated Renaissance portal has been preserved on the façade. The town arms are to be

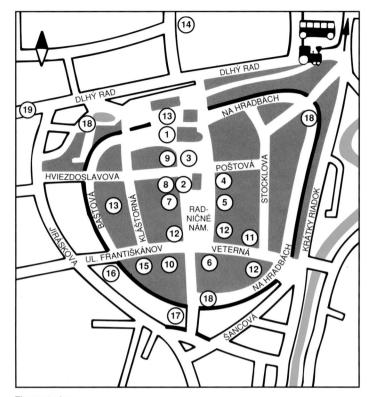

The town plan.

seen on the principal bay of the façade.

6 House No. 26: Originally built in the Gothic style on the southern side of the square, it features a preserved Gothic entrance portal. The building was remodelled to the Renaissance style and later into the Baroque style. The façade of the building is decorated with a figural painting with rocaille ornaments; it dates from 1760 – 1770.

7 House No. 40: Originally built in the Gothic-Renaissance style, this house features a medieval core which was renovated in the second half of C 16. The preserved architectural and artistic members are in the Gothic and Renaissance styles. There is a carved timber ceiling in the back pantry. The rooms on the ground floor have Renaissance vaults with stuccoed ridge ribs resting on ornamental brackets.

8 Weinhaus (No. 42): Originally a house built in Gothic style and located on a corner building-plot, the Weinhaus was transformed at the beginning of C16 into a two-storeyed, three-axial, two-wing building. Spacious cellars were used by the town for storing wine from the Tokay vineyards. The wine-tavern, which is mentioned in documents dating from 1433 – 1434, was located on the ground-floor. The idiom of the window jambs on the side façade relates artistically to the Renaissance windows of the Town Hall (from the workshop of Master Alexius).

9 The House No. 43: A corner house with a medieval core was remodelled in the first half of C17 and transformed into the Baroque style in the second half of C18. The preserved classical façade is from the first half of C19.

The Archives Bastion.

10 The Šariš Museum, Rhódy Street (No.1): A corner building originally built in the Gothic style; the projecting arcade was added in the Renaissance. The building has quadrattura decoration on its corners.

11 The Hangman's House, Veterná Street (No. 10): This building is located in former Temničná (Prison) Street which connects the square with the Hrubá Bastion. A coat of arms is located above the portal. On the first floor peculiar windows of the grain storerooms have been preserved, nowadays they are almost impossible to be found in Bardejov. This house standing near the town's prison was rented to the town's hangman.

12 Town Houses: Most of the houses in the square or in the side streets leading to the square are original, dating from the Middle Ages – from the second half of C14 up to C16. They are two-wing houses with passageways and they also feature an entrance portal and a typical entrance to cellars. Many of them have retained architectural elements of the Middle Ages (vaulted ceilings, portals, etc.).

The Šariš Museum, Rhódy Street. A corner building originally built in the Gothic style; the projecting arcade was added in the Renaissance.

During CC16 – 18 the houses were remodelled several times according to the needs and style of the period, including the renovations of the façades. Profound changes occurred when the houses were roofed afresh after the fires in 1878 and 1902 and when the design of the roofs of all the houses was altered. Since the 1970s the roofs of the houses have been returned into their original period appearance.

13 The Former Humanist Gymnasium: In the Middle Ages a school was attached to the parish church. Its existence is documented by a notice about a teacher, which dates from 1435 as well as by the date which was discovered on the first floor on the south façade of the Gymnasium "ERECTA ANNO 1508." Later the building was remodelled into the Renaissance style. Up to now well-preserved Renaissance details include a cornice inscribed "ANNO DOMINI 1612" and municipal arms cut in stone. In 1841 and 1879, the building was transformed into the classical style. A music school named after the Bardejov composer Vojtech Keller is now housed there.

14 The Evangelical (Lutheran – Augsburg Confession) Church: This church was built in the classical style in 1798 – 1808 after the letters patent on religious tolerance was passed. The interior furnishings are neo-Gothic of the second half of C19. The building has an elongated ground-plan with a semicircular apse; the nave features flat vaulted ceiling.

15 Franciscan Monastery and Church of St. John the Baptist: Originally constructed in the Gothic style after 1460, during the Renaissance renovation in the second half of C17 the sanctuary was vaulted. At the same time, the portion of the monastic complex which was connected up with the town walls was built. In 1759 the church was enlarged as well as the monastery. Other renovations were carried out in CC19 and 20. The interior furnishings, including altars, the organ, the pulpit, etc. date from the second half of C19. The liturgical ornaments date back to CC17, 18 and 19. In the monastery a Renaissance cloister, then vaults on the first floor as well as a portal and a window have been preserved.

16 The Graeco-Catholic Church: This edifice in the Eclectic style with neo-Romanesque details on the façade was built on the site of the former castle moat in 1901 – 1902.

17 The Lamp Column: This medieval column is to be found in the garden of the old hospital. Originally it was situated in the cemetery in front of the Upper Gatehouse; according to a Register of Verdicts, it is the very site where people condemned to death were beheaded.

18 The Town Fortifications: The fortification system is among the most elaborate and best-preserved medieval fortifications in Slovakia. Because of its significance, the system is enlisted in the European Fund of Cultural Heritage. Three essential stages in the construction of the fortifications stand out. In order to enhance security of the market village, King Louis I's warrant to erect the curtain walls was passed at about mid-C14. At the end of the third quarter of C14, the town appeared within stone walls with three main gatehouses on the west, the Lower Gatehouse on the northeast, and a postern for pedestrians, punctured in the middle of the northern wall. Several rectangular bastions fortified the walls, and an outer moat surrounded them.

During the second construction stage (during C15), the fortifications were rebuilt and reinforced, so that the defence spread along the curtain wall which was added a stone parapet. Another line of the walls, the widened moat, and the ramparts increased the security of the town. Stone outworks – barbicans – with drawbridges were built in front of the entrance gatehouses. The fortification system was also strengthened by semicircular or horseshoe-shaped bastions. The so-called Hrubá (Thick) Bastion, located on the eastern side of the town walls, was the largest. Bastions built in the fabric of fortifications are as follows:

Bardejovské kúpele – the bathhose Astória.

the Prašná (Powder), Veľká (Big), Červená (Red), Pravouhlá (Rectangular), Archívna (Record Office), Školská (School), and Kláštorná (Monastic) Bastions.

The next stage in the construction of the town walls was performed in the first half of C16. Huge, circular jutting out barbicans were built. Together with the gatehouses, they created an effective defensive system. In C17 an armoury was built near the Hrubá Bastion.

From C18 onwards, the importance of the town fortification system decreased; the Bardejov fortifications started decaying, but were not demolished as happened in other towns. Since the 1950s gradual repairs and reconstruction works of the walls have been in progress.

The town fortifications, including the gates and bastions, were systematically restored. The „Thick" Bastion, the most massive of them all, was restored in the years 1953 – 1957, the „Large" Bastion in 1956 – 1960. One portion of the former moat is now used as garden plots, another is built up with houses, and on the west side where the moat was filled in, a school was constructed.

19 The Former Jewish Complex: A synagogue, baths, residential houses, and a workshop built by the Jews were located in Mlynská (Mill) Street (Nos. 6 and 7), west of the fortified part of the town. This complex creating a suburb has survived of the whole area organized according to the rules of the Talmud; it dates from the end of C18. A large synagogue from the first half of C18 is the dominant of the complex. It consisted of a ritual bath, an expansion tower with a boiler room, a slaughterhouse, and an assembly house. The preserved Jewish suburb is a most-notable urban architectural unit in whole eastern Slovakia. A well-preserved cemetery with sandstone tombstones also belongs to this complex.

Bardejov had already been a very well-developed medieval town by C14. Yet, at that time the town did not possess any arms; it used a seal as a means of attesting its documents. The Bardejov seal bore an engraving of St. Aegidius, the patron saint of the parish church. The town started using arms only in C15. Being a border town, it devised the heraldic design in relation to this fact. It adopted a medieval weapon – the halberd (an ax-like blade and a spike mounted at right angles to the end of a long shaft), for its own heraldic symbol. Since the mid-C15, two crossed halberds have been the principal motif of the Bardejov arms. Ladislas V chartered them in 1453. The heraldic insignia on the shield are identical with those in the charter, which is to be seen in the enclosed illustration.

Besides well-preserved and valuable urban and architectural structures, the town was renown for the pottery by Master-Potter Frankovič, for the manufacturing of wicker baskets, fur coats, and blue-and-white print textile. Several famous scholars, educationalists, and scientists lived and worked in this picturesque town, e. g. C16 English educationalist L. Coxe, the art-historian and documentalist of the monuments of C19 V. Myskovszký, just to name a few.

When entering the town along the Bardejov – Prešov road visitors can walk through what has remained of the Upper Gatehouse, and continue their tour of the town. A visit to the church and the monastery of the Franciscans, then to the Šariš Museum situated in Rhódy Street as well as the former Town Hall may provide pleasant experiences. The best opportunity to get acquainted with the most valuable monuments of the town is to visit the parish church and have a walk along the square with delightful period burghers' houses. Not only in the centre but also in the side streets and other parts of town along the town walls there are many charming sights which enable visitors to enjoy the romantic character and the beauty of this unique historic town.

Bardejov has extraordinarily interesting and attractive surroundings. It is possible to spend several days at Bardejov Spa where the Museum of Šariš Folk Architecture is located. Zborov, 11 km distant, merits a visit as well, and so do the little wooden churches at Frička, Jedlinka, Lukov-Venécia, Hervartov, Kožany, and Tročany; all of them are located farther away from the town. The Bardejov forest park and the surrounding mountains offer various hiking opportunities both in summer and in winter.

Kežmarok

Names: L – Caesareoforum, Kesmarkinum, **G** – Käsmark, **H** – Késmárk
Latitude: 49° 07' N, **Longitude:** 20° 30' E
Elevation: average 625 m, **range:** 610 – 1226 m
Population: 17 500
Suburbs: Malý Slavkov
Means of Access: By rail: route No. 185; By road: routes No. 67 and 536
Accommodations: Club, Štart Hotels, Pension No. 1, Regent, Adria Hostel,
    bed-and-breakfast, cottages, Hostel ATC Karpaty
Information: City Information Center – tel: (++421)(0)968-4524047,
    e-mail: info.kk@kk.sinet.sk, \\www.kezmarok.sk, http:kezmarok.tripod.com

The ancient town of Kežmarok is located in the basin of the River Poprad in the northwest portion of eastern Slovakia. The promontories of the Levočské vrchy (Levoča Hills) reach the town from the east. The peaks of the High Tatras, which are 15 km away from Kežmarok to the northwest, are in range of view from the town.

The Spišská Magura mountain range separates the Poprad Basin from Poland. The town enjoys a moderately cold and humid climate with great temperature inversions. The average temperatures are of –3.5 °C to –6 °C in January and of 16 °C to 17 °C in July; the average annual rainfall is 650 – 850 mm. The Levoča Hills are rich in snow fall in winter.

Situated at a ford across the Poprad River and at a crossroads of the old long-distance trade routes from Poland by way of Levoča to the south, Kežmarok enjoyed good conditions for settlement as early as prehistoric times. Architectural finds including stone knives, scrapers, clay pottery shards, iron arrowheads, and small bronze items confirm that man occupied this territory more than 10,000 years ago.

Traces of other ancient settlements were found on Michal Hill, above the present-day train station. A row of massive stones lined up next to each other were still in place at the beginning of the C20. A cult of sun worshippers evidently met here for the summer and winter solstices.

The first written information about Kežmarok dates from 1251, where there is an unofficial reference to the year 1190 and a cloister for women which stood on the present site of the castle. And where there was a cloister, there was often a church and settlements. Archaeological research in the castle courtyard has confirmed the existence of St. Elizabeth's Church. Foundations of a large sacred building plus other buildings and a burial plot with over 250 skeletons were uncovered. The construction of the church has been dated to 1239 – 1251. Because the church's foundations and pillars were not typically symmetrical, it is presumed that it was built by the Saxons after their arrival using the foundations and walls of an older building on the site.

The manuscript dated from 1251 also mentions the church of St. Michal and the surrounding settlement. The city of Kežmarok was formed by the joining of four settlements. One was Slavonic and also included Hungarian residents who were employed to guard the border with Poland. This settlement was located in the vicinity of St. Michal. The German community was concentrated around

Kežmarok at the heat of watchmakers' guild charter. An etching by J. J. Lumnitzer, 1814.

St. Elizabeth's Church. Two more Slavonic settlements existed, one of which included the Church of the Holy Cross. Since these settlements were spread out, their safety could not be guaranteed and therefore they decided to join together. Thus the city was formed, and by 1368 it already had town walls with a moat surrounding it. There was not enough room inside the town walls for all the settlements, so only the Saxon settlement and one connected with the Church of the Holy Cross were located there. The oldest existing street, Starý Trh (Old Market) was a part of the latter one. Research confirmed that the oldest parts of the Church of the Holy Cross indeed date from the middle of the C13. During the C15, the town walls were reinforced with bastions, gates, and barbicans.

Kežmarok was granted its town charter in 1269. The Hungarian King Béla IV specified the town's rights as well as responsibilities, such as the payment of property tax. The town could elect a mayor, and had the right to hold weekly markets. The town's borders were set, and were the same as those of the Saxon settlement as mentioned in the manuscript dated 1251, and almost identical to those of present-day Kežmarok.

In 1380 Kežmarok became a Free Royal Town and in the next ten years was granted various privileges which were later acknowledged by ruler Zigmund of Luxembourg in 1435. In 1463, King Matthias Corvinus granted the city the right to use a coat of arms, as well as a red wax seal on documents. Kežmarok's coat of arms manuscript

is one of a kind in Slovakia; the coat of arms is positioned in the center of the manuscript, whereas in others it is located in the upper left corner.

These privileges brought Kežmarok success and economic growth which was disturbed by frequent conflicts between the rulers themselves, ruling aristocrats, or between the cities of Levoča and Kežmarok who fought for over 200 years with each other over the right to be able to warehouse goods. Another source of trouble was the war with the Hussites, who in 1433 crossed the border from Poland, surrounded the city, and occupied it for a short while. In that same year the Church of St. Michal, west of the city, was sacked and destroyed. The plague epidemic and frequent fires contributed their share of problems for Kežmarok as well. After the Hussites deserted the city, the citizens of Kežmarok repaired the town walls and in 1461 began to reconstruct the Church of the Holy Cross into a three-nave edifice and laid the cornerstone of the City Hall.

A castle was built at the north edge of the city in the C15, on the site of the older church and cloister. Additional construction took the form of the Gothic parish church which was built in the center of town. Next to it a Renaissance bell-tower was built, as was a high school.

The panorama of Kežmarok.

The castle became an important part of the life of the town from the architectural, urbanistic, economic, and social point of view. It is first mentioned in 1447, in reference to Jan Jiskra's army encampment in Kežmarok. The castle later became the property of the Zápoľský brothers who received it in repayment of a loan by King Matthias Corvinus. The present disposition of the castle is a result of the brothers' reconstruction work. The core of the castle, built on the site of the destroyed St. Elizabeth's Church, became a two-storey palace surrounded by fortified walls containing loopholes, bastions, and an entry gate with a draw-bridge. The water-filled moat encompassing the castle not only defined its own borders, but also a new relationship with the town. A different fate befell Kežmarok than did the other Spiš towns, because in spite of the rights and privileges it had received from the king in the past, the castle's owners became the actual rulers of the town. From 1462 this position was held by the Zápoľský family, from 1528 – 1571 the city was ruled by Polish aristocrat Laskovec, and from 1579 onwards the Thököly family was in power.

The city began to exert a great deal of effort to rid itself of the influence of these local rulers, starting in the middle of the C17. With the signing of the „Vienna" contract, the city finally bought their freedom from the Thököly family, who retained the castle, its landholdings, and 24 houses. The city was also obliged to pay a fee to the King's Chamber Court. When the Thököly family fell from power in 1687, the city took over the castle and the family's holdings.

In spite of its dependence on the local rulers, Kežmarok experienced a building boom in the C16 and C17. The city center filled in with Gothic and (later) Renaissance houses which exhibited special local architectural details, such as special portals, chamfered stone window frames, unique sill moldings, etc. A bell-tower and one-storey, block--like „humanistic" school were constructed in 1591 near the parish church. The school represented further development in the educational tradition begun in Kežmarok at the end of the C14. The new Renaissance style became evident with the completion of the castle renovations, especially as a result of the crenulated „attic" decoration on the fortified walls. This same decoration was repeated on the bell-tower and the tower of the church. Many new structures were built during the C18 on the outskirts of the city, thanks to the extremely healthy economy as a result of the brisk trade in wine, beer, salt, grain, fabric, hides, and related crafts. The Evangelical Church, made of logs, was built in 1717 in the form of a Greek cross, and the lyceum was constructed adjacent to it in 1775. A new cemetery was established south of the town center. The Pauline Order consecrated the Church of the Virgin Mary in 1747. This church is part of

The castle, CC15 – 17.

The courtyard of the castle.

The walls of the Gothic castle.

a row of houses on Hradná (castle) street where the city hall was reconstructed in the Baroque style. In 1818 the Reduta, or philharmonic hall was constructed, and it remains a dominant feature of the city to this day.

Any remaining free land within the confines of the town walls was built upon during the C19. By this time, the walls were in poor condition and lost the original purpose for their existence. On the site of the old market new apartment buildings were constructed. At the turn of the C20, several school buildings were added adjacent to the north and south boundaries of the historical center. A new Evangelical Church was constructed in 1892 in the neo-Byzantine style, adjacent to the Lyceum. On the west side of the city and on the site of the ancient settlement of St. Michal, a monumental Art Nouveau railroad building was erected. In its vicinity, prosperous flax factories

were founded in the 1860s, building on centuries old craft tradition.

No less important for Kežmarok was the development of tourism, recreation and the spa industry in the High Tatras for both the domestic and foreign markets. The first half of the C20 saw a surge of residential architecture contribute to the further development of the city. On the edge of the historic center and in place of the former town walls, especially on the south and north sides, gardens and family houses began to appear. In the second half of the C20, development again quickened its pace, with the construction of whole neighborhoods of concrete-panel apartment houses, industrial and administrative buildings, schools, health and shopping facilities.

Kežmarok has retained its historic character, as evidenced by the preserved street plan from centuries past. Many historic burgers' houses retain their original plans including the enclosed, vaulted carriage passages. These homes characteristically have three-bay facades, and are of two or three

Reduta.

The Town Hall; originally Gothic, later classical.

A town house.

storeys in height with long wings parallel to the rear courtyards.

The long tradition of historic crafts production has been revived since 1991 with the international craft fair entitled „European Folk Crafts" which takes place on a yearly basis.

The preserved urbanistic and architectural structure of the city with dominant buildings like the churches, burger's houses, schools, castle and other public buildings was a deciding factor in the registration of Kežmarok as an Urban Preservation Area in 1950.

Town houses in the square.

Craftsmen's houses.

1 The Castle: One of the most impressive monuments of the town, it was built on the ruins of a Late Romanesque settlement and on the site of the church dedicated to Saint Elizabeth (referred to in a document from 1251). Belonging to the category of so-called „town castles" built directly in the town for defense purposes, this original Gothic fortress was constructed up against the town walls which in effect serve as its entire northern (and oldest) wall. The castle was first written about in 1463, and two years later it was ready for occupancy. Over the years and with further construction phases, the number of towers and living spaces increased, one of which is a two-storey palace attached to the town walls. On the north side of the walls a polygonal bastion was built, later to be reconstructed as a chapel. Further fortification works at the castle included a second outer wall with loopholes, a water moat, and a drawbridge.

The Renaissance construction works can be divided into three phases. The first two took place under the ownership of J. Reuber in 1572, and again in 1575 in the aftermath of a fire. The third phase was in 1583 when the Thököly family was the owner.

Renaissance arcades were added to the buildings in the courtyard and the castle wall was topped off with a crenulated parapet, in fashion at that time. A four-sided residential tower built in the manner of a bastion was connected to the south

The Renaissance bell-tower, from 1586 – 1591, next to the Gothic parish church, C15.

side of the castle. An existing well in the courtyard was deepened. Gradually, the utilization of the castle changed from its original protective function to one which was more of a representative nature.

An Early Baroque reconstruction took place in the first half of the C17, and the changes were focused on making the castle more comfortable. This fact is reflected by the exterior and interior sgraffito decoration of the walls and rich plaster decoration on the vaulted ceilings.

The most valuable part of the castle is the chapel, built in 1657 – 1658. The rich plaster decoration of

its lunette vaults is assumed to be the work of Italian artists who were commissioned to execute the work by Thököly in 1657. The rare furnishings of the chapel help create the image of just how high were the standards of the interiors of Thököly's residence.

Fires in 1741 and 1787 were the impetus for major changes in the castle's floor plans, especially after the second one which caused the collapse of a sizable portion of the building. In the C19 the castle began to be used for a variety of activities, including use as an army barracks, craft workshops, an embroidery factory, and even a hospital. By the end of the C19 the idea of making the castle into a museum was being discussed. The idea became reality in 1928 – 1931. And in 1962 – 1985 a general restoration of the castle complex took place, making the necessary adaptations for the needs of the local museum.

Today the museum presents the story of the city's development from earliest times up until the present. Expositions feature: archaeology; development of local self-government, guilds, and crafts; arms and associations related to the use of arms; history of medicine and pharmacy; education and culture; a gallery of paintings, etc. Of special interest is the exposition dealing with the relationship of the city to the High Tatra Mountains; people from Kežmarok were pioneers in exploring and mapping the Tatras.

2 The Wooden „Articular" Evangelical (Lutheran) Church: This sacred building was listed as a National Cultural Monument in 1985. On the basis of Articles 25 and 26 of the Šopron Parliament in 1681, Emperor Leopold I confirmed religious freedom for Protestants and at the same time allowed the building of churches, parsonages, and schools. Churches built according to these Articles were therefore known as „articular" churches. The publication of this decree did not mean that it was possible to build immediately, but at the same time, the demand to hold worship services was great. First, the king's commissars had to mark the precise location of each future church and set conditions for the building process. This is the reason that many churches were at first temporary, and then later were replaced with newer and bigger versions. After building these small, temporary churches, church members turned to their brothers in the northern Protestant countries such as Denmark, Sweden, Saxony, Prussia, Latvia, Estonia, and Lithuania to raise money for their newer churches. Both the Danish ruler Christian V and Swedish King Charles XI personally signed decrees allowing collections to be taken in their respective countries for financing the church in Kežmarok.

The first Protestant church in Kežmarok was built in 1687 – 1688 and in its place a new wooden church with the floor plan of a Greek cross was erected in 1717, according to the design of the Nooder Kerk log church in Amsterdam. The church was built to seat 4000 people. The cross-vaulted ceiling is supported in the center of the church by four turned columns. During the building of the church in 1717 the only part used from the older building was the stone portion of the sacristy dating from 1593 which originally served as a pub and later as a school. The builder, J. Mütterman of Poprad, used wood from yew and red spruce trees to construct the church. The beautiful interior can be termed as „folk Baroque" and includes paintings which originate from the turn of the C18. When the new church was completed in 1894, the regular use of this church was discontinued. The balcony parapets are decorated with paintings from the Old and New Testaments. The vaulted ceiling features paintings of the Four Evangelists and the Twelve Apostles. The wooden polychromed altar from 1718-1727 and the pulpit dating from the year 1717 were fashioned by the Kežmarok woodcarver Ján Lerch and his apprentices. The stone baptismal font with its copper cover dates from 1690 and was one of the furnishings of the first church.

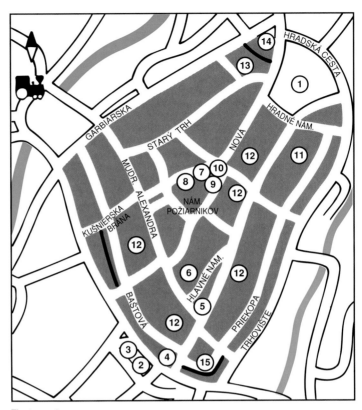

The town plan.

There are six choir lofts, one each for girls, boys, apprentices, the cantors, and two for singers. They are decorated with paintings and wood-carving. The organ was completed in 1720 by Levoča organ builder Vavrinec Čajkovský and supplemental work was finished in 1729 by Martin Korabinský. Liturgical items originate from the C17 and C18. This church served the Protestant population in the city until the end of the C19 when money was raised for a new building. At present, the wooden church is undergoing a complex restoration.

3 The Evangelical Lycée:
A National Cultural Monument; this building is located close to the wooden church. This original edifice was also made of timber wood. In 1775 construction of a one storey building begun, and in 1820 it was enlarged. After the reconstruction, there was a room for the school library and the school collections. In 1865 it was raised by another floor; in 1892 a new school was built nearby. The Kežmarok school became famous and also many outstanding professors lectured there. After 1777 the academic standard was increased as departments of philosophy, theology, and law were established here; therefore, the school could be transformed into a lycée. After 1852 the lycée was reorganized and an eight-year Gymnasium came into existence. The multi-national structure of Hungary was also mirrored in the life of the Gymnasium. Students of different nationalities studied there German, Slovak, Serbian and Hungarian fraternities. The Union of Slovak Youth was founded there as well,

The Lyceum possesses a valuable library containing approximately

The interior of the church of the Holy Cross, Late-Gothic. The high altar dates from the beginning of C16.

150,000 volumes, including 55 incunabula (books printed before 1500) and 3000 books dating from the C16.

Two painted Latin inscriptions (which include a chronogram) and several memorial plaques grace the exterior of the Lyceum building.

4 The New Evangelical (Lutheran) Church: Built according to the design of Vienna architect Theofil von Hansen, the church was constructed in the decorative neo--Byzantine style in 1894. Reminiscent of a mosque or synagogue, the interior is an example of strict symmetry. The original plans for the second tower were evocative of a minaret, but it was not built for a lack of finances. The 1000th anniversary of the arrival of the Hungarians in the Carpathian basin was celebrated in 1906. In honor of

this occasion, the remains of Prince Imrich Thököly were placed in the church. Thököly was born in Kežmarok and was a lieutenant in the uprising against the Emperor during 1678 to 1684. He died in exile in Turkey. In 1909 a mausoleum was added to the church, where his sarcophagus is located to this day.

5 Town Hall: The first Town Hall, Gothic in style, was built in 1461 but was destroyed by fire in 1515. A new Renaissance style building was constructed on the same site in 1541 – 1555, featuring a low crenulated parapet at roof level and a grand entrance portal. A tower was added in 1641, and after a second fire ravaged the building and tower, they were remodeled anew, this time in the spirit of Classicism. It was probably at this time that the allegorical fresco

entitled „Justice" was added to the south facade, a copy of which is preserved in a painting in the local museum. The last major changes in the three-storey town hall took place after yet another fire in 1922. A portion of the Late Gothic window on the south facade has been preserved as well as the original Renaissance portal crowned with a coat of arms; on the east side it is possible to see portions of Gothic and Renaissance windows.

Decorated with a painting of the city coat of arms, the Latin inscription states that the building served for guests, entertainment and sentinels (at one time a watch-tower stood on this site). The print-shop of Matthias Glaser was located here in 1705 – 1708, printing books in Biblical Czech, German, Latin, and Hungarian.

6 The Town Reduta: This two--storeyed monumental building was built in the classical style in 1818. The protruding bay features arcades on the ground-floor and pilasters with composite capitals suporting a triangular tympanum.

7 The Church of the Holy Cross: A Roman Catholic church which is a good example of the typical Spiš hall-cathedral, it was built in the Late Gothic style in 1444 – 1498 under the patronage of the Zapolya House. It is located on the site of a former chapel, later a church, which was destroyed by a fire in 1443. After the fire in 1521, the stone gallery was built on the tower. When a belfry had been built, its height was adjusted to be equal with the tip of the church tower. Late Gothic reticulated vaulting is featured in the aisled nave. The rear of the nave contains a Gothic arcaded choir from the end of the C 15.

The priceless furnishings in the church interior are from the Gothic and Renaissance periods. The main altar of the Holy Cross dates from around 1500. The Stations of the Cross sculptures were created in the workshop of Master Pavol of Levoča. The figures of Mary Magdalene, Mary and John are good examples of the Baroque style. The other altars are also worth mention: the Saint Catherine altar is dated back to 1493; the altar of the Apostles and that of Our Savior date from the years 1470 – 1480. The free--standing sculpture of the Madonna dates from the beginning of the C16. Scenes from the Crucifixion, St. Peter and Paul, symbols of the Evangelists, and the coat of arms of Kežmarok decorate the copper baptismal font (1472). The Gothic „stallae" or stalls (one with five seats from 1469 and the other with three) as well as others which are of Renaissance style (dating from 1518) are a rarity. The front parapets of these stalls are decorated with paintings of musicians.

8 The Renaissance Bell-Tower: Standing within the fences of the parish church, built in 1586 – 1591, this massive rectangular building with a decorative gable is a typical Spiš-style bell-tower. It was erected by the local master builder U. Materer, and decorated with sgraffito by an author whose initials are H. B.

9 The Humanistic Protestant School: A block-like building constructed in the Renaissance style in 1536, it is located next to the parish church on the site of a former wooden structure. It leans against the town wall. The municipality coat of arms is located on the facade above the entrance.

10 The Rectory: Dating from the second half of the C15, it became the residence of the Pauline Order in the C18, which enlarged the building. After the order was disbanded, it became the office of the Roman-Catholic parish in 1782.

11 The Church of the Virgin Mary: This Roman-Catholic, former Paulist, church was built in a row of buildings in Hradná (Castle) Street in 1747 on the site of the former Slovak Evangelical Church. This church was built by Paulists who came to the town in 1670. The one--nave church contains a straight ended presbytery with flat vaulted

The altar and the pulpit of the Evangelical Lutheran – Augsburg Confession church; the Early-Baroque interior, from the beginning of C18.

ceilings. The remarkable church interior contains many wood-carvings in the Baroque style, which are ascribed to the workshop of the wood-carver Master Engelholm.

12 Burghers' Houses: In principal streets they were built on elogated Gothic building plots as houses with a passageway and a narrow entry hall in the middle of the house or on its side. The facades show neo--Gothic or neo-Renaissance elements predominantly from the CC18 and 19, until the beginning of the C20.

13 Craftsmens' Houses at Starý Trh (the Old Market): A complex of one-storey buildings constructed with Spiš-style gable roofs covered in wood shingles, these homes feature vaulted carriage passages and wood beamed ceilings in the rooms. The residential portion

includes one room, a „black" kitchen and a pantry for storage.

Most of the houses were built in the C17 in the Late Renaissance and Early Baroque styles. The upper floors were, in this territory, used as granaries. Later they were transformed to living quarters. Even today it is possible to find some examples of facades with openings – original granary windows – on the first or second floors of the front facade.

14 Craftsmens' Houses: Recently replaced by a housing estate, these buildings originally had steep shingle roofs and stood side by side in Garbiarska (Tonners') Street.

15 The Town Walls: The first written reference to the town walls in the context with St. Elizabeth's is from 1348. The next one dates back to 1404, when King Sigismund of Luxemburg granted Kežmarok a dispence, so that it could reconstruct the damaged town walls. It is certain that the walls encircled the town completely at the end of the C14. They were high and built of stone, and the upper part contained loopholes accessible by a stone gallery from the side facing the town. Outside the walls there was a moat filled in with water from the Poprad River and the Ľubica brook. The entrance to the town was heavily guarded by three main gatehouses: the Upper Gatehouse on the road to Levoča; the Lower Gatehouse on the road to Galicia; the Kušnier Gatehouse (later also referred to as the Hussite Gatehouse). The gatehouses were rectangular, multi-storeyed blocks with a passageway. They were also defended with rectangular bastions.

After the arrival of the Hussite troops in 1433 and until the first third of the C16, the efforts of the burghers focused on improving the fortification system of the town. The gatehouses were defended with outworks and circular barbicans. The original number of the bastions was increased by the construction of the new semi-circular bastions.

A new gate dating from the first half of the C17 was created from an existing polygonal bastion. Few parts of the original town fortifications have been preserved: a part of the circular barbican of the Lower Gate near the castle; the semi-circular bastion to the west; and the rectangular three-floor bastion east of the former Upper Gate. This last bastion was repaired in 1971 – 1972 and now serves as the museum depository. The third bastion in the south-east portion of the town, not far from the former Kušnier Gate, and represents the oldest type of L-shaped bastion.

The arms of Kežmarok are very similar to Bardejov's arms. Both of them originated in C15 and were granted through letters patent. Since the Kežmarok arms were chartered by Matthias Corvinus only in 1463, that is 10 years later than the Bardejov arms, they seem to have been designed according to them. Yet the written sources discovered up to now have yielded information that the Bardejov arms were modelled after those of Kežmarok. The charges of the Bardejov arms did not alter, after they had been chartered in 1453, but the charges of the Kežmarok arms were established still in 1446.

Among the celebrities of the town there were outstanding professors of the lycée: J. Chalupka and K. Kuzmány, and former students M. Šulek, G. Fejérpataky-Belopotocký, P. J. Šafárik, S. Chalupka, D. Lichard, C. Zoch, A. H. Škultéty, J. Kráľ, J. Záborský, P. Bohúň, P. Országh-Hviezdoslav, L. Nádaši-Jége, M. Kukučín, P. Dobšinský, J. Jesenský, M. Rázus, I. Stodola, and others.

The town offers several opportunities for walks. All of them will start from the monuments of the past: the castle, the church, and the National Cultural Monuments – the Evangelical wooden church and the Lycée. Walking along the main streets of the town, visitors will reach Baštová (Bastion) Street and the Moat, where parts of the town fortifications have been preserved.

The above mentioned dignified sights of the town are the most characteristic ones; however, a visit to the museum or a trip to the surroundings, especially to the area of Jerusalem Hill, is attractive. Winter holiday-makers will appreciate good skiing conditions here. The swimming pool is an additional attraction as well as hikes to the surrounding mountains. The ambitious climbers head mostly for the High Tatras, whose shields are an irresistible objective and challenge for them.

Košice

Names: L – Cassovia, **G** – Kaschau, **H** – Kassa
Latitude: 48° 45' N, **Longitude:** 21° 15' E
Elevation: average 211 m, **range:** 193 – 850 m
Population: 241 000
Suburbs: Barca, Dargovských hrdinov, Džungla, Juh, Kavečany, Košická Nová Ves,
    Krásna nad Hornádom, Lorinčík, Luník IX, Myslava, Nad jazerom, Pereš, Poľov,
    Sever, Sídlisko KVP, Sídlisko Ťahanovce, Staré Mesto, Šaca, Šebestovce,
    Vyšné Opátske, Západ
Means of Access: By rail: routes No. 180, 169, 188, 190; By road: routes No. D1 =
    E 50 = 68, E 571 = 50, 547 and 552.
Accommodations: Hotels: Bankov, Centrum, Club VSŽ, Coral, Hutník, Imperiál,
    Slovan, U leva, Viktória Caffé; Pensions: Rozália, Pri Radnici, Dom na Šambore;
    Hostel ATC Barca, CHO Flam Hostel, Hostel Metropol, dormitories
Information: City Information Center – tel: (++421)(0)65-16186, fax: 095-6230909,
    e-mail: mic@napri.sk, www.pangea.sk

The second largest city in Slovakia is situated in the valley of the River Hornád and the Košická kotlina (Košice Hollow), at the foot of the Čierna hora Mountains in the north and the Slovak Ore Mountains and the Volovské vrchy hills in the west. From the east the Košice Hollow is bordered by the Slánske vrchy hills. To the southwest near the Hungarian border, the well-known Slovenský Karst Hills are situated.

Košice has a warm, rather dry climate typical of hollows; the average January temperatures range from –2 °C to –4 °C; average July temperatures range from 18.5 °C to 20 °C; the average annual precipitation is 600 – 700 mm. The northwestern areas at the foothills of the Slovak Ore Mountains have a warm mountain climate.

The advantageous position of the city on the crossroads of the old long-distance trade routes was the decisive factor for the development of this place of habitation on fertile soil of the river-terrace near the juncture of the Hornád and Torysa Rivers. The area has been settled continuously since the Paleolithic; an Aurignacian camp site, the earliest one known to have existed in Central Europe, was excavated at Barca near Košice.

The presence of a Slavonic community settled here in CC8 – 9 was confirmed by study of the fortified settlement site at Breh in the area of Krásna nad Hornádom. Another presumed settlement site of this type is at Hradová, where a castle was built later to control the important crossroads of the trade routes.

At the end of C11, the building of a Benedictine abbey as a centre for spreading culture was begun at this site, at Krásna nad Hornádom; it was consecrated in 1143. Another fortified site, the above-mentioned Castle of Hradová, was built in the first half of C13. Several settlements arose along the road in the river valley between these two points, which may be considered as the origins of the later town. According to existing data, by 1216 another monastery had already stood at the site of present-day Košice; the settlement itself was mentioned in 1230. It was situated at the site of Slovenská Street; the first parish church in the area was built there too. This place of habitation expanded rapidly after the arrival of German colonists; its layout followed the settlement pattern provided by other towns which had already been settled by the native folk. The German incomers appeared immediately after the Tartar invasion as new inhabitants; they founded their new homes next to the existing settlement.

Before 1249 they were granted the first privileges. Owing to them and to the advantageous situation of the settlement, it developed relatively rapidly into

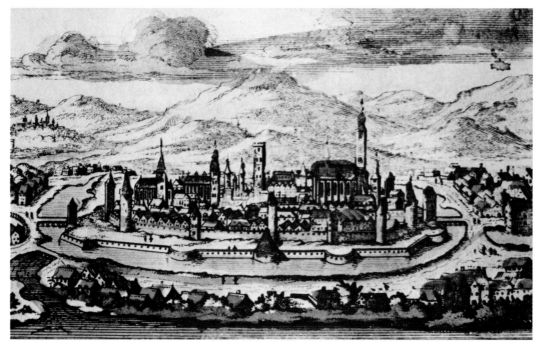

A coloured copper engraving by T. Danckerts, from 1700.

a town. The Saxons who settled in Košice achieved religious self-government very early, and in 1290 they were exempted from the jurisdiction of the archdeacon. Already by that time, the original, one-nave church of St. Elizabeth (1260 – 1280) stood in the middle of the spindle-shaped square (a typical shape for eastern-Slovakia towns). The town protective walls had been built partially by that time, as well as the Royal House and the hospital. The oldest building preserved from that period is the Early-Gothic Dominican church with remnants of the monastery located near the line of the western town walls. The presence of this religious order testified to the definite urban character of Košice at that time.

By the end of C13 markets were held in the town, which emerged as an important centre for the barter of imported goods from Prussia, the towns of the Hanseatic League in Germany, and Cracow, Poland.

At the beginning of C14 burghers of Košice showed extraordinary resolution and courage. They fearlessly rebelled against very cruel Palatine Omodej, to whom the town was donated by King Charles Robert of Anjou in 1304. Not being able to find any other possibility to get themselves rid of their feudal oppressor, they murdered him in 1311. Košice won the ensuing lawsuit with Omodej's descendents. After this event, the Omodejs joined

the opposition against King Charles Robert. The burghers of Košice played an important role in the King's victory in the decisive battle against them near Rozhanovce on 15th June 1312. Their participation in this victorious battle won Košice the charter of a Free Royal Town in 1342, and strengthened its economic and military power. Rapid development and urbanization of the town followed. At that time a major part of the forests in the vicinity were changed into vineyards, and grape-growing became one of the main occupations of the local inhabitants. Mutual cooperation treaty with Cracow was signed in 1324 as the first of this kind; it contributed largely to the steadily expanding volume of long-distance trade along the route from southeastern Hungary to the Scandinavian countries by way of Košice. These treaties document its important position in international commerce at that time. Another opportunity to improve its position was the right of storage granted in 1361. By mid-C14 Košice had only one rival in the Hungarian kingdom – the principal centre of the state and the residence of the monarch – Buda. The kings favoured Košice and paid the city frequent visits and stays. The imposing appearance of Gothic Košice was equal to its importance.

The elongated large square, orientated to the north, was bordered by ostentatiously ornamented

The square and the Cathedral of St. Elizabeth.

houses of the wealthy patricians, including
the Royal House and the so-called Levoča House.
The Town Hall stood originally in the square. The
monumental Franciscan church and monastery were
built near the northern town walls. The Gothic
cathedral of St. Elizabeth began to be constructed
on the site of an older church in about 1380. This
cathedral was of great importance to Hungarian
medieval architecture. The lodge, the masons'
workshop, set up when the cathedral was being
built, exerted great influence upon building
activity in a vast area. The master masons were
commissioned to work on various buildings,
including those at the royal court. Next to the
cathedral a detached bell-tower and a charnel-house
of St. Michael were built. By that time the town
had already more than 4,000 inhabitants, and was
protected by a ring of stout town walls.

In the second half of C14 the town expanded
behind the lines of town walls. In 1397 Košice
became a feudal authority to nineteen towns
and villages and it acquired the dominant position
in the association of eastern-Slovakia towns
– Pentapolitana. Košice was of great strategic
importance to the defence of the northeast
territories of Hungary; the strong town walls
were believed to be impregnable; therefore, the
sovereigns often committed there for protection not
only their valuables and archives but also their

The square, the western portion with town houses.

wives and children. Košice was also the seat of the
commander-in-chief of the eastern Slovakia towns'
armed forces and the captain of Košice's garrison.

In 1419 the town possessed a monopoly of
producing fustian; therefore, all manufacturers
of this cloth in Hungary had to move to Košice.
Ten years later Košice gained also a monopoly
of bleaching flax linen, which was shared with
Bardejov.

During the turbulent years of the struggle for the
Hungarian throne, Košice played an important role.

At the end of the first half of C15, under the leadership of Jan Jiskra of Brandýs (who was an *ispán,* an administrator of Šariš County, having its centre in Košice) expeditions were undertaken against the Poles and Hungarians. Loans for these expeditions flowed out of Košice's municipal treasury. All of the "Estates of the Tisza Region" submitted to Jiskra at the Diet of Seňa in 1445; Ján Talafús became a captain of Košice. The Hussites retained their power over the town also after the peace had been signed with János Hunyadi in 1450; they lost it only after their defeat at Šarišský Potok.

Patricians of the town originated of the merchant class at that period. Crafts and agricultural production had little significance apart from viticulture. The mass migration of people – especially Hungarian aristocracy – from the southern territories of the kingdom occupied by the Turks resulted in the enormous concentration of population within the town walls; the number reached 7000. At the time when Buda was seized and occupied by the Turks, Košice became the capital of the Hungarian kingdom for some time.

In mid-C16 a great fire destroyed almost the whole town; it damaged St. Elizabeth's as well as the town walls. Owing to the support of the royal court a new Renaissance town arose on the ruins of the old one. During the reconstruction works, the free grounds, which had remained on the building plots, especially behind the houses, were built up with additional buildings with the purpose to house the rising population.

The significance of Košice for the revitalization of the Hungarian kingdom in the east and southeast was also reflected in the gradual modernization of the fortifications. In CC16 – 17 the town became an almost impregnable fortress with three lines of walls and a moat. During the reign of King Leopold I, a star-shaped citadel was built in front of the southern gate; at present it may be seen only in early engravings of the town.

Košice did not escape the religious wars during Reformation and Counter-Reformation. The churches, including the cathedral of St. Elizabeth, changed hands several times. The religious unrest, the pressure of the Turkish armies, the rebellions of the Hungarian Estates as well as the loss of leadership of south-north commerce after the shift of world trade centres westwards caused a slump in both commerce and craft production in Košice and consequently in other eastern-Slovakia towns, too. After the Turkish victory, the population in that part of the town encircled by walls dropped by one third comparing to the totals in 1480. The number of houses was less than four hundred. The erstwhile second largest city in the Hungarian kingdom was stagnating.

The square, the eastern portion.

A town house in the Hlavná (High) Street.

Due to the efforts of Benedict Kischdy, the Hungarian Bishop of Eger, the Jesuitical University was estabilished in Košice in 1657, comprising the philosophical, theological, and linguistic faculties. King Leopold I issued the Golden Bule in 1660 to promote the university and make it equal to other European universities. As a part of the university a printing house was established. The University was changed into a Royal Academy in 1776, and later only the Faculty of Law had the character of a college. The Jesuitical University Church was built in 1671 – 1684 for needs of the University.

The appearance of the town was altered in C18, when a new building programme was embarked on: the suburbs were being founded as the town walls were gradually dismantled. The older palaces and monasteries were redesigned to the new Baroque and later the classical styles.

At the turn of C19 the economy revived. Manufacturer producing English porcelain, hats, and cloth appeared in the town. The population was constantly rising, especially owing to the influx of people from the villages.

The former Jesuit church, from 1671 – 1684.

Late-Renaissance Levoča House in the Hlavná (High) Street (No. 65) refaced to the Romantique style.

The theatre (1897-1899) and the „singing fountain", built in the center of the square.

At the beginning of C19 a bishopric was estabilished in Košice; the parish church of St. Elizabeth became a cathedral church in 1804.

Revival of the economy of the town was manifested in the town's architecture. The "reduta" – a ballroom, theatre, large burghers' and patrician houses, ornate aristocratic palaces, the Evangelical church, and a number of large barracks were built.

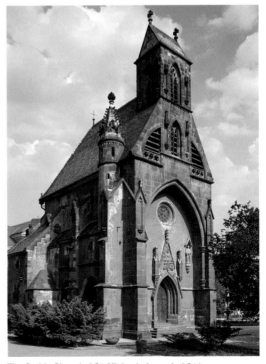

The Gothic Chapel of St. Michael; the end of C14.

Gothic St. Urbain's Tower, C15, later modified.

Mikluš Prison, consisting of two Late-Gothic town houses from C15.

The arrival of the railway, which connected Košice to Miskolcz and Budapest in 1860, and to Bohumín in 1870, provided a new mighty impulse for the economic boom of the town. Also, the construction of the railway station east of the town centre was finished in that year. On the site between the railway station and the city a large park was planted and a new street network was developed. The process of urbanization of the town was influenced by the traffic patterns of Vienna and Budapest, creating a system of circular avenues which occupied the place of demolished town walls. With the construction of new rental houses, Košice attained a metropolitan character. The river terraces westwards above the city were built up with rustic country houses grouped around small squares. The synagogue was built amidst a row of houses situated along a southern axis next to the city in the year 1866; 20 years later a Graeco-Catholic church was built in Cyrilometodská Street.

The inhabitants of Košice built a new theatre and rebuilt the cathedral of St. Elizabeth to the neo-Gothic style. At the beginning of C20 the Art Nouveau style appeared; it was applied to create romanticizing and historicizing façades. A system of suburbs, known as "glacis," was developed in C19. In 1912 the Art Nouveau City Hall was built as focal point at the end of a boulevard running parallel with the old High Street. Košice became a significant administrative, cultural and educational centre of eastern Slovakia before mid-C20.

Large blocks were constructed, new buildings of banks, post offices, the radio-broadcasting station, blocks of flats in Stará Bešeňová, and schools as well as a modern sacral building of the Roman Catholic church of the Queen of Peace. At this time the first negative interferences into the urban structure of the city appeared – new Baťa's shoe-store.

Large pre-fabricated blocks of flats built around the town centre were an answer to the rapid industrial development and the rising population in the 1960s – 1970s. Many of the big, bulky solitary buildings set directly into the centre of rows of historic houses interfered with the urban structure of the city. In general, in spite of them, Košice has preserved the historic atmosphere of Hlavná (High) Street and the circular avenues intact as well as the intimacy of the narrow lanes situated next to the former city walls.

The most significant historic, architectural, and art-historical structures of the town are situated in the centre of the large, spindle-shaped square.

The declaration of the historic centre of the town an Urban Preservation Area in 1981 was a result of the effort to save the historic environment of Košice.

The Cathedral of St. Elizabeth, Gothic, in CC14 – 15.

The Cathedral of St. Elizabeth, the interior.

The Cathedral of St. Elizabeth, the high altar.

The Cathedral of St. Elizabeth, the southern portal.

The Cathedral of St. Elizabeth, the interior.

1 The Complex of the Cathedral of St. Elizabeth:

A National Cultural Monument, it consists of the cathedral, the chapel of St. Michael, and St. Urbain Tower. The cathedral was built at the end of C14 on the site of an older building. Originally, the design was drawn for a five-nave basilica with polygonal apses and a two-tower western façade, after the church of St. Victor in Xanten on the Rhine. The mason's lodge was led by a Peter until 1420; by that time the church was erected up to the level of the main cornice. In fact, the new construction was built around an older church, which was later demolished. Other masons' lodge built another portion of the church, producing a transept which created four equal in size spaces each of which contained star vaults. Using as a model the St. Vitus' in Prague, a one-storeyed addition with a royal tribune was constructed in the southern arm of the transept. In 1470 the chapel of the Holy Cross was built under the Master of the King's Works of Masonry Štefan (Stephen), and in 1477 the chapel of the Virgin Mary was finished. The southern tower was topped with a decorative wreath and the coats-of-arms of the Royal domains of King Matthias. The stone railing around the organ balcony, removed during the restoration in 1880 and sold to Kreuzenstein, Austria, was of this period.

During the siege in 1491 the cathedral was damaged and its repair was commissioned to the Master Mason, M. Krompholz from Nissa; in 1508 he finished the constructing of the presbytery under the supervision of Master Mason Václav from Prague. After fires in 1556 and 1775, as well as after the earthquake in 1834 and flood in 1845, the cathedral was renovated. However, the causes of the cracks were not removed; the structural failures were even multiplied by a storm in 1875. A large-scale restoration was begun under F. Schmidt after a design of Imrich Steindl in 1877 – 1896, whereby not only were the structural failures corrected, but the interior space was also re-designed. The transept of the five naves was altered. The Late-Gothic chapel of St. Joseph was demolished, and also the vaulting system of the aisles was altered. The portals were decorated with new sculptures, and new stained glass was put into the windows. The crypt of Ferencz Rákóczy II was built in the church; his remains were buried into the crypt in 1906.

Fragments of Gothic wall paitings from C15 with scenes of the Resurrection, the Last Judgement, and the Twelve Apostles were discovered during the reconstruction.

The high altar of St. Elizabeth, dating from 1474 – 1477, is a Late-Gothic polyptych; it is unique in Europe as it contains the largest amount of panel paintings – forty-eight altogether – on one altar. The principal statues were created by an artist from the workshop of Dutch sculptor Nicolaus Gerhaert, who was working in Vienna. Styles of three painters influenced by the Dutch school as well as by the work of Swabian painter Fridrich Hertlin can be distinguished in the panel paintings. In 1516 M. Günther created the side Late-Gothic altar of the Visitation of the Blessed Virgin Mary. The side altar of the Last Supper in the Late-Gothic style of C15 was a donation to the Košice cathedral by the inhabitants of Bardejov in 1896. The side altar of the Virgin Mary Falling Asleep is signed by Jacobus Bleselius (1579). The side altar of *Metercia,* neo-Gothic in style, contains a Gothic panel painting from 1516 as its principal theme. The side altar of the Adoration of the Magi is neo-Gothic and dates from 1896. The side altar of St. Anthony from the first half of C16 consists of two altars which were not completely destroyed by the fire in 1556. The other altars are neo-Gothic, dating from the beginning of C20.

Worth of attention are the Late-Gothic sculptures of St. Stephan, St. Ladislas and St. Emeric dating from mid-C15, as well as the statues depicting the Stations of the Cross, dating from 1320, which are situated around the interior of the church. The liturgical ornaments are from CC15 – 16. Among them are the outstanding works of Master Szilassy, declared National Cultural Monuments.

The chapel of St. Michael, situated south of the cathedral, is a part of the complex, built towards the end of C14 as a funerary chapel in a churchyard. In 1508 it was added a northern nave which was removed in 1902 – 1904.

The chapel has cross ribbed vault. The engraved Renaissance and Gothic slabs brought from St. Elizabeth's are inbuilt into the walls of the chapel.

St. Urbain's Tower, a detached medieval bell-tower from C14 also belongs to the cathedral complex, all of which was originally surrounded by a churchyard wall until C19. The same masons who built the cathedral are supposed to have built the tower. Only the large openings on the upper storey have been preserved from the original construction which underwent a Renaissance reconstruction by M. Lindner in 1628. The Bell of St. Urbain is cast from the former one which was damaged by fire. The neo-Renaissance arcades were built on the ground-floor of the tower in 1943 – 1947. In them is located a collection of cut stones containing medieval and Renaissance slabs with epitaphs from CC14 – 17 originating from St. Elizabeth's.

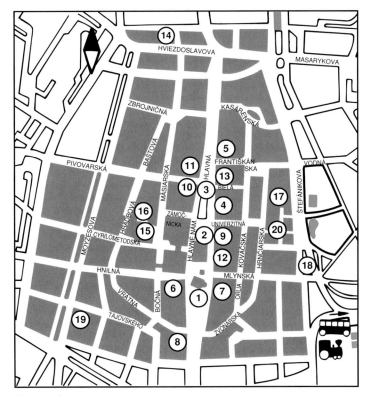

The town plan.

2 The State Theatre: Built in the middle of the square in a park according to the design in the historicizing style by A. A. Lang and Steinhardt at the end of C19. The auditorium ceiling-painting is by P. Gastgeb.

3 The Immaculata: This sculptural group is situated on the former scaffold site in the square; it was erected by builder T. Tornyossy and sculptor Š. Grimming in 1720 – 1723. The monument was restored several times, and several statues were replaced by copies.

The square is built up with palaces, burghers' houses, and sacral buildings apart those mentioned above.

4 The Jesuitical Monastery and the University Church: The church was built in 1671 – 1784 after the Gesù in Rome by Vignola. The front façade made of cut stone combines both monumentality and tranquility which are emphasized in the centre by the entrance portal and two towers. The rectangular space of the nave with radiating chapels surrounding it is vaulted by cross ribbed vaults resting on the richly decorated capitals of the pilasters. The trompe l'oeil paintings in the presbytery and chapels were created by E. Schrött at the end of C18. The interior furnishings of the church are also mostly from C18, but the central high altar of the Assumption of the Virgin Mary is from 1854; the side altars, the Stations of the Cross, and the statues of saints, as well as the liturgical ornaments, are from CC18 and 19. The chalice made by J. Szilassy has extraordinary artistic value.

The monastery was built for use of the so-called Royal House after 1654. Košice University resided in the building, and later the Jesuitical printing house was located there as well. There was also a Gymnasium founded by the Premonstratensians, the new owners of the complex, in 1811. The Academy of Law was re-established here in 1894 – 1904. There are stucco vaults in the rooms situated on the ground and first floors.

5 The Franciscan Monastery and Church: Originally a Gothic structure from C14. Located on the northeast edge of the city next to the walls, it was later incorporated into a row of houses on the spindle-shaped square. The ground-plan reflects the type of construction favoured by the friars. At its origin, the church was probably conceived as a two-nave edifice. The high standard of decoration of the church in the first building-state is documented by the reliefs above the portals and the torsos of their architecture which are strikingly similar to the stone

The City Hall, in 1779 – 1780.

Roman Catholic Rectory dating from 1804.

work of the stone masons' workshop found in St. Elizabeth's.

The Gothic vaults were abolished due to the structural failures; most likely the fire in 1556 was their cause. The Franciscans left Košice after the fire; the provisory vaulted monastery was given to the army by the Royal Chamber. In 1718 – 1724 it was converted to the Baroque style including the façade; a short time after the renovation, the church again burnt in 1775 and the next reconstruction took four years. The preserved medieval segments of the vaults, pilasters, parts of the portals, sedilia, and ornate pastophory rank among the most valuable pieces of stone work in Košice.

The high altar from the period of about 1760 is of the Rococo style; the side altars are mostly from the

1860s. The interior is added by the tomb stone of J. Renaud from 1740 and the sepulchre slabs from CC17 and 18. There is a former monastery dating from the beginning of the C15 north of the church. The present-day building dates back to 1764 – 1765. It was transformed to the classical style for the needs of the Seminary in 1810 – 1820, and in 1873 a building of the teachers' training institute was adjoined to it.

6 The Bishop's Residence
(Nos. 28, 30): Consisting of a bishop's palace and a burghers' house which was joined to the residence in 1893. The palace was built on the site of two former aristocratic homes in 1804, and was repaired after the fires in 1841 and 1867. After the burghers' house had been added, the palace

was refaced to the Baroque--classical style. The festival hall situated on the first floor is decorated with Rococo stucco ornaments. The smaller chapel in the left wing was renovated in 1939.

7 The Former County Hall
(No. 27): the Baroque-classical building from 1779 was built as a residence of the administrative offices of the Great-County of Košice; it is a work of the Court Architect J. Langer. The street front retains its original appearance from the end of C18; the County Hall is of three-wing ground-plan with a passageway. The monumental three-arm staircase runs to the Conference Hall with an ornamental stucco ceiling. There are original arcades in the courtyard.

8 Forgách Palace (No. 10): This Empire building of palace character dates from the first half of C19. The house was transformed to a bank after 1940. The central projecting bay of the façade is topped with a triangular tympanum.

9 Levoča House (No. 65): This Late-Gothic two-storeyed corner house with a passageway was a donation to the town of Levoča by Alexius Thurzo in 1542. Košice's City Council bought the house in 1569 and it was turned into an inn. In C17 the Renaissance arcades in the courtyard were added during reconstruction. Late in C18 the house was remodelled into the Baroque style, and later it was Gothicized in 1908 – 1910. The rooms are spanned over with extremely boldly constructed Gothic rib vaults.

10 Rákóczi Palace (No. 88): Built gradually through various reconstructions and additions onto a medieval Gothic base, Košice Mint was located here at the beginning of C17. It was also a residence of the captain of the Tisza region; the leader of the anti-Habsburg uprising, Ferenc

Rákóczi II, resided here in 1706
– 1707. The three-storeyed
building has a Baroque façade, and
there are also alterations from C17
preserved on the ground-floor. At
present, the building houses unique
collections of the Slovak Museum
of Technology.

11 Csáky Palace (No. 72): Also
known as Dessewffy Palace, the
Classicist three-storey palace from
the beginning of the C19 features
a balcony on the main facade and a
projecting bay. Today this building
is the seat of the Constitutional
Court.

Forgách Palace.

12 The Former City Hall
(No. 59): Built in 1779 – 1780
according to the design of
J. Langer in the Baroque-classical
style; the sculptural decoration is
by A. Kraus. A cinema was built
in the courtyard in 1927. The
staircase with a stone balustrade is
located on the left of the three-
-partite vestibule, where the ceiling
contains an allegorical painting of
"Justice" created by E. Schtött in
1781. The festival hall has the
ceiling decorated with the
apotheosis of Maria Theresa
created by the same artist.
At present the City Hall is used
by the Regional Library.

13 Andrássy-Palace (No. 81):
A Late-Baroque construction from
1899, adapted for use as a food
market in mid-C20.

**14 The Eastern-Slovakia
Museum:** A majestic edifice of
a neo-Renaissance architectural
expression, built in 1899 – 1901.
Exhibitions on eastern-Slovakia
regional development, numismatic
collections, and the Gold Treasure
of Košice – hoard of gold coins
and other gold objects – are located
here. Mikluš Prison and the
Hungman's Bastion also belong to
the museum.

**15 The Dominican Monastery
and the Virgin Mary Church:**
An Early-Gothic construction from
the period around 1290, it consists
of one-nave with a polygonal

Jakab Palace.

presbytery, and a tower projecting
from the façade. During the
Reformation the church was
used as a warehouse. When the
Dominicans, who had left after the
fire in 1556, returned, the church
was adapted to the Baroque style
and expanded by the building of
a new monastery. There is a wall
paiting from 1756 on the vault of
the church. The neo-Gothic roof of
the tower dates from 1503.

16 The Holy Trinity Column:
Located in front of the Dominican
Church and dating from 1722, it
consists of the sculptures of the
Holy Trinity placed on a slim high
column.

17 Mikluš Prison: Originating
in C17, it is composed of two
burghers' houses from C15. The

The sculptural group of the Immaculata,
built in 1720 – 1723.

original house situated on the
left had two storeys and was
illuminated through large Gothic
windows. Only fragments of this
house remain. The house situated
on the right was one-storeyed, and
raised by one floor in the second
half of C15. It has two Gothic
windows on the first floor. The
prison was referred to in 1618.
   Structurally, the building was
adapted to the needs of a prison.
After the reconstruction in 1940
– 1942, the exposition of the
town's history was located here.

18 Jakab Palace: Located next to
a former mill-race, the palace was
built by Jakab, the architect of
many Art Nouveau and Romantic
buildings. He used rejected stone
elements from renovated Saint

Elizabeth's for the construction of this palace at the end of C19.

19 The Former Synagogue:
The House of Art at present was originally constructed by the Jewish community in 1927. In the second half of C20 the synagogue was transformed into a concert hall.

20 The Town Fortifications and the Original Fortress: The building of the fortifications began towards the end of C13. In the course of C14 a continuous stone wall with loopholes was built and fortified with right-angle bastions opening towards the city; it was surrounded by a moat. The town was entered through two main gatehouses – to the north the Horná (Upper) and to the south the Dolná (Lower) which were situated at either end of the axis of the square. The Mlynská (Mill) Gate facing the River Hornád in the south was built perpendicular to the axis of the square, and the so-called

Forgáchovská (Forgách) Gate was built in the west. The projecting line of the town walls was enclosed with a lower stone rampart built in the first decades of C15. The walled fortification system of Košice was the only one in Hungary continuously modernized, not only single elements but the whole ground-plan conception was being constantly redesigned, in the course of the next centuries. By 1461 – 1471, another line of the walls situated on the periphery of the moat was built; Italian military fortification engineers took part in its construction. Another line of action-stations consisted of a high stone wall which could be defended by artillery mounted on huge bastions; their ground-plan was in the shape of an elongated semi-circle which opened towards the city. One of the bastions, the so-called Hungman's Bastion, has been preserved on the western side next to Mikluš Prison. This bastion represents the most progressive type of a bastion built in Slovakia.

The next project for improving the wall system had the character of modern Renaissance military engineering. In the second half of C16 the bastions destroyed by fire were replaced by a new bastion system. This was built under the supervision of the well-known Ottavio Baldigar. Other parts of the system appeared simultaneously with the construction of a solitary fortress situated south of the city. Construction of the pentagonal bastion fortress began in 1671, according to the project of J. L. Sich, and work on it continued until its demolition in 1713. This year was also the starting point of the gradual dismantling of the complicated wall system. Only single elements documenting its construction and character have been preserved. There is a natural-science exhibition of the Eastern-Slovakia Museum in the Hungman's Bastion, located in Hrnčiarska Street.

The arms of Košice are incontestably the most remarkable in Slovakia. Their uniqueness lies especially in that Košice acquired the letters pattent for the coat-of-arms in 1369, which is the oldest one in all over Europe. Moreover, Košice was the only Hungarian city that received four letters patents within 133 years. At present the City Council favours the earliest design of the arms, from 1502.

Košice, in the past and at present, is a significant city and centre of the eastern-Slovakia region; it was also the workplace of many eminent persons among whom was the humanist J. A. Cassoriensis; geographer J. Helszmann; poet and educationalist J. Borodáč; writer G. Fejérpataky-Belopotocký; astronomer D. Kmeť; painters J. Korponsy, K. Bauer, and the Klimkovič brothers (František, Vojtech, and Ignác); historian of art V. Myskovszky; writers G. Vámoš and J. Záborský, and others.

This eastern-Slovakia metropolis offers many possibilities for entertainment and instruction to its visitors. The extraordinarily large and lively square tempts to take long walks, and never fails to provide an attractive picture for sightseers. The cathedrale of St. Elizabeth, with its treasury and exhibition of the bells and stone details located in St. Urbain's Tower, is the most interesting part of the city to which visitors are sooner or later drawn. The churches and palaces, together with the exhibitions of the Eastern Slovakia Museum and the Slovak Museum of Technology, are also of great interest to visitors. The city has a large forest park which is a suburban recreational area; further possibilities for recreation exist at Bankov, Alpínka, Jahodná, Črmeľ, Vodnár, and Girbes. The recreational area in the valley of Myslavský Brook has a length of 5 km. The water reservoir of Ružín provides excellent conditions for water sports; it is more than 30 km northwest on the Hornád at the junction with the Hnilec River.

Excellent conditions for skiing can be found at Nad Jazerom, Červený breh, and Kavečany. Hiking paths connect the city and its surroundings with the Volovské vrchy Hills and Čierna hora forest.

Levoča

Names: L – Leuchovia, **G** – Leutschau, **H** – Löcse
Latitude: 49° 02' N, **Longitude:** 20° 35' E
Elevation: average 570 m, **range:** 460 – 985 m
Population: 13 700
Suburbs: Levočská dolina, Levočské Lúky, Závada
Means of Access: By rail: routes No. 186; By road: routes No. E 50 = 18 and 533
Accommodations: Hotels: Arkáda, Barbakan, Faix, Satel; Pensions: Maja, Kováčova Villa; Hostel ATC Levočská dolina
Information: Cultural Information Center – tel: (++421)(0)966-16186, tel/fax: 0966-4513736, e-mail: kic.levoca@netlab.sk, www.levoca.sk

Levoča, the magic centre of one of the most ancient and unique regions of Slovakia, Spiš, and a former Free Royal Town, is located in the northern part of the Hornádska kotlina (Hornád Hollow), at the southern foothill of the Levočské vrchy (Levoča Hills). Spišská Nová Ves, the county seat, is twelve kilometres to the south. Relief variations of the Levoča Hills, a chain of mountains of the Podhôľno-Magurská region belonging to the West Carpathian Arc, are astounding. They rise to a height of more than 1000 metres only to drop immediately. The Levočská dolina (Levoča valley) lies close by to the north, and with a length of twelve kilometres creates a recreational area for the town.

Levoča has a moderately cool and humid climate, following the local topography, with average temperatures of –3.5 °C to 7 °C in January and 16 °C to 17 °C in July. The annual average rainfall ranges from 600 to 850 mm. In the mountains, the snow cover lasts an average of 150 days; there are usually about 30 summer days; and the annual average rainfall is 800 – 1 100 mm.

The town and its natural surroundings create a unique amalgamate in which the entire character of the environment is a result of the historic development of this part of Slovakia as a territory of habitation.

Spiš has been inhabited since ancient times; the earliest inhabitants settled here in the New Stone Age (Neolithic; 5000 to 2500 BC). In the Eneolithic (2500 – 2100 BC), the development continued and was represented by the Baden culture, typified by its pottery with channeled decoration. The area was also settled in the Early Historic Era, i. e. in the La Tène and Roman periods.

The settlement of Spiš in this millennium is documented by discoveries of the remains of Slavonic settlement sites from the end of CC7 and 8, preceding the Great-Moravian period. Archaeological finds directly in and around Levoča date back to the Great-Moravian period and later, i. e. from CC9 to 11. The Slavonic settlement in the southeast part of the town and in the vicinity of the Košice Gatehouse was dispersed. Beyond the town walls, in present-day Stará Levoča, Pod Starou Levočou, and the Vojenské cvičisko (Drill Square), several Slavonic settlement sites have also been unearthed. All of them document the continuity of the original Slavonic settlements, which were preserved after Spiš had been incorporated into the Hungarian state in the second half of C11.

A vista of Levoča, mid-C19.

The Comitat of Spiš (aristocratic Hungarian county) was created as an independent administrative body in mid-C12. At that time non-Slavonic peoples are supposed to have started arriving here, taking over local topographic names.

The place known as the Drill Square, approximately 1.2 km south of present-day Levoča, is the site where the most remarkable pre-urban settlement existed. It was unfortified and situated on the crossroads of the long-distance trade roads; it consisted of semi-subterranean dwellings, the parish Church of St. Nicholas, and a churchyard. At the turn of CC12 and 13, the settlement most likely reached regional significance. After the Tartar invasion of the Spiš region in 1285, the settlement was abandoned. These events precipitated the growth of a medieval settlement on the site of present-day Levoča, which subsequently became an important medieval town. Levoča is recorded in a written source for the first time in 1249; in 1263 it is mentioned as a settlement which was inhabited by colonists who had the rights of holding markets and collecting tolls. In the privileges of Spiš Saxons dating from 1271, Levoča is represented as the capital of the "Community of Spiš Saxons," to

which belonged all settlements ruled according to the so-called German law.

After the Árpáds died out, the inhabitants of Levoča aligned themselves with Charles Robert of Anjou, who confirmed the privileges of 1271. Levoča advanced and became a centre in which commerce flourished; rights of storage, exemption from all tolls, as well as other privileges made it possible for Levoča to rise to the position of a great European commercial centre on the trade route from Hungary to Poland.

Becoming a free royal town in 1323, it had all the attributes of an urban centre: a parish church, town walls, a built-up area with burghers' houses, and the Minorite monastery. The magnificently designed square was a market-place and centre of commercial and social life. The main long-distance road transversed Levoča from the south, through the Lower Gatehouse, and on to the east through the Upper Gatehouse towards Košice. An essentially regular network of streets extended out from the square, dividing the entire town into twelve sections.

The original Gothic town was composed of massive one- and two-room tower and block-like

The panorama of the town from the east.

houses built on elongated building plots. The archaeological excavations show that Levoča's urban and architectural structures developed continuously until C16. The political and economic situation in the Hungarian Kingdom at the beginning of C15 caused a slight decrease in the economic output of the town. After the "Community of Spiš Towns" was dissolved, Košice, Bardejov, Prešov, and Sabinov joined together with Levoča to form the organization known as "Pentapolitana." Commercial growth in this period was restricted by threats from Hussites and the armies of the Brethrens, the followers of the Hussites. The town burnt down several times, but in the 1480s the economy advanced and building activities boomed. Representative sacral buildings with sumptuously decorated interiors were constructed; the fortifications were completed, and town houses were redesigned to contain a carriage-way and hall. These town houses filled the entire width of the medieval building plots on which they stood, leaving no free ground on their sides. The outbuildings in the rear parts of the plots were used for keeping livestock, as barns, forage-stores, and

the like. The town houses took on the form of compact blocks encircled by the system of defences.

After the discovery of America, European centres of commerce moved westwards towards the Atlantic Ocean, and the central-European road system lost its significance. The threat of the advancing Turkish armies and dynastic struggles for the throne caused a partial decline of the economy in the Hungarian Kingdom and, consequently, of the towns. After a fire in 1550, a new Town Hall and a market place, or "Kaufhaus," were built. Having supported the victorious Habsburghs, Levoča had her exclusive rights of storing Polish goods re-confirmed in 1558, which created a favourable situation for the new industrial advance and growth of the town. Town houses were reconstructed to the Renaissance style with galleries and ornamental plaster gable ends; houses arranged along the square were connected by arcades creating a covered walkway. The splendour of C16 reconstruction is evidenced particularly by the Town Hall building and burghers' houses. Fires in 1582 and 1599 ravaged the town.

The square with the Town Hall and the church of St. James.

The Town Hall, the spire and the church of St. James dominate the square.

The Gothic Town Hall, remodelled to the Renaissance style in 1551 – 1559.

The western portion of the square.

During Reformation, the inhabitants of Levoča converted to the new religious beliefs and belonged to "Confesio Pentapolitana," a "confession" of the five eastern-Slovakia free royal towns. The town became a flourishing centre of culture. Breuer's printing house located in Levoča generated significant publishing activity after its establishment in 1624, including "Orbis Pictus" by Comenius and over one thousand other books.

The period of the Counter-Reformation, accompanied by uprisings of the Estates, was characterized by stagnation of the town at the end of C17 and in C18. Re-Catholization efforts were strengthened after the Jesuits appeared in the town. They renovated the monastery of the Minorites for

their own use to the Baroque style. On the site of the previous church at the Košice Gatehouse the "new" Minorite monastery arose during 1748 to 1751.

Levoča was a significant centre of the Slovak national renaissance. Students from the Bratislava Lycée, who had left it in protest against the prohibition of Štúr's lectures, continued their studies in Levoča under the tutelage of Janko Francisci. The Gymnasium later became one of the centres of the Slovak National Revival. In C19, other contributions were made to the architecture of the town: the new County Hall in 1821, and the Evangelical (Lutheran – Augsburg Confession) Church, built in the main square, enhanced the beauty of Levoča. The town fortifications lost their significance, and there- after small private houses were built attached to the town walls from the outside; the moat was drained for gardens. The fact that the town was not joined to the new railway from Košice to Bohumín condemned the town to stagnation again, while Spišská Nová Ves, which enjoyed all the advantages of the new railway, acquired the position of the centre of Spiš. Nevertheless, the urban structure sprawled further beyond the walls, where a hospital and school were

The square: Renaissance houses, No. 43 and 44.

Thurzo House, from C16.

The house No. 43: the courtyard with Renaissance arcades typical of Levoča.

The house of Master Pavol, the Renaissance woodcarver, the creator of the high altar in St. James'.

Master Pavol of Levoča square, the Museum.

Košice Gatehouse and the town walled fortifications. In the background the Minorite church of the Holy Spirit can beseen.

built. An Art Nouveau secondary school dating from 1903 was built in the very core of the medieval town, on the site of the former Baroque wing of the Jesuitical monastery. The garrison barracks were built where a part of the walls had been demolished; the original market square was transformed into a park, which was renovated several times.

A Calvary, or Stations of the Cross, was built above the town on Levočská Hill in 1903 – 04, based on a design by A. Müller. Other building activity was focused on repairs and minor modifications of houses. In this period Levoča was an administrative centre of the Spiš district; nevertheless, the volume of successful trade ventures and craft production decreased in comparison to CC15 and 16.

The most significant, architecturally most interesting and historically most valuable buildings in the town are situated within the original town walls in and around the square. Other buildings of earlier date belong to the latest phase of the architectural development of the town in the first half of C20. Levoča was the Spiš County seat until 1923; until 1949 it was also the seat of the county court of justice; and until 1960 it was the Levoča District centre.

During the last 40 years, large housing estates were built beyond the town to the southwest; fortunately, these did not reach into the historic centre. For the past 20 years Levoča's town centre has undergone complex restoration. In 1950 Levoča was declared an Urban Preservation Area.

The interior of the church of the Holy Spirit, from the second half of C18.

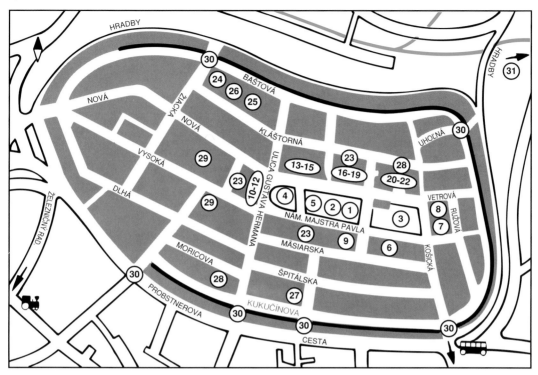

The town plan.

1 Church of St. James: This Roman Catholic parish church is one of the most splendid and noble representations of sacral art, surpassing all other achievements in Slovakia. Its exceptional value lies not only in its architecture, but in its interior furnishings as well, the most outstanding of which is the carved wood altar, a masterpiece created by Master Pavol of Levoča. The high altar of St. James is the largest Gothic altar in the world. The cathedral is a unique assemblage of artistic, historic, and architectural monuments of CC15 to 17, joining together the artistic tendencies and aesthetic feeling of those periods with the utilitarian aspects of their parameters. The church was built on the site of an older one, from which only a part of the sacristy, from 1280, has been preserved. The three-nave church was completed in 1400, together with the chapel of Saint George, which is located at the northern side and contains crossvaults and a staircase to the library. The northern antechapel dates back to the end of C15; the southern antechapel has a royal tribune from the years of 1480 to 1490. To the original columns, compound piers with capitals were attached. The wall paintings in the sanctuary and naves are from C14 and the beginnings of CC15, 16 and 17. They feature themes and scenes of Christianity – Morality, Creed, the Last Judgement, the cycle of the months, the Apostles and Prophets, the legend of St. Dorothea – and Renaissance motifs of a profane character.

The high altar of St. James, the masterpiece of Master Pavol of Levoča, dates from 1508 – 1517. With its height of 18.60 metres, it is the highest Gothic altar in the world. In addition to the central statues of the Virgin Mary, Ss. James and John, reliefs on the front sides of the altar-wings depict Biblical scenes, the Passion, and the Last Supper. Other examples of the workmanship of Master Pavol are the altar of the Nativity (1510), the altar of St. John and the altar of Mettercia (both from the year 1520), and an equestrian statue of St. George in the north chapel dating back to approximately the same time.

The other ten altars are confined to the Late-Gothic, Renaissance, and Baroque periods of sacral art; among them is the altar of "Vir Dolorum" (1476 – 1480), a rare example of older church furnishings. The baptismal font (1380), the tower-like pastofory (first half of C15), the pulpit (1627), and the Stations of the Cross (1470 to 1480), together with the Gothic senators' pew boxes (1494) constitute the basic interior furnishings of the church. The choir and the chest are by the woodcarvers K. Kollmitz and O. Hertel, from the years 1626 to 1632. K. Kollmitz also created several wooden epitaphs, including Nicholas' epitaph of M. Gosnowitzer (1669); these fine displays were his contributions to a precious set of patrician epitaphs which date back to CC16 and 17. The sculptural decoration of the tomb of Alexej Thurzo, from the year 1543, is found in the Thurzoes' chapel, which is closed

The Gothic church of St. James.

off from the rest of the church by richly decorated Renaissance grillework. The church also possesses a precious collection of liturgical objects including Gothic chalices and ciboria; chalices and monstrances executed by Baroque Master-jeweller J. Szilassy; and a set of vestments and chasubles of various periods.

The church and a part of its interior were renovated after the fire in 1849. At that time a neo-Gothic tower was added, several wall paintings were uncovered and the interior was restored. Other restorations and renovations carried out on the altars and paintings were continued in C20.

2 The Town Hall: A symbol of municipal rights and independence, the Town Hall was built after the fire in 1550 on the site of a previous Gothic building. After fires in 1599 and 1615, it was restored in the Renaissance style. An entrance portal from the previous building was preserved. The most valuable Renaissance

The western portal of the church of St. James.

showpieces of the building are: Renaissance arcades on the ground and the first floors; the reception hall with reticulated vaulting and ridge ribs; frescoes depicting the civic Vitues; the stone portal with paintings of delphines on the façade; and the Council Hall containing a carved ceiling and an oil painting of the

town council. The extensive renovation in 1893 – 1895 partially changed the appearance of the town hall; the corner columns of the arcades were changed into pillars because of structural failure, and the roof profile was changed to include high stepped gable ends. Since 1955 the building has housed the Spiš Museum. Once free-standing Renaissance belfry became a part of the Town Hall. It was modified to the Baroque. Another essential change occurred in 1824, when it took on its present-day appearance. Further renovations took place in 1895.

3 The Warehouse: The Waaghaus, or building of the former municipal weigh-scales, dates back to 1588. Originally a Renaissance house, it was renovated in C18, and in the second half of C19 it was enlarged and remodelled to the late classical style. According to the right of storage, merchants had to declare and store goods in this building. The warehouse was combined with an office which controlled accuracy of measuring and weighing. An exchange office was in this building as well. The warehouse fulfilled its original functions until the first half of C18. From that time its use was changed several times, and at present it is the Town Hall. Above the southern entrance the original coat of arms of the town has been preserved.

4 The Evangelic (Lutheran – Augsburg Confession) Church: A classical central construction dating to the years 1825 – 1837; the church was built according to the plan of A. Povolný, on the site of an earlier wooden church. The ground-plan of the church was a Greek cross with an oval altar space, with a dome over the central space, raised on a drum. The domed composition was lit through thermal windows, i. e. semicircular windows divided into three lights by two vertical mullions. A trompe l'oeil wall painting, an altar in Classical style, a Renaissance baptismal font, a Baroque organ, and liturgical ornaments from C15 to C19 remain among the interior furnishings of the church.

5 The "Cage of Shame:" The pillory is from the turn of CC16 and 17 and was used for publicly disgracing those who behaved shamefully or trespassed the law.

The most exquisite pieces of architecture in the square belonged to the most influential and richest inhabitants of the town; there were also offices of the magistrate or county administration.

6 Thurzo's house (No. 7): Originally a patrician house, created by joining together two Gothic houses, it was transformed to the Renaissance style in C16. About 1780 the courtyard wings were adapted to the Baroque style; the staircase was renovated in the first half of C19. The present-day appearance of the façade dates back to 1903 – 1904, taking on a neo-Renaissance appearance with sgrafitto adorning its steep gable and windows on the upper storey.

7 Minor County Hall: Built in the Renaissance style on the foundations of a previous building, it housed the administrative offices and Court of Justice until the major county administration building was built. The prison and the record office of the Court of Justice were subsequently established here. The façade is decorated with sgraffito, and between the windows the coat--of-arms of Spiš County may be seen. It is now used as the District Record Office.

8 The County Hall: An Empire construction built in 1805 – 1831 according to a design of A. Povolný, this corner four-wing building with an eleven-axial main façade is a row house on the square. Of all the county administration buildings in the former Hungarian kingdom, this one ranks among the greatest achievements. In this case, the building was designed to harmonize with the leading examples of historic architecture of Levoča. It represents an ideal type of administration building of the first half of C19. It was the seat of the county administration office until 1922.

Panel painting on the high altar of the church of St. James.

The church of St. James: the altar of the Nativity, Baroque, from 1752. The Crib by Master Pavol, from the beginning of C16.

9 Master Pavol's House (No. 21): Around 1510, this house belonged to Master Pavol, the great medieval sculptor and carver, whose workshop has been preserved in the courtyard to the present day. The original Gothic house was reconstructed several times. Today the restored house is the Master Pavol Museum.

10 House No. 34: Originally a medieval burghers' house, it was rebuilt several times and in 1892 – 1893 was transformed to a casino with a wine restaurant in the basement.

11 House No. 35: Originally a medieval burghers' house, it was rebuilt several times and in 1892 – 1893 transformed to a casino with a wine restaurant in the basement.

12 Breuer's Printing House (No. 36): This printing office was, in C17, originally located in a Late-Gothic burghers' house, and was enlarged and remodelled to the Renaissance style. Breuer's Printing House issued well-known calendars, and works of Tranovský

A detail of the statue of St. John the Almonder.

(Tranoscius) or Masník. In 1685, J. A. Comenius' book "Orbis Pictus" was printed here in four languages, with wood-block prints by J. Bubenko.

13 Hain's House (No. 40): Having undergone many changes, the house dates back to the Late-Gothic. It was reconstructed to the Renaissance style, then to the Baroque, and finally was given an Empire façade. In the course of C15, this burghers' house was bequeathed to the Evangelical Church by a son of the Levoča chronicler Gašpar Hain. The former Evangelical Lycée was housed here in 1752; the house was reconstructed for the needs of the school in 1793. After reconstruction in the 1970s, it was transformed into a museum.

14 Hain's House (No. 41): A Late-Gothic house , it was reconstructed to the Renaissance style; in 1784, it

was refaced in the Late-Baroque style. Together with the house next to it (No. 40), it was owned by the chronicler Gašpar Hain. The Slovak Ancient Monuments Institute is housed in the building today.

15 Old Thurzo's House (No. 42): On the site of the Post-Office stood one of three houses belonging to the Thurzo family. An original portal with Thurzo's coat of arms is located on the wall left of the entrance.

16 Mariassy's House (No. 43): The house with a Late-Gothic core was reconstructed to the Renaissance style; its spectacular entrance portal dates back to 1683. Later it was modified to the Baroque style. It is one of the loveliest and best-preserved houses in Levoča. Its courtyard with loggia and arcades on both sides is a very good example of

architectural inventiveness translated into reality and therefore of extraordinary interest.

17 Krupek's House (No. 44): Late-Gothic in style, from the second half of C15, this house was reconstructed to the Renaissance style and then remodelled to the Baroque in the second half of C18. During restoration in 1979 – 1980, a façade from C16 was discovered, featuring sophisticated Renaissance panelling and figural paintings. Its architecture and decoration makes it unique in Slovakia, and its style may be related to the architecture of Innsbruck, Austria.

18 Spillengerg's House (No. 45): Once belonging to a famous family of physicians, this house is also known as the Szenovic's or Thurzo's house. It was originally Gothic, then remodelled to the Renaissance style, then to the Baroque, and finally given the Empire façade. In its courtyard are arcades and loggia featuring beautiful wrought iron railings.

19 Okolicsányi-Zsedényi's House (No. 47): A Late-Gothic corner house, remodelled to the Renaissance style, and then renovated in the course of CC18 and 19. There is a Renaissance gallery in the courtyard. A small Gothic portal with an iron-plated door dating from mid-C15 leads to a cellar.

20 Former Town Inn (No. 54): Known as Tatra, it came into existence in the Renaissance when two buildings were joined together. Merchants who arrived in Levoča were accommodated here. The rear part of the building was transformed into a theatre in the first half of C19.

21 Former Patrician House (No. 55): Originally Gothic, with a Renaissance gallery resting on stone brackets in the courtyard; the façades were joined together in 1684. In the transverse wing is a loggia with ridge-ribs and lavish stucco decoration. The house, which was reconstructed several times, features a Late-Gothic façade with oriel windows. After complex renovation the house will be used as a hotel Jatel.

22 House No. 58: This originally Late Gothic burghers' house from the beginning of C16 was modified to the Renaissance style in 1619, then reconstructed in 1778, when it was also refaced in the Baroque-classical style. A panoramic cinema is in the building today.

23 The other houses which developed around the square are originally patricians' and burghers' houses built on earlier Gothic building-plots, and contain remnants of older houses in their essentially Renaissance structures. Most of these houses were reconstructed in CC18 and 19 as well. The original Gothic building-plots on which they stand extend to the back streets.

24 The former Monastery of the Minorites and Church: This monastic complex is built into the town walls near the so-called Polish Gatehouse. The monastic buildings were built in the course of C14. The Jesuits came to Levoča in 1671, and took over and reconstructed the church and monastery in the Baroque style. After the Jesuits left, the buildings fell into disrepair and in C19 it was necessary to reinforce the structure of the house; a Gymnasium in Art Nouveau style was built on the site of the demolished Baroque wing.

The old Church of the Minorites, dedicated to St. Ladislas of Hungary, also known as the Jesuitical or Gymnasial Church, was also called the "Black Church" in the past. It was built in three stages during C14 and consists of a nave with aisles rebuilt and furnished to the Baroque style. The main altar of 1675 was created by O. Engelholm; its centrepiece is the statue of the Madonna from 1430. Side altars and a pulpit made by the same master date back to 1694 – 1700. It was restored in 1938 – 1939. The wall-paintings (CC14 – 15) of the church and monastery are National Cultural Monuments.

25 The Gymnasium: Built in 1913 – 1915, it was built in the Eclectic style with Art Nouveau elements, and is connected to the complex of the former monastery.

26 The Church of the Holy Spirit and Monastery of the Minorites: Situated on the site of a little Gothic church that burnt down in 1747. The Baroque architecture of the church from the year 1753 is plain, and blends with the façades of row houses in the street. The well-preserved interior is decorated with frescoes by painter Ondrej Ignác Trtina of Levoča, with are of high value, and date back to the second half of C18. The painting on the high altar was created by the well-known painter J. Czauczik of Levoča.

27 The Carthousian Monastery: Originally a monastery, this theological seminary for aristocrats was used as barracks in C19. At present, it is a part of the Agricultural Technical School complex.

28 The Barracks: Built after the demolition of the eastern part of the town walls in 1885 – 1887, it served as a model barracks, constructed according to the design of Viennese architects Gruber and Völkner.

29 The Burghers' and Craftsmens' Houses: These original Gothic-Renaissance houses are mostly characterized by a one or two-storeyed ground-plans, and high-pitched roofs with unique, decorated gables. They may be found in the circular streets in-between the square and town fortifications. In the houses are partially preserved ground-plans, and various period architectural details: portals, windows, vaults, and the like. Bernolák, Nálepka, Hviezdoslav, and Jilemnický Streets show many examples of these types of houses.

30 The Town Fortifications: The town is encircled by town walls, whose extent and state of preservation rank them among the most valuable in Slovakia. Almost 80% of original length of the walls (2.5 km total) have been preserved. The fortifications consist of inner walls 2 meters wide. In front of these interior walls there is 4.5 to 6 meters of free ground, bounded by the lower outer walls or enceintes forming a Zwinger. There was originally a ditch beyond the outer wall from 3 to 4 metres deep, and 14 to 15 metres wide, which was made of masonry; in case of need it could be flooded to the level of 2 metres below the level of outer wall. The walls were strengthened by bastions and towers, their number varying according to the development of the fortification. The city was accessible through four gatehouses in the walls: the eastern walls contained the Menhard, (Vrbov), and Košice (Upper) Gatehouses, and the southern walls contained the Lower Gatehouse. The Lower Gatehouse and a part of the southern walls were demolished at the end of C19. The gatehouse had two low outworks – barbicans, as well as drawbridges. The towers and the bastions were named after the guilds which were obliged, in case of danger, to defend them – e. g. the Butcher's and Capuchins' Towers.

Levoča was already completely fortified by 1370 – 1410, and the earliest bastions date back to C14. Written records describing the defences in detail are from 1603. During C18 the walls lost their military importance and in C19 they began to be partly dismantled; the Lower Gatehouse was razed to the ground and replaced by the barracks. The walls have been under reconstruction for several years. Today an attractive restaurant is located in the Košice Gatehouse, and the Museum of the Blind is housed in the polygonal bastion next to the New Minorite Monastery.

31 The Roman Catholic Church of the Visitation of the Virgin Mary: Located on Mariánska Hill overlooking the city, this one-nave church with a polygonal presbytery and two towers was built in 1903 – 1914 in the neo-Gothic style by Levoča builder A. Müller. The altars are the work of Tyrolean sculptor F. Prinotha. The main altar features an original Gothic sculpture of the Virgin Mary from the middle of the C15. Mariánska Hill and the church are a well-known pilgrimage site where every year thousands of believers gather on the last weekend in June.

The original symbol of Levoča in the oldest town seal was the patron saint of the parish church, St. James the Elder. This is indirectly supported by the fact that a shell (an attribute of the patron saint) appears as a crest in the coat of arms of Levoča from C16. The oldest known originals of the coat-of-arms of Levoča date back to C15; their shield charges are of the same design: the double cross growing from three hills and supported by two crowned lions either side of the arms. It is supposed that Levoča's arms were chartered in C15; unfortunately, the charter was destroyed by fire in 1550. Immediately after the fire, Levoča asked the King for a new letters patent. King Ferdinand I granted it immediately, in 1550.

Apart from being a well-preserved and extraordinarily valuable historic collection of buildings, Levoča was also the birthplace and home of many outstanding men, including physicist and astronomer M. Hell; painter J. Rombauer; publisher Gašpar Fejérpataky-Belopotocký; and Štúr's followers J. Botto, J. Francisci, P. Dobšinský, and J. Matuška.

Levoča attracts many visitors who come to admire its wealth of architectural beauty. The Košice Gatehouse is the best starting point for touring the town. Beginning with a visit to the Church of the Holy Spirit and the monastery, visitors may walk down Košice Street to the square with its stately buildings such as, the museums and the church of St. James. Passing the Gymnasium, near the monastery and church of the Minorites at the Polish Gatehouse a good view may be had from this part of the fortificatons. After seeing all of the main sights, visitors may want to take another walk through the side streets, to finish at the Menhardská Gatehouse. An unforgettable and incomparable religious event takes place in Levoča in June, when one of the largest pilgrimages in Slovakia is celebrated at the church on Mariánska hora.

Besides touring the town and its sights, visitors may enjoy visits to recreational areas in the nearby Levočská Valley, and Závada. The water reservoirs provide a good combination of swimming, water sports, and fishing. Ski-lovers may enjoy winter holidays in the Levočská Valley and Závada, where ski lifts and facilities are available.

Podolínec

Names: L – Podolinum, **G** – Pudlein, **H** – Podolin
Latitude: 49° 01' N, **Longitude:** 20° 33' E
Elevation: average 572 m, **range:** 570 – 1112 m
Population: 3 200
Means of Access: By rail: route No. 185; By road: route No. 77
Accommodations: Hotels and pensions in Vyšný Ružbach and in Stará Ľubovňa
Information: Stará Ľubovňa City Information Center – tel: (++421)(0)831-4321713,
fax: 0831-433505, e-mail: mesto@sl.sinet.sk

Situated in the valley River Poprad in the borderland among the Spišská Magura mountains, the Podtatranská kotlina (Tatras Hollow) and the Levočské vrchy (Levoča Hills), Podolínec is 17 km southwest of Stará Ľubovňa.

The urban climate is influenced by the forests in its vicinity and is characterized by the difference between the cool hollow climate with temperatures varying and the mountain climate with average temperatures of –4.5 °C to –6.5 °C in January and of 13.5 °C to 16 °C in July. The annual average rainfall varies from 700 to 1 000 mm.

The earliest stage of the town begins in a settlement founded at an advantageous site on the River Poprad, on a long-distance trade route connecting the town of Poprad with Cracow. In a settlement dependent on trade and crafts, the river also served for transportation of various goods to countries on the Baltic Sea. The original Slavonic settlement was destroyed by the Tartars in 1241 – 1244. Its previous scheme was renewed by colonists in the second half of C13. Podolínec was mentioned several times in various charters dating from C13. In 1292 it was granted the town privileges. Podolínec was administred according to the Magdeburg Law Code, i. e. it had the privilege to stock goods, the "right of sword" to do the blood justice, and to erect town walls. The town

fortifications served the inhabitants of large area, including the residents of Stará Ľubovňa and Hniezdne who were required to contribute financially towards the construction. King Sigismund of Luxembourg declared Podolínec a Free Royal Town in 1412, thus promoting the town to the same level as Kežmarok and Levoča.

Podolínec was granted the right to hold weekly markets and annual market fairs.

The town's development was due to trade and craft. A boot-makers' guild was founded in 1415, and besides such common crafts as pottery, the furrier's trade, blacksmithing, shoe production and weaving mills, Podolínec was famous in Medieval and Renaissance times for the production of knives with costly ornamental handles. It was also known for the unrestricted sale of meat.

The history of the town, situated on territory of overlapping Polish and Hungarian sovereignty, was connected to events occurring in both countries. In 1235, a conflict broke out between the Archbishop of Esztergom and the Cracow bishop over the 10% fee on all contributions collected by the Church of the Virgin Mary in Podolínec. Cracow Bishop Wislaw took the matter before Pope Gregory IX to be settled.

One-half year after King Sigismund named Podolínec as a Free Royal Town in 1412, he gave

Podolínec, in mid-C20.

the town as collateral for a loan to Polish King
Vladislav. The agreement signed by both kings
influenced destiny of the town for 360 years. It
wasn't until 1772 that Podolínec returned to the
Hungarian Empire. During this period, the town's
development continued undisturbed, indeed
blossomed in comparison with other towns
stagnating from the effects of the wars against the
Turks in the C16 and C17. Podolínec had two fold
privileges, both Hungarian and Polish, and so
compared to the other 16 little towns put up for
collateral, it held an extraordinary position.

The historic center of the town with its preserved
street plan, silhouette and urbanistic structure is
a result of development in Gothic and Renaissance
times. The oldest building standing is the Chapel
of St. Ann situated in the cemetery and dating from
the turn of the C14. Originally having an octagon
ground-plan, its location north-east of the present
town indicates the considerable size of the ancient
settlement mentioned in 1279 – 1289 in connection
with Henrich, an organizer and leader of the colonists
who settled there even before the town was granted
its municipal privileges. The granting of privileges,
especially the right to build fortifications had
a strong influence on the ground-plan and borders
of the Medieval town. It is supposed that the
fortifications started in 1295 surrounded the more
heavily inhabited part of the settlement and solidified

the town on its present location. The town's
appearance was determined by a chain of separate
structures along the axis created by the road between
northern and southern gates. The market place was
located in the middle of an area surrounded by
block-like houses and tower-houses with their
respective outbuildings, situated in the center of
large lots. Close by, in the wider part of the square,
the new parish church of the Virgin Mary was built
in 1295. The archaeological excavations proved
that the urban structure was preserved until C15.
In 1409 another monumental construction appeared
in the town – a castellated fortress, which became
the centre of the Podolínec domain. Its significance
is supported by the fact that it was referred to in
a character issued by King Sigismund in 1412; it
was a place as important as Ľubovňa Castle. The
fortress was probably situated on the southern side
of the walls, more exactly on the spot where the
Town Hall stands now. Its defences consisted of
its own walls connected to the town walls.

The present-day town plan, and the street network
are a result of vigorous Renaissance building activity
in the second half of the C16 and in the C17, when
the houses were being rebuilt into two-storeyed
town houses with a passageway.

In the mid-C 17 two important buildings were
constructed – a Renaissance bell-tower next to the
parish church, and, outside of the fortifications,

The skyline of Podolínec with preserved dominant towers of the churches and the bell-tower.

The Renaissance bell-tower, from 1659, and the parish church of the Assumption of the Virgin Mary, the end of C13.

the Early Baroque Piarist monastery with a two--towered church.

The C18 Baroque appearance of the town was emphasized by onion-domed towers. At this time a new style in the building of houses appeared. The new principles were quite simple: the connection of their two wings by means of a passageway, then three-axial facades, and pointed-arch portals. The rear divisions of the plots contained various one--storeyed subsidiary out-buildings as barns, sheds, etc. The houses resembled rather free-standing farmhouse developed around the internal courtyard with a well in the middle. Importance of Podolínec lies in the concentric arrangement of lanes consisting actually of subsidiary out-buildings at the far side of the large courtyard. The preserved, romantic arrangement of concentric streets is unique in Slovakia. More recent construction activities did not disturb the Medieval character of the city, and the features of a typical Gothic-Renaissance Spiš town remain intact. Podolínec was declared an Urban Conservation Area in 1991 on the basis of its urbanistic, architectural and art-historical values.

The baroque complex of the Piarist church and monastery, in 1647 – 1651. In the foreground the town walls from C15 can be seen.

The interior of the parish church. The presbytery with Gothic wall painting.

The front of the Redemptiorists church.

The Town Hall, the western portion of the square.

The town walls with a bastion.

1 The Roman Catholic Parish Church of the Assumption of the Virgin Mary: Built at the end of the C13 and rebuilt in approximately 1360, this church underwent further renovations in Renaissance times, after a fire in the year 1684, and during the C18 when Baroque renovations included an addition. The facade, too, has undergone numerous restorations, in 1803, 1912, and 1981 – 1996. The original single-nave church was extended by the addition of two side chapels: in 1716 a chapel was dedicated to Blessed Kunikunda, and in 1720 the chapel to St. Anna was completed. The church features vaulted ceilings with stone cross-ribs which together with the Gothic stone details, window frames, and portals are the most valuable parts of the church. The presbytery contains rare Gothic wall paintings featuring biblical motifs which date from 1380 to 1430 and are rendered in several layers of paint. These paintings are listed as National Cultural Monuments. The richly decorated central altar (1700 – 1710) displays a Gothic sculpture of the Madonna from circa 1360. A Gothic baptismal font from the 2nd half of the C14 was fashioned in a bell-foundry in Spišská Nová Ves. The interior furnishings of the church are mostly Baroque.

2 The Bell-Tower: Located next the parish church, the detached bell-tower from 1659; it is built in the Renaissance style. It is a low rectangular tower with a typical Spiš Renaissance gable; it features half-circle opening and an arcaded staircase, which was added later. The bell of 1392 is highly valuable.

3 The Monastery and Church of the Redemptiorists: Built in 1647 – 1651 by the Piarist Order and under the supervision of Vienna builder Poschberger, the complex underwent a renovation of the towers in 1762, was remodeled in 1910 and 1950, and underwent modernization in 1988. The monastery is situated north-east of the town fortifications; an opening in the walls serve as its entrance. The two-storey monastery

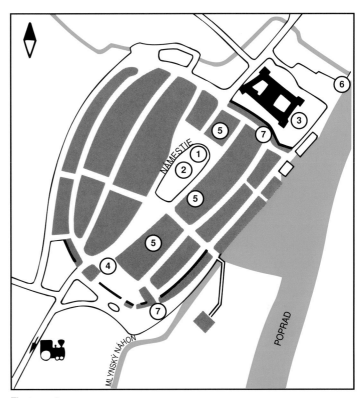

The town plan.

building has corner towers and two courtyards which are divided from each other by a single-nave church. Most of the interior furnishings of the church are Baroque. The main altar dates from 1688, the pulpit is a carved Rococo work of art, and the sacristy still contains its original Baroque furnishings and several paintings.

The Piarists established a College (or high school) where more than 52,000 students studied over the years. The Piarists left in 1919, the school was closed, and the Order of the Redemptionists occupied the complex. After the order was disbanded in 1950 – 1951, the buildings became a concentration camp for more than 600 members of religious orders. Today, a school is located on site and it is also the main headquarters of the Evangelization School and the „Light of Life" movement. The entire complex underwent reconstruction in 1988 – 1997.

4 The Town Hall: Situated on the west side of the square, the Town Hall (1903) was formed by incorporating an older building, presumed to be the original castle in the town, into the new structure. The Town Hall was restored in 1994.

5 Town Houses: Houses of merchants and craftsmen belong mostly to the Late Renaissance type of domestic houses dating from the beginning of the C17; they feature a hallway on one side, a passageway and original layout of the rooms. Later reconstructions brought about minor changes of the facades and instalment of small bathrooms. Most of the houses around the square developed in this period. Vaults with plaster decoration, jambed windows and portals inside the houses are nearly local standard.

6 The Church of St. Ann: Located in the cemetery, the oldest part of the church, the apse, dates from the middle of the C13. At the beginning of the C14 the octagonal-shaped nave was added and around the year 1600 a second nave was added. The Romanesque apse, triumphal arch, the vaulted ceiling over the octagon nave and the newer nave are worthy of attention. The interior furnishings are Renaissance and Baroque in style; the main altar dates from the second half of the C17. The entire church was restored during the years 1976 – 1993.

7 The Town Fortifications: The town of Podolínec was given the right to erect town fortifications in 1292. The towns and villages in the surroundings participated in their construction. This exemplifies the important position of Podolínec at the end of the C13. It was a place of refuge for people from the whole area in times of crisis. The relatively simple walled fortification system completed in mid-C14 consists of a high stone wall and is topped by crenellated bottlements and a parapet. Its defensive power was enhanced by original small half--cylindrical bastions, opening towards the town, with shooting galleries on the level of the parapet walk. Later they were replaced by a more advanced type of half--cylindrical bastions; one of them with loopholes and dating from the C16 has been preserved intact on the west of the former Upper Gatehouse. From the beginning, the entrance to the city was protected by two main gate-towers with carriage passages, situated at either end of the central axis of the square. The Upper Gate was at the west end and the Lower Gate at the east end. A mill-race to the south was accessible through a small gate in the walls. Outside of the walls, a water-filled moat protected the town. In the year 1408 under threat of attack by the Hussites, King Sigismund ordered a small military fortress to be built near the Upper Gate. The relatively simple fortification system together with the small fortress showed its defensive ability in 1441 when it withstood an attack by the Hussites.

The most continuous sections of the town walls and bastions still existing are located on the east side of town next to the monastery, and also on the south and west sides.

During C15, when towns boasting an ancient tradition of issuing and establishing the authenticity of charters were looking for sources of heraldic figuration of their arms, they usually employed some local motif derived from crafts, exercised in the town, or from simplified ecclesiastical motifs. They often used an attribute of a saint in the shield instead of using the entire figure of the saint. Quite often they depicted the patron saint of the parish church as before. Podolínec did not employ either of these two commonly applied figurations. It gave up using the Madonna with the Child as its symbol and began to use the letter P – the first letter of its name, thus creating unique arms. Nevertheless, these arms were abbandoned after half a-century of use, and its original symbol of the Madonna, the protector of the town, was retaken.

A tour of this picturesque little town can be started at the Town Hall and continued past the town houses towards the parish church and the bell-tower. A visit to the Piarist monastery and church with its lovely interior and a walk in some of the romantic side lanes of the town or along with the preserved parts of the fortifications afford to perceive fully the atmosphere of this typical Gothic-Renaissance town in Spiš. The church and the churchyard may also be of interest to the visitor.

More ambitious of them may take a hike along the marked hiking paths which lead to nearby Vyšné Ružbachy Spa.

Prešov

Names: L – Eperjessinum, Fragopolis, **G** – Eperies, **H** – Eperjes
Latitude: 49° 00' N, **Longitude:** 21° 15' E
Elevation: average 255 m, **range:** 233 – 481 m
Population: 93 600
Suburbs: Cemjata, Kyslá Voda, Nižná Šebastová, Solivar, Šalgovík, Vydumanec
Means of Access: By rail: routes No. 443, 446 a 447; Bus service; Local mass transportation; By road: routes No. E 50 (18) and expressway D 1
Accommodations: Hotels: Šariš, Dukla, Hviezda, Viktória, Eldorádo, Átrium, Išľa spa; Hostel OZKN, Hostel ATC Stop
Information: City Information Center, Travel Agencies Autoturist, SATUR, Tatratour, Galatour, Bustour, Jupiter, Tip-Travel

Prešov, originally the seat of Šariš County, is situated at the juncture of the Torysa and Sečov rivers in the northern fringe of the Košice hollow. Surrounded by the Spiš-Šariš foothills and the Šariš highlands, the Slanské hills are located not far to the east.

The town enjoys a moderately warm and dry to humid climate typical of valleys, with temperatures in January of –2.5 °C to –5 °C, in July 17 °C to 18.5 °C, and annual average rainfall of 600 – 800 mm.

The remnants of Paleolithic and Neolithic periods, as well as the „beech-mountain" culture document the oldest prehistoric settlements in what is today Prešov. The findings confirm that at this time there was an important road leading through the Torysa river valley along which obsidian traders traveled. The entire northern part of the Košice hollow was continuously inhabited in the Neolithic Age.

The people of the „bukovohorská" culture appear to have created the basis for permanent settlement of a large part of present-day Prešov. The earliest settlement is supposed to have consisted of pile dwellings with oblong layout and with an open fireplace in the middle of the hut. This settlement lies on the territory of the later town.

Archaeological excavation of a side of the New Stone Age revealed barrows of the eastern Slovakia type. The later level continues with discoveries of fragments of various vessels or complete ones, bronze decorative clasps and a variety of utility objects from the Early and Middle Bronze Ages and the Hallstatt period, Hillforts dating back to that period were often enclosed by earthern banks and ditches.

At the beginning of the millenium, the territory of Prešov was settled by people of the Late La Tene culture.

In the CC3 – 5, the Prešov type of dwelling was known. At that time the people contacted the Roman culture for the first time, which is confirmed by finds of hoards consisting of gold and silver Roman coins.

The dwellings of the Prešov type indicate that a farming community cultivating land and breeding cattle lived there. Next to their huts notable for stoves, open fireplaces sunken to the ground, and stockpiles, there were various sheds. Remains of kilns and shaft furnaces were also excavated. Metal technology and blacksmithery were relatively well-developed as shown by hoards of metal objects which include knives, arms, clasps, and iron slag.

Prešov in mid-C19.

These settlements are datable from the beginning of the millennium and approximately to 400 AD when the first Slavonic ethnic groups penetrated to what is now eastern Slovakia from the north through the Carpathian passes. Until C9, Slavonic settlements in the Košice Hollow and along the River Torysa valley were very rare. Situation changed only in C9 when the Slavonic peoples started arriving from the southwest. Their increased numbers were related to the expansion of the Great Moravian Empire.

A Slavonic settlement with the Prague type pottery was identified on the territory of Prešov. The earliest Slavonic settlement sites were near the River Torysa. In nowadays Prešov such a settlement was on a low terrace in the vicinity of earlier settlements. Later, owing to frequent floods, the settlement was moved to the northeast, onto a higher terrace. The next expansion of the settlement was possible only to the north, onto a terrace lying at the foot of Táborisko Hill, where the basis of today's Prešov came to existence. It did not cease existing even after of the arrival of the Hungarian forces. They were followed by Hungarian incomers who settled in the area. These people organized their own separated Hungarian settlement next to the Slavonic one at the turn of CC11 and 12. At the southern edge of present-day Prešov, a Hungarian village called St. Ladislas was founded at the beginning of C12. It became a possession of the town at the beginning of C15. The growth of the town was also supported by its key position on important long distance trade routes from Lower Hungary to Poland which intersected here the Levoča and Bardejov ones. The early medieval town expanded in two stages: in the period before the Tartar invasions and after them.

The oldest settlement was most likely situated on the site of present-day Slovenská (Slovak) Street, parallel to the square. This is also confirmed by the fact that early access roads from north and south were oriented to this street and not to the square, and only later were re-directed to the new commercial and cultural center, the present main square. The advantageous geographical position of Prešov as a natural industrial center, its traditional market, its relatively well-developed settlements offering possibilities for business and an invitation from King Béla IV were decisive factors for the subsequent immigration to Prešov by German „guests" from Saxony in the first half of the C13. They settled on the site of today's square, to the west of the Slovak settlement. The oldest written reference to Prešov is a manuscript dated from November 7, 1247 in which the king reacted to the complaint of the Cistercian monks from Bardejov, who accused the Germans from Prešov of removing boundary stones from their land. In another manuscript from 1248 King Béla IV deeded certain lands in his Šariš domain to his Saxon „guests" from Prešov. In another manuscript also from the year 1248, Béla IV gave the „guests" from Prešov various privileges. On January 28th, 1299, King Andrew III granted the „guests" from Prešov the same broad privileges which were given to „community of guests" in the Spiš region. This decree also delineated the powers belonging to courts of justice, the conditions for participation in the army, and the amount of the royal tax.

In 1342 the town was exempted from jurisdiction of the Šariš County Administrator. In 1374 Prešov was declared a Free Royal Town.

In 1347 the town began building its parish church. It may be inferred from a letter by Queen Elizabeth.

Prešov from distance.

Through this letter the inhabitants of Prešov were permitted to quarry stone for the church also on the lands of nobility living there. In 1370 the King exempted the town from jurisdiction of the regular Royal Court-of-Justice and permitted Prešov to erect town walls. Besides the charter of a Free Royal Town gained in 1374, the town was awarded further privileges and concessions. The considerable development of Prešov was supported by the acceptance of the Budín Law. The King also sent here his military engineers to construct defences. Master Ambróz of Diósgyór was ordered to direct the construction of the town walls.

Because of its economic growth in the middle of the C14, Prešov took on a dominant position over the other two towns situated on the Torysa River, Veľký Šariš and Sabinov. In 1480 Prešov became a member of the union of eastern Slovak towns, the „Pentapolitana". The beginning of the C15 was marked by war against the Turks. Since the King needed money to finance the war, he gave Prešov as collateral to wealthy aristocrats.

The urban structure of Prešov was formed in C15 when the irregular spindle-shaped square was built up on the western side and row houses were erected on the eastern side of the square. These houses belonged to the earliest part of the town which stood where Slovenská Street is today. Organization of the town into streets and town quarters was finished by mid-C15. The square started at the northern edge of the town next to the Upper Gatehouse and was closed-off by the houses next to the lanes which intersected the square. Two rows of houses in the square were separated by two lanes which thus divided the town into four town quarters. In the tax registers they were recorded by

Roman numerals, sometimes also by names of the magistrates who lived there.

In the Middle Ages, the square used to be the centre of the economic life of the town, both of trade and crafts. The houses in the square belonged to the richest burghers; very often they shared them with more tenants. They also ran their workshops there. The building plots were narrow and long; they usually stretched from the square as far as the parallel street or to the town walls. The earliest houses were built of timber. Large stone houses where mortar was employed appeared only after the big fire in 1418.

The original shapes of the long narrow plots determined the building-up of the square also in the following centuries. Stone parts of the earlier Gothic houses used to be preserved frequently with numerous architectural details; they were employed for carrying new superstructures. The Renaissance and Baroque recontructions incorporated them as well; therefore, many Gothic details may still be seen today.

The boom in building activities influenced Prešov in the second half of C15 and in C16. The town was becoming densely inhabited, especially in the town centre, which was given its present-day appearance in those times.

Aside from wars, Prešov also suffered natural disasters, the plague, and a rebellion in the C16 and C17. After the repression of the Thököly rebellion, the town became the seat of the emperor's military justice court with General Caraff at its head. He put to death numerous citizens in 1687 during the so-called „Prešov massacre". In spite of this fact, the town prospered thanks to the many craft workshops whose

A view of the historic spindle-shaped square.

Town houses in the High Street are typical of Prešov.

products sold well at the markets. In the year 1647 Prešov became the seat of Šariš county and began to grow. In the second half of the C18 the town continued to prosper, and with it came social and cultural development. At the beginning of the C18 a Calvary or Way of the Cross was built above the

town to the west, similar to the one in Banská Štiavnica.

Suburbs began to develop at the beginning of the C19, especially in the direction towards Solivar. After the railway was built and the Lower Gate demolished, a new square was created on the site of the gate. The square was soon surrounded by new administrative buildings.

In 1818 Prešov became the seat of the Greek- -Catholic Bishopric. In 1848 – 1849, the town joined in the program of the Slovak National Movement.

The current appearance of the town, especially the facades and shapes of the roofs, appeared after the largest fire in the town in 1887. A large part of the town had burnt down but in the next two years the town was rebuilt. Another destructive blow which the historic centre suffered was from bombing during World War II. After air-raids, the whole houses, rafters, and also vaulted ceilings on the second floors of many houses were destroyed.

Pitched roofs are typical of the historic centre of Prešov. They are lavishly decorated with ornamental and figural sgraffitoes. This decorative element was applied in the Baroque, too, and even at the beginning of C20 it was repeated in the Art Nouveau style.

From the point of view of urban development, Prešov represents the characteristic eastern Slovak town with a convex, lens-shaped square, a well- -developed town plan, and a large amount of artistic and architecturally valuable styles dating from the Gothic and Renaissance periods. At the present this regional capital is the administrative, industrial, cultural and university center of north- east Slovakia. It is also the center of Ukrainian and Ruthenian culture including its own Ukrainian National Theater.

A town house in the High Street.

The Town Hall, from 1511 – 1520.

Rákóczi House in the High Street.

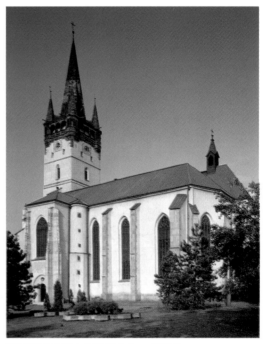

The parish church of St. Nicholas, mid-C14.

The eventful history of the town may be demonstrated by many notable architectural and cultural monuments which are situated in the main square paradoxically called High Street. The most attractive pieces of architecture are to be found in the central part of the square.

The urban scheme which had been preserved since the end of C15, and the large amount of splendid buildings embellished with many fine architectural details were the reason for to declare Prešov an Urban Conservation Area in 1950.

The interior of the parish church of St. Nicholas, the high altar is from 1696.

beginning of the C20. Other furnishings are High-Renaissance and are richly decorated. In the triumphal arch is a sculpture group of Calvary dating from about 1350 complemented by statues of the Virgin Mary and St. John. The Crucifixion by Master Pavol of Levoča dates from the beginning of C16; the organ and pulpit date from the end of C17. The chapel on the northern side contains panels of an original Gothic triptych altar dating from 1490. Liturgical ornaments include a set of chalices of CC18 and 19, a monstrance of the beginning of C18, and vestments of C18. Intarsia in patron stalls dating from the beginning of C16 are assigned to Master Gregor of Kežmarok.

2 The Evangelical (Lutheran) Church: Situated between the parish church of Saint Nicholas and the former Evangelical college, this church is an example of Late Renaissance architecture dating from 1637 – 1642. Renovations took place in the beginning of the C18 and in the years 1850 and 1947. It is a one-nave church with a polygonal presbytery, a sacristy on the north side, and balconies on both sides of the nave, serving as choir lofts. The interior furnishings are Renaissance and Baroque. The altar is neo-Romanesque and dates from 1865, the baptismal font dates from 1714, and the pews are from the C17 and C18. A Renaissance stallum (bench) from the C17 and the organ from the second half of the C17 are also worthy of mention.

3 The Former Evangelical College: Built in the centre of the square, this Renaissance complex originated in 1666 – 1668 and has an addition of the fourth wing of 1724. During CC18 and 19 the building was elevated by the third floor, and after a large fire in 1887 it was renovated in the then-favoured neo-Romantic style. It consists of four wings arranged around a central courtyard. At the time when it was erected, it had two floors and three wings; the fourth side was closed up by a wall

1 St. Nicholas Church: This Roman--Catholic parish church was built in the middle of the C14 as one-nave church, originally surrounded by a cemetery. Undergoing reconstruction during the entire C15, the new three-nave edifice was finished in the year 1515 under the management of J. Brengyszeyn. During the Reformation, a balcony for the choir was added and later removed. In 1788 after a devastating fire, the church was renovated and at that time the classical entrance portal appeared. The tower of the church was Gothicized in 1903 – 1904. F. Schulek was commisioned to head the construction works. In the interior of the church many Gothic architectural elements have been preserved: reticulated vaulting, brackets with masks, and original Gothic window tracery. The tower projecting from the western side of

the church is accessible through a Gothic portal with a pointed arch. In the fabric of the northern wall of the church, there is a little portal with a Gothic carved door. Fragments of wall paintings date from C15, and those in the nave are from C17.

The main altar, dedicated to Saint Nicholas, dates from 1696 and is a symbiosis of Gothic and Baroque sacred art. The altar features a central Gothic cabinet with sculptures dating from approximately 1506, attributed to wood-carver J. Weiss. Statues of angels at the top of the altar are from the workshop of Master Pavol of Levoča and date from the early C16. This altar is among the most beautiful sacred artistic-historic works in Slovakia. The side altars are Baroque and go back to the CC17 – 18 and several date from

with windows and a gate. The first floor featured arcades open to the courtyard. The present day layout is considerably different. In the new wing, a monumental staircase leading to the upper floor was introduced. The ground floor possesses large halls spanned with vaults supported by a central column. Other rooms have barrel vaults with lunettes, and the later added flat ceilings. The exterior is decorated in the neo-classical style with elements inspired by the eastern-Slovakia renaissance style. A memorial to the victims of the Prešov massacre in 1687 was erected on a corner of the building in 1908.

4 The Holy Trinity Column: Situated in a park behind the building of the Evangelical college, the Holy Trinity Column is a sculptural work of art dating from 1738.

5 The Neptune Fountain: Located in the park in front of the parish church, the fountain was built in 1829. This area of the square was transformed into a park with a fence and benches.

6 The Town Hall: Built on two older Medieval building lots in 1511 – 1520, the Town Hall is located in a row of buildings on the square. A major reconstruction in the Classicist style took place from 1780 – 1788. After a fire in 1887 one floor was added with a new roof in the neo-Baroque style. A portal is preserved in the side entrance hallway.

The so-called Caraff House, adjacent to the Town Hall on Jarkova Street, was built in 1624. This object was renovated in the C20. Gothic portals, Renaissance staircases, balconies and a loggia have been preserved.

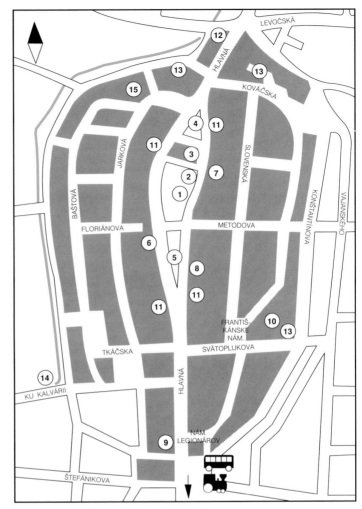

The town plan.

7 The Rákóczi House: The house was created when two older houses built on medieval plots bought by Transylvanian Prince Sigismund Rákóczi at the end of C16 were connected. The house is located in the middle of the eastern side of the square. The reconstruction transformed the house into a state palace. A spatial entrance hall was treated with ridge-ribs springing from columns. After the fire in 1696, vaults were again introduced into the rooms on the first floor. The house was renovated in C18. During reconstructions in 1951 – 1955 it was converted into a museum.

The Rákóczi House is two-storeyed with an intricate ground-plan and two closed up courtyards. The courtyard wings were later connected by an arcaded hallway on the ground-floor and a gallery on the upper floor. The façade facing the square features oriel windows and a lavishly decorated gable. The Renaissance sgraffito ornaments and plant motifs have been restored. This gable decoration is typical of other burghers' houses in Prešov. This building houses a museum of natural sciences and fire protection and fire fighting.

Greek-Catholic church of Alexander Nevski.

ground-plan of the cathedral was turned. Thus a one-nave church with side chapels was created; the tribune on the eastern side is vaulted. The original presbyteries contain Gothic reticulated vaulting. The front with a tower is lavishly decorated with stuccoes; the gable features statues by J. Hartmann. The Rococo wall paintings in the interior are from mid-C18. The iconostasis in front of the high altar was installed at the beginning of C20; the pulpit dates from the end of C18; the bishop's stall dates from after 1817; the candelabra date from C18, and the grill dates from mid-C18. The southwest side of the church adjoins the original medieval building of a monastery, renovated at the beginning of C17. In 1848 it was reconstructed for the Graeco-Catholic Bishopric. A cloister with Renaissance vaults and plaster decoration connected the Bishopric with the church plaster decoration. Its front, which is divided by a bay window, columns and a pediment, complements the structure of the street.

10 The Franciscan Monastery and Church: Situated in the northeast part of the city next to the walls, this complex is of Gothic origin (from approximately 1380) and was remodeled in the second half of the C17. Complete reconstruction took place in 1709 – 1718, under the leadership of Košice builder T. Tornyossy. The monastery was built after 1671 and is connected to the church at its northern side. St. Joseph Church is a one-nave building with the main facade featuring twin towers, and designed according to the Jesuit church in Košice. The sculptural decoration of the facade was executed by Š. Griming (1734). Lavishly decorated Baroque altars from the first half of the C18 adorn the interior. The main altar of the Holy Family is a reproduction of the original which dated from 1732 and burned in the fire of 1870. Located near the church is a statue depicting Saint Rochus from the year 1730 by sculptor Š. Griming.

8 The Former J. Záborský Theatre: Located at No.1 Hlavná (Main) Street, this building was built in the second half of the C19 on several Medieval lots as a pub and amusement hall. The main facade blends in with the houses in the row. The courtyard wings are flanked by a separate hall whose neo-Renaissance wall paintings feature plant motifs.

9 The Cathedral of Saint John the Baptist: This Greek-Catholic church is situated in the southern part of the city in the vicinity of the former Lower Gate. It was built on the site of a small hospital church of the Carmelite Order which dated from before 1429. This Gothic construction was reconstructed in the Baroque style in 1753 – 1754 under the direction of Prešov builder G. Urlespacher and then again in 1835. The church was promoted to a cathedral church in conjuction with the establishment of the Greek-Catholic Bishopric in Prešov in 1881. During the Baroque reconstruction the

11 Burghers' Houses: These Late-Gothic houses in the historic centre are built on long, narrow plots and create row houses with three-axial façades and two storeys with a side passage. They belong to the type of burghers' houses with a tap-room. Characteristic for them are also the pillared staircases in the middle of the entrance hall which lead through the building. The houses in the square have long wings projecting into the courtyard. They were introduced as extensions in CC16 and 17, but sometimes they were built at the same time as the central building. The courtyard wings are also two-storeyed; the rooms are accessible from galleries supported by stone brackets. Single plots were separated from each other by high walls - the back walls of the courtyard wings. Many architectural and artistic elements have been preserved from the earliest period, when they originated, throughout Gothic, Renaissance, Baroque, and historicizing styles. Each of the periods respected previous fine details and employed them when the houses were being reconstructed. Several new houses appeared after two older ones had been joined by means of some architectural devices to create another unit. Another typical architectural element is the treatment of façades, and individual gables notable for their lavish decorations.

Neptun Fountain in the park, in the centre of the square.

A preserved part of the town walls with a bastion, from the beginning of C16.

12 Bosák's Bank: An Art Nouveau state edifice of the bank was built on the corner of Hlavná and Levočská Streets in 1923 – 1924 by V. Glasz. Sculptures illustrating Peace, Love, Abundance, Trifteness, Saving, and Science, and an allegory of the Four Seasons, besides reliefs of steam engines and an airplane adorn the façade. The corner pieces of the building are ended in domes.

13 The Town Fortifications: In 1374 the town embarked on erecting the walled fortifications which were finished only in C15. The protective walled system consisted of triple curtain walls, a moat, bastions, and gatehouses on the south which guarded the access roads to the town. There were two additional gatehouses on the west and east, and one of them, the Floriánska Gatehouse, has been preserved. The main gatehouses were strengthened with outworks; the small gatehouses with bastions. The town walls were fortified by additional bastions and a moat. Today, parts of the fortifications on the northern side have been preserved – the Blacksmith's Bastion, walls near the Franciscan Church, the minor Floriánova Gatehouse, and the so-called Water Tower on the north.

14 Calvary: The Way of the Cross complex is located above the town and to the west beyond the Torysa River, and dates from the C18 and the C19. The central Church of the Holy Cross was built according to the designs of F. Perger in 1721 – 1753, together with 12 individual chapels, which are designed as niches containing the Stations of the Cross. Another neo-Gothic chapel is situated to the south. The interior of the church has trompe l'oeil wall paintings from the second half of the C18, the work of O. Trtina. The central altar dates from 1759 and other interior furnishings and liturgical items are from the C18 and C19, including chalices, a monstrance, candlesticks, etc.

15 Orthodox Synagogue: The most beautiful synagogue in Slovakia which is still in use, it was built in 1898 as a sacred building in the Moorish style with many Oriental decorative elements. The entire interior is decorated with beautiful ornamental paintings by A. Grazel. Bárkány's collection of Judaica is located in the womens' gallery on the upper floor.

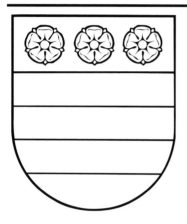

The first local heraldic symbol of Prešov dates from the beginning of C15. It is a strawberry, a speaking figuration derived from the Hungarian name of the town – Eperjes/Strawberry. The burghers of other than Hungarian origin were very mighty and influential in mid-C15. They refused to use this symbol and when its design was being debated they suggested three roses as a new and neutral one. In 1453 King Ladislas V issued a charter confirming those arms. The new municipal arms were immediately accepted. They are considered to be the most accurate and most employed Prešov municipal arms since those times up to now.

Prešov is the native town of many eminent personalities not only in terms of the region but also in the European context. The educationalists E. Fortamus and J. Matthalides worked here, and J. A. Comenius, too, visited the town. Among others, it is necessary to mention the historian of fine arts K. Divald, the geographist and historian Ján Matej Korabinský; the Hungarian poet F. Kerényi-Christman, the film director and actor J. Borodáč. Other outstanding writers and poets worked and studied here, for example, J. Záborský, J. Francisci, M. Ferienčík, J. Chalupka, M. M. Hodža, P. O. Hviezdoslav, and J. Gregor-Tajovský, J. Jesenský, M. Rázusová-Martáková. The Hungarian politician Lajos Kossuth studied here, as well as the composer M. Moyzes.

Visitors to Prešov may best appreciate this singularly charming town when walking through the spacious square, going to wonderful churches and the museum. The museum exhibition is extraordinary for its part dedicated to fire protection, which is unique all over Slovakia. In the side streets, Jarková or Floriánska, the visitor may see the preserved parts of fortifications, or take a rest in the Blacksmith's Bastion. From the top of the Calvary, a nice prospect of the historic centre may be enjoyed. The Dúbrava, a forest park, or the spas of Cemjata and Kvašná Voda draw for further walks. Technology admirers should not miss Solivar on their walks as the building of the salt-works and the equipment, then a church, and other places of interest are listed as National Cultural Monuments. Free time may be spent in recreational area at the Delňa swimming pool, Sigord, or in the former spa of Išľa or in the Svinka Valley.

The Šarišská vrchovina (Šariš Highlands), Čergov, and the Slánske vrchy (Hills) are accessible by hiking paths from the town and its surroundings.

Rožňava

Names: L – Roznavia, **G** – Rosenau, **H** – Rozsnyó
Latitude: 48° 35' N, **Longitude:** 20° 32' E
Elevation: average 318 m, **range:** 280 – 1291 m
Population: 20 000
Suburbs: Nadabula, Rožňava, Rožňavská Baňa
Means of Access: By rail: route No. 160; By road: routes No. E 571 = 50, 67
Accommodation: Hotel Šport
Information: Tourist Information Center – tel(++421)(0)942-7328101,
    fax: 0942-7324837, e-mail: tic@roznava.sk, www.roznava.sk

The old mining town of Rožňava is spread in the Rožňava hollow, along the valley of the Slaná river and on the foot of the Volovské vrchy hills. Rožňava is an administrative and economic centre of the Gemer iron-ore mining district with rich deposits of iron-ore, antimony, and mercury.

The bottom of the hollow and the promontories of the hills stretching along the Slaná to the Gemerská Poloma mountains have a warm, moderately humid climate with average temperatures of –3 °C in January and of 12 °C to 16 °C in July.

The first document related to the town and its surroundings was issued by King Andrew (Endré) III, the last ruler of the Árpád House, and it was dated in April 1291. By this letter of covenant the King gave the territory to Ladamér, the Archbishop of Esztergom. Since the very beginnings, Rožňava has been a mining town due to its mineral wealth, especially the deposits of gold. King Louis I confirmed Rožňava's town privileges in a charter dating from 1382, including the rights to elect the magistrate and organize markets; both rights influenced greatly the town's growth. The nearby villages of Nadabula and Čučma were incorporated into the town, as may be deduced from another charter of 1414. King Sigismund of Luxemburg confirmed the old municipal charters in 1418;

Rožňava became more significant due to the ore mines. The original settlement, which was located southwest of the present town-centre, gradually expanded and later the centre transferred to the site of the present main square. Most of the houses in the square have gothic cellars. The settlement grew in the direction towards the village of Čučma, and the houses with receding façades created an interesting continuous street line.

The second half of C15 represented the climax of the town's development. The beginning of C16, and especially the period after the Battle of Mohácz, signalled real danger of a Turkish invasion; for this reason the ore-mining began stagnating and consequently also the town fell into decline. In 1555 the town was occupied by the Turks; they left only in 1594.

A new stage of development of Rožňava started during Rákóczi's uprising because the town became the centre of arm production. Nevertheless, mining stagnated and even various concessions and special privileges granted upon the town by its owner, the Archbishop of Esztergom, could not return Rožňava to its former prosperity and glory. The decline of mining made the inhabitants start dedicating themselves to craft production. In C18 the economic character of Rožňava was exclusively dependent on crafts and trade, becoming also

Rožňava in mid-C19.

a centre of commerce for the entire region. The increasing number of inhabitants caused the growth of the town, the building-up of free grounds, and the development of new town sections. The town stretched mainly to the north and to the south towards the hamlet of Brzotín. The great fire in 1711 destroyed almost all of the houses in the town centre. After their reconstruction the character of the square was fundamentally changed. The above-ground parts of the original Gothic houses, in which timber played important part, were transformed in the spirit of the new Baroque style.

In 1776 Maria Theresa founded the Rožňava bishopric and thereby the position of the town was altered again; Rožňava became a free bishop's see. The steep growth of cultural and educational activities should be mentioned as new schools were established here; small manufacturers appeared in the area of the town and craft guilds became more numerous. A tannery was founded in 1782; the paper mill began operating in 1779; and the manufacture producing pottery opened in 1810.

At the turn of CC19 and 20, the town was connected to the railway and telegraph networks. At the same time, building activity boomed: administrative and school buildings were erected and even the whole quarters of little villas designed in the Art Nouveau style. The new increase of Rožňava's economic life was due to the revived mining. The town school was situated to the north, and in the south a new industrial district developed.

In the second half of C20 a new wave of building encroached upon the original urban and architectural structure of the town and damaged the historical compactness of the town centre. Because of new large housing-estates built of pre-fabricated blocks, previous urban structure was systematically liquidated. These new buildings have completely encircled the historical centre. In spite of this, the square has remained a dominant cultural and social centre where all significant art-historical and architectural landmarks of the town are concentrated.

The Town Tower in the centre of the square.

A look from the Town Tower.

The Church of St. Anna and monastery. In the background the Church of the Assumption of the Virgin Mary can be seen.

The northwest portion of the square.

The former hospital, Betliarska Street (No. 6).

1 The Church of the Assumption of the Virgin Mary: This Roman Catholic church originating from the beginning of C14 was rebuilt at the turn of CC15 and 16; its two-nave space is closed-off by a polygonal presbytery. The north chapel was added to the church at the beginning of C16. The interiors were remodelled after 1776 when Rožňava had been declared the bishop's see. The parish church was transformed to a cathedral; it was added new altars, a pulpit, pews, and stallae – the benches of church dignitaries. The tower was erected in 1776 – 1779.

The high stone altar made of stone was created by J. Gode in the Late-Baroque style in 1776. It contains sculptures of Sts. Peter and Paul, and kneeling angels. The sculptural group of the Holy Trinity is located in the altar superstructure. The Baroque baptismal font dates from about 1770. A sculpture by A. Rigele is located on the side altar of the Sacred Heart.

2 The Franciscan Monastery and the Church of St. Anna: A Late-Baroque architectural complex modified in the classical style; the exteriors of both the church and monastery were damaged by fire in 1845, and after another fire in 1890 the interiors were damaged as well. Their renovations lasted until 1906. A new organ from Salgótarján, Hungary, was installed in the church. The sculptures and other altar adornments were brought from Tirol, Austria.

The one-nave church with side chapel has a presbytery with straight ending and contains three sections of flat vaulted ceiling. The liturgical objects are by the famous goldsmith, J. Szilassy of C18.

3 The Church of St. Francis Xavier: Built by the Jesuits in the Baroque style in 1658 – 1687, the church arose on the site of the former old town hall and a Protestant school; nowadays it stands in the very middle of the square. This one-nave building with a polygonal-ending presbytery, the church is connected up to the town tower. A semicircular chapel is situated on the western side. All interior spaces contain cross-vaults.

The church was originally furnished with Baroque furniture, but only the side altar of St. Aloysius Gonzaga dating from the second half of C18 has been preserved. The other pieces of furniture date from the beginning of C20.

4 The Evangelical (Lutheran – Augsburg Confession) Church: The classical building dating from 1784 – 1786 was built in an enclosed space just outside the square. Access to the church was through the houses on the southern side of the square and through the parish garden. The church was built as a Protestant hall cathedral-church with a tribune running around the inner space; it possesses barrel vaults.

The former Evangelical Gymnasium.

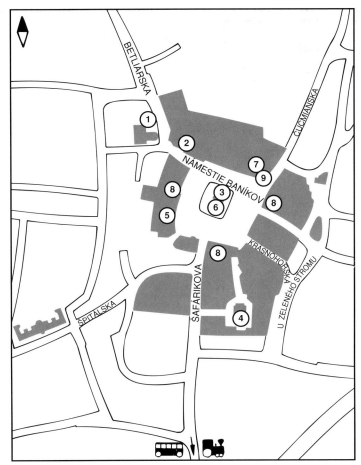

The town plan.

The classical altar created by J. Gode features a relief of the Last Supper. The liturgical ornaments and the altar frontals are even older, dating from CC17 and 18.

5 The Town Hall: Originating in 1711 through the connection and subsequent rebuilding of two houses, the Town Hall is located in a row of buildings on the western side of the square. At the beginning of C20, the original building was elevated by one floor and then refaced in the neo-classical style. The ground-floor rooms are vaulted; in some of the state rooms are exhibition halls.

6 The Town Tower: Built in the Late-Renaissance style in 1643 – 1654, the tower originally belonged to the old town hall. The tower had a Renaissance gable-end which was altered at the end of C18 when the tower was roofed with a low, bell-shaped helmet.

7 The Bishop's Residence: The Baroque, two-storeyed architectural complex was created in 1776 – 1778 when the former Jesuit monastery and a neighbouring house were joined together. The classical façade features a three-axial bay, a flat parapet cornice with an inscription

and the date of its origin. In the rooms there are barrel-vaults with lunettes and cross-vaults. Paintings from the former monastery are shown there. The interior furnishings of the chapel originated from C19.

8 Burghers' Houses: These well-preserved town houses in the square are situated directly above former mining galleries and shafts of the medieval gold mines. Gothic elements have been preserved in their cellars. Two great fires in 1566 and 1711 damaged almost all of them. Extensive renovations which followed were executed in the Baroque style; the façades were

remodelled again at the beginning of C20. The three or multi-axial houses have mostly two storeys and simply treated façades. The interiors are very often embellished with wall paintings.

9 The Plague Column: Designed in the Baroque style and erected after the plague epidemic in 1710, the column was located in front of the bishop's residence and was remodelled several times. The Baroque sculpture of the Immaculata surmounts the column. Its square pedestal was added two sculptures – St. John of Nepomuk and St. Florian in 1730.

From the end of C16 to mid-C19, Rožňava used the arms which became the model for those ones used in C20. The arms consisted of a blue shield charged with three green hills and with three gold roses. Two crossed miners' hammers were in the centre of the shield. The arms are a good example of the connection of two symbols: professional and interpretive. One earlier form of the Rožňava arms was discovered by accident. An impression made by an impact of a seal originating from the first half of C15 was found in a charter dating from 1438. These arms were of better quality. The roses did not grow from the three hills; but the most interesting is the fact that the miners' hammers were put into the shield eccentrically. In this atypical configuration, the Rožňava arms were more attractive, interesting, and artistic in the execution. The arms in this form are unique and are not comparable with any other municipal arms.

Besides the above mentioned well-preserved art-historical and architectural monuments, churches, burghers' and craftsmen's houses, the Mining Museum is a point of interest. The museum is staged in a classical house in the square where the first Rožňava tannery was originally situated. The exhibitions on folk art of the Gemer region, mining and smelting, and on the natural environment of the Slovak Karst comprising samples of minerals and other items are staged there.

The area surrounding Rožňava offers unrepeatable experiences: visits to the National Cultural Monuments – the Mansion of Betliar and the castle of Krásna Hôrka, situated not far from the town.

Hikes are possible in summer as well as in winter, and swimming-pools and the skiing grounds of Strelnica are available for recreation. Rožňava Spa with a small lake and a forest park, Rožňava Valley in the Volovské vrchy hills only 2 kilometers from the town are popular recreational centres. The Mladý baník Centre with a swimming-pool open throughout the year is situated north of Rožňava.

Spišská Nová Ves

Names: L – Iglovia, **G** – Neudorf, **H** – Igló
Latitude: 48° 55' N, **Longitude:** 20° 35' E
Elevation: average 430 m, **range:** 430 – 1266 m
Population: 39 500
Suburbs: Novoveská Huta, Spišská Nová Ves
Means of Access: By rail: route No. 180; By road: routes No. 536, 533
Accommodations: Hotels: Metropol, Preveza, Šport; Nemo Pension, Chata
Okresného úradu; Spišské Tomášovce Hostel
Information: Tourist Information Center – tel: (++421)(0)965-16186,
fax: 0965-4428292, e-mail: brantner@spinet.sk

Spišská Nová Ves, the present centre of Spiš, is situated on the River Hornád in the basin of the Hornád, bordered on the south by the Volovské vrchy Hills and the Slovenský raj Mountains, a National Park, in range of view from the town. This unique landscape is created by a complex of coniferous and deciduous forests with picturesque meadows on an original plateau, now deeply furrowed by erosion.

Spišská Nová Ves is situated on the boundary of a moderately warm and a moderately cold climate typical of a basin region with average January temperatures of –2.5 °C to –6 °C, and average July temperatures of 16 °C to 18.5 °C; the annual average precipitation varies from 600 to 650 mm.

Favourable natural conditions have fostered habitation in this part of Slovakia since pre-history. Archaeologists discovered settlements datable to the La Tène period and Great Moravia.

The earliest written source about Spišská Nová Ves is from 1268, in which it is called "Villa Nova." It was already a relatively well-developed settlement with an important parsonage. In C13 German colonials settled next to the older settlement. The following process of amalgamation of both settlements into one culminated at the beginning of C14. The settlement acquired the character of a mining town. In 1271 King Stephan V gave the Saxons living in Spiš rights which were confirmed and modified by Charles Robert of Anjou in 1317. This was very important, as it declared their right of self-government. All Saxon communities and towns in Spiš were exempted from the jurisdiction of the royal county administrator; they formed a union with an official elected by them. Among economic rights, the most important one for the town was the right of extracting ore. A great number of mines for copper, iron, and silver, as well as foundries and forges had already been developed within the town area by C14. The mining and metallurgical industry flourished mainly in C18 and mid-C19.

Just when the town began flourishing, it was pawned by Sigismund of Luxemburg as a pledge for 37 000 Bohemian groschen borrowed from the Polish King Vladislav; he needed them to prepare a military campaign against Venice. Spišská Nová Ves was not the only town put into pawn for this money. The period when Spišská Nová Ves was held in pledge lasted for more than three centuries, until 1772. Pawned towns; as a result of their special position, were protected from subjugation

Spišská Nová Ves at turn CC19 – 20.

by the county authorities or mighty feudal lords. This was the case of other towns from the former Community of Spiš Saxons in C15. Because they were not possessed completely either by Hungary or Poland, they stood aside during frequent violent conflicts and wars of that period. Spišská Nová Ves itself received various privileges, not only from Hungarian but also from Polish kings. This was of great advantage to the town, and its development was also actually bolstered by that fact. Spišská Nová Ves acquired the leading position among the pawned towns, and in 1778 it became a centre of the Province of Sixteen Spiš Towns, holding this position until the Province was abolished in 1876.

As regards the development of its urban structure, Spišská Nová Ves stretched along the road from Spišské Vlachy to Spišský Štvrtok. By the widening of this road and the building of town houses on narrow, long building plots, a large spindle-shaped square was formed. It was much larger than the squares of a similar type in any of the towns in eastern Slovakia. Originally the town was walled in, but the defences were abolished in the first half of C19. Two-storeyed town-houses, generally three or four-axial and built of bricks,

stood freely on the plots. They were richly decorated with Baroque and Rococo plaster sculptural elements. The cores of the town houses are medieval in substance, consequently remodelled and extended towards the back part of the plots. At the rears of these long plots, which once contained gardens, other domestic houses and administrative buildings were built towards the end of C19. The town began to expand and several new buildings were added in the very centre, in the square, during C19 and at the beginning of C20.

In C19 the mining of ore was renewed, and so Spišská Nová Ves came to be ranked among the busy industrial centres of Hungary. Manufacturing, metal processing, wood-working, china and paper-production factories were built. The process of industrialization was accompanied by an influx of people and the rapid growth of the town, which has been retained up to now. As a result, new buildings sprawled into the historical centre; still, it is a valuable urban formation boasting many beautiful cultural monuments.

The church of the Assumption of the Virgin Mary with its slender spire is a famous landmark of the town. The Redute-building and the Town Hall,

The houses in the square are typical of the town.

The classical Evangelical (Lutheran – Augsburg Confession)
church, from 1790 – 1796.

both built in C19, also dominate the wide and very
long square. Around the historical town, little
villas built in the Art Nouveau style developed,
as well as several schools in the Eclectic, Art
Nouveau, and Functionalist styles.

The economic growth supported the growth
of educational and cultural facilities. The oldest
document concerning the existence of a school
dates back to C14. The earliest record of a town
school is from 1481; the school existed until 1918.
Among others, T. Polluciou, a well-known teacher
of the Greek language, poet, and orator, held
a position there in mid-C17.

The most important buildings of the town are
situated in the middle of the square.

A Late-Baroque house in the square was used for province administration.

The Reduta, from 1900 – 1905.

The southern portal of the parish church, the beginning of C14.

The tower of the parish church.

A view of the neo-Gothic high altar across the nave; from the end of C19.

1 The Parish Church of the Assumption of the Virgin Mary: Built in the second half of C14 on the site of an older church dating from C13. The chapel of St. Michael was added in 1395. In 1435 a fire destroyed the roof and ceilings of the church. It was temporarily covered with a flat wood ceiling which collapsed during an earthquake in 1441. About the year 1445 the church received a cross vault and polygonal pillars in the aisled nave. The church was renovated several times: in 1742, in 1771 – 1772, and in the last third of C19 after the design of J. Steindl when the church tower acquired its present shape. The last extensive renovation of both the interior and exterior was completed in 1954 – 1958. The "incorrect" C19 additions were rejected and removed from the stone triumphal pointed arch in favour of the original Gothic elements; later, overpaintings on the stone ribs, pillars, and walls were removed as well. The original Late-Gothic polychrome of the stone elements was uncovered, and a discovered Early-Renaissance wall-painting from 1460 – 1470, with figures of the Evangelists, was restored. The vault had to be made stable, and the 86 meter-high spire acquired its characteristic appearance at that time.

The church is a three-naved basilica; the polygonal ending of the presbytery was added at a later date. A huge tower projects from the front. The northern side chapel of St. Michael is the oldest original part of the church. Gothic and Renaissance architectural elements in both the interior and exterior, mainly the portal with the relief of the Coronation of the Virgin Mary dating from the end of C14, create the monumental and dignified character of the church.

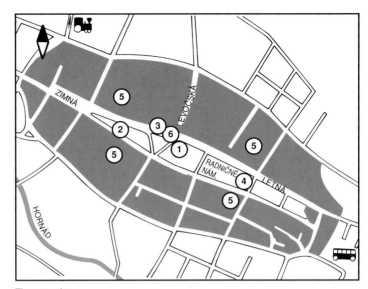

The town plan.

The interior furnishings are rich in highly precious pieces by old Masters. Especially unique are the Late-Gothic Stations of the Cross by Master Pavol of Levoča from about 1520; the Gothic panel-paintings of the Virgin Mary and Vir Dolorum, dating from about 1490 and produced by the workshop of Master Martin; the Gothic reliquary cross from mid-C14; and the Gothic bronze baptismal font from 1549. Several altars of later origin are neo-Gothic in style, from C19. Pews are classical, by the wood-carver T. Thern, and date from 1797.

2 Evangelical (Lutheran – Augsburg Confession) Church: This church, built in 1790 – 1796 in the classical style after the design of architect F. Bartel, is a free-standing building based on the plan of the Greek cross, with balconies decorated in Louis XVI festoons. The vaults are resting on pilasters. Among the original interior furnishings, the altar painting of Jesus on the Mount of Olives by J. J. Stunder, from 1797, is the most valuable. The altar, the pulpit, the baptismal font, and the pews are from C18.

3 Town Hall: This free-standing Classicist building, constructed in 1780 – 1820 has four storeys with a central bay and a balcony on the south facade. The balcony opens into a large hall with an ornamental painted ceiling. The two-winged staircase with columns, pilasters and rich ornamentation adds to the monumental character of the building's interior.

4 The Reduta: An Art-Nouveau building built in 1900 – 1905 according to a design by architect K. Gerster. It has an oblong plan with a large protruding ground-level semicircular foyer on the western side. At the corners of the building there are four towers richly decorated at the roof level. The building was restored in the 1980s. It is used for cultural and social events, and houses a café, a polyfunctional hall, etc.

5 Town Houses in Letná and Zimná Street: Dating from CC17, 18, and 19, several of these houses have Gothic cores from C15. These two-storeyed houses, with three or four axes, and with rich architectural decoration, show the influence of the Renaissance in the vaults, portals, and window jambs. Baroque and Rococo styles predominate in the street façades. The houses contain mostly barrel vaults with lunettes and ridges.

Sedilia – stone benches – are preserved in the passageway of several of the houses. The Art Gallery of the Spiš-Region Artists is located in the town house at Zimná Street No. 46.

6 Letná Street No. 50: The so-called Provincial House, it was the former seat of the Community of Sixteen Spiš Towns; today it houses the Ethnographic Museum. Medieval in its core, it was renovated in 1763 – 1765 in the Rococo style. Its main façade shows copious stucco decoration with rocaille ornaments and six allegoric reliefs. In 1443 Jan Jiskra of Brandýs and King Vladislas signed a peace here.

In towns of the same character – in this case ore-mining towns – changes of the components of their arms often occurred in certain periods. This happened when two towns had very similar or identical arms; intensive correspondence between them caused the need to change the symbol of one of them. Until C16 the contents of the arms of Spišská Nová Ves and Rožňava were identical. Therefore, Spišská Nová Ves adopted a new symbol - three roses set in a vase. As the heraldic elements of the earliest seals of these two towns were different, Spišská Nová Ves only returned to its original arms.

The town is a birthplace of painters J. Kolbenheyer, J. J. Lumnitzer, O. Ember, D. Simo; the painter J. Hanula, who worked here, is buried in the local cemetery.

A walk in Spišská Nová Ves square – the largest square of the spindle-shaped type in Slovakia – will take the visitor to the parish and Evangelical churches, the Reduta, and the Provincial House, with its expositions of history, archaeology, and natural science. In the Art Gallery, his paintings and works of contemporary art from the whole of Spiš are displayed.
   This beautiful town and its surroundings offer pleasant holidays: in winter, trips to the skiing-area of Ferčekovce; in summer, walks in Modrý Hill forest park, which is a Protected Area for the rare species of flora and fauna which occur here. Nearby there is also a thermal swimming pool. The tourist centres of Čingov, Plejsy, and Hrabušice, not far from the town, are singularly charming resorts. Marked hiking paths lead from the town to the Volovské Hills and to the Slovenský raj National Park, with its gorges, canyons, waterfalls, karst formations of tremendous beauty, and rare varieties of flora and fauna.

Spišská Sobota

Suburb of Poprad

Names: L – Mons S. Georgii, **G** – Georgenberg, **H** – Szepesszombat
Latitude: 49° 03' N, **Longitude:** 20° 20' E
Elevation: average 672 m, **range:** 670 – 943 m
Population (Poprad): 52 900
Suburbs of Poprad: Poprad, Kvetnica, Matejovce, Spišská Sobota, Stráže pod Tatrami, Veľká
Means of Access to Poprad: By air: Slovair, Tatraair; By rail: routes No. 380, 400, 420; Bus service; By road: route No. E 50, local mass transit
Accommodations in Poprad: Hotels: Satel, Poprad, Európa, Gerlach, Alfonz, Eden, Zimný štadión, Club Hotel Olympia; Pensions: Dagmar, Elizabeth, Irena, Klára, Tatratour, hostels

Spišská Sobota is the most interesting and historically-colorful part of the city of Poprad, which is the administrative and economic center of the region at the foot of the High Tatras in the south-west portion of the Poprad valley. The Poprad River with Nová Voda and Velický Potok tributaries flow through the town. Poprad was created from five originally independent towns and villages. The area surrounding the town is a relatively wide valley, which, in the north, is bordered by the majestic cliffs of the High Tatras and the High Tatras National Park. The Low Tatras National Park, the Low Tatras and Slovak Paradise („Slovenský raj") lie to the south of the valley. Part of the Hranovnická dubina nature preserve is located directly in the town of Poprad.

The surrounding mountains and the town's location combine to create its climate in which the average annual temperature is 5.9 °C, with average temperatures of 14.5 °C to 17 °C in July and –4.5 °C to –6 °C in January. The average annual rainfall is 600 – 900 mm. Poprad and its suburbs serve as the main corridor to the High Tatras.

The history of this rather complicated settlement is entwined with the original independent towns which now constitute the town of Poprad: Matejovce, Spišská Sobota, Stráže Pod Tatrami and Veľká.

Spišská Sobota is located 1.5 km from the center of Poprad. This originally independent small town is spread out over a moderately raised terrace of land above a bend of the Poprad River, which served as its southern border in the past. This originally Slavonic market colony grew in a strategically advantageous locality where the old trade road ran to the East and was named „Via Magna", crossing the border between the Hungarian Empire and Poland. German colonists settled along this road after the Tatar invasion. The name of the market colony was „Forum Sabbathe" according to the oldest written reference originating from 1256. In other documents dated from 1271 and 1273, the town was named „Sanctus Georgius", according to the patron saint of the church which was a dominant building in the market place on the square.

In 1380 Louis (Lászlo) I the Great confirmed the right to hold weekly markets here on Saturday. Since then the town has preserved its medieval urban structure, developed around the spindle--shaped elongated market-place, which later became the square.

We do not know what the earliest houses in the town looked like; if we may deduce their appearance from traditional folk architecture, which is the prototype for the first burghers' houses, we

Spišská Sobota. A reproduction from the "Spišské Karpaty" a C19 painting.

come to the conclusion that the early settlements must have been built of wood. The medieval cores revealed in preserved houses are dated only from the CC14 – 15. The earliest buildings were built as one-space block-like, ground-level houses with entrances in the rear. When they were subsequently enlarged, their ground-plan and a street line, which became typical of them, developed. In the C15, the houses featured three-axial facades which overlooked the square. As they were built on long narrow medieval building plots, the houses were entered through a side entrance or through a passageway. The back parts of the plots were closed off by a barn, pigsty, cowshed, etc. This standard medieval domestic house layout was typical of Spišská Sobota. In turbulent times these out-buildings acquired fortification functions and served the needs of defending the town against assaults. They were connected with each other to form portions of the then missing town-walls.

The economic development of Spišská Sobota was positively influenced also by the fact that it had been given as collateral for a loan, together with twelve other Spiš towns, to the Polish king Vladislav. Even though these towns remained as a part of the Hungarian Empire, the Polish sovereigns granted

them economic privileges in order to reap the largest profits possible. The architectural boom of the C15 was also affected by the war for the Hungarian crown; in 1491 Spišská Sobota was damaged by the armies of the Jagellovs.

The most convincing proof of this fact is the parish church which was enlarged around the middle of the C15. In place of the small old sanctuary, builder Juraj Steinmetz of Spišská Sobota created the two-nave church featuring cross and star vaulted ceilings which spring from a central column. The narrow slotted windows were enlarged, the whole interior was decorated with wall paintings and representative furnishings were installed.

The period of development when the inhabitants – the craftsmen and tradesmen – enlarged and remodeled their houses can be imagined according to the preserved Gothic details of the town houses.

The building activity did not diminish even in the C16. The rich townspeople began another reconstruction of the parish church. During 1502 – 1514, the Saint Ann Chapel was added to the north side of the church and thereby the two-nave church was changed to a three-nave church and more interior furnishings were added. By the middle of the C16, the town inhabitants had built a road to

A view of Spišská Sobota. In the background the High Tatras can be seen.

Restored Renaissance town houses in the square.

Three-axial houses with gable roofs.

Poprad, constructed the stone bridge over the river, and a new road leading to the Spišská Sobota Upper Gate. This road crossed the square to the east and led to the Lower Gate towards Matejovce. New suburbs began to form around the road.

The market hall was built on the square by the middle of the C16. A fire in 1545 damaged the creative efforts of the citizens, destroying one-half of the town. Despite that, many beautiful details of the town's architecture have been preserved from that period. The disposition of the houses did not change, but stone and stucco decoration around the windows appeared on the previously plain facades.

In 1567 Spišská Sobota was given another privilege – besides the weekly markets, it could also hold two fairs. The Town Hall built in 1574, and the water-supply system in the next year were signs of the town's great economic surge. In 1598 a typical dominant feature of the Spiš towns – a representative Renaissance bell-tower – was added to the square.

Originally a Romanesque parish church of St. George, rebuilt in 1464, and a Renaissance bell-tower, from 1598.

The interior of the church of St. George. In the foreground the Calvary, C15.

As there were no town walls, the burghers decided to fortify the town at the beginning of C17, fearing an assault of Bethlen's insurgent troops. There were four gatehouses built to guard the entrances to the town from the main roads: The Upper Gatehouse, leading to Poprad; the Lower Gatehouse, on the road to Matejovce; the Velická Gatehouse, which protected the road to Veľká; and the Slavkovská Gatehouse, facing Veľký Slavkov. The burghers built bastions as well; and the town walls were constructed by connecting the barns and granaries and other out-buildings at the rears of the long building plots. A moat and a mill race completed the unusual defences to the north and east; the southern side was protected by a steep hill, a brook, and a river. Nothing remains today of these peculiar town fortifications. They were dismantled during C19. The reconstruction of the rectory and the Town Hall went on simultaneously with the fortification works before mid-C17. An alms-house and town baths were built not far from the town walls, near the stone bridge.

The high altar of St. George by Master Pavol of Levoča, from 1516.

The altar of St. George. The Last Supper.

In C18, the period of prosperity ended slowly, accompanied by diminished building activity. Spišská Sobota shared the same fate of many eastern-Slovakia towns – they lost their position which had been based on long-distance trade along the roads connecting the traditional commercial centres in the North and South. The gradual decline of these significant and busy centres of urban life was caused by the shift of the world-trade centres from the East to the West, and beyond the Atlantic to the New World. Any building activity took place only out of necessity; for example, the burnt houses were renovated after the fire in 1775. Just before the fire (1772), Spišská Sobota, together with other mortgaged twelve Spiš towns, rejoined the Hungarian Empire; the Saint Mary column placed in the square in that same year is a memorial to that event.

Some Baroque details appear on the facades of the houses rebuilt after the fire, and the Baroque influence is seen also in the rectory's mansard roof. The Evangelical Church was built in 1777. It is part of a row of buildings in the east portion of the town and was built according to rules set forth at that time for the building of Protestant churches – that is, it was built without a tower.

The economic stagnation of the town was fully manifested in C19. Building activities were restricted only to minor repairs and modifications of façades; paradoxically enough, the shortage of money saved the valuable architecture and medieval urban structure of Spišská Sobota from changes. Fortunately, even the earthquake in 1813 did not damage the buildings seriously. According to the written records, only a vault in the northern nave of the church collapsed. The old, unused churchyard around the parish church was abolished at the end of C18 and a new one was established in the western portion of the town. A part of the square used in the past for markets was changed into a park.

The general decline of the town culminated when the railway built in 1871 bypassed Spišská Sobota. The district office moved to Poprad, and the once-bustling town started to stagnate.

After 1945 Spišská Sobota became a part of Poprad. The town, however, is a magnet for tourists; not only because of the intact architecture and nearly original town plan, but also because of the wonderful surroundings and the unforgettable wild scenery of the High Tatras in the background. Spišská Sobota is an Urban Preservation Area from 1950.

The altar of the Virgin Mary.

1 Church of St. George: The parish Roman Catholic church, originally built in the late Romanesque style about mid-C13, was referred to for the first time in 1273. From the original one-nave building of a supposed rectangular shape, only the southern outer wall has been preserved. The receding entrance portal, with small columns having capitals with floral motifs, is also a remnant of these original walls. Under the local builder and surveyor of the works, J. Steinmetz, the church was radically rebuilt in 1460 – 1464. On the site of the previous sanctuary, a longer and wider one was built. The space of the nave has vaults springing from a central column; in this way the two-nave hall was achieved. St. Anna's chapel and the sacristy were added

to the church at the same time, in 1502 – 1512. The wooden organ chest on the western side of the nave and the choir on the northern side were built in the second half of C17. The antechapel with stucco adornments on the façade was built in front of the Romanesque southern entrance in the C18. After the earthquake, the badly-damaged Saint Ann Chapel received new vaulted ceilings, the wood screen was replaced by a stone screen, and most likely all the paintings except for one – the trompe l'oeil architectural painting above the pastoforium on the west side of the sanctuary (originating from the C15) – were whitewashed. The church was renovated in the second half of the C19 and in the first third of the C20.

The rich and valuable interior

St. George from 1516, the equestrian sculpture of St. George, and the scene of the Last Supper, are by Master Pavol of Levoča. The altar of the Virgin Mary dates back to 1464. The altar of St. Anthony, depicting the legend of St. Anthony, was made by Master Pavol in 1503; the principal sculpture was produced in the sculpture workshop in Spišská Kapitula. The altar of St. Anna of 1503 has a neo-Gothic superstructure. At the same time, the altar of St. Nicholas was built. The minute portable altar depicting the Crucifixion dates from 1480 – 1490, and the Late-Gothic Stations of the Cross located in the cornice of the triumphal arch are from 1489. The altar of St. Joseph in the northern chapel was created in 1755 in the Late-Baroque style. The pulpit, choir epitaphs, the organ chest, and the screen in front of the high altar were executed in the Early-Baroque style in the workshop of local wood-carver P. Gross in mid-C17.

2 The Renaissance Bell-Tower: Located on the site of a former wooden building, it was erected in close proximity to the outer wall in 1598. Kežmarok's Master Ulrich Materer supervised the building of the bell-tower. It was vaulted in 1657. During the transformation into the Baroque style in 1728 – 1755, the original Renaissance gable was changed, too. The bell-tower windows were also remodelled. The collection of bells in the tower is original. The oldest bell dates from C14; the next oldest one was made by a bell-founder J. Wagner in 1511, and the last two bells were made in 1564 and 1779. The bell-tower was renovated in 1956.

3 The Immaculata Column: Built in the square in 1772 to commemorate the return of the Spiš towns which were pledged to Poland back to Hungary, the sculpture of the Immaculata surmounts the top of a tall column capped with a Doric capital. This column is fenced with a stone balustrade; it is one of the dominant constructions of the square.

4 The Rectory: This house was build on two three medieval building plots in 1638 – 1640. The huge mansard roof originating from a Baroque reconstruction changed the complex composition into an imposing unit. In the interior, Renaissance and Baroque details prevail; they were added during the renovation after 1775. The back parts of the building plots on the River Poprad are closed off by a stone wall, which serves as another example of the local type of town fortifications.

5 Evangelical (Lutheran--Augsburg Confession) Church: This Baroque-Classical structure was built in the eastern portion of the town in a row of houses in 1777. The style of the interior harmonizes with the exterior, though it originated only in the C19. The painting in the main columned altar, Jesus Christ on the Mount of Olives, was created by J. Czauczik in 1852.

6 The Former Town Hall: Located in the square east of the parish church, it was built on older foundations as an one-storeyed, compact block-like building with a central corridor. After the fire of 1775 the building was remodelled and the facade was executed in the style of Louis XVI.

7 The Burghers' Houses: Creating the most characteristic element of this Urban Preservation Area, these houses stand on narrow Gothic building plots. The street facades are mostly two- and three-axial with a long passage or carriage-way on the side. Originally, grain was stored in the rooms on the first floor; their small windows in the facade overlooked the street. These rooms were transformed into living spaces

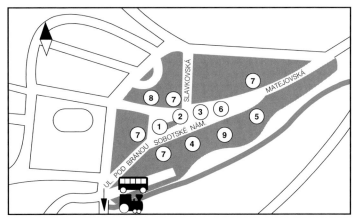

The town plan.

A panel painting on the altar of St. Anna.

during the C19. Twin-houses, which are interesting because of their ground-floors, arose on two building plots No. 33 is a good example of this type. Only a few buildings which served as merchant houses with shops remain. One of them is house No. 22, located in the north-west side of the square. Its location shows that it originated some time after the road to Vyšný Slavkov was built. An oriel window seated on three brackets is on the first floor just above the Renaissance entrance.

The houses in the street starting with No. 54 form a row of typical domestic constructions on the northern part of the square. Their shingle gable roofs characteristic of folk architecture have been preserved. In the past each house possessed a gargoyle, a water spout made of wood and projecting from the roof gutter, which collected rainwater and directed it into the road.

8 House No. 16: This original Gothic house on the western side of the square, originating in the second half of the C15, deserves special attention. It was remodelled to the Renaissance style in the second half of the C16, and again in the C17. The rich stuccoed supraportum and suprafenestra and the decorative lattice are the results of the Baroque transformation of the facade.

9 House No. 25: This Late Gothic house from the mid-C15 located on two medieval plots is said to have hosted King Matthias Corvinus during his visit to Spiš in 1474. The house was remodelled to the Renaissance style in the C17; Gothic and Renaissance details were employed only secondarily. The house was rebuilt in the CC18 and 19 and restored in 1921 and 1966.

There were two reasons for choosing an ecclesiastical motif for the municipal arms of Spišská Sobota: firstly, St. George was its patron saint, and secondly, Mons Sancti Georgi was the most commonly used name for the town in the Middle Ages. At the beginning of C15 two town seals existed. In the smaller one, St. George is pictured as a knight mounted on a horse, slaying a dragon with his spear. The larger town seal is very unique and interesting; Saint George is depicted standing and straddling the dragon. The back-ground of the seal is filled with stars. It is supposed that the likeness of Saint George in the larger seal was influenced by the original statue on the altar, later replaced by the newer equestrian carving made by Master Pavol of Levoča in 1516, and which exists to the present day.

Baroque sculptor J. Brokoff, naturalist Samuel A. ab Hortis, Czech ethnographer J. Vydra, naturalist and doctor Ján Dercsényi, architect Gedeon Majunke, historian Michal Schmank, and painter Eugen Wallacky rank among the important personalities who lived in Spišská Sobota.

The visitor to Spišská Sobota usually enters the town from the centre of Poprad through the area of the former Upper Gatehouse. Besides a pleasant walk through the square with the picturesque houses, a visit to the church of St. George with sumptuously furnished interior is recommended.

The small town Spišská Sobota together with the centre in Poprad boosts extraordinarily attractive surroundings. The Tatras and Slovenský raj Mountains have excellent facilities and conditions for an unequalled holidays all the year round. Hiking, skiing slopes, visits to spas, and sightseeing tours of other places of interest are generally the main destinations of visitors to this wonderful region at the foothill of the High Tatra Mountains.

Spišské Podhradie
with Spišská Kapitula
and Spiš Castle

Latitude: 49° 01' N,
Longitude: 20° 47' E
Elevation: average 430 m, **range:**
   420 – 611 m
Population: 3 700
Suburbs: Katúň
Means of Access: By rail: route No. 187;
   By road: routes No. 18 and 547
Accommodation: Sivá Brada Pension,
   bed-and-breakfast
Information: City Hall –
   tel: (++421)(0)966-4541495;
   Pension Sivá Brada –
   tel/fax: 0966-4542292

**Spišské Podhradie
with Spišská Kapitula and Spiš Castle
Names: L** – Scepulsium,
G – Kirchdorf, **H** – Szepesváralja

**Spišská Kapitula
Names: L** – Mons sancti Martini,
G – Zipser Kapitel,
H – Szepeshely, Szepesikáptalan

The towns of Spišské Podhradie and Spišská Kapitula are located in the valley of the River Hornád, which is bordered by the Levočské vrchy (Levoča Hills) in the north and by Branisko in the east. Towering above Spišské Podhradie on a travertine cliff in the height of 634m is Spiš Castle. In the vicinity of the town is Dreveník, a travertine knoll 609 meters high. This geological structure was declared a State Nature Reserve. It is the largest travertine formation in Slovakia and includes limestone rocks and twenty-four caves. It supports both thermophile and mountain plants there. The Peklo (Hell) Gorge and the "rocky town" known as "Rocky Paradise" are the most impressive parts of the Reserve.

Spišské Podhradie and Spišská Kapitula enjoy a moderately cold and humid climate typical of basins with average temperatures of –3.5 C to –6 °C in January and 16 °C to 17 °C in July. The average annual rainfall is of 600 to 800 mm.

Three different territorial administrative organizations played an important part in the development of whole Spiš: first, border Spiš Castle which originally represented the royal power and later it represented an administrative aristocratic district; second, the town community with its headquarters in Levoča; third, a priory – the kapitula, and the canons' cloister – the centre of the Spiš community of religious persons, located in Spišská Kapitula.

Traces of the oldest settlement site in this area were found in a travertine quarry above Spišské Podhradie (Paleolithic, 500 000 years BC). The precincts of Spiš Castle and Dreveník had been settled by 5000 BC (Neolithic Age), Dreveník in the Eneolithic Age (2600 – 1900 BC); it became the centre of this culture in the whole Tatra Mountains region.

At the turn of the millennium, this site was occupied by people of the Púchov culture. The hillfort built atop the hill gives a picture of density and extension of the settlement.

The other densely populated settlement site of the hill dates from the Great-Moravian period. The principal Slavonic hillfort on Dreveník had fulfilled its function of an administrative centre until the

Spišské Podhradie in C19.

region was incorporated into the Hungarian kingdom in C12. Its function was taken over by Spiš Castle. The new settlement of the hill after C10 was connected with the building of the earliest parts of Spiš Castle (turn of CC11 and 12). Its fine strategic position predestined it to control and guard the roads running to Spiš from three directions: from the east through Branisko Pass, from the north through Prašivá, and along the road in the valley of the Hornád, leading from Gemer through the Slovak Ore Mountains. In 1209 the castle was a seat of Spiš Royal County.

SPIŠSKÉ PODHRADIE was built on the western hillside below Spiš Castle. Most likely, its beginnings are datable back to the times when the hill was reoccupied and the fort rebuilt. This dating is supported by archaeological excavations in Spišská Kapitula. According to the discoveries it was inhabited in C11. After the second half of C12, when German colonists played an important role in inhabiting Spiš, the town possessed its own church and a priest (referred to for the first time in 1174). In that time the small town developed as a community below the castle, mentioned in 1249 for the first time. Its development as a centre

independent of the castle and as a free town belonging to the Community of the Spiš Saxons began approximately at the same time. From the beginning its layout was determined by the road leading from Levoča to Prešov and to Spišské Vlachy and forked because of the castle hill. The church, situated on the northern border of the complex of a later-constructed parish church, was the centre of the original settlement. After the Tartar invasion in 1241, Spiš was again peopled by colonists, their most important enterprise was the building of the parish church (1258 – 1273) dedicated to the Virgin Mary. Since that time the complex of the parish church has represented the centre of the town. The domestic houses developed in continuous rows along roads radiating from this centre. The town charter granted to Spišské Podhradie in C14 encouraged its economic development. Since 1321 it had been denoted as "a town." In the first third of C14, it had its own hospital, first mentioned in 1327. In the second half of C14, the town plan expanded. At the foot of the hill new continuous rows of two-storeyed burghers' tower houses of stone were built by the colonists who built this type of domestic houses over whole Spiš.

Spiš Castle and the settlement bellow castle, across from distance.

In the first half of C15 the economic prosperity of the town increased because of the fact that thirteen towns and villages were pawned by King Sigismund of Luxemburg to Polish King. Spišské Podhradie belonged among those more important towns which exerted great influence over the community of the Spiš pawned towns. General prosperity generated extensive building activity, which shaped essentially the appearance of the town. The new, broad oblong square surrounded by town houses was designed south of the church. The street line on the western side of the square respected the building complex of the hospital. The first written record about a Latin school in the town dates from 1450. In 1456 the town was granted the right to organize weekly markets. The second half of C15 was marked by the presence of late-Hussite troops, which devastated the parish church; during the reconstruction in 1462 – 1497 it was fortified and then used as a refuge for the local population during war times. The C16, which clang to the spirit of Reformation, did not bring about essential changes in the town-planning. The greatest building activity in mid-C16 concentrated on the reconstruction of the former town spital. In 1650 the Mercedarians arrived in the town and took possession of this spital, which had served several purposes, being also a poorhouse and an orphanage. They transformed it into a hospital. Simultaneously, they rebuilt the whole complex and also joined a neighbouring town-house with it. On the northern side of the square an original Gothic burghers' house was rebuilt into the Town Hall in 1547; the portal with the municipal arms has survived on this building up to now.

The town was damaged by fire in 1583. The subsequent renovation of the original Gothic burghers' houses was carried out in the Renaissance style.

The relatively peaceful C18 provided a good opportunity for the revitalization of the town's economy. The Baroque period left its mark on the town plan. Houses having two- or three-wing ground-plans were built in the southeast part of the large square. A two-storeyed school and three burghers' houses were built on the eastern side of the square in 1787. The church and the monastery of the Mercedarians, located on the western side of the square and including two older burghers' houses, were baroquized. The Marian Column was erected in the square in 1726; at the same time, also the Town Hall was renovated.

A new dominant structure, the Evangelical church, was built in 1799 – 1808 and attached to a row of houses on the eastern side of the square. The façades of the majority of the houses were unified to the Baroque style.

Owing to the extensive building activity in CC18 and 19, a new street plan with one-storeyed houses in the town's suburbs came to existence. The shingle gable roofs ended in a tip, which were typical of eastern Slovakia's towns, had been preserved until mid-C19. The complete reconstruction of the parish church in 1824 – 1829 was the most important change in the town. The original projecting tower from the front preserved from the first building phase was included into the new one-nave church.

The connection of the town to the Spiš-Bohumín railway at the end of C19 did not cause profound changes in the town's economy. Spišské Podhradie retained its agricultural and artisan character of a provincial town.

The building activity during the first half of C20 had impact on the period outlook of the square. The community centre the "House of Culture" – was built in 1930's, close to the Gothic entrance to the complex of the parish church; the Municipal Building was built in the southern part of the square in 1937.

1 The Church of the Virgin Mary: This Roman Catholic, one-nave parish church was built sometime after 1258. In 1462 – 1492 it was rebuilt, a side chapel was added, and the church was encircled by a stone wall with a quadrangular gatehouse. It burnt out in 1794. In 1824 – 1825 the church nave and the presbytery were remodelled into the classical style. The quadrangular tower is vaulted with a cross-ribbed vault; dentils and a frieze on the tower façade have been preserved from the original church. The Gothic Virgin Mary triptych altar, originally the altar of St. Catherine, dating from 1521 is the most valuable work of art in the church interior. The central sculpture of the altar is that of the Virgin Mary; the altar paintings were restored in 1906. The Rococo pulpit dates back to the first half of C18 and the Gothic baptismal font by J. Weygel dates from the end of C14.

2 The Monastery and Church of the Mercedarians: This complex, first alluded to in 1327, was originally a spital. It was rebuilt and expanded in 1653 – 1658. After 1671 it came under Mercedarians, who enlarged the entire complex of the church and the monastery. They annexed two town-houses to the monastic complex and then baroquized it. The interior spaces of the oldest part of the monastery and the one-nave church contain cross-ribbed vaults. The façade of the church features Baroque paintings of St. John of Nepomuk and St. Nicholas both in decorative stucco frames; a chronogram of 1636 is in the painted cartouche above the entrance. The interior furnishings date mostly from CC18 and 19; the high altar with a central painting of "The Veneration of St. John of God" was created by M. Speer in 1737.

3 The Evangelical (Lutheran – Augsburg Confession) Church: Built in 1799 – 1809 in the classical style and renovated in 1889, it is a large hall-type church with a slightly singled out transept and a segmental end; it also possessed a tower. The three-axial façade with a gable is emphasized by double pilasters; the ornamental painting dates from 1889. The picture of Christ on the Mount of Olives, painted by J. Czauczik, adorns the altar. Most of the interior ornaments is from C19.

4 The Old Town Hall: Located in Marian Square No. 6, it is a Renaissance, three-storeyed house built in 1546 and rebuilt in 1785. The Renaissance portal with an architrave containing the municipal arms has been preserved on the façade. The interior spaces have been modernized.

5 The Municipal Hall: The Hall was built in the square after a design by an architect J. Kováč from Kežmarok in 1937.

6 The House No. 10: Located in Paleš Square, it was originally a Gothic house built in C15, then in 1609 rebuilt to the Renaissance style; in the second half of C18 remodelled to the Baroque style. The two-storeyed house has a passageway which is vaulted with cross-ribbed vaults and lunettes. Many Gothic and Renaissance stone details have been preserved in the interior of the house.

7 The House No. 16: This original Renaissance house from the first half of C17 was reconstructed in the first half of C20. The two-storeyed house has a passageway, which is vaulted with cross-ribbed vaults along the living quarters. The courtyard wing was remodelled into the classical style in the first half of C19 and refaced into the neo-Gothic style in the second half of C19.

8 The House No. 39: This Renaissance house dating from the second half of C16 was remodelled in the first half of C17, and transformed to the Baroque style in C18. The two-storeyed house has a three-wing ground-plan with a two-axial section projecting to the street. The remains of a Renaissance fireplace and a Renaissance portal with a hand hammered door have been preserved in the passage, which is spanned with a flat vaulted ceiling. Profiled timber beam ceilings dating from the beginning of C17 have been preserved in several rooms.

9 The Marian Column: This Baroque column dating from 1726 was restored in 1861. The railing dates from the first third of C20. The stone sculpture of the Immaculata surmounts the column seated on a three-sided pedestal featuring corner volutes.

10 The Cemetery and the Holy Cross Chapel: Built at the beginning of C19, the chapel contains a painting of the Crucifixion created by J. Czauczik in 1835. The figural tombstones of the Lux and Hermatt families were sculptured by A. Lux, a native of Spišské Podhradie.

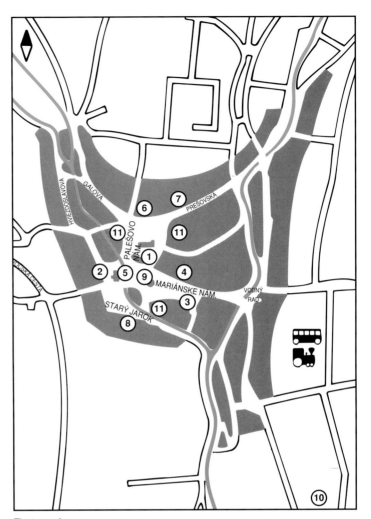

The town plan.

11 Burghers' Houses: Representing majority of historical buildings, they are mostly two-storeyed with a well-preserved ground-plan of medieval houses with a passageway. The passageways feature ridge-rib vaults with lunettes; the living rooms had artistically treated timber ceilings mostly of C17 and related to the ceilings of the canons' houses in Spišská Kapitula. What was specific of the town in the past were shingle roofs with wooden gables and a gambrel facing the street; they have not been preserved.

Spišská Kapitula in C19.

SPIŠSKÁ KAPITULA developed as a fortified settlement on the hill opposite Spiš Castle. It was located above the settlement around the castle. In the neighbourhood was a monastery, which is at present known as the archaeological site at Pažica. The specific character of the town was derived from its being a religious centre of Spiš Priorate and the canons' cloister. Spišská Kapitula became the see of the Bishop of Spiš to which the districts of Liptov and Orava belonged later.

From the beginning it was considered a *locus credibili* and the members of the priory were endowed with special political and judicial functions by the Hungarian sovereigns. As a religious centre, Spišská Kapitula performed a variety of services in culture and education as it was usual in the medieval society.

According to pottery obtained through archaeological excavations, the earliest settlement of this area may be dated back to C11. Closely connected with this settlement was a rotunda. This sacral building was built between mid-C11 and 1273, when it was mentioned for the first time in a testament of prior Muther; it was referred to as a pilgrimage chapel of the Virgin Mary. The site

of this first sacral building determined the location of all the edifices which were later built in Spišská Kapitula.

The existence of a fortified monastery at Pažica in C11 (located west of today's Spišská Kapitula) can be seen as the reason for organizing a significant religious administrative centre here. The fortified monastery was situated directly on the vitally important ancient long-distance trade route (*Via Magna*) leading from Šariš through Spiš to Levoča and to Poland, farther on to western Europe. The monastery served as a religious centre of Spiš in C12.

The priory was established in 1198; the town of Spišská Kapitula developed soon thereafter.

Historical sources tell us about the disastrous Tartar assault in 1241 – 1243. Spišská Kapitula was plundered and completely razed to the ground. However, the extent of the damage is not known. The afore-mentioned rotunda known in 1273 as the Virgin Mary pilgrimage chapel was preserved until C18; the existence of St. Martin's Monastery in C14 and partially in C15 was proved as well. The extent of damage to the monastery was most likely the impulse to begin extensive building activity.

The Cathedral of St. Martin, from 1245 – 1273, and the walls.

Soon after 1245, a cathedral, located near the rotunda and less than a hundred metres from the above mentioned monastery, was begun.

In 1249 the Hungarian King allowed the prior to built a palace within the castle walls while he and the religious institution were stationed at the castle; building activities continued in Spišská Kapitula and in 1275 the cathedral was completed after the northern tower had been erected. The prior's palace was contemporary with the cathedral; when it was finished, Spišská Kapitula became the seat of the Prior of Spiš in 1281.

At that time only an earth road led from the settlement around the castle, intersected the then-unfortified Spišská Kapitula to connect the cathedral and the prior's palace. The urban structure of Spišská Kapitula developed when Prior Lukáš (Lucas) established six new canons' houses in 1282 in addition to the four already existing ones.

Spišská Kapitula fell a victim to several smashing attacks at the end of C13. Therefore, the prior decided to fortify the wealthy town. A stone wall with crenellated battlements was erected in the second half of C14. It enclosed the cathedral, the prior's palace, and the rotunda. Since it followed the contours of the terrain, the town plan acquired the shape of an irregular oval.

The Chapel of Corpus Christi was attached to the southern wall of the cathedral; it was consecrated in 1382.

The growth of the settlement to the east outside the fortified central part of the town in the C14 was an important stage in the development of the settlement of Spišská Kapitula. The individual buildings of the canons were built on both sides of the road leading to Spišské Podhradie.

The development of the town of Spišská Kapitula had been completed by the end of C14, the town being divided into building plots which were allotted to individual canons. The elaborate structure of canons' houses did not differ very much from afortified medieval manor. Their growth and improvement of their economy were tied to the economic boom of whole Spišská Kapitula. This favourable development ended during the first half of C15 when J. Jiskra's troops invaded the region.

Building activity revived only in the second half of C15. It concentrated on the long-planned reconstruction of St. Martin's Cathedral, which was

The Lower Gatehouse and a canons' house in
Spišská Kapitula, C15.

begun in 1460. The nave and aisles arose from the
original basilica's three naves. The large-scale
renovation was accomplished by the building of
additional stone walls on the north and south. Using
as a model the French Sainte Chapelle, a large
funerary chapel of the Zapolya family and then
a library were built on the site of the former Chapel
of Corpus Christi in 1468 – 1493. The southern part
of the prior's palace was added a new wing.
This building phase terminated the medieval
development of the fortified centre of Spišská
Kapitula.

Outside the defensive walls, the existing canons'
houses were refurbished and several new ones were
added. Their appearance of a fortified manor was
retained.

The next extensive building phase occurred in
C17. A new concept of a canons' house was
devised at Pazmány's special request in 1629: he
demanded from any canon to have two servants at
least. Therefore, the servants' living quarters,
mostly one-storeyed houses, were built parallel to

the canons' houses in the opposite corner of the
grounds. Both the façades of the new buildings and
the façades of the older ones overlooked the street.
They were connected up with a wall in which was
a gateway for carriages and a postern for
pedestrians. Each canons' house represented an
economically independent unit protected by a wall.
The back part of such typical grounds was enclosed
by a large back yard containing a barn, a stable,
a pigsty, etc.

In 1647 during the Counter-Reformation the
Jesuits built a monastery complex in the southern
part of the town, most likely on the site of the
former poorhouse. A year later, the Jesuits also
established a Gymnasium in the wing of the
building; the school lasted until 1671 when it was
moved to Levoča.

The prior's palace did not avoid constructional
changes, either. It was added a west wing in
mid-C17.

The defensive walls encircling the whole urban
unit were built in 1662 – 1665 and became the most
extensive structure in the town. After Spišská
Kapitula had appeared within the protective walls,
the canons had no need to preserve the original
defensive functions of their houses. Therefore, they
were transformed to comfortable ornate dwellings
of a Renaissance manor house type.

After a very turbulent period of development,
the economy of Spiš revived again in C18. Years of
peace allowed Spišská Kapitula to revive building
activity which, fortunately, did not interfere with
the previous plan of the settlement. The garden of
the priory was remodelled according to Baroque
ideals of the ornamental style favouring low shrubs
surrounding ornamentally arranged flower beds.
The terrain was trimmed into terraces. The garden
had an entrance in the form of a clock tower
(built in 1739). The polygonal bastion of the
fortifications, which was located opposite the clock
tower, was transformed into a garden house.
The Baroque garden which was introduced here
reflected the period taste and emotional fervour.

The period of 1753 – 1776 was marked by an
essential reconstruction of the prior's palace, which
was enlarged. The façades were renovated, the new
monumental Baroque stairway was installed, and
also a Baroque chapel was added. The entire

Zapolya's funerary chapel, next to the Cathedral of St. Martin.

The high altar in the funerary chapel, Gothic, 1499.

structure was covered with a gambrel shingle roof. In 1776 when Maria Theresa promoted the priorate to a diocese, the former prior's palace was transformed into the bishop's residence. After 1776 interiors of the palace were remodelled with the same creative energy as the exteriors.

Almost all of the canons' houses were transformed to the new style and refined. The continuous street line was obtained when the free-standing houses became interlinked with a wall. Shingle gambrel roofs on all of the canons' houses became unifying architectural members of the whole town. Two sculptures of St. John of Nepomuk became an inseparable part of the period appearance of Spišská Kapitula.

In 1810 – 1815 the former Jesuit monastery was rebuilt into a theological seminary and later into a teachers' training institution. Its façades were remodelled to the classical style.

The 18th century appears to have been the last significant period which impacted the architecture of the town; since that time, the appearance of Spišská Kapitula has remained nearly intact. Only one edifice disturbed the original town plan and composition of the whole urban structure: in 1927 a huge building was built for the needs of a teachers' training college which was later on transformed into the College of Ministry of Interior.

In 1950 Spišská Kapitula was declared an Urban Conservation Area.

Spišská Kapitula, Spišské Podhradie, and the Spiš Castle together form the complex which was declared a UNESCO World Heritage Site.

12 The Cathedral of St. Martin:
Being the very core of the whole town, the cathedral was built in 1245 – 1275. Constructed on the Romanesque basilica scheme as a three-nave structure with a western choir and two-tower façade; it also possessed the Chapel of Corpus Christi, which was added to the south nave of the cathedral and consecrated in 1382. The rebuilding of the cathedral began in 1460. The apses which closed each of the naves were demolished and replaced by an elongated polygonally-ended presbytery; the walls of the lateral naves were elevated, thereby creating a three-nave hall.
A precious stone pastophory was built in the presbytery which was spanned with a reticulated vaulting, the side naves have lièrne vaults. A two-storeyed sacristy and a library were attached to the south wall. The spiral stone staircase with a gabled portal leading to the room of the records is located opposite the sacristy, in the corner of the north nave. In 1488 – 1493 the Chapel of Corpus Christi was replaced by the funerary chapel of the Zapolya family. The elongated nave contains reticulated ribbed vaulting. The original Gothic stone parapet of the choir has been preserved on the western side. Dating back to the Late--Romanesque period, are the pillars, which are crowned with little columns topped with bulbous capitals on which the nave vaults rest, then the west part with two towers and an entrance portal. In 1770 – 1777 the church was renovated and in 1873 – 1889 it was gothicized under F. Storn.

The high altar from 1470 – 1478 was then modified. The altar of the Adoration of the Magi, the altar of St. Michael dating from 1470, and the altar of the Virgin Mary Falling Asleep dating from 1477 – 1478 are the most valuable among the side ones. The triptych altar of the Coronation of the Virgin Mary, created in 1499 and restored in 1655 by F. Lang, is located in Zapolya's Chapel. The Late-Gothic panel paintings removed from the

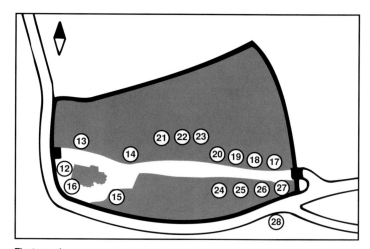

The town plan.

altars of the parish church in Spišské Podhradie are displayed here in the sacristy. The Late-Gothic and Renaissance funerary slabs, tombstones, and mortuaria dating from C17 are also to be seen in the cathedral. "Leo Albus," a Romanesque stone sculpture originated in the second third of C13, and a wall painting dating from 1317 are the most valuable ornaments in the church. The painting depicts a secular scene – the coronation of Charles Robert of Anjou the King of Hungary.

Among rare liturgical ornaments incorporating chalices dated to CC14 – 19, a crozier and a crown, plagues of C19 and a baroque thurible, a monstrance of 1740 made by J. Szilassy is the most precious one; it was declared a National Cultural Monument.

13 The Bishop's Palace: The original prior's palace, it was built simultaneously with the cathedral and was completed in 1281. The palace was rebuilt in CC14 and 15, creating the core of a Renaissance palace, renovated in 1652. This palace was remodelled to the Baroque style in 1753 – 1766; subsequent renovations were carried out at the end of C19 and at the beginning of C20. The Renaissance palace was built on the U-shaped ground-plan; several

rooms have been preserved, featuring cross vaults resting on central column. The most important outcome of the Baroque reconstruction is the staircase with the preserved balustrade. The chapel on the ground-floor containing painted vaults dates from 1760 and is the best known interior space of all of the stately halls. The Holy Trinity with allegorical figures of Faith and Hope are included into the modern painting created by M. Klimáček in 1946. A stone sculpture of the Madonna dating from 1753 is placed on the façade, in a niche above the entrance; another Baroque sculpture of the Madonna dating from about 1760 is on the façade of the palace which faces the garden.

14 The Clock-Tower: The quandrangular entrance gatehouse into the former ornamental garden of the prior's palace dates from 1739. The tower has two protruding oval terraces and a well-preserved, richly decorated Baroque iron grillework which protects the entryway.

15 The Former Seminary:
Located on the site of a former inn referred to in 1510, given to the Jesuits in 1636; they established a school on this site; later they built a monastery there in 1647. The

monastery is a two-storeyed building with a central cloister-garth, called also "paradise," and a protruding lateral wing into which the school was housed. In 1810 – 1815 the structure was rebuilt into the classical style according to the needs of the newly established seminary. Since 1819 a teachers' training college was located in the seminary building, which necessitated the addition of another storey. The central part of the building with a wall painting dating from 1731 by I. Forza has been preserved from the original building. It was modernized in 1932 – 1934 when the protruding wing was replaced by a new multi-storeyed modern building.

16 St. John's of Nepomuk Sculpture: Situated in front of the western façade of the cathedral, the sculpture dates from 1732.

17 Canons' House No. 2: Originally built in the Gothic style after 1460, this house was rebuilt in 1657 and enlarged by out-buildings at the end of C18 and the beginning of C19. A Gothic two-storeyed structure of a manor house type, it has a four-room ground-plan, which forms the core of the present house. The original ground-plan was preserved during the Renaissance rebuilding; the entryway with a pointed arch stone portal was included into the structure as an addition. During the rebuilding, the façade was altered and given Renaissance windows, and an oriel window on the second floor. A chronogram showing the date "1657" is located between the two windows on the first floor.

18 Canons' House No. 3: This Renaissance building was built on the site of a former Gothic structure in 1662. It is a block-like building of a hall-type. It is reached by outside steps leading to the front entrance and decorated with sculptures of lions. To the east of this block is situated a one-storeyed out-building. Both buildings are connected by a stone

The altar of the Coronation of the Virgin Mary.

wall with a postern gate for pedestrians and a gateway for carriages. To emphasize the street and courtyard façades, windows with Late-Renaissance decorative jambs were employed. In the niche on the façade is a Baroque sculpture of the Virgin Mary with Child; the sculpture is standing on a pedestal decorated with a relief of putto.

19 Canons' House No. 4: A medieval building dating from C14, this structure was renovated in the second half of C15 and rebuilt into the Renaissance style in the second half of C17. It is

a two-storeyed, eleven-axial three-wing structure. The passageway in its centre contains flat vaulted ceilings. A Gothic stone portal has been preserved near the entrance to the basement. A wide, two-armed wooden staircase with Empire balusters leads to the second floor. From the basement plan it is evident that originally two medieval structures stood on the building plot.

20 Canons' House No. 5: Originally a Gothic building dating from C15, this structure was rebuilt into the Renaissance style in the first half of C17 and then to the

The altar of the Virgin Mary Falling Asleep. Gothic, from 1470 – 1478.

21 Canons' House No. 6:
A Renaissance house from the first third of C17, it was built on older medieval foundations and was remodelled to the Baroque style in 1741. The residential two-storeyed house has a three-wing ground-plan with a central hall. A two-armed staircase leads to the second floor. The six-axial street façade is treated in the Renaissance style. A Baroque sculpture of St. Anthony of Padua is located on the façade in a niche on the second floor. The rectangular entrance portal is Renaissance in style.

22 Canons' House No. 7:
Originally a medieval house, it was rebuilt in CC17 and 18; then for the last time in 1874. The two-storeyed L-shaped edifice overlooks the street. The classical façade is five-axial on the first storey, and six-axial on the second. The house is accessed through a portal with a large segmental arch above which is a chronogram.

23 House No. 8: Built as a chapel at the end of C17, the house was renovated in CC18 and 19; later on it was occupied by the parish clerk. This two-storeyed structure neighbours with the garden of the bishop's palace on the western side. The building has an oblong, three-wing ground-plan. The five-axial façade faces the street. The Early-Baroque portal with a broken-apex pediment is situated in the central axis of the façade; a painted sun-dial from C18 is located between the windows on the first storey.

Baroque style in C18. The one-storeyed house is connected by a wall with a two-storeyed out-building. In the middle of the wall is an entrance ended in a pointed arch; its keystone shows an inscribed date of 1746. The Gothic core of the house occupies its front portion; it also contains pierced loopholes and original windows. The main two-axial façade features Renaissance windows; between the windows on the second floor is a Late-Baroque painting of St. Michael in a Rococo frame.

Leo albus.

24 Canons' House No. 14:
Originally a Gothic house built in C14, it was first renovated in C15; later on it was rebuilt into the Renaissance style in 1616. It underwent further transformations in CC18 and 19. The block-like building has three wings with a centrally situated entrance. A classical three-armed staircase ascends to the second storey. The out-building, parallel to the living quarters, was built in C17. Both structures are connected by

a wall in which is a rectangular Renaissance portal for the pedestrians and a semicircular-arch gateway for wagons.

25 Canons' House No. 15:

Originally a Gothic house which was rebuilt in the second half of C17, and whose façade was renovated in C18. The two-storeyed structure encompassed the entire width of the V-shaped building plot. The arch above the entryway is formed by a segment of a large circle with cornices. The keystone shows an elaborate classical coat of arms. An Early-Baroque sculptural group depicts the Coronation of the Virgin Mary and is located in a niche above the entrance.

26 Canons' House No. 16:
This Renaissance structure from C17 was remodelled into the Baroque style in 1744. An out-building is located next to the living quarters, and both buildings are connected by a wall. An entrance with a semicircular arch features a sculpture of St. Michael placed in a niche above the keystone.

27 Canons' House No. 17:

An original Gothic building dating from the beginning of C14, it was remodelled in C15 and rebuilt into the Renaissance style in the first half of C17; Baroque and classical remodelling were executed later. The residence is two-storeyed with a protruding bay. The trompe l'oeil wall painting preserved in one room on the second storey dates from C19. The one-storeyed out-building built in C17 is located parallel to the canons' house. The buildings are connected by a wall containing a wide entrance with a semicircular arch and a postern for pedestrians. The building plot borders with the southeast corner of the town walls. The garden wall features rich Baroque trompe l'oeil paintings, adorning the original ornamental garden.

28 The Town Fortifications:

Surrounding the centre of the town, they were built in C14. In 1587 – 1589 they were added a gatehouse tower on the western side. In 1662 – 1665 the entire town was fortified. The western gatehouse tower and a section of the walls of the earlier fortification system were included into to the new one, which was composed of a simple stone wall with loopholes, and small circular and semicircular bastions open to the town. They were accessible directly from the canons' houses. The two-storeyed gatehouse with a passageway was built on the eastern side of the main road. From the southwest, the town was entered through a gateway with a semicircular arch built directly into the fabric of the town walls.

Spiš Castle: A National Cultural Monument. The imposing silhouette of a castle built on the summit of a precipitous hill belongs to one of the largest castles in Central Europe; it dominates Spišské Podhradie and the surrounding country. The castle together with the towns of Spišské Podhradie and Spišská Kapitula creates a historically developed unit. A huge circular keep standing in the middle of the upper fortified ward was the principal element of the Romanesque county castle in C12. The original keep was replaced by a new one after the earthquake in the first third of C13. The new keep was situated close to the old one and has survived up to the present days. A Romanesque three-storeyed palace was built simultaneously with the tower, on the most remote spot of the entryway. The ground-floor served for accommodating the livestock, or as barns, service rooms, and the like; the upper floor was employed for defence, and the first floor comprised the living quarters. They were accessible from a courtyard, and consisted of only one state hall divided by two rows of stone columns with capitals which supported a timber ceiling. The hall which was lit through seven windows divided by mullions contained a fireplace and a prevet, a medieval type of toilet accommodated in little bay. The upper floor was accessible by an

Chapel below the Castle.

exterior staircase. After the Tartar invasions, King Béla IV allowed the Prior of Spiš to build a palace and a tower on the grounds within the castle for walls, the Spiš "prepošt" or cleric. The churchman chose a place situated to the west of the keep and slightly below it, bordered by a stone wall with crenellated bottlements and a quandrangular entrance gatehouse. North of the access road his living quarters developed. This piece of domestic architecture possesses square ground-plan. From its upper floor the keep was approached by a wallwalk. Owing to the extensive building activity of Prior Matthew, the precincts of the castle essentially expanded, partially outwards of the encircling walls, between 1250 - 1260. The temporary stay of the Prior in the castle is connected with the building of a Romanesque chapel in the upper keep. Its tribune was accessible from two sides by the wallwalk. The artistic design of the Romanesque palace and the chapel on the precincts of Spiš Castle, the prior's palace in Spišská Kapitula, and the parish church in Spišské

Podhradie is associated with the presence of Italian stone-cutters who settled in nearby Spišské Vlachy. In C14 a new large space protected by a stone wall with crenellated battlements was added to Spiš Castle on the west side. The main entrance was situated to the southern side, where a two-storeyed gatehouse with a barbican was built to protect it. At the same time another gatehouse with a barbican defending the entrance to the castle was built on the west side.

A separate fortlet used as living quarters by the commander of Jiskra's troops was built in the centre of the courtyard in the mid-C15. The new owners of the castle, the Zapolya family, attempted to transform the upper keep to an aristocratic seat. During the construction work it was added new buildings and also a new chapel was built in the middle of the upper courtyard. The lodge of the stone-masons building the castle also participated in the building of the family's new

funerary chapel in Spišská Kapitula. In the Renaissance the castle belonged to the Thurzo and Csáky families, who expanded the upper castle by adding some more buildings. The castle burned down in 1780. The complex reconstruction of the castle-ruin has been in progress since 1970. Spiš Castle and cultural monuments in the surroundings were recorded on the List of World's Cultural and Natural Heritage by the UNESCO.

The municipal arms date from C15. They belong to a rare type of local symbols, the so-called "talking arms," in which the heraldic figuration corresponds with the name of the town. Its source may be seen in Spišské Podhradie's which was also called Kirchdorf (Church Village). Other possible explanation is that the ecclesiastical motif in the coat-of-arms is derived from a patron saint whose attribute was a church standing on the palm of hand. This hypothesis has not been confirmed yet.

The name of the town of Spišská Kapitula indicates that it developed mainly as a religious institution – a *locus credibilis* and a centre of secular canons. Such places were a specialty of the feudal Hungarian state. The religious corporations of secular canons and also convents issued and authenticated documents on various private law-suits and judicial matters and verified various warrants at the request of the sovereign or high county administrators and juristic persons. That is why the arms of Spišská Kapitula are considered a symbol of a *locus credibilis* from C13. This can be affirmed by the original name of the settlement, Mons Sancti Martini, and the fact that Spišská Kapitula had been a *locus credibilis* for more then 700 years, and authenticity of a great amount of charters was guaranteed by the town's seal.

Today, a museum displaying various artifacts documenting the history of the hill as a place of habitation during centuries is housed in the rooms of the Renaissance and medieval palaces. Other restored parts of the castle are open to public.

This extensive collection of some of the most interesting monuments in Slovakia offers the visitor several excellent possibilities for longer walks. After a tour of Spišské Podhradie one can take a slightly ascending road to Spišská Kapitula, the charming and unique religious centre. Entering through the passage way in the gatehouse, the visitor can immediately see the only one street of Kapitula, at the end of which stands the monumental cathedral with its pair of towers on the western side, and the bishop's palace. Passing through the postern gate, one comes to a road on the northern side which leads back to Spišské Podhradie along the town walls. A longer walk from Podhradie takes the visitor to the castle; a visit to the museum will provide additional knowledge of this highly attractive place. The view from the upper castle, a famous and impressive landmark, of valleys and mountains in the surrounding is breathtaking.

Hiking paths lead to Dreveník or further on to Žehra or Spišské Vlachy. The beautiful surrounding mountains – Volovské vrchy, a mountain pass of Branisko, and the Levočské vrchy Hills – are particularly suitable for hiking and vacations both in winter and in summer.

BIBLIOGRAPHY

Adamec, V.– Jedličková, N.: Slovensko. Turistický lexikón. Bratislava, Šport, 1991.

Autoatlas Slovenská republika 1:200 000 a 1:100 000. Prvé vydanie. Harmanec, VKÚ.

Bardejov. Mestská pamiatková rezervácia. Bratislava, SÚPS, 1991.

Cestovný poriadok ŽSR 1999 – 2000.

Dejiny Prešova I. Košice, 1965.

Holčík, Š.: Bratislava. Bratislava, ČSTK – Pressfoto, 1990.

Hotel Guide SR. Komárno, Hepex, 1999.

Hriadeľová, R. – Hromadová, Ľ.: Bardejov. Bratislava, Tatran, 1977.

Hromadová, Ľ.: Levoča. Bratislava, Tatran, 1979.

Jankovič, V.: Národné kultúrne pamiatky na Slovensku. Martin, Osveta, 1980.

Kováč, D.: Dejiny Slovenska. Bratislava, SAV, 1988.

Križanová, E. – Puškárová, B.: Hrady, zámky a kaštiele na Slovensku, Bratislava, Šport, 1990.

Lehotská, D.: Dejiny Modry, Bratislava, SAV, 1961.

Levoča. Mestská pamiatková rezervácia. Bratislava, SÚPS, 1990.

Oriško, Š.: Kremnica, Bratislava, Tatran, 1984.

Puškár, I. – Puškárová, B.: Spišská Sobota. Bratislava, Tatran, 1977.

Puškár, I. – Puškárová, B.: Kežmarok. Bratislava, Tatran, 1979.

Puškár, I. – Puškárová, B.: Spišská Kapitula. Bratislava, Tatran, 1981.

Puškár, I. – Puškárová, B.: Bratislava. Bratislava, Tatran, 1992.

Slovensko. Dejiny. Bratislava, Obzor, 1978.

Súpis pamiatok na Slovensku, I. – IV. diel. Bratislava, Obzor, 1967 – 1978.

Sura, M.: Banská Bystrica. Bratislava, Tatran, 1982.

Šášky, L.: Kamenná krása našich miest. Martin, Osveta, 1981.

Šášky, L.: Umenie Slovenska. Bratislava, Tatran, 1988.

Špiez, A.: Slobodné kráľovské mestá na Slovensku v rokoch 1680 – 1780. Košice, Východoslovenské vydavateľstvo, 1983.

Vlastivedný slovník obcí na Slovensku, I. – III. diel. Bratislava, Veda, 1977 – 1978.

Výsady miest a mestečiek na Slovensku: 1238 – 1350. Bratislava, Veda, 1984.

Závadová, K.: Verný a pravý obraz slovenských miest a hradov ako ich znázornili rytci a ilustrátori v 16., 17. a 18. storočí. Bratislava, Tatran, 1974.

Žudel, J.: Stolice na Slovensku. Bratislava, Obzor, 1984.